YANKEE INDIA

YANKEE INDIA

American Commercial and Cultural Encounters with India in the Age of Sail 1784–1860

✦

SUSAN S. BEAN

PEABODY ESSEX MUSEUM • MAPIN PUBLISHING

PRASHANT H. FADIA FOUNDATION

The publication of Yankee India *has been supported by a generous grant from the*
Prashant H. Fadia Foundation.

Published in the United States of America
in 2001 by
Peabody Essex Museum
East India Sq.
Salem, MA 01970 USA
and
Grantha Corporation
80 Cliffedgeway, Middletown, NJ 07701

Simultaneously published in India
in 2001 by
Mapin Publishing Pvt. Ltd.
in association with
Peabody Essex Museum

Mapin Publishing Pvt. Ltd.
Chidambaram, Ahmedabad 380013 India
www.mapinpub.com

Distributed in North America by
Antique Collectors' Club
Market Street Industrial Park
Wappinger Falls, NY 12590
Tel: 800-252-5321   Fax: 914-297-0068
www.antiquecc.com

Distributed in United Kingdom & Europe by
Art Books International
1 Stewart's Court
220 Stewart's Road
London sw8 4UD
Tel: 020 7720 1503   Fax: 020 7720 3158
email: sales@art-bks.com

Distributed in Asia by
International Publishers Direct (S) Pte Ltd
240 Macpherson Road
#08-01 Pines International Building
Singapore 348574
Tel: 65 7416933   Fax: 65 7416922
email: ipdsing@singnet.com.sg

Text © Susan S. Bean 2001
Principal photographers: Markham Sexton and Jeffry Dykes
at the Peabody Essex Museum

ISBN: 81-85822-83-2 (Mapin)
ISBN: 1-890206-29-6 (Grantha)
LC: 00-111446

Design by Katy Homans, New York
Edited by Philomena Mariani, New York
Processed by Reproscan, Mumbai
Printed by Tien Wah Press, Singapore

Table of Contents

Foreword

DAN L. MONROE

EXECUTIVE DIRECTOR, PEABODY ESSEX MUSEUM

The publication of *Yankee India* coincides with the revitalization of the Peabody Essex Museum's 200-year connection with India, its art and civilization. Several of the museum's founders were pioneers in the East Indies trade at the beginning of the nineteenth century. They formed close commercial ties with India, which, in turn, led to the establishment of sustained personal friendships with leading Indian merchants. Through these connections, the museum began to collect what were, at the time, works of contemporary Indian art and culture. While trade between India and America decreased over time, and the museum itself underwent many transformations and changes over the ensuing two centuries, the Indian collections continued to grow. These collections now encompass a rare mix of works of art on paper, textiles, paintings, furniture, decorative arts, photographs, and manuscripts that together represent a broad spectrum of Indian art, history, and culture.

Recently, the museum has renewed its early interests in India through several major acquisitions, exhibitions, and publication projects. Most notably, we were fortunate to acquire the core of the internationally renowned Chester and Davida Herwitz Collection of Contemporary Indian Art. The museum's Herwitz collection includes more than 800 works created by India's leading artists between 1960 and the late 1990s. This acquisition, combined with the existing collections of Indian art, has established the Peabody Essex as one of the world's leading museums for the art of India from the colonial period to the present.

Working with the Victoria and Albert Museum, we have organized an important exhibition and published a pioneering volume on Anglo-Indian furniture based on the holdings of the two museums. Finally, to extend our exceptional strengths in nineteenth-century Asian photography, the museum has acquired a large collection of Raja Lala Deen Dayal photographs from Harvard University. Dayal is widely considered to be one of India's finest nineteenth-century photographers.

As part of the $100 million expansion of the museum now underway, contemporary and historical collections of Indian art and culture will, for the first time, have a permanent place in the Peabody Essex Museum galleries. It is within this context that we are pleased to present *Yankee India*.

Dr. Susan Bean has mined the rich and complex collections of the Peabody Essex Museum, spanning the holdings of several curatorial departments, to create *Yankee India*. In keeping with the museum's commitment to interweave art and culture in innovative ways, Dr. Bean has combined archival materials, works of art on paper, decorative arts, paintings, textiles, and other materials to illuminate the early, and little studied, relationships between the United States and India in the early decades of the nineteenth century.

The relevance of this endeavor transcends scholarly interests alone. South Asians, and their cultures, are playing an ever more visible and important role in the life of contemporary America. South Asians now comprise an important and rapidly growing economic force in American business. Indeed, the Prashant H. Fadia Foundation, which has so generously supported this publication, is a leading example of the new engagement between South Asia and America. Many elements of South Asian art and culture have been adopted by Americans and integrated into American life—influences that are certain to expand in the future. *Yankee India* helps to reveal the rich historical and cultural underpinnings of these connections by illuminating the strong, but until now largely forgotten, ties that once bound Yankee New England and India.

Foreword

PRASHANT H. FADIA

DIRECTOR, PRASHANT H. FADIA FOUNDATION

The study of encounters of Western civilization with India is a subject of great interest and profound significance. European colonialism fractured a nation and its psyche and yet it sent winds of change that breezed through the vastness of India. By contrast, America did not have any colonial ambitions in India. The origins of the 200-year relationship between the two great nations are based on friendship and equality.

In 1785, the *United States* was the first American vessel to reach India at Pondicherry—a French port on India's southeastern Coromandel Coast. It is a little known fact that from 1795 through 1805, total American trade with India exceeded that of all the continental European nations together. Today, at the gateway to the twenty-first century, we are amidst an information-technology revolution driven by the entrepreneurial spirit of multitudes of young minds from the two nations, working together and making history.

Nineteen years ago in California, I founded Abacus Software Group, and in 1991 Sierra Systems Asia in Mumbai. In the year 2000, Abacus was nominated as one the "100 leading pioneering technology companies in the world" in Davos, Switzerland, and in 1999 as the eleventh fastest-growing private company in America. Through the establishment of the Prashant H. Fadia Foundation, it has been possible to support important projects in the arts, technology, health, and the environment, both in the United States and in India. I am pleased that these enterprises are continuing the tradition of commerce and cultural exchange between India and the United States begun when the first American ship sailed to India over 200 years ago.

As a member of the board of trustees and overseers of the Peabody Essex Museum, I am gratified to be involved in the production of *Yankee India*, a historical study of great significance, which presents for the first time the gripping story of the very beginnings of the Indo-U.S. relationship. The Prashant H. Fadia Foundation congratulates Dr. Susan Bean for this unique achievement, which will make this important formative period of Indo-U.S. relations better known and better understood. This book will also serve as an invaluable resource for scholars, students, and others interested in the development of the engagement between India and America. I thank Dan L. Monroe for the opportunity to participate in this exciting time of rapid growth and revitalized engagement with India at the Peabody Essex Museum.

Acknowledgments

Though it may seem odd, the first recipients of my thanks are not actual people, but life-size clay portraits—of Rajinder Dutt, Raj Kissen Mitter, and Durgaprasad Ghose (figs. 11.12, 14.5, and 14.9). I first encountered them tucked away in a remote storage room, partially clothed, and if I remember rightly, lying on their backs. When I learned that they were portraits of Calcutta merchants, specialists in the American market, and had been in the collection of the Peabody Essex Museum for nearly a century and a half, most of that time on display, I was enthralled. Who were these Bengalis whose fragile clay portraits had been so carefully preserved? What did they and the Yankees who had founded the museum in 1799, after a decade of successful trade with the East Indies, think about each other and their culturally and geographically distant civilizations?

I soon realized that this encounter had been important economically and also as an ingredient in the development of Americans' ideas about themselves and their place in the world. When the descendants of Raj Kissen Mitter inquired about the portrait of their ancestor, I was drawn in more deeply. Kunal Mitra, Raj Kissen's descendant, visited the museum and later I met his father R. K. Mitra in Calcutta. They were generous with their time, hospitality, and information. After my research had led to an article on Rajinder Dutt, I heard from his descendants as well. Ranen Dutta and his wonderful family have since hosted me on several visits to Calcutta, taken me to family events at their ancestral residence, the home of Rajinder Dutt, and helped me learn more about the artists who made the portrait statues. In Mumbai, Roshan Kalapesi found new information about Nusserwanjee Maneckjee Wadia and connected me to his very knowledgeable and helpful descendant, A. R. Wadia.

My first trip to Calcutta, twelve years ago, was made possible by an invitation to participate in a symposium from the late Ashin Das Gupta. He was among the few who had investigated and written about U.S.–India trade in the age of sail and understood its significance. In Calcutta, I was fortunate to make the acquaintance of Ruby Palchoudhuri, Honorary General Secretary of the Crafts Council of West Bengal. She introduced me to the community of potters and sculptors in Krishnanagar whose ancestors had made the museum's portrait statues. We also began a stimulating and productive association that has led to exhibitions and events in Calcutta and Salem. Along the way, historian of Calcutta Jaya Chaliha, her daughter Joyoti Chaliha, and her associate Bunny Gupta have provided invaluable information and assistance.

I am deeply grateful to a number of colleagues whose continuing encouragement has helped sustain my enthusiasm as this project grew and suffered multiple interruptions—especially Pratapaditya Pal, Janice Leoshko, Robert L. Hardgrave, Edward C. Dimock, Ainslie T. Embree, and Dane Morrison. At the Peabody Essex Museum, many colleagues have made crucial contributions, large and small, including those associated with my own department—Alyssa Langlais Dodge, Cynthia Cort, Michelle Tolini, Aimée Moisan, Rebecca Larsen, Nancy TenBroeck; and those in other departments—Paula Richter, Dean Lahikainen, George Schwartz, Daniel Finamore, H. A. Crosby Forbes, librarians Kathy Flynn, Will LaMoy, John Koza, as well as Christina Hellmich, Lucy Butler, William Barton, and William Phippen. The museum's photographers, Markham Sexton and Jeffry Dykes, and the department's staff, Heather Shanks and Marc Teatum, have brought the book visually to life. Staff at other institutions have been generous with their time and guidance, particularly the Yale Center for British Art, the Baker Library of Harvard Business School, the Houghton Library of Harvard College, the Massachusetts Historical Society, the Boston Athenaeum, the Salem Athenaeum, and the Oriental and India Office Collections of the British Library. I have been fortunate in the astute editing skills of Philomena Mariani, the elegant vision of designer Katy Homans, and the committed interest of publisher Bipin Shah.

I am grateful to Dan L. Monroe, director of the Peabody Essex Museum, for making it possible for this project to come to completion. To Prashant H. Fadia, I extend my deep and abiding gratitude; without his enthusiastic support, this book might never have seen the light of day. Throughout the long time this project has taken, through all the ups and downs, John and Edie sustained and encouraged me. Whatever is good here is theirs too.

—Susan S. Bean, January 2001

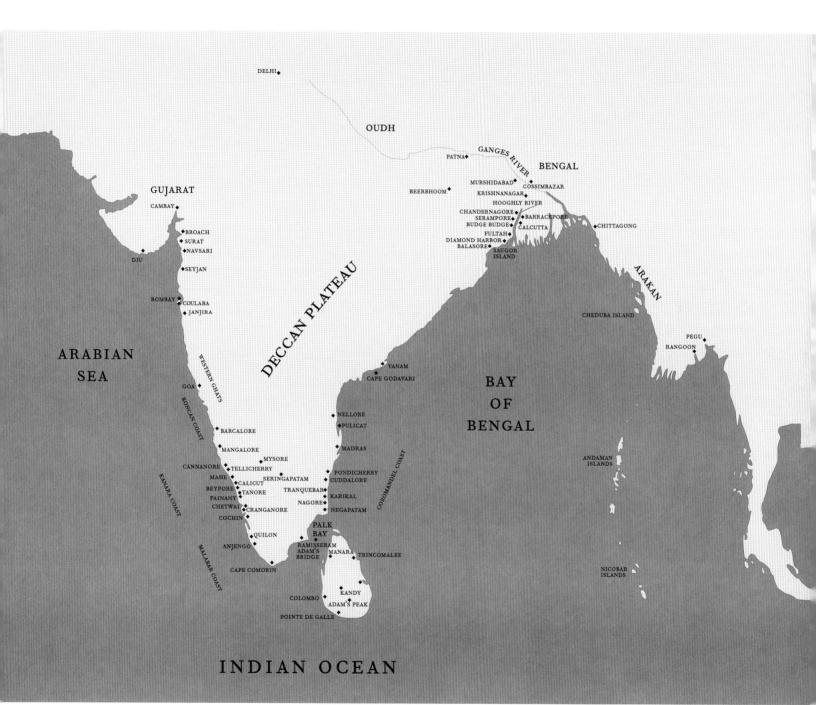

DELHI ◆

OUDH

GANGES RIVER

PATNA ◆

BENGAL

GUJARAT

CAMBAY ◆

MURSHIDABAD ◆ COSSIMBAZAR
BEERBHOOM ◆ KRISHNANAGAR
HOOGHLY RIVER
CHANDERNAGORE ◆
SERAMPORE ◆ ◆ BARRACKPORE
BUDGE BUDGE ◆ ◆ CALCUTTA ◆ CHITTAGONG
FULTAH ◆
DIAMOND HARBOR ◆
BALASORE ◆ ◆ SAUGOR
ISLAND

◆ BROACH
◆ SURAT
◆ NAVSARI

DIU ◆

◆ SEYJAN

ARAKAN

BOMBAY ◆ ◆ COULABA
◆ JANJIRA

CHEDUBA ISLAND

PEGU ◆
RANGOON ◆

ARABIAN
SEA

DECCAN PLATEAU

WESTERN GHATS

GOA ◆

BAY
OF
BENGAL

YANAM ◆
CAPE GODAVARI ◆

KONCAN COAST

◆ NELLORE
◆ PULICAT

◆ BARCALORE

ANDAMAN
ISLANDS

MANGALORE

◆ MADRAS

KANARA COAST

CANNANORE ◆ ◆ MYSORE
MAHE ◆ ◆ TELLICHERRY
BEYPORE ◆ ◆ CALICUT ◆ SERINGAPATAM
PAINANY ◆ ◆ TANORE
CHETWAI ◆ ◆ CRANGANORE
COCHIN ◆

PONDICHERRY ◆
CUDDALORE ◆
TRANQUEBAR ◆
KARIKAL ◆
NAGORE ◆
NEGAPATAM ◆

COROMANDEL COAST

◆ QUILON

PALK
BAY

ANJENGO ◆

RAMISSERAM ◆
ADAM'S ◆ MANARA
BRIDGE ◆ TRINCOMALEE

MALABAR COAST

CAPE COMORIN ◆

NICOBAR
ISLANDS

COLOMBO ◆

KANDY ◆
ADAM'S PEAK ◆

POINTE DE GALLE ◆

INDIAN OCEAN

Fig. I.1 Crowninshield's Wharf, Salem (detail), signed "George Ropes, Junr. Salem, 1806."
At the wharf are Crowninshield vessels, including *America*, *Belisarius*, and *Fame*, all of which made voyages to India.
Oil on canvas, 82.5 x 241 cm; Peabody Essex Museum M3459.

American Encounters with India in the Age of Sail

In the age of sail, scores of American merchant vessels, most of them a modest few hundred tons, voyaged to India from ports along the eastern seaboard (fig. I.1). The commodities brought back—cotton and silk textiles, sugar, indigo, ginger, saltpeter, leather, jute, linseed—were stocked in American shops and re-exported in immense quantities to Europe, South America, and Africa. In the first decades after Independence, this commerce played a significant role in American life. The trade generated federal tax revenues, helped relieve the war debt, and raised capital to build up nascent industries. But the significance of this trade with India surpassed its commercial impact. Especially in coastal cities and towns, India—its products, its civilization, its religions—touched the lives and imaginations of countless Americans. Voyages to the East were a window on the world beyond Europe for the new United States of America. They became the context in which Americans encountered the distant and exotic cultures of Asia and the Pacific.

Men and boys who ventured to the East Indies saw amazing things. They regaled friends and families with their adventures, recorded their experiences in letters and journals, and brought home "curiosities" from the places they visited. Mariners' experiences in India provided a dramatic foil for Americans' developing ideas about themselves and their place in the world—about the commercial and political status of the United States among the Western nations, about the rise and fall of civilizations, about the moral and intellectual character of Protestant Christianity and Hindu polytheism, about the characteristics and inherent capacities of the races of humankind, and about the place of their young republican nation in human history.

An unexpectedly rich record of this first encounter between India and America survives in mariners' logs, journals, letters, and business papers, in Indian commodities, and in mementos brought home. Mariners' manuscripts and gifts brought for loved ones—Kashmir shawls, gossamer cottons,

statues of Hindu deities, fantastic hookahs with long snakey smoking tubes—can still be found in museums, libraries, and private collections. Through these narratives and objects, Yankee mariners articulated their experiences, for themselves and for their families and communities, providing complex, if fragmentary, illumination of this initial American encounter with the East.

In their time, these documents, artifacts, and images were important sources of knowledge, each preserving memories, impressions, and experiences in different ways. In their journals and letters, mariners formulated stories of their experiences for themselves and a very select readership of family and fellow voyagers. The pictures and models they brought home, in a similar way, constructed a view of the East that allowed those who hadn't been there to visualize sights, events, and people. By contrast, "curiosities" were actual fragments of mariners' experiences. Displaced from their original contexts, they were put before viewers to contemplate and to bestow with new meanings. Whether in the homes of mariners or on public display, these curiosities were palpable links to India, manifestations of life there. They stood for India's history and geography, religions and social mores.

MARINERS' WRITINGS

Captains of sailing vessels routinely kept logs of their voyages, recording longitudes and latitudes, winds and weather, sightings of land, and arrivals at port (fig. I.2). Most shipmasters stopped making entries while their vessels were in port; rarely, a port journal was kept to record cargoes discharged and loaded, and repairs done (see James Briggs' journal, chapter 13). While mariners' time ashore was consumed by dispersing and gathering cargoes, and refitting vessels for the voyage home, the curious among them delved into the places they visited,

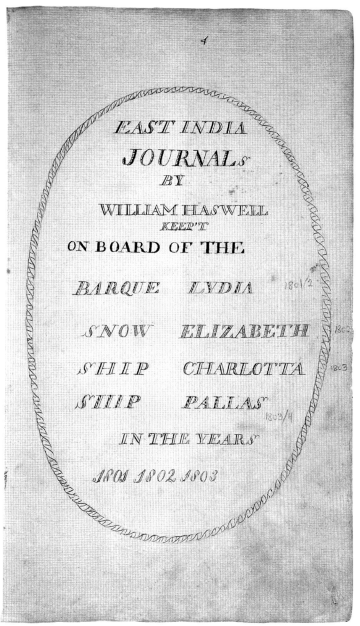

Fig. I.2 Title page of the journal kept by William Haswell recounting his voyages to the East Indies between 1801 and 1803. Peabody Essex Museum Library.

traveling a little, picking up souvenirs, observing and sometimes joining in local society. A few recorded their experiences, observations, and impressions in journals—usually like their logbooks in form.

The largest single collection of such logs and journals, held in the archives of the Peabody Essex Museum, contains accounts of nearly three hundred voyages to India. Most are the obligatory, prosaic reports kept for merchants and insurers with little to indicate the experiences of distant ports and alien civi-

lizations. Among those extending beyond routine subject matter are five of particular significance, spanning the era of the American India trade in the age of sail—from Independence to the Civil War, a time of enormous change in both India and the United States. Each journal is the unique product of an individual's experience; yet each reflects the state of Indo-U.S. commerce at the time of writing, and all are united by a common orientation of Yankees trading in Indian ports. All of the writers sensed an enormous gulf separating their new, republican, Protestant, Anglo-Saxon nation from what they perceived as the ancient, heathen, dark, conquered peoples of India. They were also acutely sensitive to the contrast they saw between themselves and their powerful, monarchist, former British masters. These five narratives form the backbone of this study. Each, presented in a substantial excerpt to impart its author's particular experience and orientation, is illuminated by contemporary images and mementos that convey how India was envisioned and imagined in America.

The earliest of the journals was kept by Benjamin Carpenter, master and supercargo of the *Ruby* on a voyage from Boston in 1789, five years after the first American ship set sail for India. It is an account of a man conscious of his pioneering role and intent on the business of developing a profitable trade in the Indian Ocean. A decade later, Dudley L. Pickman, scion of a prominent Salem family who kept copious journals of his five long-distance voyages, sailed as supercargo (business agent) on two India-bound vessels, to Madras in 1799 and Calcutta in 1803. Both voyages took place during the Napoleonic wars, when American merchant vessels prospered as neutrals carrying much of the international trade, but always in peril of hostile and marauding British and French warships and privateers. In 1817, William A. Rogers, a young attorney fresh from an apprenticeship in a law office, a stint as a very junior member of the diplomatic delegation in France, and an education at Harvard College, set out to finance his own law practice by serving as supercargo of the ship *Tartar* on a voyage to Bombay. Rogers filled the pages of his journal with commentary on his young republic, the old monarchies of Europe, and the ancient, decaying civilizations of the East. In 1832, James B. Briggs, a pillar of the Salem East India Marine Society and its museum of "natural and artificial curiosities," sailed as commander and supercargo of the brig *Apthorp* on a voyage to Calcutta. He arrived there to find a severely depressed market, and his port journal concentrates on the extensive work of readying the vessel for its homeward passage and the unloading and reloading of cargoes. Briggs seems to have thought he needed to justify his actions to the *Apthorp*'s owners in Boston at a time of poor business conditions at home and in Calcutta. The last of the journals is the 1854 chronicle of Edwin Blood, a nineteen-year-old supercargo's clerk from Newburyport, Massachusetts, with an appetite for adventure.

All of the authors belonged to port towns in New England. Of them, only Carpenter and Briggs spent most of their working years as merchant mariners. For Pickman and Rogers, from families whose men were lawyers, ministers, and prominent merchants, these voyages were a means to capitalize other ambitions—a law practice in Rogers' case and business ventures in Pickman's. Both served as supercargoes, managing the buying and selling of goods. The youngest of the group, Blood was sent to sea by his father, for his health and to complete his education before starting life as a merchant in Newburyport and Boston.

CURIOSITIES, VISTAS, AND PUBLISHED ACCOUNTS

Many Yankee mariners, whether or not they preserved their experiences in journals and correspondence, brought home curiosities and gifts for loved ones from their voyages. For them and for their contemporaries, such souvenirs were tangible representations of the places they had visited, sometimes more evocative than their recollections, letters, and narratives. In the late eighteenth and early nineteenth centuries, "curiosities" were a particular class of object comprising the unfamiliar, unusual, and exotic. The word *curiosity*, connoting novelty and fascination, designated both the object and the beholder's response to it.[1] Curiosities were distinct from commodities, useful things like cloth and sugar that were easily assimilated into familiar categories and bought and sold in the world market. By contrast, curiosities were singles, individual items, to be looked at, held, and contemplated as products of nature or artifice. More often than not, they had little monetary value: some were simply picked up, like shells or fragments of ancient monuments; others—fans, smoking devices, images of deities—were purchased very cheaply in the bazaar (figs. I.3, I.4). Sometimes curiosities were specially commissioned—some statues and figurines, for example. Occasionally they were acquired at considerable cost. Each curiosity was informative, revealing something about its place of origin: the peculiar flora and fauna, the strange devices used in everyday life, the religious paraphernalia linked to "heathen" beliefs and practices.

Because curiosities were actually *from* far-off places, unlike recollections or journal descriptions that were merely *about* those places, they embodied real connections to their places of origin. In a sense, they transposed those places—and the Yankee experiences of them—to the home front. But they did so in a way that was ambiguous, raising more questions than could be answered about their original contexts and encouraging viewers to answer those questions as best they could, with their own resources. People who had never been to India had to connect exotic things they saw to what they already knew, believed, or imagined about the world's creatures, civilizations, or arts. Mariners might provide some information about how things were made or used (to the extent they knew), but many of the contexts in which these curiosities belonged were simply unknown in the United States. No one knew how to make or play the musical instruments brought back from India, and very few knew anything of the legends and rituals associated with images of Hindu gods.

Most curiosities were carried home to share with family and friends. Some found their way into museums, newly established late-eighteenth-century civil institutions, where collections were available for public viewing. In Salem, Massachusetts, a group of mariners joined together in 1799 to establish such a museum so that curiosities brought back from their worldwide voyages could be shared with fellow citizens. Transported to settings such as the Salem East India Marine Society's museum, curiosities acquired new meanings. Unlike journals or letters, texts with strong narrative structures, curiosities were displaced objects, alienated from their original contexts and ripe for adoption into new narratives. Some of these were supplied by the donor, who provided a description of what he gave, but viewers also relied on their own knowledge and experiences to interpret an object. The museum setting, in which curiosities were grouped and juxtaposed, also created new contexts for understanding. By displaying objects together, viewers were encouraged to make comparisons. For example, musical instruments from different parts of the world could be looked at together and implicitly contrasted with familiar Western ones; agricultural implements and artisans' tools encouraged viewers to evaluate different technologies and

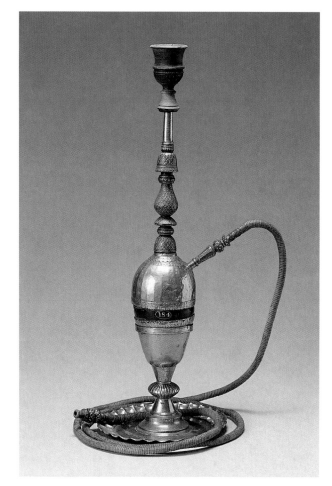

Fig. I.3 "Bengal god" (Balaram), Krishnanagar or Calcutta, c. 1800, entry #143 in the manuscript register of the East India Marine Society (Peabody Essex Museum Library). The designation "god" was later stricken and "idol" was written in its stead. Clay and pigment, height 50.5 cm; Peabody Essex Museum E7692, Gift of Captain Joseph White, 1800.

Fig. I.4 "The instrument used in smoking tobacco in Bengal, vulgarly called hubble-bubble," Calcutta, c. 1804, entry #184 in *The East India Marine Society of Salem* (Salem, Mass., 1821). Brass, coconut, leather, silk, height 70 cm; Peabody Essex Museum E7386, Gift of Captain John Barton, 1804.

modes of production. For the men who gave these objects, as well as for visitors to the museum, curiosities—actual fragments of exotic cultures—were potent ingredients for imagining far-off lands and the people who lived there.

The East India Marine Society's museum displayed "natural and artificial curiosities, particularly such as are to be found beyond the Cape of Good Hope and Cape Horn";[2] it was the first museum in America to take the East as its special domain, although rare and interesting objects from Europe and America were also collected and shown there. The members of the East India Marine Society intended their museum to exhibit the remarkable things found in their travels in order to inform fellow members and visitors about the marvels of the world's natural and human diversity. Many of these objects were

brought from India, including "idols," "hubble-bubbles" (water pipes), "punkahs" (fans), mounted insects, and preserved flowers—about two hundred objects in all. Most were brought back and donated to the museum by New England mariners, although some were given by Indians and Englishmen. Other museums of the day, such as the Charleston Museum in South Carolina, the Newburyport Marine Society in Massachusetts, and C. W. Peale's museums in New York, Baltimore, and Philadelphia, may also have included objects from India, but the collection of the East India Marine Society with its Asian emphasis was by far the most extensive. Today, this collection, built between 1799 and 1865, is of singular significance because so much of it has survived, along with catalogues giving object descriptions, donor names, dates of acquisition, and sometimes

Fig. I.5 *View of a Mosque at Moorshedabad with Representation of a Bazar or Indian Market* by James Moffat, 1805.
The East India Marine Society's museum displayed several engravings by Moffat, probably including this one.
Aquatint, 34 x 51 cm; Peabody Essex Museum M3103a, Gift of Miss Frances R. Morse, 1927.

associated documents that convey how these objects were perceived at the time.

Pictures of scenery and people, painted by European and Indian artists, were another valuable resource for the project of imagining India. In the eighteenth century, the appetite for such images was satisfied by two distinct styles of work. Western artists, principally Britons, portrayed romantic ruins, dramatic mountains, and cityscapes (fig. I.5). Many such views were reproduced as prints, published in London or Calcutta, and widely circulated. At the same time, Indian artists were commissioned by European patrons to portray monuments like the Taj Mahal, types of "natives" such as the *khansama* (butler), *nautch* (dancing) girl, and *fakeer* (religious mendicant), as well as studies of flora and fauna. Indian painters worked on paper,

and also on more exotic surfaces such as mica and ivory (fig. I.6). Potter-sculptors fashioned clay figurines dressed in cloth costumes depicting different "native types." Works in exotic media served double duty: as curiosities because of their unusual materials, and as representations of life in India. In this era before photography, such depictions were all that was available that could be brought home to show what the land and its people looked like.

Mariners' impressions of India were shaped by what they read, saw, and heard before they ever sailed into port. Most of them were acquainted with Indian products; they probably owned cotton or silk cloth made there and had seen curiosities brought home by others. They read accounts of events in India carried from time to time in local newspapers. Most of these

Fig. I.6 Brahman almanac keeper and wife, Tanjore (Thanjavur),
c. 1800, entry #379 in *The East India Marine Society of Salem* (Salem,
Mass., 1821). Gouache on European paper, 34.7 x 24.6 cm; Peabody
Essex Museum E9943, Gift of Captain Solomon Towne, 1805.

nica, which, he noted, corroborated his own observations (see chapter 7). Of course, novices also learned much from fellow mariners already experienced in the India trade, especially during the long ocean voyage. Edwin Blood complained of endless talk about India—most of which he later found to be woefully inaccurate (chapter 16). By the middle decades of the nineteenth century, more books about India were being published; many of these were illustrated with prints drawn from the work of numerous amateur and professional European artists. While most of these were still published in Calcutta and London, more and more were being printed in the United States.[3]

THE UNITED STATES AND INDIA IN THE AGE OF SAIL

U.S. trade with India became possible immediately after Independence when American shipowners, no longer prohibited by the British East India Company's commercial monopoly, were free to trade directly with the East. At the time, "India" was understood to designate a region of the "East Indies," which extended from India to Southeast Asia and the Malay Archipelago, sometimes encompassing China and Japan. Europeans had been active in the maritime East Indies trade since the Portuguese pioneered it in the late fifteenth century. Americans were the last Westerners to pursue long-distance ocean trade, following routes established by the Portuguese, Dutch, and British connecting far-flung corners of the world, bringing crops, manufactures, religions, administrative systems, and modes of production to places thousands of miles from their original homes. By the time of American participation, the industrial revolution, already underway in Britain, had set in motion the transformation of this trading world. India's commercial relationship with the West would be turned upside down: from a source of manufactured goods, principally textiles, India would become a market for Western manufactures—principally textiles.

When the 1783 Treaty of Paris ended the American War of Independence and the Indian Ocean was opened to American vessels, Yankee merchants and shipowners were quick to take advantage of the new opportunities. A few, including Benjamin Carpenter (whose journal is excerpted in chapter 3), were eager to establish an American trading company following British, Dutch, Danish, and French models. But most preferred to trade independently, each ship pursuing its own advantage, going

stories, based on reports in British newspapers, described battles and marked the progress of British victories over Indian rulers—Tipu Sultan of Mysore, the king of Kandy, and the Mahrattas—all of which took place far from the Anglo-Indian ports where Americans traded. Navigational charts and gazetteers, routinely acquired from London, were a ubiquitous part of seaport life. William Rogers wrote in his journal about ports he never visited as the *Tartar* sailed by on its way up the southwestern Malabar Coast of India (see chapter 10). His references almost certainly depended on a gazetteer kept aboard the ship.

Other publications on India were available, if scarce, in the first half of the nineteenth century. Dudley Pickman, for example, supplemented his description of Hindu society with a long passage copied from the 1797 edition of the *Encyclopedia Britan-*

wherever a profitable market could be found. The first two American ships embarked for Asian waters in 1784: the *Empress of China* left New York bound for Canton and the *United States* set sail for India from Philadelphia. The *Empress of China*, the first American vessel to reach Canton, produced a 25 percent profit for its investors when it returned in 1785.[4] American participation in trade with the East Indies increased rapidly in the wake of such news. Within a few years of its inception, this trade had yielded substantial revenues to the new nation and brought increased prosperity to its port cities.

The *United States*, the first American vessel to reach India, arrived in December 1785 at Pondicherry, a French port on India's southeastern Coromandel Coast. At Pondicherry, the ship and its crew were watched closely by French and British officials and by the nawab (governor) of Arcot. The British feared a new competitor joining the Dutch, Danish, and French companies whose factories dotted the coastline. Nevertheless, they were eager for the silver Americans would bring to trade, especially to help fund military actions, and they knew American ships could be useful in furthering the private trade of East India Company employees. Company officials did not want to exclude Americans from the India trade, but they did want to control their participation. In 1794, just a decade after the opening of the trade, the British succeeded in negotiating the Jay Treaty, which excluded American merchants from carrying goods to Europe and from the port-to-port "country trade" in India. American ships were permitted to trade only at British-controlled ports, and their voyages were to return directly to the United States—limitations accepted by the American government but resented by Yankee mariners. Before the Jay Treaty shut them out of the coasting trade, Yankee vessels had found it profitable to carry cargoes between ports in the Indian Ocean for freight charges and to supply commodities where they were most in demand; even after the treaty forbade such voyages, some shipmasters continued to engage in them when they could.

When war again erupted between France and England in 1793, eventually enveloping all of Europe, American shipowners found themselves in the enviable, if dangerous, position of neutrality—theoretically able to pursue trade with all the nations at war. American merchants flourished as neutral traders. A lucky few made large fortunes in the Asia trade. Elias Hasket Derby of Salem reputedly became America's first millionaire. Between 1795 and 1805, total American trade with

India exceeded that of all the continental European nations together.[5] At the end of the eighteenth century, the ports of India were the most frequently visited in Asia. More American ships carried on trade with India than with China.[6] Cotton and silk textiles were the most important exports from India to the United States. India was also a principal source of sugar, ginger, indigo, and drugs. The duties levied on these imports provided much needed revenues to establish a stable federal government, and profits from the trade helped to finance an American industrial revolution, funding the construction of mills, canals, railroads, and steam-powered vessels.

As the European war intensified, British and French attacks on American shipping increased—each side trying to prevent American commerce from benefiting the other. By 1807, these depredations became so severe that the Jefferson administration, hoping to pressure the British and French into respecting American neutrality, enacted an infamous embargo on all foreign trade. After a year and a half, the prohibition had failed in its purpose but was devastating in its impact on American coastal communities. Pressure from their representatives, and from prominent shipowners and merchants, forced its repeal in 1809. Foreign commerce revived quickly, but the upswing was short lived because the source of the conflict remained: British and French interference continued unabated. A few years later, in 1812, the United States declared war on Great Britain, and trade was halted again, this time for three years.

The economic isolation of the war years, which prevented vast quantities of imported goods from reaching the American market, had the unintended and beneficial effect of stimulating the growth of domestic industries. At the war's end in 1815, newly prospering textile manufacturers demanded legislation to protect them from the resumption of foreign competition. The very next year, Congress enacted a tariff that effectively barred from the U.S. market the inexpensive textiles that had been the mainstay of trade with India. As industrialization advanced with the help of government protection, and the United States expanded westward, the economic impact of trade with India declined dramatically in relation to growth in domestic commerce, manufactures, agriculture, and transportation. Despite these changes in the nation's economy, dedicated East India merchants, especially in New England, continued to find the trade a profitable pursuit.

After 1820, no longer holding out the promise of bountiful

returns, U.S. trade with India contracted and became the preserve of experienced Boston and New England merchants who had developed the Indian market as a specialty.[7] These Yankee traders learned to concentrate on raw materials needed to supply rapidly growing domestic manufactures—leather for shoes, indigo for textile dyeing and printing, saltpeter for explosives, linseed for oil-based paints and varnishes, and jute for baling. American trade concentrated at Calcutta, India's principal port and the source for linseed and jute. Boston became the main U.S. outlet for these goods. By the 1840s and '50s, American trade in these raw materials was again on the rise and the value of imports from India increased dramatically, as did the number of American voyages to the Indian Ocean.[8]

BEING IN-BETWEEN

Yankee mariners, who made their way and sometimes their fortunes around this trading world, operated in special locales—in-between places or contact zones.[9] For months at a time on the high seas, a mariner's society was limited to his shipmates. The crew comprised a dozen or two men and boys, often of several nationalities, some of whom spent their lifetimes voyaging, others who were there for the adventure and a chance to seek their fortunes. The ship's master or captain commanded with absolute authority. Hierarchy and strict discipline enabled these tiny worlds to move across great oceans where wind, weather, and currents required a closely orchestrated division of labor. A few officers, also of privileged rank with better quarters and food, assisted the captain in navigating the ship and directing the crew. On many American vessels, a supercargo, charged with the voyage's business, was second only to the captain in precedence. The captain, officers, and supercargo were often part owners of the vessel and its cargo, though even ordinary seamen might take a small "adventure" (speculation)—silver dollars with which to buy; something to sell—and make a little profit themselves.

In port, these shipboard societies came apart. Some hands remained with the vessel to refit it for the homeward voyage and assist in the gathering and dispersing of cargoes. Others went their own way, and the homeward-bound crew was usually reconstituted with much change in personnel. While in port, seamen stayed on the ship or, less frequently, lodged at boardinghouses near the waterfront. Captains, supercargoes, and officers usually set themselves up in the relative comfort of hired living quarters with staffs of servants. Most of them limited their contacts in port to the business of unloading and loading their vessels, buying and selling cargoes, and refitting their ships. Their exposure was restricted to functionaries of this contact zone, especially their "native" agent and household servants.

The ports visited by American mariners in India, especially the ports of British India—Calcutta, Bombay, and Madras—were quintessential contact zones, designed to facilitate relations across social and cultural chasms. In India, the British built their ports as forts and factories, places they controlled, where ships could be received and unloaded, goods brought from the hinterland, and commodities traded. The services of special brokers were required to facilitate exchanges and accommodate temporary foreign residents. At Calcutta, the first such middleman to be encountered was the British pilot and his "native" assistant who navigated ships up the treacherous Hooghly to port; at harborless Madras, it was the local boatmen who ferried crews and cargoes to shore from their anchorages a mile or more out in the roads. In port, there were chandleries to supply the ships, grogshops and brothels to indulge pleasures usually constrained at home, and houses rented to ships' officers providing living quarters on the upper level, a godown (warehouse) below, and an exotic array of servants for the weeks or months in port.

The masters of these contact zones, without whom the chief business of trade could not be conducted, were local specialists, *dubashes* and *banians* (see chapter 1) who brokered relations between foreigners and native merchants and suppliers. They spoke English and employed clerks (*sircar, conicopoly*) who managed English and Bengali or Tamil correspondence and accounts. Many of them made fortunes and used their resources to advance their standing in their own communities by building temples, sponsoring great religious ceremonies, and promoting reforms such as education for girls and political participation for "native" men.

Many American mariners were keenly aware of being in an alien world. Perhaps the sense of difference was intensified by the long ocean voyages in the limitless realm of sea and sky confined to their small, 250 to 600 ton vessels and their twenty or thirty shipmates, often for months without a stop in port. The contrast between the familiar and the foreign sharpened, motivating some to describe their surroundings and to compare the exotic scenes they encountered to the familiar ways of home. Some, like Dudley Pickman, William Rogers, and Edwin Blood, ventured out to learn what they could of their surroundings. American mariners' glimpses of Indian civilization happened in these contact zones, engendering a distinctive view of India, its inhabitants, and civilization. Yet, as they reported on their experiences in these foreign ports they were also depicting themselves. In their journals and letters, they tried to portray the alien, exotic civilizations they encountered and in the process expressed their own sense of identity—as men and as Americans.

YANKEE IMPRESSIONS OF INDIA

Residents of American ports were accustomed to seeing goods from India, China, Italy, and England—even occasional seamen from the Pacific Islands, Europe, or Asia walking about their towns. In these places, Asia was not so far away; here was an atmosphere hospitable to the beginnings of American interest in Indian civilization. In Salem, Boston, Newburyport, Providence, New York, Philadelphia, and Baltimore, even ordinary residents were familiar with Indian fabrics—serviceable cottons and luxurious silks differentiated by their qualities of weaving, places of origin, patterns, and colors. An enormous variety of Indian textiles was advertised in local newspapers and available in many shops (fig. I.7). Inexpensive Indian cottons were widely used as staple textiles for sheeting and shirting. Women with means wore the soft, warm, delicately patterned woolen wraps known as Kashmir or camel's hair shawls.

The vessels that carried commodities also facilitated a broader engagement. They brought books and pamphlets, some published in Calcutta, some in London. Local newspapers reprinted news of India from London papers and from reports brought home by mariners.[10] Americans could follow the progress of British conquest in southern India against the armes of Mysore and the Mahrattas. Trading voyages also facilitated religious and philosophical encounters. Merchant vessels carried the first American missionaries to India in 1812.[11] A few years later, they brought back the publications of Rammohun Roy, Calcutta's leading religious and social reformer. The close relationship of his ideas to the tenets of Unitarianism attracted an interested audience and prompted commentaries that

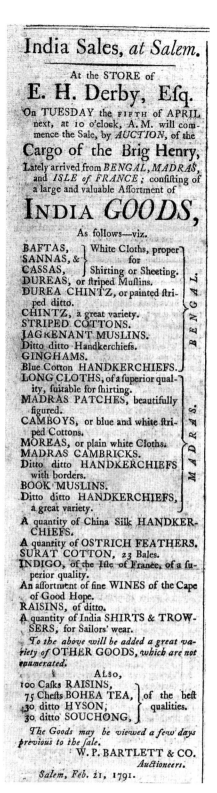

Fig. I.7 "India Sales, at Salem," advertisement printed in the *Salem Gazette*, March 22, 1791, listing a variety of Madras and Bengal textiles for sale at the store of E. H. Derby. The goods had been brought in the brig *Henry*, on the same voyage that the vessel's supercargo Benjamin Crowninshield (fig. I.10) witnessed and described sati, the ritual suicide of a widow, in Calcutta (see chapter I).

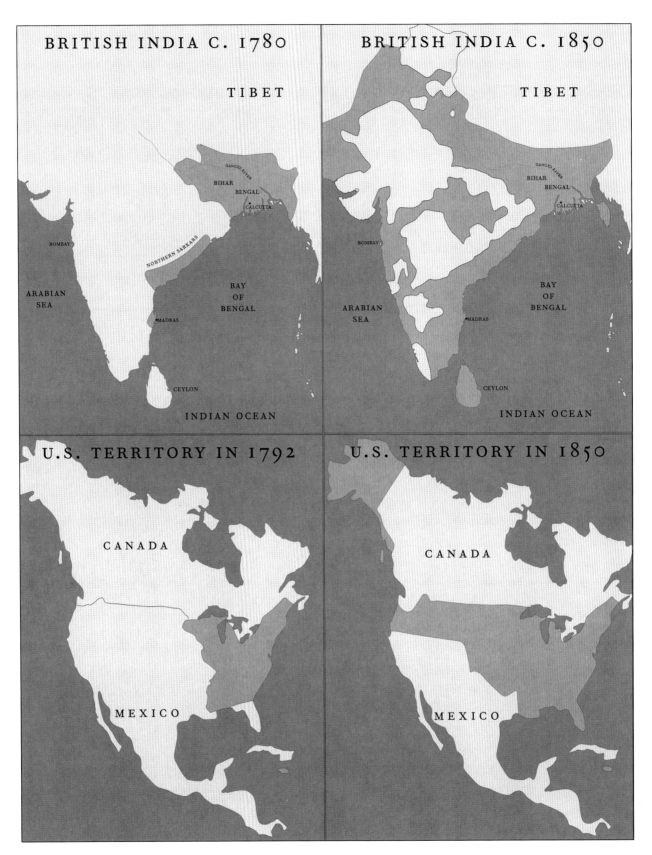

Fig. I.8 Maps comparing the geographic extent of the United States and British India in the 1780s and 1850s. Sources: C. Collin Davies, *An Historical Atlas of the Indian Peninsula* (New Delhi: Oxford University Press, 1959), pp. 52, 66; Tomas Lopez, *Atlas Elemental Moderno* (Madrid, 1792), pl. 22; Alexander G. Findlay, *A Modern Atlas*, 4th ed. (London: William Tegg, 1850), pl. 26.

appeared in the *North American Review* in 1818 and in the *Christian Register* during the 1820s. By the second quarter of the nineteenth century, these trading voyages were also bringing the translations of Sanskrit literature and religious texts that were becoming more widely available.[12]

In the early decades, especially before 1820, New England merchants who prospered in the trade held prominent positions in government and society and made their knowledge of the East a national resource. Jacob Crowninshield, for example, who brought the first elephant from India to the United States in 1797, prepared a memorandum on trade with India for the Jefferson administration, was elected to the House of Representatives, and received an invitation from Thomas Jefferson to serve as secretary of the navy. Nathaniel Silsbee, founder of a firm that would trade with India for a hundred years, served in the House of Representatives from 1816 to 1821 and in the Senate from 1826 to 1835. Benjamin W. Crowninshield was secretary of the navy under President Madison. The experiences of these men informed official American perspectives on the East.

In the 1820s, Emerson, Thoreau, and others of their circle became serious readers of Indian literature in translation, finding congenial ideas and inspiration in the sacred texts of Hinduism and Buddhism. In *Walden*, published in 1854, Thoreau made explicit the interplay of commerce and culture. As Thoreau watched Irish laborers cutting ice from the frozen pond for shipment to India, he considered the "stupendous and cosmogonal philosophy" of the *Bhagavad Gita* and imagined, literally and figuratively, "the pure Walden water . . . mingled with the sacred water of the Ganges."[13] The American Oriental Society, the first scholarly association concerned with Asia, was founded in Boston in 1842; its first president was John Pickering of Salem. Elements of global culture, blending and transforming Hindu and Christian philosophies, were being formed in Boston, Concord, and Calcutta in the first half of the nineteenth century.

The American experience of India coincided with the formation of national sensibilities. When Americans first came on the scene in the East Indies, the trade was dominated by the British. During the period of American trade under sail, the British East India Company transformed itself from a commercial concern into a political and military arm of the Crown, and British control of India expanded to the entire subcontinent. In 1784, when the first American ship landed at French Pondi-

cherry, the British had territorial rights to Bombay (granted in 1603) and a small surrounding area on the west coast, as well as a strip of land from the southern tip of India up the east coast to Bengal and inland along the Ganges River. Victory in the 1757 Battle of Plassey had made the East India Company the effective rulers of Bengal. The British pursued territorial expansion vigorously and, a century later, in 1857 when a major rebellion against British rule was put down and authority was transferred to the Crown, virtually the entire subcontinent was under British control (fig. I.8).

For Americans, the progressive subjugation of India by the British—their closest cultural kin and erstwhile masters—contrasted sharply with their own nation's dynamic economic, territorial, and political expansion. During the same period, the United States of America, having won its freedom from the British, grew from its original thirteen colonies into a continental power with settlements beyond the Mississippi, territory on the Pacific coast, and, through the Monroe doctrine, hegemonic claims on the entire Western Hemisphere. Americans contrasted their young, energetic, expanding civilization with the ancient, declining one they saw in India and felt their own superiority.

At the time, the nature of human diversity was a charged topic for Americans, especially the relationship of African slaves and Native Americans to the new American polity. Though it was widely believed that physical, intellectual, and cultural characteristics were inextricably linked, there was discussion about how much or how little it was possible to change or reform other peoples. Some believed that all human beings, as children of the same creation, shared in godliness; others that some human groups had become degraded since creation. Some believed that different races had existed from the beginning; others that the races had evolved. However Americans of European ancestry differed in their explanations of human racial diversity, it was universally recognized that diversity itself was highly significant and that the races were of unequal qualities. Their own race they held to be superior in intelligence and civilization to all others on earth. In India, Americans did most of their business in British-built ports where race was an organizing principle. At Madras and Calcutta, there were forts where the Europeans lived and worked and a native section often known simply as "black town." At Madras, Dudley Pickman noted in his journal, no "blacks" were permitted inside the fort in a palanquin (chapter 6). Most Americans considered the racial character of Indians a factor in their subjugation by the British.

Yankee mariners' views of the world's religions were similarly centered on themselves. Nearly all Christians of conviction, they were secure in the superiority and singular truth of their own religion. Even so, there was room for widely differing attitudes toward Indian religions. Some were tolerant; others condemning. Some advocated proselytizing to save the millions of heathen souls; others were skeptical of missionary motives and competence. Staid, conservative New England Congregationalists and rationalist, liberal Unitarians expressed distaste for the religious zeal of evangelical Protestants (mostly Baptists and Methodists), and were critical of the sharply segregated religious organization of most Indian churches.

In their presumption of moral and racial superiority, these New Englanders were much like the British in India. But the Yankees were by no means mere reflections of the British in all their attitudes. In these first decades after independence, Americans felt their attachment to ideals of liberty, self-government, and republicanism strongly and set themselves apart from the monarchical, hierarchical British. Their burgeoning nationalism occasionally led them to sympathize with the plight of Indians as subject people and to oppose the spread of British rule (for example, Dudley Pickman in chapter 6 and William Rogers in chapter 10).

THEN AND NOW

Two centuries have passed since the beginning of American trade with India. Opinions about the legitimacy of diverse religions, the equality of races, and the connection between race and culture have been fundamentally altered, if not entirely changed. Yet, there remain haunting similarities between American views then and now. In the early nineteenth century, Americans noted ancient wonders such as the caves of Elephanta and judged India a civilization in decline. Nearly two hundred years later, India is often characterized by a qualitatively similar notion: underdevelopment. Both perspectives support the belief, widely held by Americans then and now, of their own national superiority.

The fascination with India as an icon of the deleterious effects of exploding population and economic underdevelop-ment, assumed to be a twentieth-century phenomenon, was already present in only slightly different form in the journals of American visitors to eighteenth-century India. The responses to Indian poverty, particularly the practice of "begging," also have an uncanny resemblance to comments made by late-twentieth-century American visitors to India. Dudley Pickman, for example, at Tranquebar on the southeast coast in 1799, remarked on the great many beggars on the streets, some deformed, all "most pitiable objects" (chapter 6). Virtues of self-reliance, work, and individual effort were integral to the Protestantism of New Englanders, and everyone was expected to earn a living by a Western conception of honest labor.[14] In India, the beggars, jugglers, dancing girls, and snake charmers had an accepted place. Depending on the generosity of others was a customary way of life for many who were diseased or crippled. Jugglers and snake charmers, considered lowlife tricksters by Europeans, were appreciated for their illusionist skills and earned their livelihoods amusing passersby. Dancing girls, considered morally suspect by Westerners, were essential participants in many religious festivals and celebrations. To most Yankee mariners, the everyday presence of such people was a demonstration of the degenerate state of Indian society.

Indian religious teachings have attracted followers in the United States since the impact of Swami Vivekananda at the 1893 World Congress of Religions in Chicago; today, Hindu philosophy and practice is well established with large numbers of adherents who are not of South Asian origin. Nevertheless, as the uproar over Southern Baptist missionary literature in the autumn of 1999 demonstrated,[15] there are still many in America who believe that Hinduism is wrong and its followers are damned. In the same vein, for decades in the first half of the twentieth century, South Asians were excluded from "the land of opportunity" on racial grounds. From the beginnings of the trade with India, Yankees grouped Indians with others of dark complexion, and understood this as a racial classification entailing biological and psychological differences. The racial discrimination still encountered from time to time by Americans of South Asian origin is part of an entrenched culture of race with which Americans of all backgrounds still struggle.

Though the early U.S. encounter with India through commerce is all but forgotten, its significance cannot be diminished. At the beginning of the nineteenth century, the trade was a leading source of U.S. custom duties, and many prominent leaders of the new nation learned about the world and America's place in it from their experiences in the India trade. Yankee vessels brought admirable textile manufactures, especially cotton goods, whose utility and beauty would spur Americans to devise methods for producing satisfactory imitations. As the trade narrowed and was concentrated in Boston, sailing ships continued to serve as conduits, transporting missionaries and ice to India and returning with exotic curiosities and coveted Kashmir shawls as well as intellectually engaging and challenging translations of Sanskrit literature. Throughout this period, when the East was four months or more away from the United States and information was very limited, far-off exotic India provided an opportunity to envision dramatic differences—in religion, race, economy, and geography—and in doing so, to serve as a foil in the shaping of American identity. The encounter between America and India in the age of sail warrants a closer look—for its important economic and cultural impacts in the nineteenth century and for its illumination of long-standing, deeply ingrained American attitudes toward morality and civilization.

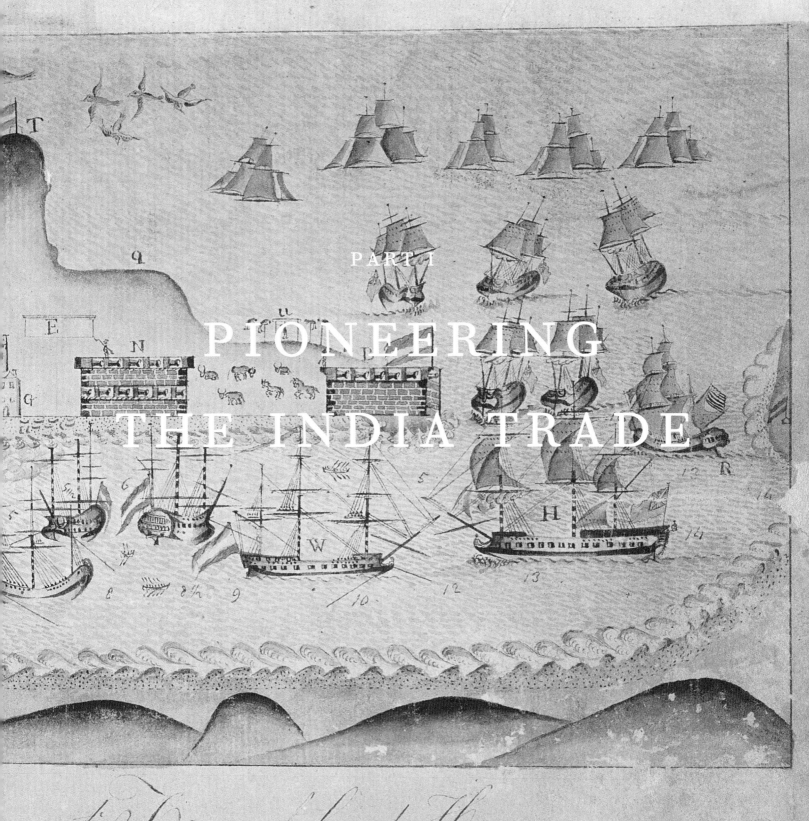

PART I

PIONEERING
THE INDIA TRADE

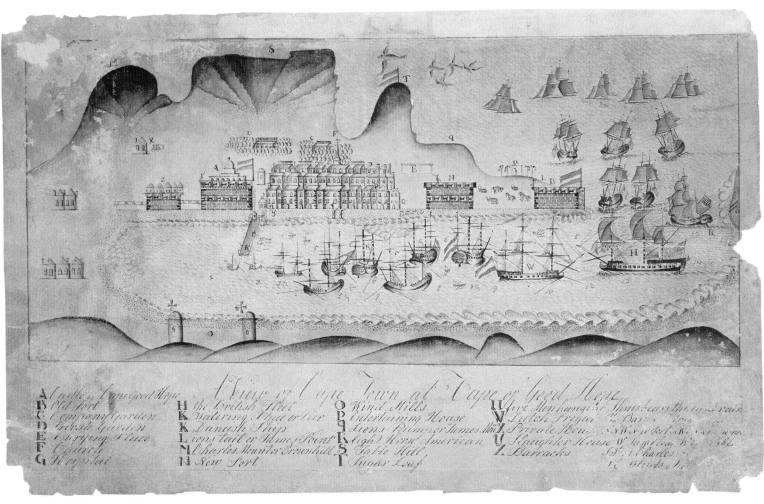

Fig. 1.1 *A View of Cape Town at Cape of Good Hope*, attributed to a member of the crew of the *Light Horse*, c. 1788.
In the alphabetical key, letter "R" indicates the Derby bark *Light Horse* of Salem, which stopped at Cape Town during its
trading voyage in the Indian Ocean.
Ink and wash on paper, 19.3 x 31.5 cm; Peabody Essex Museum M15748, acquired 1974.

CHAPTER I

Bridging the Divide

The first Americans who sailed to Asia navigated their ships in unfamiliar waters to trade in alien ports. They crossed a boundary that had been created by the British East India Company's monopoly on trade with the East (fig. 1.1). Private traders in the colonies, as in Britain, were prohibited from taking part. This boundary, which became obsolete with the end of British rule in 1783, was a palpable marker for Yankee traders. In Salem, Massachusetts, for example, the founders of the East India Marine Society honored a decade of successful enterprise in 1799 by forming a society limited to masters and supercargoes of vessels that had sailed beyond the Cape of Good Hope and Cape Horn, where no American ships had ventured before; they saw themselves as pioneers, passing into new, partially charted territory, exploring unfamiliar ports and markets.

The border that had been created at the Indian Ocean marked a divide that was technological, commercial, and cultural. American shipmasters needed the knowledge and experience to navigate the Arabian Sea and the Bay of Bengal. They needed to know about commodities and markets at ports they had not visited before. They needed to know how to deal with Eastern merchants, suppliers, and commercial agents, as well as the rules and regulations that governed trade.

The background they built on to sail into the Indian Ocean was considerable. Americans had been part of the British colonial world. There were some whose lives spanned the Eastern and Western colonies of the British empire, including Elihu Yale, a governor of Madras, born in Boston in 1649, who helped found the college in New Haven that bears his name, and Lord Cornwallis, who lost the American colonies and just a few years later secured Indian ones. Colonial newspapers carried accounts of events in other parts of the empire, including India. Indian goods, chiefly textiles, were already important commodities, acquired through London and sold widely in the colonies. American mariners were experienced in the West Indies and European trades. They could extend their range using published navigational charts and gazetteers, and the

guidance of experienced foreign crew members who had navigated the Indian Ocean. In India, American ships usually visited British-controlled ports, where there was a shared language and some familiarity with business practices. But Yankee merchants knew that to succeed in the Indian Ocean trade, they had to learn quickly and develop new trading strategies. Benjamin Carpenter's journal of the *Ruby*'s 1789 voyage to Calcutta, excerpted in chapter 3, is a lucid exposition by one of these self-styled pioneers.

BRITISH COLONIES: INDIA AND NORTH AMERICA

In the seventeenth century, America and India became odd step-siblings, brought together by the colonial ambitions of Great Britain. In the 1630s, Boston was settled under royal charter by the Massachusetts Bay Company and Madras was founded as a trading fort by the East India Company with permission from the nawab of Arcot. In the 1660s, Bombay, given to Charles II by the Portuguese as part of his marriage settlement, was turned over to the East India Company, and New York was taken by the British from the Dutch. Philadelphia was settled as a proprietary colony by Quaker leader William Penn in 1682 and, in 1690, Calcutta was selected by Job Charnock to be the English trading settlement in eastern India. For about 150 years, from the establishment of these first colonies until the United States gained independence in 1783, North America and India were increasingly drawn into the sphere of British political and commercial ambitions.

The situations confronting the British in these regions were radically different. North America offered a land of temperate climate, not unlike the British isles, suitable for settlement and sparsely populated (both because of Native American settlement patterns and seventeenth-century wars and epidemics that had decimated the population of eastern America). Settlement was organized by private companies (the Plymouth Company, the Council for New England, the Massachusetts

Fig. 1.2 David Octherlony (1758–1825) at a nautch, Delhi, ca. 1821.
David Octherlony was born in Boston in 1758, attended Governor Dummer Academy in Byfield, Massachusetts, and went to India in 1803,
where he began a distinguished military career that eventually brought him a knighthood and a monument in Calcutta erected in his honor.
Gouache on paper, 22.4 x 32.1 cm; By permission of the British Library.

Bay Company, among others) and individuals (William Penn, Lord Baltimore, Roger Williams) who were granted land and charters by the Crown. British settlers migrated to North America for the opportunities of acquiring land and to live and worship as they wished.

India, by contrast, was densely populated and produced pepper, ginger, and textiles much sought after in Europe, Southeast Asia, and China. India's tropical climate would not support a transfer of British agriculture. The heat, monsoon rains, and endemic diseases made permanent settlement by Britons less feasible and far less attractive. Instead, a monopolistic corporation of merchants, the East India Company, was organized to control trade and supervise the military enforcement of British interests.

During the eighteenth century, British hegemony extended dramatically in both regions. This common colonial background created a realm of shared experience. There were many men whose careers bridged these widely separated colonies. Elihu Yale made his fortune as an employee of the East India Company. His career in India was noted in the American colonies. The *Virginia Gazette*, for example, printed an account of a visit to Yale from a Mughal emissary "of a majestic Form . . . the Magnificence of his Dress in Pearls and Diamonds, is beyond Description."[1] Yale, who later retired to the English countryside as a great "nabob," was persuaded to contribute toward the founding of a college in the American colonies. His endowment consisted principally of textiles—including calicoes and muslins from India—which were sold in Boston.[2] Another New Englander who served in the East India Company was Nathan Higginson, born at Guilford, Connecticut, in 1652. Higginson left for India when he was about thirty and became a prosperous member of the council of Fort St. George, Madras. He later served as mayor, and in 1692 was appointed governor. Higginson resigned in 1698 and spent the remainder of his life in London.[3] David Octherlony, born in Boston and educated at Governor Dummer Academy in Byfield, Massachusetts, went to India in 1803 to serve in the army, where he distinguished himself as a military leader. Octherlony was made a baronet and memorialized in a monument on the *maidan* (town common) in Calcutta (fig. 1.2). William Duer's colonial journey took him in the opposite direction. Born at Devonshire in 1747 and educated at Eton, Duer was sent to an old family friend, Robert Clive, to serve as his aide-de-camp in 1764. Duer was not long in Bengal before he became ill and returned home. He left the army and went into a business that soon took him to America in search of a more abundant supply of lumber. What Duer found was beyond his expectations; he settled in New York near Saratoga and built a lumber mill into a very successful business. He became an active participant in the independence movement, serving as a delegate to the Provincial Congress in 1775, a member of the Committee of Correspondence, and the Continental Congress.[4] He was an investor in the first American voyage to the East Indies, the *Empress of China*, which left New York for Canton in 1784.[5] Besides these men of renown, there were scores of seamen, soldiers, and adventurers whose unrecorded experiences crossed the expanse of the British colonial world.

Of all those whose lives bridged the growing British dominions, perhaps one best represents the diverging fortunes of the Indian and American colonies. In October 1783, Major-General Charles Cornwallis surrendered to General George Washington at Yorktown, opening the way for the independence of thirteen North American colonies. This defeat notwithstanding, five years later Cornwallis was appointed governor-general of India and commander in chief of British forces there. During his tenure, he reformed the revenue and civil service administrations of the East India Company, and advanced a fundamental shift in the purpose of the company, transforming it from a commercial corporation to the revenue-collecting ruler of British-controlled India. Cornwallis also achieved the military fame that had eluded him in America: in 1792, he defeated Tipu Sultan of Mysore, who had been the principal obstacle to British supremacy in southern India (fig. 1.3). Tipu gained worldwide notoriety as a gifted military commander and adversary of the British. As early as 1769, Salem's *Essex Gazette* reported on his negotiations with the nawab of Arcot, who had recently driven the British from posts on the Coromandel Coast.[6] Had Tipu Sultan been as successful in his efforts to gain French support against the British as George Washington had been in the American war, Indian history might have taken a very different course.

INDIA SEEN FROM THE AMERICAN COLONIES

North American colonists were ambivalent about British India. Many traded in India goods; some served as soldiers or administrators in the expanding British establishment in India. Religious leaders such as Cotton Mather championed bringing the gospel to the heathens of the East Indies.[7] Colonial newspapers carried occasional reports from London on the progress of the East India Company in India. In 1774, the *Boston Evening Post* published an account of "the city of Tanjour being taken by storm by the Company's troops under the command of General Spencer." The king of Tanjore, like the ruler of another unnamed province, was taken prisoner and released for a considerable ransom, nearly half of which was sent back to London "as a remittance to the Company." "Our affairs in India," the article concluded, are "in a most flourishing condition."[8]

As revolutionary fervor increased—especially after the Tea Acts made the East India Company beneficiary to colonial exploitation in America—more Americans found common cause with the people of India as fellow victims of colonial greed.[9] In 1773, Parliament granted the East India Company the right to bring its tea, and the tax burden that came with it, directly to the American colonies.[10] For the growing American independence movement, this was an intolerable abuse of the colonies. Later that year, the *Dartmouth* and the *Beaver* sailed into Boston Harbor and were attacked by a party disguised as "Red Indians" and "Negroes." The tea they carried was dumped overboard, wantonly destroyed. The Boston Tea Party, as it became known, motivated the British Parliament to pass punitive laws that in turn led inexorably to confrontation and war.

Fig. 1.3 *Marquess Cornwallis Receiving the Sons of Tippoo Sultan as Hostages*, engraved by Daniel Orme, London, December 21, 1793, after a painting by Boston-born artist Mather Brown. In the late eighteenth century, Tipu Sultan was the strongest challenger to British hegemony in India. Cornwallis, whose defeat at Yorktown in 1783 ushered in American independence, went on to a distinguished career in India, defeating Tipu Sultan and serving as governor-general, 1786–93.
Engraving, 46.6 x 61.3 cm; Peabody Essex Museum M18833, Gift of John Dominis Holt and Frances Damon Holt, 1980 (see fig. 4.21).

Voicing the growing resentment against the government-backed East India Company, John Dickinson, a renowned penman of the Revolution, published as a broadside in 1773 "A letter from the Country, To a Gentleman in Philadelphia." Not only did he place the American rebellion in the global context of British imperial ambitions, but he also expressed sympathy for fellow victims of British rapacity:

> Their conduct in Asia, for some years past, has given ample Proof, how little they regard the laws of Nations, the Rights, Liberties or Lives of Men. They have levied War, excited Rebellions, dethroned Princes and sacrificed Millions for the Sake of Gain . . . they have, by the most unparalleled barbarities, extortions and monopolies, stripped the miserable inhabitants of their property, and reduced whole provinces to indigence and ruin. Fifteen hundred thousand, it is said, perished by Famine[11] in one Year, not because the Earth denied its Fruits, but this Company and its Servants engrossed all the Necessities of Life and set them at so high a rate, that the Poor could not purchase them. Thus having drained the sources of that immense Wealth . . . they now, it seems, cast their eyes on America . . . But thank GOD, we are not Sea Poys, nor Marattas, but *British Subjects* who are born to Liberty, who know its worth, and who prize it high.[12]

In 1774, the *Boston Evening Post* printed a similarly sympathetic view reported from London: "A correspondent observes, with concern, that the cruelties and rapine practiced by the East India Company in Bengal have roused the indignations of the public against the East India Company themselves."[13] American colonists increasingly saw themselves and the natives of India as fellow victims of British exploitation. A member of Congress in 1777, remarking on the latest news from India, declared: "It is reported that the East Indians have risen upon their oppressors, and taken Madras. This is all good news. It seems as if the time [is] coming when Great Britain is to be called upon to make severe retribution for her infamous destruction of the human species in India. Let us be wise and virtuous from her example that we may avoid her fate."[14]

THE INDIAN PRESENCE IN AMERICA: COMMODITIES

During the colonial period, American merchants and their customers were familiar with Indian products. Although few had any direct experience with the subcontinent, many used the ginger, pepper, and other spices that came from India and knew and admired the products of its dyers and weavers. In the early eighteenth century, India's fine silks and cottons with vibrant, colorfast patterns were superior to European and American products. Some textiles made in India, such as the gossamer cottons woven of the finest yarns spun with a simple drop spindle, were known to be of extraordinary value (fig. 1.4). On January 4, 1770, the *Massachusetts Gazette and Boston Weekly Newsletter* reported, "In the magnificent present, which the Nabob of the Carnatic has sent to his majesty, there is among other things of very great value, one piece of muslin which, we are credibly informed, is the finest that ever came to Europe; the texture of it is of a very peculiar nature, and the whole is remarkably fine. It cost exactly 7800 rupees, which is about 975 £."

Indian textiles came to the American colonies—often in American vessels—from London, where they were imported by the British East India Company. All sorts of Indian cloth was used, for household furnishings (upholstery, window curtains, bedcovers) and every kind of garment (neck cloths, waistcoats, petticoats, dresses) by people of all social strata. The quality and value of the textiles ranged from coarse goods for servants' clothing to fine muslins valuable enough to be insured. India goods were listed in newspaper advertisements by name. For

example, the 1767 *Pennsylvania Chronicle* advertised *humhums*, a plain cotton cloth of stout texture woven in Bengal.[15] Evidently Anglicized Hindustani terms were widely known and in common use until the years of the Non-importation Agreement in the 1770s, when American colonists boycotted textiles that came to the colonies through British East India Company trade.

Household inventories, merchants' papers, and newspaper advertisements, as well as examples preserved in museum collections, indicate the range of Indian textiles available.[16] Calicoes, good-quality cottons originally from Calicut on the Malabar Coast, were put to many uses. For example, a Salem household inventory of 1677/78 lists two painted calico tablecloths as well as plain calico tablecloths and calico shirts, and a Boston inventory of 1684 lists white calico bed curtains, chair covers, sideboard cloths, and cupboard cloths as well as a flowered calico quilt. In 1707, Thomas Banister of Boston ordered fifty pieces of wide blue book calicoes (named for the way they were folded). In New York (until 1665 the Dutch colony of New Amsterdam), the household inventory taken for Margarita van Varick in 1695–96 listed clothing of calico including nightgowns, neck cloths, aprons, quilted waistcoats, white and flowered petticoats, and "clouts," and furnishings of calico including carpets, quilts, curtains (both white and colored), valances, napkins, pillow covers, bibs, children's beds, and blankets, as well as a set of white flowered muslin curtains (fig. 1.5).

Striped and checked cloths of cotton or mixed silk and cotton were popular too, and many different kinds of cloth were imported as "handkerchiefs"—multipurpose squares used for neck cloths, bundle wraps, and wipers. A Boston inventory from 1695 includes "3 handkerchiefs of *allejars*," probably a striped cloth of cotton or cotton mixed with silk, usually red or blue with white, sometimes flowered or decorated with gold and silver thread, woven in Gujarat and on the Coromandel Coast. In 1726, William Trent of New Jersey owned

Fig. 1.4 "A machine used in spinning by the natives of India," eastern India, c. 1803, entry #292 in the manuscript register of the East India Marine Society (Peabody Essex Museum Library). This kind of spindle was used for making the very fine yarns required for weaving the most delicate, gossamer cottons. Wood and iron, length 32.7 cm; Peabody Essex Museum E7796, Gift of Captain Benjamin Crowninshield, 1803.

Fig. 1.5 Palampore, Coromandel Coast, 1700–1750. This bedcover was owned by the Van Rensselaer family, and was probably in their possession before the Revolutionary War. Painted and printed cotton, 258.8 x 224.8 cm; Courtesy Historic Cherry Hill Collections, Albany, New York.

three pairs of window curtains made from seersucker (a striped fabric of mixed silk and cotton, with a rippled texture). A runaway servant in Boston was described as wearing "a narrow striped cherrederry [a silk and cotton textile woven in stripes or checks] gown, turned up with a little flowered red and white calico, striped homespun quilted petticoat, plain muslin apron." In 1729, Thomas Fitch, a Boston merchant, noted the poor sales of *betilles* (South Indian white, red, striped or flowered cottons, often used for neck cloths) sent from London. Connecticut merchant Samuel Boardman's account book of 1772 includes silk *lungi rumals* (large square designs originally made for men's wrappers) for neck cloths.

In the American colonies, these products of weavers' looms and dyers' artistry transmitted a sense of India. In an age when all textiles were handmade and fibers such as cotton and silk were often difficult to obtain, textiles were highly valued trade goods whose special features—the softness and washability of cotton, the colorfastness of the dyes, the luster and smoothness of silks and the brilliance of their colors—were much admired. In Britain, it was efforts to reproduce the effects of Indian cotton weaving and dyeing that brought about the industrial revolution.

During the Revolution, American merchant shipping had directed its energies to privateering: 626 letters of marque were issued to American privateers, whose success in preying on the British enriched their crews and supplied Revolutionary forces. During the last two years of the war, however, the British strengthened their blockade and captures increased until the New England fleet was decimated and bankrupt.[17] Moreover, at war's end, the British closed their West Indian ports to the U.S., halting legitimate trade with markets that had been vital to Yankee commercial prosperity. Southern ports recovered fairly quickly from the blow because of the unflagging British demand for tobacco, rice, and indigo. But northern ports, which had depended on the West India trade and on building ships and selling them to Britain, languished.[18] It was northern shipowners, spurred by financial hard luck, who began to look East.

During the late 1780s and '90s, when the East India Company was preoccupied with Tipu Sultan's challenge to its dominance of southern India, merchants of the new United States reinvented American commerce. Independence released American vessels from the restrictions of the East India Company's monopoly on trade with India, inaugurating a period of commercial exploration and unfettered experimentation. For the first time, American ships were free to ply the ports of the East Indies. The federal government, to ensure an advantage for its own merchants in foreign trade, taxed goods imported on American vessels at preferred rates. The duty on tea, the most sought after Asian cargo, was less than half for American-owned vessels than for foreign ships. The U.S. government thereby secured trade in East Indian commodities for Yankee shipowners.[19]

At first, American vessels sailed only as far as Cape Town and Île de France (Mauritius) to exchange their miscellaneous cargoes of provisions—flour, beef, butter, cheese, fish, rum, Madeira, candles, tobacco, tar—for tea brought there from China. American traders also purchased coffee, sugar, spices, porcelains, and silk and cotton goods from China and India. They soon found profitable opportunities to carry freight. On occasion, a vessel was sold if no profitable cargo or freight could be found, or if an irresistibly advantageous offer was made.[20] But the market at these entrepôts was not always satisfactory, and Yankee ships soon began to venture farther into Eastern

waters. Between 1784 and 1786, three American ships—two from New York and one from Salem—reached China; one Philadelphia ship arrived on the Coromandel Coast of India.[21] These voyages contributed to a revival in American shipping. By 1787, the West India trade had improved. French ports were reopened to Americans and ways were devised to evade prohibitions on trade with the British West Indies—for example, by sending cargoes via Nova Scotia.[22] By 1794, U.S. tonnage exceeded that of all Western nations except England.[23]

THE FIRST YANKEE VOYAGES TO INDIA

The first United States vessel to trade in Asia was the *Empress of China*, which departed New York for Canton on February 22, 1784, with a cargo of silver specie and ginseng. *Empress* returned the following year with tea.[24] The *United States* cleared Philadelphia a month after the *Empress'* departure and became the first U.S. vessel to arrive in India. The ship carried a mixed cargo of lead, copper, iron, ginseng, tobacco, twine, pitch, tar, staves, and cordage. Reaching French Pondicherry on the southeast coast in December 1784, ship surgeon Thomas Redman recorded in his journal of the voyage:

> passed close under the guns of the fort, with the 13 stripes flying which caused much speculation to the inhabitants what country our flag belonged to, as this was the first ship that ever hoisted the American colours on the coast of Coromandel. December 26, Sunday . . . came to anchor in Pondicherry road being exactly 9 months and 1 day from the day we joined the ship at Chester until we cast anchor at Pondicherry. . . . [The commandant, Marquis de Bussy] received us with the greatest demonstrations of pleasure and satisfaction and mentioned that every indulgence and privilege should be shewn our ship that a French ship was entitled to.

The log includes a brief description of Pondicherry, recording the first Yankee impressions of India:

> Pondicherry is one of the most healthy Settlements on this Coast, its situation is high and airy and stands on a bank fronting on the sea. . . . The town including the black one is near two mile in length and about the same in depth, the white town is separated from the black by a canal. . . . In the centre of the white town stands a most superb house, which is called the government house,

where lives the commandant, it fronts an elegant parade which is planted all round with a double row of trees, forming delightful walks, and seats fixed at different parts of it, which [are] filled every evening with both sexes taking the air. The sun is so entirely hot during the day that you see no person in the street except those who are in their palanquins, which are carried by the black boys on their shoulders, which is the way you travel all through India. Here is the old observation made (if I mistake not) by Montesquieu that one half the world are born with saddles on their backs, and bridles in their mouths, for the other half to ride them to death. The blacks here are in the most abject state of slavery and bondage to the Europeans, but amongst themselves are arbitrary and tyrannical, one to the other . . .[25]

Perhaps the most striking thing about this description is the salience of race in describing the inhabitants of Pondicherry. Americans readily perceived race as a key feature of the social order in European trading settlements, with their "black towns" where the natives lived and kept their business and the "fort" where Europeans lived and worked. Coming from a newly established nation in which republicanism, freedom, and equality had been instituted, in sharp contrast to monarchical Europe, Yankees were ambivalent about the fact that their own system encompassed only part of the population. Race remained basic to relations with vanquished Native Americans and enslaved Africans. In commenting on the racial basis of Anglo-Indian society, Thomas Redman managed to condemn both the "abject state of slavery" of blacks and their tyrannical relations to each other (presumably a reference to caste hierarchy).[26] Remarks on the racial order of British India recur often in American journals throughout the age of sail. The natural separation and inherent inequality of races remained a perennial of American perspectives on India. Redman's commentary indicates the significance of India not only for its valued commodities, but for its utility as a topic of discourse illuminating the particular qualities of American identity.

Nearby in Madras, the British closely observed the arrival of Americans on the Coromandel Coast. On January 30, 1785, an East India Company letter from Madras to London sounded the alarm—the Indian Ocean had been penetrated, Americans had come to trade, and the British East India Company now had to figure out how to deal with the interlopers:

The separation of America from the British dominions . . . seemed, among other important consequences to portend a considerable revolution in the commerce of India. An American ship is now upon the coast with merchandize, and as this was the first attempt from that quarter to explore the advantages of Oriental commerce, every information was now given which Lord Macartney [governor of Madras] could procure: On the 26 December arrived on the Coast the American ship *Independent States* [sic], Thomas Bell commander. Her burden from 350 to 400 tons [actually 200 tons]. She mounted eight guns and was navigated at her departure from America by 39 men. . . . Her cargo besides Madeira consisted of tobacco, Virginia ginseng, naval stores of all kinds, copper, and some private adventures of hardware, together with a considerable sum in dollars. The name of the supra cargo was James Moore, said to have been born at Glasgow. . . . He had taken a warehouse at Pondicherry and meant to land his cargo there and to remain himself in India. The principal owner was a Mr. Willing of Philadelphia, whose son was on board. After delivering her cargo, it was expected the ship would return to France.[27] The captain came recently on a visit to Madras by land, and waited on the Nabob [nawab] of Arcot, by whom he was well received. It was once affirmed that the captain had brought a letter from the American Congress addressed to the Nabob that it was presented and that the answer was not favorable . . . the Nabob gave Captain Bell reason to hope for a settlement on the coast. Mr. Willing, it was said had projected an East India company, and an establishment at Porto Novo was the point he wished to establish in this quarter.[28]

The governor of Madras, Lord Macartney, discredited the reports of offers from the nawab and plans to form an American trading company.[29] But if Thomas Willing did contemplate an American East India Company, he was not alone among Yankee pioneers of the Asia trade. It was to be expected that Americans would consider following the pattern already well established by England, Holland, France, and Denmark. In his journal of the *Ruby* (excerpted in chapter 3), Benjamin Carpenter expressed similar thoughts when he found himself amid the disarray at French Chandernagore during France's revolutionary year, 1789. Chandernagore, in utter turmoil, was apparently being abandoned by the French, and Carpenter proposed the town, upriver from Calcutta, as an ideal site for an American factory: "If we can conquer the silly jealousies subsisting between the American merchants and persuade them to unite their property to establish a factory here, I am fully persuaded they would realize forty percent per annum on their stock." But Americans never did unite; they continued to pursue the East India trade as independent merchants creating a niche for their family firms and their smaller vessels, both easier to man and to fill and dispose of cargoes.

The entry of American ships into the India trade was facilitated by navigational charts published in Britain and Europe, and by the skills and expertise of crew members with prior experience, most often British subjects, like the Scottish supercargo of the *United States*. This participation of foreigners in the first American voyages to Calcutta makes it difficult to pinpoint the opening of American trade there. The ambiguities of these first voyages demonstrate how merchants operated across a maritime borderland, between the jurisdictions of states, regularly manipulating or simply ignoring regulations to suit their advantage. In 1784, the same year the *United States* arrived at Pondicherry, the *Hussar*, flying Danish colors but believed by the East India Company to be American property, sailed up the Hooghly to Calcutta. The next year, the first ship actually flying the American flag, the *Hydra*, dropped anchor at Calcutta. But the *Hydra* was jointly owned by English and American merchants. When the authorities in Calcutta were unsure how to receive the vessel, the commander conveniently raised a French flag (for its supercargo had a French as well as an American commission), and the *Hydra* was admitted to the port. The next "American" entrant into Calcutta was the *Chesapeake* of Baltimore. Despite its dubious status, having an Irish owner and a British crew, the *Chesapeake* was welcomed by Lord Cornwallis.[30] Cornwallis, erstwhile foe and now governor-general of British India, determined that permitting Americans, who brought silver specie to trade, was advantageous and declared that "the vessels belonging to the citizens of the United States of America, shall be admitted and hospitably received, in all the sea ports and harbors of the British territories in the East Indies." Cornwallis "gave orders that American vessels should be treated at the Company's settlements in all respects as the most favored foreigners," and the *Chesapeake* was exempted by the Supreme Council of Bengal from paying duty on its cargo.[31]

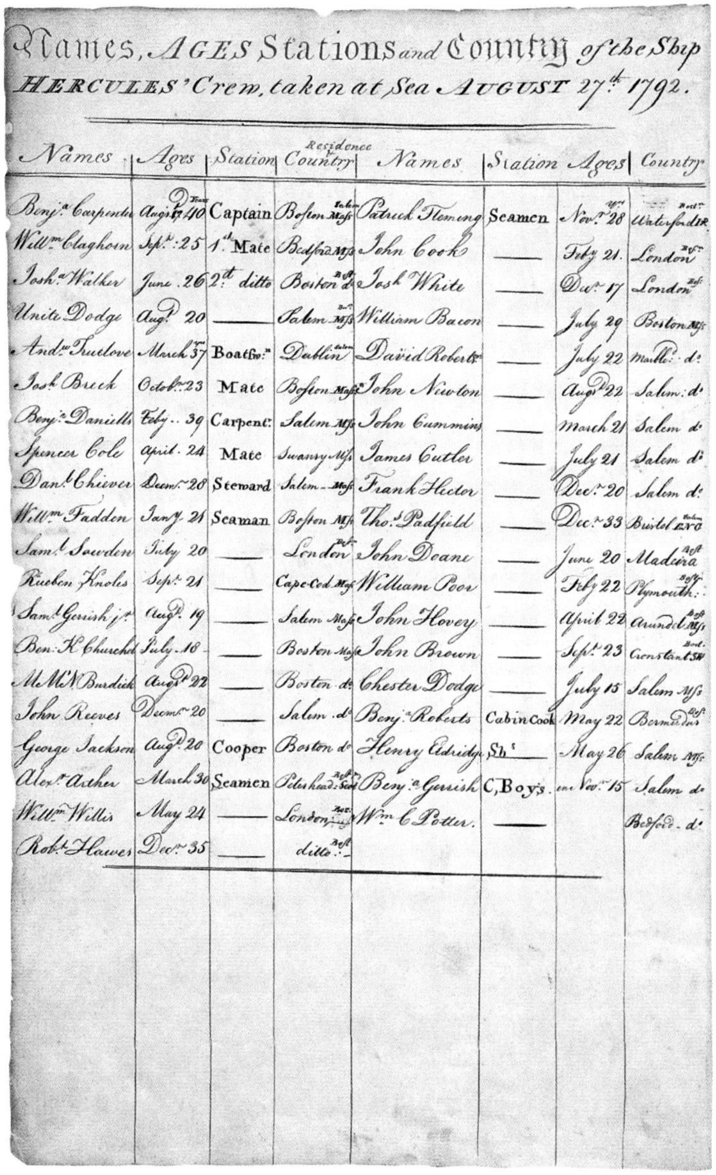
Names, Ages Stations and Country of the Ship HERCULES' Crew, taken at Sea AUGUST 27th 1792.

Names	Ages	Station	Residence Country	Names	Station	Ages	Country
Benj.a Carpenter	Aug. 40	Captain	Boston Mass	Patrick Fleming	Seamen	Nov.r 28	Waterford IR
Will.m Claghorn	Sep.r 25	1st Mate	Bedford Mass	John Cook	——	Feby 21	London
Josh.a Walker	June 26	2d ditto	Boston do	Josh White	——	Dec.r 17	London
Unite Dodge	Aug.t 20	——	Salem Mass	William Bacon	——	July 29	Boston Mass
And.w Truelove	March 37	Boatsw.n	Dublin	David Roberts	——	July 22	Marble: do
Josh Breck	Octob.r 23	Mate	Boston Mass	John Newton	——	Aug.t 22	Salem: do
Benj.a Daniells	Feby 39	Carpent.r	Salem Mass	John Cummins	——	March 21	Salem do
Spencer Cole	April 24	Mate	Swanzy Mass	James Cutler	——	July 21	Salem do
Dan.l Chiever	Decem.r 28	Steward	Salem Mass	Frank Hector	——	Dec.r 20	Salem do
Will.m Fadden	Jan.y 21	Seaman	Boston Mass	Tho.s Padfield	——	Dec.r 33	Bristol ENG
Sam.l Sowden	July 20	——	London	John Doane	——	June 20	Madeira
Rueben Knoles	Sep.r 21	——	Cape Cod Mass	William Poor	——	Feby 22	Plymouth:
Sam.l Gerrish jr	Aug.t 19	——	Salem Mass	John Hovey	——	April 22	Arundel Mass
Ben: K Churchel	July 18	——	Boston Mass	John Brown	——	Sep.t 23	Cronstant SW
M. M.N Burdick	Aug.t 22	——	Boston do	Chester Dodge	——	July 15	Salem Mass
John Reeves	Decem.r 20	——	Salem do	Benj.a Roberts	Cabin Cook	May 22	Bermudas
George Jackson	Aug.t 20	Cooper	Boston do	Henry Eldridge	Sh.s	May 26	Salem Mass
Alex.r Arther	March 30	Seamen	Peterhead: Scot	Benj.a Gerrish	C. Boy's	Nov.r 15	Salem do
Will.m Willis	May 24	——	London	W.m C Potter	——		Bedford do
Rob.t Hawes	Dec.r 35	——	ditto				

Fig. 1.6 Crew list from Benjamin Carpenter's journal of the ship *Hercules* on a voyage to the East Indies in 1792. Peabody Essex Museum Library.

AMERICAN VESSELS, CARGOES, AND CREWS

One feature that soon distinguished American vessels in the India trade was size. The ship *United States*, for example, at 200 tons[32] was less one-quarter the size of a typical British East Indiaman. The ship *Ruby*, commanded by John Rich and owned by Ebenezer Lane of Boston with Benjamin Carpenter serving as supercargo (the voyage described in chapter 3), was 230 tons, with three masts, two decks, a square stern, and a figurehead. The *Belisarius*, on which Dudley Pickman served as supercargo in 1799 (when he wrote the journal excerpted in chapter 6), was

Fig. 1.7 Silver specie, the currency of world trade in the eighteenth and nineteenth centuries. Center: Spanish dollar, Carolus IIII, minted in Mexico City, 1796 (diameter 3.9 cm). Top and bottom: overstruck Spanish dollars, a double Arcot rupee minted in Calcutta between 1811 and 1822 (diameter 3.8 cm), and a half-pagoda struck at the Calcutta mint, 1811 (diameter 3.5 cm). Peabody Essex Museum, Robinson Coin Collection.

260 tons. In the early decades of the trade, Yankee vessels typically between 250 and 350 tons were manned by crews of 25 to 45. In comparison, typical vessels of the British East India Company were 800 to 1,000 tons with crews upwards of 100.[33]

A few years after the voyage of the *Ruby*, Benjamin Carpenter commanded the *Hercules* on another voyage to Calcutta and kept a journal which opens with a crew list (fig. 1.6). The *Hercules* carried 4 officers, 9 petty officers, and 25 seamen: 38 men in all. They were young, mostly in their teens and early twenties. The *United States* in 1784 was manned by 35 men: a captain, Thomas Bell, a chief mate, two midshipmen, a carpenter, boatswain (in charge of sails, rigging, anchors, etc.), carpenter's mate, sail maker, cooper, and 21 seamen. Also

aboard were the supercargo, surgeon, steward, and two cooks. A few men were discharged at Pondicherry, Achen, or Madeira; four died on the passage. Four new seamen shipped at Pondicherry and four at Barbados.

In the late eighteenth century, the lure of the sea was enhanced by better wages and the prospect of profit on an adventure, especially for those entitled to some space for trade goods on the ship. Wages for ordinary seamen were $5 to $10 a month, for able seamen $7.50 to $18, and for petty officers up to $24, with no living expenses while at sea. Shore wages were low by comparison: between 1800 and 1810, about a dollar a day for ordinary labor, and steady work was not assured. Masters and mates received $20 to $25 in the China trade, and each officer had the privilege of one-half to five tons cargo space on the homeward passage for private adventures. Officers also received a commission of one to eight percent on the net proceeds of the voyage. The supercargo usually received a 2.5 percent commission on the funds sent out.[34] Prospects for officers were so promising that the young men who served as supercargoes were often well educated and from prominent families, hoping to accumulate sufficient capital in a short time to establish their own firms. Even for lesser officers and ordinary seamen, the pay and prospects for profit were good enough to attract ambitious boys from all backgrounds, some of whom garnered the beginnings of substantial fortunes from this start.[35]

Silver dollars, Madeira wine, and naval stores became staples of the U.S. trade in Asia until the 1820s, when industrial production began to yield goods for export—especially textiles, clocks, and glassware—and commercial paper, bills of exchange, took the place of treasure. The naval stores, pitch, tar, and lumber were mostly American products. Madeira, which had become fashionable among the British in India,[36] was purchased en route or re-exported from the United States. Foreign goods like wine became important in U.S. trade; by 1801, more than half of U.S. exports were foreign products being re-exported.[37]

During the first decade of Indo-U.S. trade, the British were tolerant of the American newcomers; their business was small and remained ancillary to the China trade until war broke out in Europe in 1792–93. They brought much-needed silver with which to trade, and expanded foreign markets for Indian goods. It was silver specie, not products, domestic or foreign, that dominated these outgoing cargoes (fig. 1.7). Spanish or Mexican dollars were the mainstay of the first decades of

American trade, before there was much in the way of domestic manufactures, and Yankee merchants had little other than the products of their forests (ginseng, lumber) and farms (butter, cheese, flour, beef) to trade. Silver made American trade with India attractive to the British. The East India Company was perennially short of treasure to fund its administration and military operations in India, and the silver Americans brought to purchase cargoes was greatly needed. American vessels also provided a means for East India Company servants to trade privately with Europe and to transfer their wealth home to England.[38]

AMERICAN STRATEGIES IN THE INDIA TRADE

A voyage to India from a port on the east coast of the United States took three to four months. With a month or two needed in port to exchange cargoes and repair a vessel for the return journey, a minimum of nine months could be expected before arrival at home port. However, direct voyages to India and back were just one strategy followed in the early years of the trade. For example, Brown and Francis, a Providence firm, sent four ships to India before 1790.[39] The first ship dispatched was the *General Washington* in 1787. The 1,000-ton ship was huge by American standards. But it carried the typical merchandise—anchors, sailcloth, munitions, claret, porter, cider, hams, chocolates, cheese, and spermaceti candles—as well as silver specie. The *General Washington* stopped at Madeira to pick up wines; it engaged in the coasting trade between Pondicherry and Madras (which the British did not like), and it continued on to Malacca, sailed back to Madras, then on to Canton, returning to Rhode Island via the West Indies. This was the kind of circuitous voyage advocated by Benjamin Carpenter in his journal of the *Ruby* (chapter 3), as much dependent on freight and port-to-port trade as on cargoes brought directly to and from the United States. Even when foreign products were brought home, as likely as not they would be re-exported in some future voyage. As an early chronicler of American trade wrote: "This trade, called the carrying trade, in some years, exceeded in value, the trade of the United States in articles of domestic produce."[40]

In 1787, the same year that Brown and Francis of Providence sent the *General Washington* to the Coromandel Coast, Elias Hasket Derby in Salem, Massachusetts, launched his family firm in the India trade. Under the immediate supervision of his son Elias Hasket, Jr., the trade was pursued with singular vigor and remarkable flexibility. Harvard-educated Hasket, after a stint in the European trade to master French and English business practices, embarked from Salem on the *Grand Turk* for Île de France. There he sold his cargo, principally American products. He also sold the ship for twice its U.S. value and with the proceeds purchased two other vessels, the *Peggy* and the *Sultana*. Hasket made Île de France his base for the next three years. From there he directed the trade of these and other Derby vessels. The *Peggy* and the *Sultana* were engaged in the country trade in India, stopping at Bombay, Colombo, Tranquebar, Nagapattinam, Madras, and ports on the Malabar Coast.[41] Cargoes arrived from Salem at Île de France in 1788 on two more Derby vessels, the *Atlantic* and the *Light Horse*, which his father sent out about six months after the departure of the *Grand Turk*. At Île de France, the cargoes were sold for bills of exchange and the ships were sent to Bombay for cotton and blackwood to be delivered to Canton. A few months later, in December 1788, the brig *Henry* was dispatched to Île de France. Derby sold the cargo and followed the *Sultana* in the *Henry* to Madras and Calcutta, where the *Sultana* was sold. The *Henry* was loaded with India goods for Salem, arriving there with Hasket aboard in December 1790. The profit from his three-year absence was almost $100,000.[42]

By 1789, there were forty American ships trading in Asian waters.[43] Benjamin Carpenter's *Ruby* (chapter 3) was one of these. Carpenter saw enormous opportunities for his countrymen: "There is so many advantageous ways of employing such a ship in India that I scarcely know which to recommend. I will here mention several which from my own experience I know must be very beneficial." As supercargo of the Boston ship *Ruby* when it sailed into the Indian Ocean in 1789, Carpenter took the ship from port to port to exchange cargoes and take on freight, much as Elias Hasket Derby, Jr., had done. There was a special freedom in these years. The trade was so new that it had not yet become subject to treaty regulations. Yankee captains and supercargoes tried ports and markets as they wished. Derby had found Île de France, then rapidly growing under French control, an ideal base for trading in the Indian Ocean. Carpenter devised a circuit of the Indian Ocean dictated by commodities, winds, and markets. These forays were exploratory. Pioneering Yankee mariners, from the last Western nation to enter the Asia

Fig. 1.8 Gopaul Kissen Mitter, Calcutta, c. 1840. Gopaul was a
son of Radha Kissen Mitter whose family firm specialized in the
American trade at Calcutta. The portrait was one of a set presented
by the Mitter family to John T. Morse of Boston around 1840.
Gouache on ivory, 15.2 x 11.4 cm; Peabody Essex Museum M5628.

trade, focused their attention on navigation and business strata-
gems. Carpenter's journal amounts to a guide to the Indian
Ocean trade, written to be shared with select partners in future
voyages.

By the early 1790s, there had been enough successful voyages to make the British wary of American competition and to
motivate the American government to seek security for its trading privileges. In 1792, President Washington appointed the
first official representative of the United States to India.
Benjamin Joy of Newburyport, Massachusetts, was sent as consul to the East Indies at Calcutta "and other ports and places on
the coast of India and Asia."[44] Joy recommended that there be
official representation also at Madras and Bombay, where many
American vessels stopped. However, during his three years in

Calcutta, Joy was unable to obtain official recognition as consul
from the British authorities. He remained at Calcutta until 1795,
when illness compelled his return home. Although a number of
others were also sent as consular representatives of the U.S.
government, the British did not formally recognize any of them
until 1851.

The first decade of American trade with India and the East
consisted of experiments in carrying freight between Asian
ports and marketing Eastern cargoes in Europe and America.
While British officials were glad to have Yankee silver, they
were disturbed by American vessels' access to the private fortunes the British were illicitly transferring to England. The East
India Company also had concerns: it did not want American
competition in the coastwise "country trade" in India or in supplying Indian goods to Europe—privileges it preferred to retain
for itself. The East India Company wanted American trade limited to direct voyages between the United States and India.

BROKERING COMMERCIAL AND CULTURAL BOUNDARIES

In the ports of the East Indies where Americans went to trade,
commerce with the West had extended the already complex mix
of languages, nations, cultural expectations, and codes of conduct from distant parts of the globe. Ships landed with officers
and crew unable to understand local languages, unfamiliar with
local practices, and at best only roughly acquainted with local
law. Accustomed to different legal and moral systems, these
men had to yield to regulations and accommodate themselves to
local practice, but often enough they flouted laws, defied accepted behavior, and passed judgment on native customs. In the
same way, the men with whom they did business helped the foreigners understand local markets and business practices while
they took advantage of their ignorance.

Because there was so much ignorance on both sides, particularly of the local and foreign values of commodities, there
was ample opportunity for sharp practices to generate good
profits. Yankee merchants' and sea captains' keen awareness of
their dependence on "native" middlemen was often expressed in
a passionately felt ambivalence. The Browns of Providence,
Rhode Island, for example, sent their ship *General Washington*
to Madras in 1787–88. The supercargo reported that "the whole
life and study of the Indians is to cheat you," yet he himself suggested that future shipments of New England rum be labeled

"West Indian" because the Indians could not tell the difference.[45] In these transactions, which crossed the boundaries of moral systems, tactics for resisting, circumventing, and avoiding inconvenient expectations and requirements were readily devised and exploited by all parties.

In this in-between space, the service of middlemen who brokered the commercial and social interactions between foreigners and local authorities and markets was crucial. In British India, the origin of these brokers as translators, a kind of boundary negotiator, was transparent in some of their titles. In eighteenth-century Pegu (now in Myanmar), they were called *linguists*, but functioned as business agents, not mere translators. In Madras, they were called *dubash*, from Tamil for "two languages,"[46] though the Anglo-Indian meaning of the term was "business agent." By the time Americans entered the scene, the *hong* merchants at Canton, the dubashes at Madras, and the banians[47] at Calcutta had established roles (fig. 1.8). They spoke English and sometimes other European languages. They were familiar with European markets—British, French, Danish, Dutch, and Portuguese. They knew how to locate and purchase suitable commodities, and how to find buyers for imported cargoes. They knew something of the business practices and social mores of foreigners and, in India, the East India Company rules that regulated commerce. They made it possible to connect buyers and sellers, and accommodate local and foreign expectations for transacting business.

Calcutta banians, Madras dubashes, and Pegu linguists all found a new demand for their services with the coming of the Americans. In Calcutta, the largest and most active port in India during the late eighteenth and early nineteenth centuries, a class had arisen of these new men who made their fortunes as intermediaries for the British East India Company. These men and their families became the elite of nineteenth-century Calcutta. As the founders of Indian modernity, they blended the Western with the indigenous, creating new cultural forms. When American vessels appeared on the scene in the late 1780s, some of these banians turned their attention to the needs of the newcomers and made the American market a specialty. In British Indian ports, there were also private British agency houses where Americans could go for the same services. But Yankee merchants tended to avoid these whenever possible, since the British agency houses in turn relied on "native" agents as middlemen, and the costs of dealing with them were necessarily

Fig. 1.9 Reverend William Bentley (1759–1819) by James Frothingham. Reverend Bentley kept a diary of all that transpired in Salem from 1784 to 1819 and described the first native of India to visit Salem in 1791. Oil on canvas, 64.1 x 54 cm; Peabody Essex Museum M4474, Gift of Lawrence W. Jenkins, 1936.

higher. For a commission of a few percent, Indian middlemen would sign customhouse bonds, find buyers for incoming cargoes, purchase and deliver commodities for export, arrange housing, and supply *sircars* or *conicopolys* (clerks) and domestic servants. American supercargoes like Benjamin Carpenter (who discusses the role of middlemen in his 1789 journal of the *Ruby* in chapter 3) were keenly aware of their importance to a successful trading voyage. At Pegu he advised: "The first thing after your arrival will be to procure a linguist." At Madras he noted, "The *dubash* is useful when you are at a loss for a market and will frequently dispose of your articles, when you have made every effort without success. . . ." It was not only their knowledge of the markets and ways of doing business that made these middlemen valuable. They also often extended credit to their clients, which made it possible for cargoes to be purchased when resources were limited. Especially in Calcutta, Yankee sea captains and supercargoes were often in debt to their native

Fig. 1.10 Benjamin Crowninshield (1758–1836) by Carta, 1803. Oil on canvas, 87 x 66.5 cm; Peabody Essex Museum M2224, Gift of Elizabeth Lambert Clarke and Katherine F. Clarke, 1941 (deposited 1917).

agents. The middlemen, because they knew doing business depended on good personal relations, sometimes befriended their American clients and entertained them, inviting them to domestic celebrations and religious festivals. These middlemen were the source of the most intimate connections Yankees had with "native" society.

FIRST IMPRESSIONS

Opportunities to experience Indian civilization in the United States were minimal during these years. News of India was usually garnered second hand and from a British perspective, through reports published in London and reprinted locally. Published prints of Indian scenes by European, especially British, artists were just beginning to be disseminated, as were English translations of Hindu scriptures and Sanskrit literature (following the organization of the Asiatic Society of Bengal in 1784). Visitors from India to the United States were exceptional.

For many Hindus, ocean travel was explicitly prohibited and punishable by expulsion from one's family and caste. In 1791, one of the first Indians to visit the United States arrived in Salem, Massachusetts.[48] His name seems not to have been recorded, but he was from Madras and employed as a servant to Captain John Gibaut.[49] When Reverend William Bentley, the town's unofficial chronicler from 1784 to 1819, encountered this visitor from Madras, he recorded in his diary (fig. 1.9):

> Had the pleasure of seeing for the first time a native of the Indies from Madras. He is of very dark complection, long black hair, soft countenance, tall, and well proportioned. He is said to be darker than Indians in general of his own cast, being much darker than any native Indians of America. I had no opportunity to judge of his abilities, but his countenance was not expressive. He came to Salem with Capt. J. Gibaut, and has been in Europe.[50]

During the first decade of trade, American energies were consumed in exploring markets throughout the Indian Ocean, experimenting with diverse outgoing cargoes, trying out American products and foreign goods to offset the quantity of treasure needed for trade. By 1794, hundreds of Americans, nearly all young men, had been to India on sailing ships. Though preoccupied with the business of trade and preparing their vessels for the long journey home, they came back with experiences, souvenirs, and commodities. Interest in India and opinions about Indian society and civilization developed as familiarity and experience were gained by increasing numbers of American mariners. They stopped at the Cape of Good Hope, Île de France, Pointe de Galle, Surat, Madras, Calcutta, Pegu, Achen, Canton, and even Nagasaki—any ports with good prospect for sales or freight to carry. From India they brought home sugar, to replace the supply from the British West Indies, and textiles, available directly for the first time. They learned the range of quality, color, and design, and the cheapest sources for the home market and for re-export to Europe, the West Indies, and Africa. Americans became leaders in the world market for Indian textiles during the remaining decades before Western industrial production became dominant and Indian textile production declined precipitously.

Besides pioneering the Asia trade for the United States, Yankee mariners also became the conduits for the beginnings of distinctly American perspectives on Asia. The first glimmerings of a Yankee India, a vision of India different from the British

Bramenes cum mortuus est secundum eorum legem crematui uxor autem eius, præ amore sese viuam in ignem cum illo conijcit

De Bramene doot wesende wort nae haer wet verbrant. en zyn vrouwe wt liefde haers mans, verbrant haer levendich met hem.

58 en 59

Fig. 1.11 Sati, the ritual suicide of a widow on her husband's funeral pyre, from *Itinerario*, 1595–96, by Jan Huijghen van Linschoten, engraved by Joannes a Doetechum. Benjamin Crowninshield concludes his description of a 1789 sati: "whether it is right or wrong, I leave it for other people to determine . . . [I]t appeared very solemn to me. I did not think it was in the power of a human person to meet death in such a manner." Hand-colored engraving, 27.9 x 39.4 cm; Peabody Essex Museum M15383, Gift of Frances Damon Holt, 1972.

and distinctly American, were developing. Already, at the end of the colonial era, Americans occasionally saw themselves, along with the natives of India, as fellow victims of British colonial power. Now they began to experience life in this remaining colony of Britain, and they were not sure what to think. One of the most extraordinary records of these early cultural encounters occurs in the midst of an otherwise routine log recording a voyage to Calcutta on the brig *Henry* in 1789, the same year as Benjamin Carpenter's voyage in the *Ruby*. The *Henry* had been sent out from Salem by Elias Hasket Derby and its trade was directed by his son Hasket. Benjamin Crowninshield, commander of the *Henry* and keeper of the log, sailed to Calcutta as part of Hasket's complex strategy (fig. 1.10). While at Calcutta, Crowninshield witnessed a *sati*, the ritual suicide of a widow on her husband's funeral pyre. He was evidently taken to the event

by another foreigner, an Irishman, perhaps with more experience in Calcutta than Crowninshield had yet acquired. Crowninshield recorded what he saw in extraordinary detail and with great sensitivity. Such measured accounts of Hindu religious practice were unusual. More typical was Benjamin Rush's diary entry reporting a discussion with a Mr. Stewart: "October 8 1791. This morning Mr. Stewart breakfasted with me. He spoke with horror of the religion of the Gentoo nation which admitted of women burning themselves on the same funeral pile with their husbands. . . . He saw one of these sights . . . ."[51]

Crowninshield's report is quoted in full (fig. 1.11):

November 28, 1789: On this day I cannot help remarking that which I was eyewitness to myself—with respect to the manner and customs of the natives of Bengal in burning a woman on the funeral piles [pyre] of her husband at

Calcutta. The operation was performed at twelve a.m. and, I believe, [it] is the custom, in general to burn at that hour. Previous to this I had information of the barbarous operation to be performed. M. Derby (Elias Hasket, Jr.)—two Irish gentlemen and myself set out for the place and arrived about three-quarters of an hour before she went on to the piles. The place where the piles was prepared was on the banks of the river four feet from the water's edge. The place was down fourteen or fifteen steps to the river, and on the lower step, the poor object sat on a cot frame alongside of her husband, a corpse, with her two little sons about her and a large crowd of the natives of both sexes. As soon as they saw us coming they immediately made way for us to see. We advanced within four or five feet of her, where we saw her with her hand lifted up, seemingly at prayers. With her two little sons by her, one about six years of age, the other about four. They seemed to be highly [?] that their mother was going to the regions of bliss in so honorable a manner and fully persuaded in a manner that she was acting right. When we got within about four feet of her she turned her head toward us, got up on her feet and paid her obeisance to us then ordered her two little sons to step forward and do the same. The Brahmins that were around her appeared all the time persuading her to go on with courage. At the distance of ten or fifteen feet from her, five or six old men were preparing the pile. All the women that were there, I observed, stood in the water up to their middles. The method they took to prepare the pile was this, as near as I can recollect. They made a hole in the clay about four feet long for to let air underneath the pile. They then took four large sticks of wood and made a square, drove down stakes each side of them, then pile[d] on light brush until they had got it about four feet high. Then they took some flax and wet it in the river. Two of the Brahmins twisted it together, then laid them across the pile about four feet apart, which was to tie the man and wife together, which finished the pile to receive the poor objects. They then took the cot on which they sat, brought them within three feet of the . . . place on which they were to be consumed. The natives paid great respect to us and made a way for us so that we got within a fathom or two of the pile and would not suf-

fer anyone to be before us. Two of the Brahmins, or high priests, uncovered the dead corpse and set it up with his face towards her back while two women, which appeared to be her sisters, went into the river and brought out two pots of water and washed her feet. Then two of the Brahmins brought [the] two pots and emptied [the water] over the corpse. The poor woman, looking round, saw her husband with his face towards her, put on a resolution and gave out word that she was ready. She got upon her feet on the cot, was steadied by two old men that appeared to be masters of the ceremonies. In a few moments one of her relations brought a little basket with little shells and three small boxes. The poor creature sat down on the couch and took the basket and gave out to three of her nearest relations a box each containing red paint. A Brahmin took one of the boxes with red paint and, with his finger, rubbed it on her forehead. The oil of coconut was then running out her hair. I could not help smiling to see that as soon as the cloth was taken off the corpse that had been two days and smelt disagreeably, a dispute [arose] between the men and women [concerning] who should have it. But finally the women got the cloth. The poor object then got upon her feet with a small basket in her hand, assisted by the Brahmins. Then four men took the dead corpse and laid it on the pile with his head to the northward. The unfortunate woman, assisted by the two principal men, stepped off the cot frame with an intention of going round the pile three times on which her husband lay. The first time, in going round, she stooped at his feet and hove about a number of little shells which everyone seemed eager to get. The second time, going round, she did the same. She being too feeble and I suppose that she had been taking opium, so that she could not perform the third round. It was surprising to see the persuasions and art the Brahmins made use of to get her to go on the piles. She then stepped on to the piles and laid herself down alongside of her husband with her right hand under his neck, his right arm over hers, his right leg over her. They immediately hove on brush and wood. There were four men stood by with green bamboos to hold her down in case she should not be able to stand the flames. After they had got on brush enough, they hove on some oil and flour of brimstone in order to make it burn more fierce. After all this was done, her two little sons came round the pile with lighted torches. The eldest of them set fire to the pile towards her head and the other towards her feet. Immediately the natives made such a noise that I could not hear the last groan, but I observed, when the pile was all in flames, that she turned over on her back. Thus ended a most horrid sight, and whether it is right or wrong, I leave it for other people to determine. There is this in it, it appeared very solemn to me. I did not think it was in the power of a human person to meet death in such a manner.[52]

Benjamin Crowninshield's narrative indicates that American mariners sometimes experienced deeply affecting, profound encounters with Indian culture that altered their conventional ways of understanding. Crowninshield's description of sati is remarkable for its author's unwillingness to judge. It is an indication that, even in these opening years of trade, the enormous gap separating Yankee and Hindu moral sensibilities might be bridged.

Fig. 2.1 Benjamin Carpenter (1751–1823), Italy, c. 1785.
Carpenter was a pioneer of the American trade with India, and master and supercargo
of the *Ruby* on its voyage to India in 1789 (chapter 3). Oil on canvas, 97.8 x 73.7 cm;
Peabody Essex Museum M351, Gift of the family of Benjamin Carpenter, 1880.

CHAPTER 2

Benjamin Carpenter, Master Mariner

I know nothing so profitable as a ship in the country trade. A ship of three to five hundred tons coppered, well-manned and armed,
with a skillful navigator, may never have an idle moment during his stay in India.[1]

When perhaps not quite thirty, Benjamin Carpenter stood for his portrait, a large oil painting, which depicts him as a prosperous, scarlet-coated merchant with one hand resting on a globe (fig. 2.1).[2] Like many adventurous young men of his generation, he had served on privateers during the American Revolution, received a mariner's education, and amassed some capital. Unlike most, Carpenter used this experience to begin a lifelong career as a merchant mariner. For more than thirty years, he commanded vessels to ports around the world, managing the business of trade himself. Although he was prosperous enough to have his portrait painted as a young man, to own a ship, and to leave his widow a mansion and four acres on Brattle Street in Cambridge, Massachusetts, he never abandoned the sea for the safer life of a sedentary merchant, as did most of his successful contemporaries. Carpenter's passion for the pursuit of trade is conveyed in his journal of the voyage of the *Ruby*, excerpted in the following chapter.

There is no record of when Benjamin Carpenter's career at sea began, but it was in full swing when he was in his mid-twenties during the Revolutionary War. He and his wife had left Salem, Massachusetts, for England at the beginning of the war when he had Tory leanings. In London, he applied to the British government for a pension. When it was denied, he returned to Salem and joined the war for independence.[3] Having made this decision, he became a staunch supporter of the new nation. Like many New England mariners, he served the cause of freedom—and his own future—on a privateer, sailing as a lieutenant on the *Oliver Cromwell*, fitted out in Beverly, Massachusetts, in 1777 and commanded by Benjamin Cole, one of more than a dozen owners.[4] During the war, he commanded the first ship sent to England with captured British officers.[5] Immediately after the war he entered the India trade. He was "the first" to carry "the thirteen stripes around the Cape of

Good Hope after the peace of 1783 and exhibited them on his return to St. Helena."[6] During his long career, he commanded many vessels out of Salem and Boston in both the European and India trades. Although he was the owner of at least one, the brigantine *Two Brothers*, he usually sailed as the commander of vessels owned by others.

Benjamin Carpenter was born in 1751 in Rehoboth, Massachusetts, the youngest of twelve children. The fates of Carpenter and his family epitomize the uncertainties of life in the eighteenth century, whether at sea or on land. When Carpenter died at the very respectable age of seventy-two, he had outlived two wives and four children. He married Esther Gerrish in 1774 when they were both twenty-three years old. She died at the age of forty-three, having borne four children; one son and two daughters died young. The other son, George, was lost at sea in 1810, and Carpenter never recovered: "a deep and aggravated domestic loss (his only son was left to perish on a wreck at sea) broke down a strong constitution."[7] One year after Esther's death, in 1795, Benjamin married her older, widowed sister Abigail. They were together twenty-seven years, until her death. In 1822, at the age of seventy-one, Benjamin married forty-two-year-old Deborah (Lee) Austin. He died less than a year later, leaving Deborah a widow for a second time.

Despite long absences from home and an intense preoccupation with business, Carpenter had the interest and energy to be active in the civic life of Salem. His involvement indicates how, through organizations formed in the new United States, the experiences of individuals were brought to bear on the organization of civil society. Carpenter joined the Salem Marine Society in 1791, when Salem was the seventh largest town in the country and its merchant mariners were leading citizens. In the same year, he also joined many of Salem's professional men and merchants as a member of the Essex Lodge of Freemasons.

Fig. 2.2 Ostrich egg from the Cape of Good Hope, length 16 cm.
Peabody Essex Museum, gift of Captain Benjamin Carpenter, c. 1805.

A few years later, in 1796, he and a few others formed a committee to improve the Salem water supply by constructing an aqueduct.

In 1799, Carpenter and twenty-one other entrepreneurs who had succeeded in making Salem prominent in the East Indies trade organized a marine society exclusively for the captains and supercargoes of Salem vessels that had navigated Cape Horn or the Cape of Good Hope. The Salem East India Marine Society became one of Carpenter's lifetime preoccupations. In 1804, he presented a pair of Venetian glass chandeliers to illuminate the Society's meeting hall. When in 1824 the East India Marine Society erected a grand building, elegant foliate ceiling medallions were carved and installed to receive the chandeliers at each end of the great meeting room (where they can be seen today). Carpenter collected many other items of interest that were eventually displayed in the Society's museum, including a conch shell from Île de France (Mauritius), a pair of lady's slippers from Persia, a woman's shawl from Otaheite (the Society Islands), an ostrich egg from the Cape of Good Hope, and an Indian stone mortar from the Salem turnpike (fig. 2.2). He served on the Society's governing Committee of Observation from 1799 to 1806. He was twice president, from 1806 to 1810 and from 1811 to 1812. Carpenter may have had other grand ambitions for what the Society might become—an American trading company like the British, Danish, or French East India companies. In his journal, he warmly endorses the idea of an American factory at Chandernagore, north of Calcutta, "if we can conquer the silly jealousies subsisting between American merchants."

In 1789, Carpenter sailed from Boston as supercargo of the ship *Ruby* on a voyage to Ceylon (Sri Lanka) and India. Carpenter's journal of this voyage is bound to the end of another account, kept when he commanded the ship *Hercules* to Calcutta in 1792–93. The journal of the *Ruby* was probably copied from some more perishable form into the space left in the fine, leather-bound volume. The two accounts are remarkably different. The *Hercules* journal is a typical captain's chronicle of a voyage, recording locations, winds, weather, unusual events, and brief port entries. Its only outstanding features are Carpenter's fine calligraphy and occasional sketches of shore views. The journal of the *Ruby*'s voyage is a supercargo's detailed record of trade in the Indian Ocean. An extraordinary document, not at all typical, it is a manual for the East Indies trade, focused sharply on the coastwise "country trade" in Asia. The entries are written in the second person, but no intended recipient is identified. Most likely, Carpenter's observations and instructions are addressed to imagined partners in future trading ventures, and to himself, as a memo or plan for future voyages.

The *Ruby* was owned by Boston merchant Ebenezer Lane and commanded by John Rich. The ship, which had been built at Milton, Massachusetts, the year before the voyage, was just under 230 tons, with two decks, three masts, a square stern, and a figurehead. The *Ruby* was typical of the relatively small vessels (compared to British East Indiamen of 800 tons and up) that Americans preferred. Smaller vessels, as Carpenter explains in his journal, were less expensive to man and to load with cargo, and they were faster. When Carpenter set sail on the *Ruby*, he was a skilled navigator, commander, and soldier. He was also, as is so apparent in his journal, a trader with considerable experience in world commodities and markets. Sometimes he traded in established markets and sometimes he tried out new ones. He seems to have especially relished exploring new markets, when his task was to discover or create exchange equivalencies between inexpensive items like seal furs, and goods highly valued at home such as silk textiles or tea. The mode of trade that he promotes in his journal was known as the "country trade" in the Indian Ocean—moving cargoes from port to port for freight charges or to profit on the sale of goods more in demand at other ports than at their place of origin.

In the British ports of India, procedures for trade, values, and currencies were well established. In Burma and on the Nicobar Islands, there were no currencies and barter was the rule. Carpenter was acutely aware that knowledge of commodities and demands for them were not the only keys to success in the Indies trade. He was also a keen observer of English, Dutch, and "native" traders' expectations. His journal advises on proper behavior at various ports, providing helpful details on the correct approach to local authorities and emphasizing the importance of conformity to their expectations. Carpenter's concern for correct conduct seems to have come from a pragmatic perception of trade as an activity on the social margins, where one's own mores were inapplicable and even irrelevant. Carpenter knew that in this situation, traders often acted rashly to get what they wanted—ultimately to their own detriment. He advocated a prudent course of acquiescing to local custom and counting on a mutual desire for trade to bring profit to both parties. However, Carpenter's astuteness about commercial encounters had another side. While he took great care to observe local proprieties, he did so only to ensure his ability to carry on trade, not out of an appreciation of the merits of other social worlds.

Like most Americans, Carpenter was certain of the moral supremacy of Western civilization. And like most Yankee merchants, he expected to take advantage of his trading partners' limited knowledge of markets and commodities, as long as doing so would not jeopardize his ability to trade. As a result, he was caught in a contradiction that he could not see, but that is obvious to readers of his journal. When at Madras, for example, he rails against the thievery of the boatmen, he also reports with equanimity that European traders regularly deceived and overcharged native buyers. With profit as the principal motive, it seems inevitable that merchants dealing in commodities and markets only partially known to their trading partners would try to get away with whatever they could to increase their sales. Their own sharp practices could be rationalized by perceptions of the others as naturally dishonest, even morally corrupt, and their presumption of moral superiority protected them from perceiving their own questionable behavior.

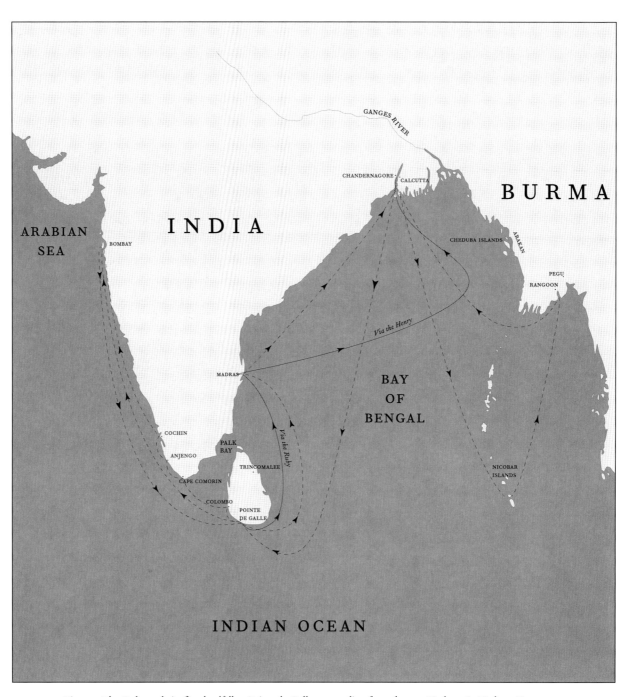

Fig. 3.1. The *Ruby* made its first landfall at Pointe de Galle, proceeding from there to Madras. At Madras, Carpenter took passage to Calcutta on an English country ship, the *Henry*. While in Bengal, he traveled upriver to Chandernagore. The dotted lines represent other voyages recommended by Carpenter in his journal for an American ship during a two- or three-year stay in the Indian ocean, carrying freight, and buying and selling cargoes.

CHAPTER 3

From the Journal of the Ruby, *1789–90*

BENJAMIN CARPENTER

The Ruby *left Boston bound for Madeira and the East Indies on the 24th of December 1789. On January 22, they made Madeira, where they stayed until February 12, moving on to Tenerife in the Canary Islands. Both ports were sources of wines to sell in India. On March 7, they anchored at Port Praya, Santiago, in the Cape Verdes: "a very miserable hole destitute of every convenience." On June 16, 1790, they landed at Port Louis, Île de France (Mauritius), expecting to trade but finding everything in confusion: "liberty is the cry and every man has his uniform and sword by his side. No prospect of a market for our tobacco etc. All business at a stand and nothing else but a reformation of government will appease the Democrats." The French Revolution had arrived at its colonies and trade was impossible. The* Ruby *soon left, bearing for the island of Ceylon (Sri Lanka). Shortly after June 28, 1790, Carpenter began his port entries (fig. 3.1).*

When you are within a league of Point de Galle,[1] you will take a pilot who will be very solicitous to carry you into the harbor, but I think it best first to send your boat on shore to try the market. For unless you can meet with tolerable sales, it is not worthwhile to carry your ship in, as the expense of anchorage is very high and by this precaution may be saved. The passage in is rather difficult, but the Dutch who are very attentive in this respect have taken care to have a number of boats stationed on each side [of] the channel. So by keeping in [this] way you avoid all danger [fig. 3.2].

On your arrival at Point de Galle it is customary to visit the Governor, Lieutenant Governor and Fiscal [sheriff]. You will find Mijnheer Sluiskin, the Governor, a pleasant man, free of access and by no means ostentatious. You will probably dine with him once or twice a week, and on every Thursday evening you will receive an invitation to his concert. If you will endeavor to render yourself agreeable you can never be at a loss for society, nor obliged to eat dinner alone at a hotel. It is necessary you should give the Governor the refusal of your cargo. He will probably trade with you, but if he should not, it can be of no determent and it is a respect which men in high office always expect. Don't omit giving the Fiscal some trifling present. By this means you gain his friendship and then little matters are overlooked.

I have always made this a rule. Let me be in what port I may, not to neglect this attention. And I have ever found my account in it. From the Governor to the meanest citizen I have made it my study to please. Let a man's occupation be what it will, you may have occasion for his aid. I have known a small present of ten pence to be the means of saving a hundred pounds. Good language will have the same effect therefore exert yourself as much as possible this way and set apart twenty pounds for these purposes. I know of no place where this attention is so necessary as in India. I have too frequently seen the old saying verified: "We let out at the bung to stop the spoil." A degree of address familiarity in conversation and attention to your person is no less necessary.

Point de Grace [sic, Galle] is a small place of little commerce, however I think it an object for vessels bound to India to touch at. You can sell the amount of 200 pounds sterling to very good advantage and the returns will turn to good account on the coast. Remember that the person you deal with is to pay the duties and charges of landing. You will be obliged to hire a cable from the shore which will cost you 100 rupees. The swell that renders this necessary bears into the harbor. You must run this cable astern. Weigh the anchor at your bow. Sheet home your topsails and then slip your stern cable and away you go.

Fig. 3.2 *Vue de Point de Galle*, 18th century. Copperplate engraving, 23.5 x 32.4 cm; Peabody Essex Museum M14054.

Point de Galle is not only a market for provisions etc. from America, but for rice and niter [saltpeter] from Bengal. Advantageous freight may always be made from Bengal to this place. Let ships bound for India touch at the Isle of Ceylon for the purpose of selling the following articles if they have time. Colombo is the capital, consequently the better market. But if they are late in the season Point de Galle is the only place: thirty pipes Madeira or good Teneriffe wine will fetch 300 rupees per pipe [126 gallons].

		RUPEES
80 cases gin	12 barrels	12 Rs
10 ton Philadelphia iron		220 Rs
40 casks nails assorted per [lb.?]		75 Rs
50 barrels beef		30 Rs
50 barrels beef		30 Rs
20 hogsheads porter		60 Rs
50 Boxes spermaceti candles		1½ [Rs] per lb
10 pipes brandy		250 Rs
10 hogsheads tobacco		20 [Rs] 100 lbs.

Sundry other articles such as hams, tongues, cheese, etc. dry goods are at present in great demand, and I am informed, will always pay a good freight. These articles would readily sell at Point de Galle, and I am told double the quantity at Colombo. Several persons at Point de Galle would have contracted to have received many of these articles and obliged themselves to pay the same prices.

Colombo is a little out of your way and would cause a detention of ten days. But if you plan your time of sailing from America so as to give sufficient time to touch here and arrive on the coast before the change of monsoon,[2] I think you would find your account in it. But as for Point de Galle you may stop there without the least determent to your inland voyage. Let your cargo consist of what it may, it will fetch fifty percent more here than on the coast.[3]

In return for the articles you sell at Ceylon, you will take the produce of the Island, consisting of the following articles—

coir [coconut fiber] cordage at	7 Rs the 100 Dutch lb	
arrack [palm wine]	100 per leaguer of 150 gallons	
cocoa nut oil	150 per leaguer of 150 gallons	
pepper	144 per candy [unit of weight in India] of 500 lbs English	
areca nuts	22 per ammonam [unit of volume in Ceylon], or 24,000 nuts	

Some few nutmegs, cloves etc. may be procured but the risk is greater than the object. The articles are sure sale and will fetch about twenty percent on the coast Coromandel or in the Bay of Bengal.

Trincomalee is nothing more than a garrison. Therefore it is not an object to stop there. We are offered a freight for the ship, of rice, from Bengal at two and a half rupees per bag or we can contract to deliver a cargo to the number of 6,000 bags at five rupees the bag. Fifty tons of niter would readily sell at 150 rupees the ton. A quantity of coarse blue and white cloth would fetch about fifty per cent.

We left Point de Galle the 10th August and on 15th saw Negapatam [Nagapattinam; see fig. 6.9] bearing west two leagues distant. We stood in fifteen fathoms all night and in the morning we were abreast of Cuddalore. And at meridian next day we came to anchor in Madras roads in nine fathoms about a mile from the shore.

On your arrival at Madras you will take your Manifest Register and Clearance and wait on the master intendant where you will make your entry [fig. 3.3]. This being done you will ask permission for as many boats as you can employ in discharging your cargo. For the surf is [so] high on shore that you can do nothing with your own boats. It is very expensive landing a cargo. Their boats will carry but two pipes or hogsheads [sizes of casks] a trip and their pay is a rupee. You must be careful to send one of your people in each boat, for the natives are so much given to thieving that unless you use this precaution, you must expect to lose many things. Your goods after they are landed are carried to the Custom House where they are inspected. From thence you may take them where you think proper.

The duties are not exacted until you have finished your sales when you pay five percent on the sales. Your expenses, excluding duties, store-rent, anchorage, etc. will be about ten percent. When you first land at Madras you will have a number of the natives about you who will [be] very solicitous to serve you as a dubash or broker. It is necessary to have one of their people, but not to be too precipitate in your choice. They are in general a [set?] of artful men and require well looking after. Pauls Vincaty is the best dubash in Madras. He has served me in two voyages and I have no reason to be dissatisfied with him. He will procure you a store and everything you are in want of. He will also supply you with cash to a considerable amount. You will also want a conicopoly [clerk] who will be of service to you in many little matters, such as supplying you with coolies, receiving your money, etc. The dubash is useful when you are at a loss for a market and will frequently dispose of your articles, when you have made every effort without success. It is better to take a small house and preferable to living at the tavern and vastly more convenient. Your house expenses will be about a pagoda [Madras currency worth 8 shillings, or 3½ rupees], whereas at the Tavern two pagodas a day. The sun is so powerful and the heat so excessive that you cannot live without a palanquin. This will cost you two rupees. After your sales are finished and accounts settled, if your dubash has

Fig. 3.3 *Madras sur les Côtes de Coromandel aux Indes*, engraved by Bergmüller, Amsterdam, c. 1785.
Hand-colored engraving, 28.6 x 41.9 cm; Peabody Essex Museum M18805,
Gift of John Dominis Holt and Frances Damon Holt, 1980.

behaved himself well and has been faithful to you, you will pay him about 30 pagodas; and the conicopoly 20.

There is a number of commercial houses in Madras, but the most respectful, and with whom it is probable you may do business is Messrs. Balfour, Spalding and Co., Mitchael Amos and Bodwin Seertoin and John Hall. They are men of property and carry on an extensive trade. Mr. Hall is very liberal in his dealing and is very attentive to strangers. He is the principal purchaser of wines and European goods. He is well informed and will give you every information respecting your proceedings while in India. To gain the friendship of such a man is by no means a small acquisition, especially in India, when you are

liable to so many impositions. Before you make any contracts or do any business of any kind it is best to consult him. He will inform you of the state of the market and the customs of the place necessary to be complied with. An attention to your person as well as uniformity of conduct is necessary to make you appear in any favorable light to the haughty Indians [i.e., Anglo-Indians] who have a very miserable opinion of the Americans, and their ignorance and shameful behavior hitherto has justly merited their censure.

General prices of Europe Goods at Madras—October 1790

		PAGODAS
Porter	in casks at	14
Ale	ditto	15
Cider	per dozen	2
[Perry?]	ditto	3
Claret English		6
ditto French		5
Pickled tongues	12 tongues [per?] cask	10
Salmon in hides		———
Hams		very high
Cheese		
Gin	12 bott. per case	4
Brandy	per gall	30 fanams
Flour, superfine	per barrel	6
Tar	ditto	3
Pitch		3½
Bar iron	2½ inch broad & 14 feet long	22/500 lbs
Lead	in sheets	14
ditto	in bars	14
Copper in sheets		
Japan [copper?]	in bars	
Shot of different sizes	per candy	18
Whale Oil		5 per barrel
Spermaceti candles	25 lb	6½ per maund [unit of weight]
Nails, every size, [?] sail		30 per lb.

(A few spars for top-masts and yards, and a few pieces of oak for anchor stocks would do well)

Russia duck		10 per bale
Ravens ditto		8 ditto
Europe cordage		7 per lb.
Saffron		3 per lb.
Gold thread		2 ounce

Dutch gold leaf on or rather copper imitation any quantity

| ready sale | | 2 Rs/book |

Cowbear—a small hard substance from the gall of bullocks and is used as a medicine in India—it is in great demand at 120 pagodas per maund

An invoice of piece goods well assorted would at this time sell for fifty percent advance but the markets are so fluctuating with dry goods that I think it dangerous to meddle with them. Every kind of eatable or drinkable is in general demand and if in good order seldom fail[s] to command a good price. Merchandize in general and especially dry goods are sold by invoice at a certain advance according to the demand. It is customary for the India captains to add twenty percent on the prime cost and then sell at twenty-five percent on the foot of the invoice so that instead of twenty-five they gain forty-five percent on the whole amount. The natives are unacquainted with the cost of goods in Europe and are easily deceived this way.

The amount of 200 pounds in garden seeds from the Cape of Good Hope would fetch 100 percent. A very considerable quantity of raisins from ditto would readily sell at four fanams per pound.

The currency of Madras is in pagodas, fanams, and cash—80 cash is one fanam; 45 fanams is a pagoda [fig. 3.4]. A pagoda is worth 8 [shillings] sterling. Fanam 2 [pence] lawf[ul?] cash. Duties at Madras are five percent on your sales.

Price current of Batavia goods at Madras Oct. 1790

		PAGODAS	
Cloves 1st qual	90	per pecul 133 lb
ditto 2nd	75	ditto
Cinnamon	55	per candy of 500 lbs
Pepper	48	ditto
Sugar 1 qual	14	ditto
" 2 "	12	ditto
" 3 "	10	ditto
Sugar Candy	28	ditto
Sugar Candy 2nd qual	23	per candy of 500 lbs
Coffee	22	
Nutmegs	60	per maund 25 lbs
Mace	70	ditto
Rice		50 per garce [unit of volume for rice] of 9256 lbs
Arrack		30 per leaguer of 150 gallons

China goods in general fetch about fifty percent advance—you may reckon with safety on this advance, on fine teas, nankeens, sugar candy and rather more on china ware. These articles are in great demand and will at all times readily sell. It is so much out [of] the way for China ships homeward bound to go to Madras that it is by no means an object. But if you are bound from China to Bengal in the southwest monsoon,[4] I would advise you to dispose of part of your goods at Madras. Your goods will fetch the same price here, and you have the advantage of ten percent on your bills. The universal use of umbrellas in China would, I should think, cause a demand for whale bone, and, as we have no market for it in Europe, we ought to endeavor to find vent for it in Canton.

Fig. 3.4 Coins used in Madras, from top: pagoda (diameter 2.5 cm), fanam (diameter 2 cm), cash (diameter 1 cm). Peabody Essex Museum, Robinson Coin Collection.

Price current of sundry articles [from] Ceylon at Madras 1790 viz

		PAGODAS
Arrack	per leaguer	36
Coconut oil	ditto	38
Coir cordage	ditto	12
Cinnamon	per lb	
Cloves	per lb	1
Pepper	per candy	55
Arrack nuts	per ammonam of 20,000	10

The current prices of sundry merchandize, the produce and manufacture of Bengal at Madras—Octo. 1790

			PAGODAS
Table rice	1st qual.	per garce of 9256 lbs	80
ditto	2nd ditto		60
Cargo rice	ditto		50
Pease	ditto		70
[Minamaloo?]	ditto		50
[Persaloo?]	ditto		60
Wheat	ditto		50
ditto	from Yanam[5]		75
Ghee [clarified butter]		per candy of 500 lbs	27
Sugar	1st quality	ditto	15
ditto	2nd	ditto	13
ditto	3rd	ditto	10
Jaggery [palm sugar] in its natural state ditto			8
Cumin seeds, black		ditto	6
[Mintotoo?]		ditto	8
Ginger		ditto	10
Cumin Seeds	1st qual	ditto	18
Cumin seeds, split,		per candy 500 lbs	14
Taffeties	1st qual	per corge of 20 pieces	60
ditto	2nd	ditto	50
ditto	3rd	ditto	45
Malda[6] cootanies,[7] 18 cubits long			50

[Sidabad?]	ditto	9	ditto	17
Radanagar[8] raw silk		per maund of 25		33
Cossimbazar[9]	ditto	ditto		27
Mugga [wild silk]		ditto		10
Muggatooties		ditto		11
Opium		per box		150
Tincal [borax]		per candy of 500 lbs.		70
Long pepper		ditto		20
[Sanigaloo?]		per garce of 9256 lbs.		60

There are many other articles suitable for the Madras market, but as it is customary to sell these goods by invoice at a certain percentage, I don't think it necessary to enumerate them here. It is a general rule, established by the merchants in India, that all piece goods from different parts of the coast should be sold at twenty percent advance. It is invariably attended to.

[*Omitted: prices of Malay goods at Madras*]

A person of abilities in the mercantile line with a ship 300 to 500 tons, copper bottom and a fast sailor may be sure to do well in the country trade provided dispatch is made and economy observed. He must be determined to stay in India two or three years, and make himself well acquainted with navigation and the prevailing winds. He will be sure to behave himself in such a manner as to gain the acquaintance of the principal merchants and pay the strictest attention to keeping your ship in order. By this means you will not only have the refusal of freights, but very frequently get a number of passengers. There is so many advantageous ways of employing such a ship in India that I scarcely know which to recommend. I will here mention several which from my own experience I know must be very beneficial.

Freights are high, and as it is a certain profit, I should rather prefer it [than] to load on my account, but it frequently happens that a profitable voyage may be made with certainty. In that case it would be advisable to embrace the opportunity. Let your ship sail from Bengal the first of November with a cargo of rice. She will proceed to Point de Galle where if she meets a good market, dispose of the cargo and take in return arrack, oil and some spices. With these articles proceed on to Bombay where you will sell your arrack 130 Rupees, oil 180, and the spices at about fifty percent; let your cargo [be] from Point de Galle, as it is the best article and surest sale at Bombay. Having disposed of your cargo you may then take a freight of cotton for Madras. After you have delivered your cotton you will take freight of salt for Bengal, where after it is discharged and all accounts settled, you will have finished your first voyage.

This voyage will take three and a half months provided you sail the latter end of one and beginning of the other monsoon [i.e., November/December]. You will then have time for another such one, before the cotton season is over. This I think is the best thing you can do at this season. You will then take in your cargo of rice at Bengal and proceed exactly as you did on your former voyage. By the time you have finished your second voyage it will be June, which is the end of the Bombay and commencing of the Pegu [in Burma] trade. You will doubtless after being seven months at sea want some few repairs which may detain you at Bengal till the first of July which is the best time for a voyage to Pegu.

In a voyage from Bengal to Ceylon you have many advantages arising from the general demand of rice at every port on the Malabar coast. For instance, suppose you were disappointed in a market at Point de Galle, you have then Colombo, Anjengo, Comorin and Cochin [fig. 3.5]. These are places where you may never be at a loss to sell at. A cargo of rice I should prefer selling at Point de Galle and taking in return arrack, etc. for Bombay. It is not necessary for your ship to anchor at either of these ports, unless you have a prospect of sales. But when you arrive in sight of the place, hoist your boat and go on shore to learn the state of the market. If you should meet with encouragement you may bring your ship too, but till then it is quite needless.

The plan of this voyage will be as follows. The ship will be about three to five hundred tons, coppered and a good sailor. She will carry ten or twelve guns with every apparatus necessary for them with thirty men, a gunner, two mates and provisions for five months. She will then be in a situation for any part of India. The expenses of such a ship per month in India including insurance, hire[d] seamen's wages etc. is as follows viz:

Fig. 3.5 *A View of Gingeram [Janjira] on the Malabar Coast* by Benjamin Carpenter.
The drawing is bound in the volume containing the journals of his voyages on the *Ruby* and *Hercules* (1793).
Ink on paper, 8.9 x 19 cm; Peabody Essex Museum Library.

	RUPEES
Capt. wages per m[onth]	300
Chief mates	50
Sec^d ditto	35
Gunner	20
30 Seamen	200
	———
	605
Provisions for above crew, viz.	
10 bags rice	30
dall [lentils], ghee and salt	12
Beef, pork, pease etc	70
	———
	717
Wages, provisions etc. brought here	717
Candles, oil lamps, etc.	25
Wood and water	12
Sundries	12
Expenses of ship includg officers and wages	766
wear and repair	766
Insurance	400
Charges of ship per month	1932 Rupees

The ship will carry 6000 bags rice which will cost at Calcutta 1½ Rupee per bag:

say 6000 Bags rice.	at 1½ Rs	9000
Pilotage down river		500
Charges of weighing		500
		———
Sicca Rs		10,000

By sales of 6000 bags rice at Point de Galle @ 5 Rupees (which is a moderate price it is now selling at 7 & 8 at Bombay 9 Rs per bag)	30,000
Expenses of anchorage etc to be deducted	1000
Net amount of sales at Point de Galle	29,000
Net profit on sales	19,000

With the net profit on the sales you will purchase the following articles, viz.

200 leaguers arrack	at 100 Rs	20,000
50 ditto oil	at 150	7,500
spices		1,000
charges		500
		———
	Rs	39,000 [sic 29,000]

With this cargo you will proceed to Bombay where you will sell at price as follows—

200 leaguers arrack	120Rs	24,000
50 ditto oil	180Rs	9,000
spices		1,250
		34,250
Custom duties, coolie hire & leakage 10 pct		
		2425
		31,835 [sic, 31,825]
Net profit on this sales at Bombay		2835 [sic, 2825]

Your ship is now empty and you may either load with cotton on your own account or take freight to Madras. I should advise by all means the freight. Your ships will carry 100 bales, the freight of which will be

10 Rs pr bale	10,000 Rs
Expenses of anchorage etc.	1000
Net profit of the freight from Bombay	9000

After you have discharged your cotton at Madras you will then take a freight of salt to Bengal. Your ship will carry 1000 garce, the freight of which will be Rs 60 per garce Rs 6000

Pilotage up river and sundry other expenses 1500
Net profits of freights to Bengal 4500

Thus in three and a half months you will have performed this voyage. Let us see the result of it. The charges for the ship including officers' and seamen's wages, wear and repairs, insurances etc. for three and a half months will be.

	7,000Rs
Supra cz	
By profit gained in the sales at Point de Galle 19,000	
ditto at Bombay	2,835 [sic, 2825]
ditto freight from ditto	9,000
ditto on salt to Bengal	4,500
	35,335 [sic, 35,325]
Charges of ship to be deducted	7,000

The profit arising from this voyage will be 28,335Rs. [sic, 28,325]

Suppose the ship to be supplied with sails and rigging sufficient for three years. I have made no charge against her, for any of those articles, but should it so happen that she would be in want of them, they will be very expensive.

You are now in Bengal with a property of 28,000 rupees. If you wish to perform another voyage to Point de Galle and Bombay, which no doubt you will, you have for this sum 10,000Rs [which] will answer all your purposes. You can then either remit your money home, or lend in Bengal at twelve per-cent—but if you wish to make a voyage to the Malay Coast, you will want the whole property and some more added to it. (For the plan of such a voyage [see] a few pages further.)

If you make a second voyage to Point de Galle and Bombay you will again arrive at Bengal in July, which is the exact season for a voyage to Pegu where another advantageous voyage may be made. Let your investment consist of the following articles Viz! Coarse blue cloths, cutlery, tobacco, sword blades, hatchets, pewter spoons, small looking glass[es] and a few other trifling matters with about 500 Rs in gold. Having all things in readiness you will make the best of your way for the Nicobar Islands where with this investment you will purchase a full cargo of coconuts. From thence you will proceed to Rangoon, Pegu. This cargo of nuts will purchase at Rangoon a full load of timber, which will net a handsome profit on the Coromandel Coast or at Bengal.

Memorandum of a cargo suitable for the Nicobar Islands, Pegu, and in what manner you are to proceed on your arrival in Rangoon.
Viz.,

	RUPEES
Coarse blue cloths	300
Cutlery	400
Sword blades	100
hatchets	100
small looking glasses	100
	1000
Pewter spoons	100
Beads, jews harps & rings	100
20 gold mohurs	320
Amt of cargo for Nicobar Islands Rs	1520

Exclusive of this, take in the value of 500 Rs in tutinage [tutenag, a white metal alloy] and spices for the purpose of purchasing elephants teeth and wax. Pilotage and charges of landing 700 Rs. Cost of the cargo with charges at Bengal 2220 Rs. This cargo of 2220 Rs. will purchase at the Nicobar Island 280 thousand nuts which are worth at Pegu forty rupees per thousand. This cargo of nuts will purchase at Rangoon a full load of timber.

Say sales of 280,000 coconuts	at 40 Rs	11200.
Net profit on your sales at Rangoon		Rs 8980.

The timber at Rangoon will cost	7871
Expenses, & charges of the ship with duties, etc.	1109
The cost of the timber at Rangoon with charges	8980
Sales of the timber at Bengal	11301
Pilotage and other charges to be deducted	1000
	10,301
Net profit on the sales of timber at Bengal	1321

This finishes your sales of nuts at Rangoon and of timber at Bengal—the net profits of which is 10301

Let us see the proceeds of the tutinage and spices and sales of elephants teeth, etc.

NB. the timber is very low in Bengal at this time owing to the vast quantity brought this Season—it is generally worth forty or fifty percent more than I have computed it at, in the above calculations.

Tonage, spices etc. the prime cost in Bengal is	500 Rs
Sales of these articles at Rangoon	1454
Charges, duties, coolie hire etc.	150—1304
Net profit of Sales at Rangoon	804
Cost of elephants teeth and wax at Rangoon	804
Sales at Bengal after paying the duties, etc.	1135
Net profit on sales of teeth & wax in Bengal	331
Net profit of the sales of tutinage etc on the return to Bengal	
	1135

Charges of this ship including the seamen's wages, wear and repair, insurance etc. for two months (which is the time the voyage is performed in) will be 3125 Rs
Supra Cz

By the net profit	on the sales at Rangoon	8980
ditto	on the timber at Bengal	1321
ditto	on elephant teeth	1135
		11,436
The profit of this voyage is		8311 Rupees

This will bring you to the middle of September. You may then make a short trip to Madras or Point de Galle and return again to Bengal the first of November. It will then be a good time for a voyage to Batavia—several islands off [the] west coast of Sumatra and Mocha [seaport in Yemen]. I will presently give the plan of such a voyage. But first a little advice respecting your transactions at Pegu.

On your arrival at Pegu you will meet with a number of the natives who will want to trade with you. Pay no attention to them till you have settled the duties and have permission from the prince so to do. The first thing after your arrival will be to procure a linguist. Inquire of an old man by the name of Francisco. He is an honest fellow speaks the English tongue perfectly well and will serve you faithfully. He will immediately on your arrival take you to the prince or Mahoon to whom you will render an exact list of your ships company: stores, guns and the invoices of your cargo. After he has examined your invoices etc., he will ask you if you wish to trade. If you do, he will demand one or two of your topsails and sometimes your rudder as security for your good behavior and to prevent your going off without paying the duties. These being in his custody and some trifling presents made him he will grant you liberty to sell your cargo, and to purchase timber or anything else, except precious stones with which notwithstanding the country abounds. They are not allowed to send any of them away. Be careful to appear very condescending [i.e., humble] while in the presence of the prince, and not assume any haughty airs during your stay there. If you strictly attend to this conduct, you may expect to find the greatest hospitality. But should you offer the least insult to any one of the inhabitants, you must expect to be severely handled.

Your cargo when landed is put in the king's godown [warehouse] and when you have finished unloading several officers will go on board to search your ship. Endeavor to find out the day they intend to visit you and make some little preparation to give them a good reception. This small attention will often have a very good effect. This business being over you will go with them to the prince and then settle the duties which will amount to about thirteen percent. You have then fully conformed to the customs of the place and are at liberty to commence your traffic. You will find no difficulty in a speedy sale. I should advise you to accept the first offer—if any ways tolerable—for the arrival of a second ship frequently reduces the price fifty percent. If you can persuade the officers to let your cargo remain in the king's godown till you can find a sale for it, you will [save] the coolie hire which is very high.

Timber is plenty and they have generally great quantities on hand. Should you want any carpentry work done apply to an old man named Achad. He is a good workman and reasonable in his charge. They have no coin at Pegu. Their pieces [of silver] are in different shapes and valued as in China. When you make a bargain be sure to mention the quality of silver and ready money on delivery of the goods. Do not credit any of them. You will take a cash keeper or Shroff [money changer] who will examine the silver and prevent any impositions. You will pay him one percent on all you receive and pay. He is answerable for any deficiency and, in case of embezzlement, the law is often where you can obtain immediate satisfaction. Their accounts are kept in silver trials of the value of 125 percent and arrals: 100 arrals is a trial.

Coolies and workmen are paid in silver of forty percent value. Duties, anchorage, etc. is silver of twenty-five percent. A trial of twenty-five percent is the value of an Arcot rupee.

Having your cargo on board and all things in readiness—you will make application for permission to depart. They will then demand the duties, and anchorage and other charges which will amount [to] 1100 trials of twenty-five percent or Arcot rupees. When this is settled you have leave to quit the place.

[*Omitted: section on costs and prices at Pegu and advice on a voyage to Prince of Wales Island*]

A good freight may be made from Bengal to Ceylon or Bombay [fig. 3.6]. [A] good ship from three to five hundred tons may never be at a loss for a full freight to either of these places. A ship of 300 tons will carry 5,500 bags the freight of which at a very moderate computation would be 82,500 rupees. This voyage is performed in five weeks. To Bombay the freight would be 1100 Rs which would take two m[onths]. The expenses of such a ship in India, including seamen's wages, wear and repair, insurance etc., will be 2,000 Rs. per month. If you should choose to take a load of rice on your own account in preference to a freight, there are several good markets and where you may [be] sure to meet a speedy sale. The consumption of rice is so immensely great in India and consequently in general demand that you are never at a loss to find a ready market.

Cargo of rice at Bengal will cost one and a half rupees per bag. At Madras it will sell for four; at Ceylon, Cape Comorin or Cochin at five, and at Bombay six and a half per bag. At Madras you receive specie in payment. At Ceylon they have no silver nor gold, of course you will receive the produce of the island, consisting of arrack, coconut oil, areca nuts, pepper, coir cordage, and some few spices. [At] Comorin, Cochin and Bombay you will be paid in rupees. The articles from Ceylon will sell at Bombay at about ten percent advance. At Madras for twenty percent and at Calcutta for twenty-five percent advance. At Bombay you may be pretty certain to obtain a freight of cotton to Madras or China provided you arrive there any time between the 15th May and 15th July. A ship of 300 tons will carry 600 bales cotton the freight of which to Madras will be ten rupees per bale and to China twenty rupees. There is a certain quantity of cotton sent yearly from Bombay to Madras on account the India Captains take it from thence to China.

I know nothing so profitable as a ship in the country trade. A ship of three to five hundred tons coppered, well-manned and armed, with a skillful navigator, may never have an idle moment during his stay in India. There has no vessel been sent from America though it is so evidently advantageous. If you have not sufficient funds to employ the ship and cargo in India, it is an easy matter to remit the proceeds of the cargo home and let your vessel pursue the freighting business. The only object is to get a ship in India and if you are obliged to send her out in ballast, even then you may be sure to accumulate a very pretty property. For if the country ships that sail at three times the expense of our ships make such rapid fortunes, surely we cannot fail to find our account in it.

Fig. 3.6 Bombay, printed in Paris, 18th century. Hand-colored engraving, 43.2 x 26.7 cm; Peabody Essex Museum M17717, Gift of John Dominis Holt and Frances Damon Holt, 1978.

I have here stated an account of the expenses of a country ship which I took passage in from Madras to Calcutta in order to show the immense differences of her charges and ours—Ship *Henry* burthen 800 tons.

[*Omitted: charges for the ship* Henry; *advice for voyages to the coast of Arakan (now Rakhine, in Burma) and the Straits of Molucca*]

Having completed the sales of the *Ruby*'s cargo, and settled all accounts at Madras this morning, October 25, I took passage on board the *Henry*, a large English country ship of 800 tons burthen bound for Bengal. It being late in the season and the monsoon about changing we, in order to avoid the easterly winds and current on the Coromandel Coast, stood over to the opposite shore, and in sixteen days made the coast of Arakan, about

Cheduba islands. We there took the variable winds and in twelve days struck sounding off the eastern brace in the River Bengal. At 8 pm being in the latitude 20° 40', longitude 88° 30' we sounded and found bottom with 40 fathom line, soft mud. Stood in all night towards Balasore roads and shoaled the water very regular. As per journal annexed. At 7 am saw the Nelligree [Nilgiri] Hill from the dock bear from NW by W to W NW distant 12 leagues; 18 fathoms sand and mud. Stood in to 9 fathom soft mud. Middle hill bearing NW by W distant 7 leagues. At meridian tacked ship and stood [?] the outer edge of the western sea reef.

[*Space left in original for a sketch*]

Thus appears the Nelligree Hill bearing from W by N to NW distant 10 leagues fifteen———fathom———and dark sand.

———— The bearing and distance of the buoys, with instructions for sailing into Bengal River in case of an emergency and you have no Pilot on board—

[*Omitted: sailing instructions with information on buoys and depths*]

On your arrival at Calcutta you will proceed as at Madras—the manner and customs are the same with this difference only—the inhabitants are more sociable and friendly. You will find them ready to assist you in everything. They are very liberal and deal on honorable terms. On my arrival at Bengal I was an utter stranger to every person there—and notwithstanding I was destitute of even a line of recommendation, I found the greatest hospitality and very soon became acquainted with the principal merchants there.

The produce and manufactories of Bengal are every way suited for the American market, but as the trade to this country is a very recent affair, they have not those goods on hand which we are most in want of. For this reason our ships are obliged to wait three or four months for a cargo. This inconvenience is easily remedied by a previous order. You may then be sure to have your goods in readiness on your arrival, and then your detention may not be more than three weeks or a month. You ought to plan your voyage so as to arrive in Bengal at the end of the southwest [monsoon] and sail from there at the beginning of the northeast monsoon.[10]

A voyage from America may be performed in fourteen months—and a person well acquainted with a suitable cargo will seldom fail to make a good voyage. Their sugar and niter will ballast your ship, you can fill her with dry goods. The sugar is of a superior quality to the West India sugar[11] and is sold at six rupees per maund of eighty-two pounds English. The country abounds with a great variety of drugs of the first qualities. They are seldom brought down to Calcutta, but are easily procured about Patna.[12] They are sold astonishingly cheap, and if care is taken in choosing them they will turn to very good account in Europe. There is many articles in Bengal which would answer well in America that we are not yet acquainted with. There are also many things [that are] the produce of America that would net good profit and would be a sure remittance in India. My stay was so short in India that I had not time

to gain every information I could have wished, but such as come within the compass of my inquiries I will here mention.

America abounds with furs of different kinds, any quantity of the various species would very readily sell in Bengal at 100 percent profit.[13] They purchase them to send to China, which is by far the best remittance they can make. It is a little surprising that [given] the number of ships we have sent to China that none of them should think of furs. They are certainly the best article they can carry. They pay but a small freight and net at a handsome profit. The sea otter from the northwest coast of America sells in China for fifty Spanish dollars per each skin. Surely there cannot be such astonishing differences in the price of American furs as to render them unprofitable. If not it is an unpardonable neglect of our supercargoes not to have made themselves acquainted with their value in China. I had conceived before I left Boston that furs might constitute a very considerable part of our remittance to India and China and from the information I have received from several merchants in Calcutta I have by no means formed a wrong idea, they are used by every class of the Chinese and consequently must be in general demand.

3000 barrels whale oil would readily sell in Calcutta for 20 Rupees on the barrel which is double the price it sells at in America. [*Omitted: advice on hunting whales and seals; comments on potential sales from American birch bark (used for dye), and American-made gin, duck, and nails*]

After duly considering the advantage arising from this trade, there is no one can venture to affirm that the commerce with India is prejudicial to America. [*Omitted: prices current at Calcutta of imports and exports, and charges at Canton*]

Having contracted for a quantity of chintz to be manufactured at Chandernagore (a French factory about 30 miles from Calcutta) [fig. 3.7].[14] In order to choose patterns and expedite matters, I this morning hired a buggerow[15] and made an excursion up the river. The rapidity of the current carried me at the rate of eight miles an hour and in four hours I arrived safe at Chandernagore.

I found everything in the greatest confusion. The Patriotic Party had gained the victory over the Aristocraties and taken possession of the [French East India] Company's treasures,

CHANDERNAGORE

Fig. 3.7 *Chandernagore* by James Moffat from his series of ten views of India and China. Published at Calcutta, 1800–1803. Aquatint, 33.7 x 49.5 cm; Courtesy of the Yale Center for British Art, Paul Mellon Collection.

warlike stores etc. which caused a total stagnation to every kind of business. The situation of this delightful spot and its vicinity to the different manufactures suggested the idea to me that it would be a most excellent place to establish an American factory. I conversed with many of the principal men there who all gave me to understand that the place would shortly be abandoned. If so would it not be an easy matter to make interest with the Court of France for liberty to establish a factory there for a trifling yearly quota [i.e., a share]. I have not doubt such a privilege would readily be granted. Within a very few miles of the manufactures, how easy would it [be to] procure goods on the most advantageous terms. The natives are much dissatisfied with the French agents and if we were once established there on a respectable footing we should very soon be overflowed with the choicest goods. It is almost incredible the difference in the price of goods at Chandernagore and Calcutta.

I lived six days with Mr. Ward, a gentleman in the [British East India] Company's service, who had resided fifteen years in the country and was superintendent of one of the principal English Factories at Beerbhoom [Birbhum]. He had retired from business and was living at Chandernagore to avoid the noise of the Town. He had by him muster of every specie of goods manufactured within 5,000 miles. He was kind enough to present me with a few of them—with their original prices.

These I carefully kept, and on comparing them with some of the same kind at Calcutta, I found seventy-five percent od[d]s [difference] in the prices. Among his musters he showed some patterns of silks of the finest fabrication and far superior to any English or China silks I ever saw. And also a variety of medicinal drugs very valuable in Europe, and in Bengal are sold for a mere trifle.

Mr. Ward was a very intelligent man and gave me a great deal of good information. He was kind enough to offer me a letter of recommendation to any and every part of the country. He strongly advised me to tarry in Bengal over the season and to take a tour through the country and visit the manufactories, where, he told me, I could make contracts to the greatest advantage. The people in Calcutta, says he, have not the least idea how cheap the goods are manufactured at a little distance up the country. The factors [traders] can find no vent for their goods in the country and are obliged to send them to the merchants at Calcutta for sale. They invoice their goods at fifty percent above prime cost and make the people in Calcutta believe it is the primitive cost. Where as if a person should, with his cash in hand, go up the country himself, he would purchase this same goods at ten percent.

The navigation to Chandernagore is perfectly safe and there is a sufficient depth of water for a vessel of 1,000 tons to anchor within a cable's length of the shore. If we can conquer the silly jealousies subsisting between the American merchants and persuade them to unite their property to establish a factory here, I am fully persuaded they would realize forty percent per annum on their stock. This is certainly a far greater profit than they can gain on their Europe, West India or any other trade whatever.

[*Omitted: advice on the Bengal–West Africa and Persian Gulf trade; information on seals and whales; recommendation of pickled oysters and lobsters as cargo from America; notes on voyages to New Holland and Batavia; memo on drugs for sale in America; note on Spanish galleons; prevailing winds and weather*]

Carpenter's journal ends abruptly. He may have rejoined the Ruby *for the voyage home or he may have taken passage on another vessel. Reverend William Bentley noted Carpenter's presence in Salem on March 11, 1791, at a meeting held to reorganize the Essex Lodge of the Masons.*[16]

handsome Figures and to be procured if not, this Su[m]
had better be laid Out in the Articles beforementione[d]

Recapitulation

~~other side~~

2000	Dollars in Mock Pulicat Handkerchiefs	
5000	D° in Beerboom Gurrahs	
3000	d° in Illiabad Sannas, Jallipore Malmedy, Tanda[s]	
2000	Nabob Gungy	
1500	Oud Cossahs	
1500	Foolpoore D°	
1500	Salam. D°	
1500	Guzzenahs	
2000	in by d° Pieces of Chintz or in the foregoing Art[icles]	
20,000.		

I shall inclose in this the Patterns of such Cottons, as [I]
happened to have in Our Store of which you will obs[erve]
I have recommend only One Kind, We had most of th[e]
other Sorts that I have recommended, and they have
been dispos'd of — their having met with so read[y]
a Sale is the Surest proof, of their being the best Calcul[ated]
for the Markett — If the above information Shou[ld]
prove of any Service to you, I shall be happy, that it
may not lead you into any error, you will please ca[re]
-fully to compare it with what you may derive fro[m]
other Sources —

I am Your Friend & hum: ble Serv[t]

B. Pickman Jr

To Israel Thorndike Esq[r]

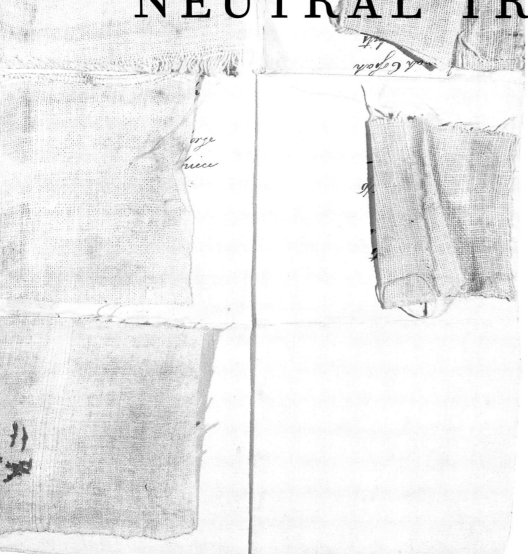

PART II

HALCYON DAYS OF NEUTRAL TRADE

The Mount Vernon of Salem comanded by Capt. S: Elias Derby = 1789

Fig. 4.1 *The Mount Vernon of Salem Commanded by S: Elias Derby, 1789* [sic, 1798] by Michel Felice Corné.
The painting commemorates Elias Hasket Derby, Jr.'s capture of a French privateer near Gibraltar during the
undeclared war between the officially neutral United States and France, 1798–1800. Watercolor, 40.6 x 54.4 cm;
Peabody Essex Museum M1975, Gift of John Morris, 1865.

CHAPTER 4

Heyday of the India Trade

THE CHALLENGES OF NEUTRAL TRADE

In 1793, when war broke out in Europe, President George Washington issued a proclamation asserting that the United States "with sincerity and good faith, [would] adopt and pursue a conduct friendly and impartial toward the belligerent powers."[1] The president also decreed that dealing in contraband and aiding or abetting the hostilities were punishable offences. As citizens of a neutral country, American merchants and sea captains were expected to pursue their trade impartially with all parties to the conflict. During war, their activities were supposed to be constrained by the so-called rule of 1756, devised by British courts and accepted by other Western powers,[2] which obliged neutrals to abide by existing restrictions, so that trade closed to foreign shipping in peacetime remained off-limits in wartime. Accordingly, American ships could continue to trade, for example, at both London and Marseilles, as long as they dealt in the usual goods.

But wartime upheavals produced new conditions and opportunities. As more of Europe was drawn into the war and British naval supremacy created a virtual blockade of the continent, the French and their allies were unable to bring products home from their colonial possessions. Before the war, Americans had operated under stringent, if often disregarded, restrictions in the West Indies. The British banned many U.S. products and allowed others, subject to high duties, only in British vessels.[3] Similarly, the French required that trade at their colonies be carried in French vessels. During the war, the French and their Continental allies, cut off from their West Indian colonies by the British blockade and the depredations of the British navy and privateers, willingly allowed Americans to bring goods to their West Indian possessions and transport cargoes to their home ports. Because these voyages pursued trade that had been closed to Americans in peacetime, they were in violation of the 1756 rule of war. To take advantage of this opportunity while maintaining the appearance of compliance

with the rule, products of the French, Spanish, and Dutch West Indies were first landed at U.S. ports. Goods intended for Europe were later reloaded and shipped with new papers.[4] The U.S. government sanctioned and facilitated these "broken voyages" by refunding duties on the goods that were re-exported.[5]

Other marginally licit and illicit opportunities were also energetically pursued. For example, the Dutch, preoccupied by the war in Europe, used Americans to keep up their trade with Japan—in this case skirting Japanese restrictions that allowed trade with Europe only through the Netherlands—by chartering U.S. vessels that then sailed into Nagasaki as Dutch. In their eager pursuit of the neutral carrying trade, many American sea captains went further, flouting the "rule of war," by taking cargoes, for example, from British India to French Mauritius (Île de France). On the vast oceans that belonged to no country and in the ports of alien nations, American mariners followed others' rules when necessary and disregarded them when there was an advantage to be gained. This was a risky strategy, but the prospect of substantial payoffs was irresistible. During the Napoleonic wars, hundreds of American merchant vessels pursued their fortunes, capitalizing on their position as outsiders to the conflict.

Yankees' suspected transgressions of neutrality and their perceived services to the other side soon elicited hostile responses from both the British and the French. The British stepped up pressure on American shipping by ruling that enemy property, even in neutral vessels, was liable to seizure at sea. They detained and searched Yankee vessels for English-born seamen to be pressed into service.[6] In the United States, many saw these British actions as intolerable violations of national sovereignty, especially considered alongside British efforts to impede U.S. expansion by colluding with Native Americans on the western frontier. The U.S. Congress wanted to retaliate, but President Washington, in hopes of averting war, sent Chief Justice John Jay to London in 1794 to negotiate a settlement.

Most Yankee merchants were loath to be at war with

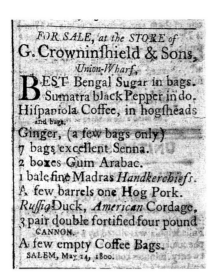

Fig. 4.2 "For Sale at the Store of G. Crowninshield & Sons," advertisement in the *Salem Register*, May 15, 1800, indicating the global reach of New England shipping.

England and hoped Jay's mission would be successful. American foreign commerce was heavily dependent on London banking houses, which facilitated the expansion of U.S. world trade by supplying credit that was honored almost everywhere. But the Jay Treaty resolved little. Compensation was offered for vessels, cargoes, and crew seized in the West Indies, but there was no settlement of the British presence on the western borders of the United States. And while the treaty gave formal sanction to American commerce in the East Indies, new restrictions on port-to-port trade and on American voyages between India and Europe were a major blow to American commercial interests. The carrying trade in the Indian Ocean extolled by Benjamin Carpenter (chapter 3) suddenly became illegal.[7] The treaty was a double failure. Not only did it leave American discontents unsettled, but it angered the French, who saw in the treaty between the U.S. and Great Britain the inevitable abandonment of their 1778 alliance of "amity and commerce" with the United States. In response, France set its privateers on American shipping.[8]

Throughout the Napoleonic wars, from 1793 until 1815, the relations between putatively neutral Yankee merchant vessels and the warships of the belligerents remained precarious. The risky position of so-called neutral traders in this world at war was chillingly experienced by Dudley Pickman and related in the journal he kept of the homeward passage of the *Derby* from Calcutta in 1804 (see chapter 7). Four months into the voyage, he recounted:

September 7 in latitude 31 degrees north were boarded from the French privateer ship *Calibri*, 22 guns, 250 men, from Bordeaux, three months out on a cruise and were detained by her eighteen hours during which time the Frenchmen had possession of our ship and endeavored by threats, promises, etc. to induce our sailors to declare the vessel or cargo "English property." Our crew were all taken out, as also the captain and myself, on board the privateer where we were kept for the night. We were suffered to pass with little injury from the plunder. It was to me a night of extreme anxiety.

"TO THE FARTHEST PORTS OF THE RICH EAST"[9]

Despite these obstacles, during the European wars of the early nineteenth century, American shipping expanded globally. In little more than a decade from the opening of the Asian trade, merchants, sea captains, and supercargoes of the new United States of America became cosmopolitan masters of world trade (fig. 4.2). Yankee vessels were occupied in the Baltic, the Mediterranean, the Indian Ocean, and the Pacific. Shipowners, captains, and supercargoes regularly took freight or purchased goods in one port for delivery or sale where there was a demand, turning over cargoes several times during the course of a single voyage.

Despite the risks and uncertainties, despite harassment from French and British naval vessels and privateers, the years of the European wars were immensely prosperous ones for Americans, trading across the globe in their small, maneuverable, armed vessels. Between 1795 and 1806, U.S. exports rose from $67 million to $108 million. Almost all of this increase was derived from the re-export of foreign goods.[10] The growth of U.S. foreign commerce was a direct outcome of the opportunities to trade as neutrals in foreign goods which were landed at U.S. ports and then reloaded for export, and to carry freight between ports in the Caribbean, Baltic, Mediterranean, and Indian Ocean. In addition, profits were made from carrying freight or buying and selling cargoes abroad—returns that were not recorded, as imports, exports, or duties.[11]

Neutral trade proved to be a critical means for Americans to build capital. The increase in wealth provided the resources for some to invest in fledgling industries, establishing the financial foundation for the American industrial revolution. Dudley

Pickman (chapter 5), for instance, used the profits from his ventures as a supercargo to invest in textile manufacturing. The expansion of American commerce had other far-reaching effects on the home economy. Shipbuilding flourished. Shopkeepers were supplied with desirable merchandise from around the world. Farmers found a market for products that could be exported to Europe and its colonies. In Newburyport, Massachusetts, for example, the value of personal holdings tripled between 1793 and 1807.[12]

AMERICAN TRADE IN INDIA DURING THE EUROPEAN WAR

Trade with India was a key component of this era of American commercial expansion. Although the Jay Treaty conferred legitimacy on direct trade, practiced since the time of Governor-General Cornwallis, it disallowed the coastwise country trade cutting into the profits of merchants such as the Derbys of Salem, and Brown and Francis of Providence, and negating the advice of Benjamin Carpenter in his 1789 journal of the *Ruby* (chapter 3). The powerful British East India Company actively sought to prevent American trade with India from competing directly with its own interests and from providing a means for British residents in India to evade regulations and get their property home to England.[13]

The wording of the Jay Treaty specified that Indian cargoes be brought directly back to the United States and thwarted Yankee merchants who had developed a successful carrying trade in the Indian Ocean. But the treaty gave Americans more leeway than the British intended. Indian cargoes could be landed in the United States and then re-exported. Besides, American merchant mariners, accustomed to operating on the peripheries, where jurisdiction was often hazy and regulations easy to evade, ignored the Jay Treaty's provisions when it suited them. In the British East India Company's Board of Control papers, there are numerous references to alleged violations of the treaty. For example, in 1797, the ship *Five Brothers* was prevented from exporting piece goods from Surat to Mauritius; in 1797, Jacob Crowninshield of Salem was accused of infringing the treaty by engaging in the coasting trade; in 1803, Jacob Benners, commander of the *Dispatch*, was reported to have contravened the treaty by trading with a Danish vessel.[14] Yet, on the whole, East India Company officials dealt leniently with American merchants' infringements of the treaty. British merchants retained a sense of fellowship with these traders from the United States, so recently their countrymen. Besides, they wanted the silver currency that Americans brought. They needed ways to send home the proceeds of their own private trade, and they did not want to divert American trade to other European companies.[15]

In 1807, an East India Company official reported that the American trade surpassed "everything of the kind recorded in the Commercial History of British India. . . . A trade which seven years ago did not exceed S.Rs. 6,718,992 [approximately $3.5 million] or Sterling 839,784 had advanced in the year under Report the enormous sum of S.Rs. 20,020,432 [roughly $10 million] or Stg 2,502,554, exceeding . . . the total amount of our Private Trade with Great Britain."[16] Despite the restrictions imposed by the Jay Treaty, American trade with India flourished. In the decade following, American trade exceeded that of all the Continental European nations combined.[17] In 1804, the year Pickman's *Derby* visited Calcutta (chapter 7), more than forty other American vessels stopped there to trade.

Many prosperous merchants, shipowners, and sea captains who engaged in this wartime worldwide commerce were also prominent among the political elite of the new nation. Almost continuously until 1816, Massachusetts was represented in the U.S. Senate by a merchant from Suffolk or Essex counties. Dudley Pickman served in the Massachusetts legislature. His fellow Salem merchant mariners Nathaniel Silsbee and Jacob Crowninshield were U.S. senators. Fisher Ames of Dedham, a sedentary India merchant, served in the U.S. Congress for almost a decade. Benjamin W. Crowninshield served as secretary of the navy. These men saw themselves as building American commerce and making a place for the new United States among the old established trading powers—Great Britain, France, the Netherlands, Spain, Portugal. Most of them were allies of Alexander Hamilton, who, as secretary of the treasury from 1789 to 1795, shaped national policy to protect property and to support commerce and industry. Hamilton believed that a stable, strong federal government needed a firm foundation which could be had by taxing imported goods. In 1791, 92 percent of U.S. revenues were generated from impost and tonnage duties.[18] This first experience of national prosperity, derived from far-flung voyages and exotic cargoes, provided a measure of financial stability to the federal government, and brought with it a sense of cosmopolitanism—a peculiarly American cosmopolitanism that prized independence and noninvolvement

Fig. 4.3 Jacob Crowninshield (1770–1808) by Robert Hinckley after an early miniature. Oil on canvas, 78.7 x 63.5 cm; Peabody Essex Museum M360, Gift of the Crowninshield Family, 1888.

In his memorandum, Crowninshield described the India trade, distinguishing the opportunities at its two principal ports, Bombay and Calcutta. According to Crowninshield, Bombay had been an important source of cotton for Americans to provide the Canton and European markets—until the Jay Treaty forbade it after ratification in 1795. Since then, because few products were manufactured in the region around Bombay, the port was of little interest to Americans. Crowninshield noted that, although the treaty had expired in 1803, the British "pretend to consider the restriction in the British treaty as in force."[21] The prohibition on American trade from port to port in India and from India to Europe was a source of considerable annoyance and resentment, especially because Danish and Swedish vessels were permitted these routes. Crowninshield took pleasure in reporting that American ships had profited from carrying freight to Europe for Britons who wanted to move their wealth home. He knew that British India benefited from American imports of treasure, the scarcity of which was a perennial problem for the East India Company. With some pride, he reported that although Americans were required to bring their cargoes to home ports before re-exporting them to the Continent, when they did so, they still beat British prices.

Crowninshield described Calcutta as the premier Indian port, a principal source of cotton and silk textiles, sugar and indigo, and a supplier of rice to other parts of India. On American trade, he reported:

> We send from 30 to 50 ships annually to Calcutta. The outward cargo is chiefly dollars, iron, lead, brandy, Madeira and other wines. . . . [I]t is estimated that we have imported in some years at least three millions of dollars worth of goods from Calcutta. The white cotton manufactured goods were cheap at first hands; similar goods could be had at other foreign and native settlements, but the prices might be a little higher. We buy our cargoes of the native merchants and not of the English residents because they come to us at a lower price through this channel.[22]

BANIANS & DUBASHES: MASTERS OF THE CONTACT ZONE

When Americans traded in Indian ports, they preferred, as Crowninshield reported, to work with Indian commercial agents, because doing so saved them money. Although it might be easier to buy and sell cargoes through British mercantile

while asserting American rights to engage in commerce in all the corners of the world.

When Thomas Jefferson was elected president in 1800 on a platform favoring agrarian over commercial interests and pro-French over pro-British policies, Jacob Crowninshield was among the few East India merchants to support the Republican party. Crowninshield's pro-Jefferson position grew partly out of a local rivalry with the Federalist Derby family and partly out of his family's success in the French and Continental markets: their fleet had grown from three vessels of less than 100 tons to nine, ranging from 250 to 500 tons. Jacob Crowninshield (fig. 4.3) was elected to the U.S. Senate on the Republican ticket, and Jefferson chose him—though illness prevented him from serving— as secretary of the navy at a time when the fledgling navy existed principally to protect and support the merchant marine.[19] In 1806, at the height of the neutral trade, Jacob Crowninshield wrote a long memorandum on U.S. foreign commerce to James Madison, then secretary of state.[20]

houses, the cost was higher because the British, too, needed to employ native agents to operate in the local markets. By the end of the first decade of American trade, there were men at each of the principal ports, banians at Calcutta and dubashes at Madras, who provided American sea captains and super-cargoes with the information and services they needed to trade. These men, already experienced in dealing with foreigners, principally British, were masters of the contact zone, specialists in bridging the commercial, linguistic, and cultural gulf between American merchants and local practices. They were the most crucial and intimate links Yankees had to India. They managed the arrangements for American vessels in port—facilitating compliance with official regulations, finding laborers to unload and gather cargoes. Their knowledge of local markets—sources for commodities and buyers for imported goods—was indispensable to their American clients. By the end of the eighteenth century, the wealthiest among them also provided capital for Yankee transactions. Such dependency fostered trust when transactions were successful and suspicion when they failed.

By the turn of the nineteenth century, with a decade of American experience in India behind them and a marked increase in American activity in Indian ports, Yankee traders had established relationships with the middlemen at the ports they visited. In 1800, Dudley Pickman, supercargo of the *Belisarius* (chapter 6), found the situation at Madras much as Benjamin Carpenter reported a decade before. One could deal with British, Armenian, or Portuguese agents. There were only a few dubashes experienced in the American market. Pickman described two of them: "Paulem Yagapah Chitty (called by his second name) does a considerable share of the business with Americans. He is a contractor with the East India Company for piece goods and is said to be rich, but we found him much in want of money. He is a Gentoo, and appears a fair man. . . . Paulem Mutiah Chitty, brother to Yagapah and concerned with him, is not so good a man as the other. This is the only native merchant of importance I dealt with." Mutiah and Yagapah were Chettiars, members of a widely scattered Tamil-speaking caste in southeastern India, whose men for centuries had specialized in long-distance trade, especially in Southeast Asia.[23] They were experienced in dealing with foreigners. Many of them, like Paulem Yagapah Chitty, worked with the British East India Company to supply their cargoes.

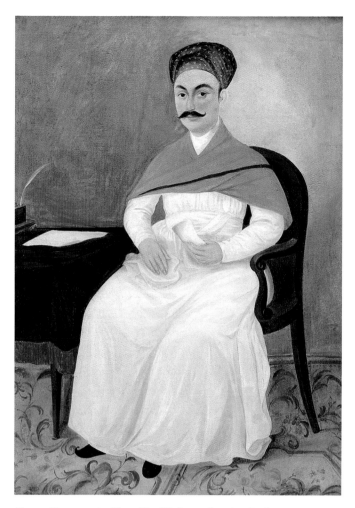

Fig. 4.4 Nusserwanjee Maneckjee Wadia, attributed to Spoilum (Canton), c. 1800. Nusserwanjee was the leading agent for the American trade at Bombay. Oil on primed cloth, 99 x 73.7 cm; Peabody Essex Museum M245, Gift of John R. Dalling, 1803.

At Bombay, Nusserwanjee Maneckjee Wadia was without rival in handling the American trade (fig. 4.4). Nusserwanjee was from a prominent Parsi family. His father and grandfather built ships for the British. Through family influence he became the agent for the French trade, which he facilitated so satisfactorily that his portrait was installed in the Marine Office in Paris and he was awarded the Legion d'Honnaire by Napoleon Bonaparte.[24] George Nichols of Salem was one of Nusserwanjee's clients; their relationship indicates the importance of personal ties in negotiating the vagaries of business transacted without the reassurances of shared practices. It is also evidence of Nusserwanjee's success in dealing with foreigners. In about 1800, Nichols, who was soon to be married, came to Bombay to trade and engaged Nusserwanjee. The two developed a cordial relationship on this trip. Nusserwanjee found Nichols a superb

Fig. 4.5 India mull dress, c. 1800, later alterations. George Nichols purchased the fabric for his fiancée's wedding dress in 1801 from Nusserwanjee Maneckjee Wadia for five dollars a yard. White cotton brocade, length 126 cm; Peabody Essex Museum 123571w, Gift of the Nichols Estate, 1938.

fabric, "a beautiful striped muslin, very delicate, made in Bombay for some distinguished person," suitable for his fiancée's wedding dress (fig. 4.5). Nichols purchased the cloth from Nusserwanjee at five dollars a yard. Nusserwanjee also presented Nichols with "a camel's hair shawl, quite a handsome one,"[25] for his bride-to-be (fig. 4.6). Nichols "returned the compliment by presenting [Nusserwanjee] with a set of Mavor's *Voyages*."[26] Later, Nusserwanjee gave Nichols another shawl "of larger size and handsomer."[27] Gift exchanges like these built relationships in the contact zone, where expectations were imperfectly understood and legal constraints were treated pragmatically.

At Calcutta, where many more Yankee vessels went to trade, there were more native Bengali agents who attended to the American market. When Dudley Pickman visited Calcutta in 1803–04, he assessed the abilities and standing of several of them, recording in his journal (chapter 7):

> Ramdulolday [Ramdulal Dey] (who is also banyan to the very respectable English house of Fairlie, Gilmore and Co.) . . . does most of the southern and some of the New England business, is very shrewd and capable, extremely avaricious, and possesses great talents for business. He is considered to be worth three to five millions rupees. Ram Chunder Benorjea, a Brahmin, does some southern and a considerable proportion of the northern business. He is said to be worth five to ten lacs rupees and is a very smooth tongued man.[28] Collisunker [Kalisankar] and Doorgapersaud [Durgaprasad] Ghose do some southern and more northern business. The latter is a shrewd man and industrious when pressed by business. They are about as rich as Ram Chunder, and I was satisfied with the manner in which they managed the business I entrusted to them.

Business acumen, reliability, and available capital, which might be tapped to finance American transactions, were the crucial qualities in a "native" commercial agent.

Ramdulal Dey (fig. 4.7), mentioned above by Pickman (as Ramdulolday), was the first, most prominent, and wealthiest of the specialists in the American market. During the height of the American wartime trade, he was also the most esteemed business contact in Calcutta for Americans. The Lees in Boston named one of their ships *Ramduloll Day*,[29] and in 1801, a group of American merchants expressed their appreciation by presenting Ramdulal with a life-size portrait of George Washington (fig. 4.8).[30] The choice of subject, the father of their new nation, spoke not only of their pride in Washington's leadership but also of their new republican polity, independent of Britain and its monarchy. Their separation from the British colonial world and its regulations placed Americans in a particularly enviable light for more than a few Bengalis.

Like many eighteenth-century Bengalis who made their fortunes as bilingual business agents and culture brokers for foreign clients, Ramdulal Dey was a man from a modest background who found ways to take advantage of the new center of economic and political power in British Calcutta. Ramdulal was something of an outsider, skillfully combining good fortune

Fig. 4.6 Moon shawl, Kashmir, c. 1800. Nusserwanjee Maneckjee Wadia gave this shawl to his Salem client George Nichols as a gift for George's bride. Goat fleece, 164 x 167 cm; Peabody Essex Museum 123590.2, Gift of the Nichols Estate, 1938.

with entrepreneurial acumen. He grew up as a poor relation in the household of Mudden Mohun Dutt, *dewan* (chief officer) of the Export Warehouse for the British East India Company, a man who had made his fortune in the service of the new European masters of Bengal. When he was about sixteen, Ramdulal went to work as a bill sircar (clerk) delivering invoices and collecting payments.[31]

Ramdulal's biographer makes much of his entrepreneurial talents, which were soon displayed when his low bid won a sunken ship lying near the mouth of the Hooghly. Ramdulal made the purchase in his employer's name with his employer's money, but without his knowledge. Almost immediately he resold the wreck to an Englishman at a handsome profit.

Mudden Dutt, stunned and bewildered by Ramdulal's integrity, blessed him and said, "Ramdoolal the money is yours."[32] Like others of his time, Ramdulol Dey succeeded by taking risks in the radically altered, often precarious circumstances of British commercial and political ascendancy. His success became a model of entrepreneurship in Bengal that endured through the nineteenth century, as increasing numbers of non-Bengalis gained positions of prominence in Calcutta.

Despite mutually profitable business transactions and well-meaning gift exchanges, the relationships between native merchants and Yankee traders were intrinsically fraught. The social and cultural gap between them was enormous and relationships soured easily. An 1806 letter to Ramdulal Dey from

Fig. 4.7. Ramdulal Dey (1752–1825), copy 1954 by Srimati Mamata Deb of a portrait in the family's possession. Ramdulal Dey, who pioneered the American market in Calcutta at the end of the eighteenth century, became one of Calcutta's wealthiest men. Oil on canvas, 91.4 x 66 cm; Courtesy of the Anath Nath Deb Trust.

Patrick T. Jackson, a Newburyport merchant, clearly expresses the deep ambivalences of both sides in dealing across this cultural chasm. The letter responded to a protest from Ramdulal about slowness in payment and lack of appreciation for loyal service, including extending generous credit: "I believe you Dololl, will acknowledge that you have lost nothing by your acquaintance with [me] and with some members of my family. You have not only got considerable business from us, but some more from our recommendations. I am certainly obliged by the confidence you shew in giving me so large a credit, but you know I could have . . . found others who would have done the same had I given them my business . . ."[33] While Jackson was confident enough to recommend Ramdulal's services and grateful for credit allowed him, he did not want to appear beholden and he felt wary of being overcharged.

The relationships formed by Yankee sea captains and supercargoes with their brokers, the closest ties between India and America in the early nineteenth century, were riddled with incongruities. Their financial entanglements created intimate connections; their fortunes were mutually dependent. Yet, they encountered one another across a moral chasm, deep in linguistic, religious, racial, and social difference. In this situation, loyalty, gratitude, distrust, and condemnation were closely connected. Americans' first direct impressions of India were formed in this context. The banians, dubashes, and other native agents, for their part, became discerning operators managing the terrain between moral systems. In their dealings with Americans, outsiders both to native and to Anglo-Indian society, they came to know men very like the British in appearance and language, but assuredly distinct in the markets they represented and in their distance from the power structure of Anglo-Indian society. For a few, their relationships with ex-colonial Yankee republicans nurtured their own resistance to British domination.

REPRESENTING INDIA IN AMERICA THROUGH CLOTH

In the period of neutral trade, cotton and silk textiles were the most important commodities imported for the American market. In this era, India continued to be regarded as a source of admirable manufactures. Especially in demand were modestly priced cotton goods of ordinary quality suitable for everyday use at home and for garments. Cotton was not yet the ubiquitous fiber it would become. Cotton textiles from British mills were just beginning to make an impact on the U.S. market and cotton production in the U.S. was in its infancy. Wool and linen, the native fabrics of Europe and America, were neither as soft as cotton, as comfortable in a range of temperatures, nor as receptive and retentive of a wide variety of colors.

In the colonial period, Indian textiles had reached America indirectly, through the British East India Company's imports to London. As direct trade with India grew after independence, piece goods dominated the cargoes brought to the United States. By the turn of the nineteenth century, an enormous variety of Indian textiles had become available, especially in the ports along the eastern seaboard. This increased availability and familiarity of Indian cloth was reflected in auction notices and newspaper advertisements that included lists of Indian textiles enumerated by place of manufacture, type, and quality—

cossah bafta, gurrah, mamoody, from Oudh, Alliabad, Dacca, Gaurypore, etc. The enumeration of cloth types in American merchants' papers is very detailed. The correspondence of Boston merchant Henry Lee, for example, contains references to more than fifty kinds of Indian textiles.[34] American buyers were familiar with types and qualities of Indian textiles, and the reputations of various weaving centers.

Of all the textiles imported from India to America, versatile white cotton goods were by far the most numerous. Their names designated the place of manufacture and indicated qualities of the cloth—color, design, fineness of weave, and size. In most cases, it is no longer possible to precisely describe the particular kind of cloth the names were intended to designate. Few of these textiles can be positively identified today. A rare set of samples survives in a 1796 letter from Benjamin Pickman of Salem to Israel Thorndike of Beverly, Massachusetts. Six specimens of white goods are named and given with dimensions and price: *Oud Cossah, Marath Sanna, Marath Gangy, Manuikpore Gurrah, Jannah Cossah,* and *Laquire*.[35] A close look at these examples indicates the attention paid to the evenness and fineness of yarns, and the tightness of weaves (fig. 4.9 and pages 64–65).

American importers specialized in lesser qualities of white and blue cloths and brightly colored checks, stripes, and prints. They supplied U.S. and European demands for utilitarian textiles, sheeting and shirting, and goods for the African slave trade, as well as provisions for plantation slaves. White goods might be dyed or printed to order, before export; occasionally white goods were exported for printing in America. For the African trade, dyed piece goods, for example, brown *gurrah* or blue *guineas*, were especially in demand. A sample of blue guinea cloth, made in southern India for the African trade, is preserved in a letter to Boston merchant Henry Lee. The swatch is of a coarse cloth dyed a dark blue, described in the accompanying letter as copper blue, like the throat of a pigeon.[36]

Yankee merchants, of course, had a deeper knowledge of this vast array of textiles than did the buying public. Some of them understood that the desirablity of these cloths derived from more than their intrinsic qualities. The textiles embodied the oriental mystery of distant, exotic India. Some of the appeal was carried in their strange-sounding names. Fully aware of the importance of naming for the success of their sales, the Lee firm of Boston wrote to its representatives in Calcutta that, when

Fig. 4.8. George Washington (1732–1799), attributed to William Winstanley, c. 1800. This life-size portrait was presented to Ramdulal Dey of Calcutta in 1801 by a group of grateful American clients. Oil on canvas, 238.1 x 149.9 cm; Courtesy of Washington and Lee University.

buying *emerties*, "We would have you divide into two parts the longest ones and invoice by some other name."[37] Regarding other goods, the firm advised "Do not invoice these goods by the name of Meergungee, but call them Shazardpoer, Tilpah or some other name. The buyers are sick of the sound of Meergungee and it really affects the value of the article."[38]

Next to ordinary cotton goods in popularity were handkerchiefs, large square cloths used as neck cloths, head coverings, and bundle wraps. Many were cottons, such as *sooty romals, lungee* handkerchiefs, and checked *pulicat* handkerchiefs, both

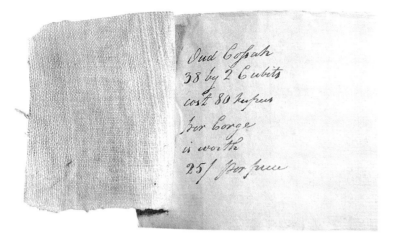

Fig. 4.9 Sample of a cotton textile, *Oud Cossah*, with notations giving size, cost, and value. The sample was included in a 1796 letter from Benjamin Pickman, Jr., to Israel Thorndike recommending purchases of cotton textiles at Calcutta (letter reproduced on pages 64–65). White plain-weave cotton; Courtesy of the Beverly Historical Society, Beverly, Massachusetts.

Fig. 4.11 Block-printed (*choppa*) handkerchief, c. 1825. Plain-woven silk (*kora*), 78.2 x 66 cm; Peabody Essex Museum R682, Gift of the Ropes Estate, 1989.

Fig. 4.10 Bandanna handkerchief, c. 1820. Embroidered "A.R." in a corner by the owner Abigail Ropes (1796–1839). Tie-dyed indigo plain-woven silk (*kora*), 94 x 91.4 cm; Peabody Essex Museum R678, Gift of the Ropes Estate, 1989.

Fig. 4.12 Detail of a palampore (bedcover), Coromandel Coast, c. 1800. Brought from India by Salem merchant William Dean Waters between 1817 and 1845. Painted and printed cotton, 264 x 216 cm; Peabody Essex Museum 123328, Gift of William C. Waters, 1938.

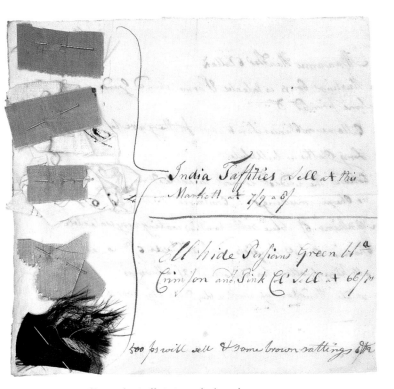

Fig. 4.13 Silk samples (taffaties) attached to a letter, c. 1790.
Peabody Essex Museum Library, Crowninshield Family Papers,
John Crowninshield Business Papers.

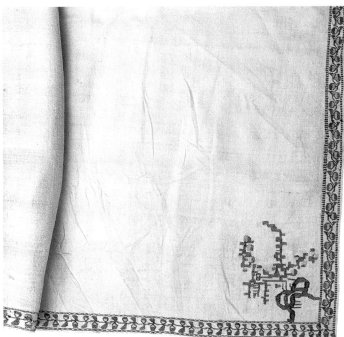

Fig. 4.14 Detail of a Kashmir shawl, c. 1800. The shawl, which
belonged to Elizabeth Clarke of Salem, was among the first imported
to the United States. The weaver struggled to adapt his tapestry-
weaving technique to accommodate a European bow motif. Twilled
goat fleece, 137.2 cm square; Peabody Essex Museum 109680.

real (made in Pulicat on the Coromandel Coast) and mock (imitated in other production centers), as well as *madras* handkerchiefs that became standard issue for plantation slaves. The
most popular handkerchiefs were silk squares from Bengal
known as *bandanoes* or *bandannas*, terms derived from indigenous words for "tie-dyed." These smooth, glossy silk handkerchiefs, dyed in spotted patterns on a yellow, blue, chocolate, or
scarlet ground (fig. 4.10), were produced in the region around
Cossimbazar and Murshidabad, the old Mughal capital of
Bengal, upriver from Calcutta. In the eighteenth century, the
designation *bandanna* was extended to include printed silk
squares (*choppa rumals*) in exotic floral designs of red, beige,
and black (fig. 4.11). Silk bandannas were widely affordable—
simultaneously luxurious and utilitarian.

Besides the handkerchiefs and plain cottons, there was a
broad array of fashionable cloths in cotton, silk, or a mixture of
fibers. Merchants' families and others of means had bedcovers
(*palampores*) of bright colorfast painted and printed cotton (fig.
4.12). For use in their finest garments, fashionable women purchased weblike fine cotton *mulmuls*, sometimes plain, striped, or
figured (*jamdani*), and occasionally decorated with silver. The

influence of Indian style on America was also evident in dress:
in 1800, George Nichols' bride wore her gown of very fine,
striped muslin with a headdress made of a "white lace veil, put
on turban fashion" (see fig. 4.5).[39] Silks, especially *taffaties* in a
wide range of colors, were imported as dress fabric (fig. 4.13).
Of all Indian textiles, goat-fleece Kashmir shawls—luxurious,
soft, and warm—were the most esteemed and expensive. One
of the earliest shawls imported to the United States was owned
by Elizabeth Clarke of Salem around 1800 (fig. 4.14). The
shawl, of very fine goat fleece, was purchased for the then-enor-
mous sum of sixty dollars. Mrs. Clarke embroidered her name
in the corner near one of the awkward bows executed by the
weaver to suit Western taste.

Handspun, handwoven, dyed, printed, and painted textiles
from India were admired and sought after in the United States.
They could be exotic or ordinary, inexpensive or costly, utilitarian or luxurious, plain or highly decorated, coarse or fine.
The array of textiles available was vast, and India produced
goods that could not be found anywhere else. The demand for
these textiles fostered a high regard for India and its native
manufactures.

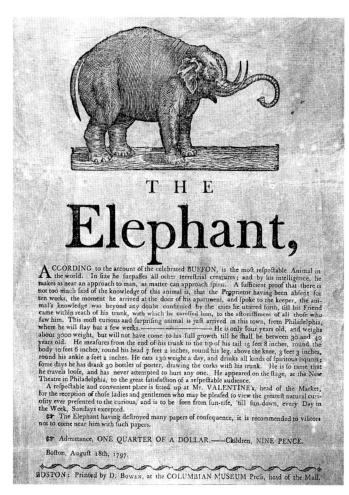

Fig. 4.15 *The Elephant*, broadside inviting the public to the
Columbian Museum in Boston to see the first elephant ever in the
United States. The elephant was brought by Jacob Crowninshield
in the *America* from India to New York, where it was sold for
$10,000. It delighted crowds for "one quarter of a dollar—children,
nine pence." Printed paper, 28.6 x 24.1 cm; Peabody Essex Museum
M4589, Gift of Mrs. William C. Endicott, 1938.

ENVISIONING INDIA

American trading voyages brought more than commodities
back to the United States. Along with the textiles, sugar, ginger,
and indigo came seamen's accounts of their experiences, books,
pictures, and an expansive array of curiosities. All of these
became ingredients in the images of India constructed by
Americans in the first decades of direct contact. Among the
more spectacular and singular representations of India was an
elephant which arrived in New York in 1797, brought by Jacob
Crowninshield on the *America* and sold for the princely sum of
$10,000. The elephant's new owners took it on tour, charging

25 cents per person for the privilege of viewing it (fig. 4.15).
When Salem chronicler Reverend William Bentley saw the
beast, he recorded in his diary:

> Went to the market house to see the elephant. The crowd
> of spectators forbad me nay but a general and superficial
> view of him. He was six feet four inches high. Of large
> volume, his skin black, as though lately oiled. A short
> hair was on every part, but not sufficient for a covering.
> His tail hung one third of his height, but without any
> long hairs at the end of it. His legs were still at the com-
> mand of the joints, but he could not be persuaded to lie
> down. The keeper repeatedly mounted him but he per-
> sisted in shaking him off. Bread and hay were given him,
> and he took bread out of the pockets of the spectators. He
> also drank porter and drew the cork, conveying the lic-
> quor from his trunk into his throat.[40]

Bentley's description conveys the sense of novelty and
wonder in an encounter with the exotic that pervaded American
experiences of India in the first few decades of trade, when
information and contacts were scarce. In these years, visions of
India were constructed out of fragments: impressions shared by
mariners with their friends and relations, exotic souvenirs like
fans and hubble-bubbles, luxurious gifts like ivory carvings and
Kashmir shawls, occasional books brought home like Raynal's
history of India[41] and Sir William Jones' translation of the play
Shakuntalam published in Boston's *Monthly Anthology* in 1805,
and news reports—mainly from British sources—carried from
time to time in local papers.

The most concerted effort to represent the East was organized in 1799 by the Salem East India Marine Society. After
fifteen years of direct trade with Asia, a group of captains and
supercargoes joined together to create a museum dedicated to
displaying "curiosities" from the East. The Society was modeled partly after other marine societies, well-established social
and benevolent institutions dedicated to the exchange of navigational information, the support of needy families, and good
fellowship—one had been in existence in Salem since 1766. But
these entrepreneurs of the East Indies trade believed that what
they had seen and learned on their voyages to the East should be
shared with fellow citizens. Unlike any other marine society,
this one established "a museum of natural and artificial curiosities, particularly such as are to be found beyond the Cape of
Good Hope or Cape Horn."[42] Members were enjoined by

the bylaws to collect. While membership was open only to those who had "navigated the seas near the Cape of Good Hope or Cape Horn, either as master or commander or as factor or supercargo,"[43] they invited the public to view their museum.

Members of the Society saw themselves not just as merchants and navigators, but as pioneers of commerce and world explorers. At their periodic dinners, they toasted their vision and their forebears: "Natural History. May Commerce Never Forget its obligations"; "Vasco da Gama, What genius performs may genius immortalize."[44] They commissioned a portrait of Captain James Cook to hang in their meeting hall (fig. 4.16). Along with cargoes of commodities and special gifts for family and friends, they brought home curiosities, unusual objects—many of them never before seen in New England— that demonstrated the marvelous diversity of plants, animals, weapons of war, musical instruments, and religious paraphernalia. These objects, like the experiences of Yankee mariners in distant ports, were acquired to expand knowledge of the world and contribute to the edification of the people of Salem and the many visitors to their busy port. The collection they established became the most famous repository of East Indian (and other) curiosities in the country, visited by tourists from abroad and presidents of the United States.

The museum also accepted contributions from local residents, Bostonians, and even foreigners. The first foreign donors to the museum were Nusserwanjee Maneckjee Wadia of Bombay and Durgaprasad Ghose of Calcutta, commercial agents through whom so many of the Society's members had carried on their business. In 1803, Nusserwanjee presented a "complete Parsee dress" consisting of shoes, robe, shawl, and turban. In the same year, John R. Dalling gave the museum an oil portrait of Nusserwanjee, the work of a Chinese artist (see fig. 4.4). Using the portrait as a model, the Society commissioned a mannequin carved of wood in Nusserwanjee's likeness to display the clothing. The same year, Durgaprasad Ghose presented the Society with two musical instruments, a *dholak* (drum) and a *tambura* (stringed drone), and a *kittishal* (a large parasol used for sheltering a palanquin) (fig. 4.17). No doubt they had been told by their Salem clients about the new society and its mission of displaying curiosities from the East Indies to enlighten Americans about distant civilizations. In making donations to the collection, Nusserwanjee and Durgaprasad went beyond gestures of friendship that cement business relations. They

Fig. 4.16 Captain James Cook (1728–1779) by Michel Felice Corné, c. 1802. The East India Marine Society considered Captain Cook, mariner and explorer, a model to emulate. His portrait was commissioned and displayed in the Society's museum. Oil on canvas, 69.9 x 50.8 cm; Peabody Essex Museum M3385, Gift of Thomas W. Ward, 1803.

attempted to traverse the great distance separating their civilizations and to participate in the representation of their world to foreigners in a country halfway around the globe.

Durgaprasad's gift of musical instruments and a large umbrella was given to complement another donation from five members of the East India Marine Society who were all in Calcutta in 1803. Together they purchased a large silver-trimmed black palanquin with four-and-a-half-foot carrying poles at each end (fig. 4.18). They intended their gift to be carried in the Society's processions through the town, as well as to be exhibited in their museum. Each year, members of the Society, attired in oriental splendor and carrying curiosities from their collection, marched through the streets of Salem. The palanquin, its donors jovially suggested, would "gratify the

Fig. 4.17 Drum (*dholak*) and stringed drone (*tambura*), c. 1802. The instruments were presented to the East India Marine Society's museum in 1803 by Durgaprasad Ghose, banian for the American trade in Calcutta (see fig. 11.12), to be carried in the Society's processions through the town. Wood, gourd, leather, pigments, drum height 30.5 cm, drone height 109.5 cm; Peabody Essex Museum E7445 (drum) and E7447 (drone), Gifts of Durgaprasad Ghose, 1803.

Fig. 4.18 Palanquin, Calcutta, c. 1800. In 1803, five Salem sea captains purchased this palanquin in Calcutta for the East India Marine Society, to be displayed in their museum and carried in their festival day processions. Wood, silver trim, cushion upholstered with English chintz, height 108.5 x width 79.5 x length 460 cm; Peabody Essex Museum E14329, Gift of Captains Benjamin Lander, Edward West, William Mugford, Joseph Orne, and Moses Townsend, 1803.

Fig. 4.19 *Southeast View of the New Government House*, drawn and engraved by James Moffat, Calcutta, 1803.
Aquatint, 47 x 58.4 cm; Peabody Essex Museum M15590.1.

curious, show the method of travelling and answer a very good purpose on festival day in case any accident should happen [to] a member."[45] The palanquin was carried in at least one Society procession a year for nearly two decades and sporadically thereafter. Durgaprasad's gifts were intended as additional props for these processions, which he no doubt understood as a kind of festive gathering.

To members of the Society, most of whom had been to Calcutta, palanquins like this one were very familiar. During a stay in port, an American would have to hire one, along with a team of bearers, to carry him about the city as he made arrangements for the disposition and gathering of cargoes. For observers who saw the palanquin in the Salem processions and for visitors to East India Marine Hall, it was a curiosity, an exotic mode of transport in which men acted the role of draft animals. In 1823, the *Salem Register* reported, inside rode "a boy appareled in the most gorgeous habitments, borne by black-fellows, sweating under the unaccustomed burthen, in the East

Indian dress attended with fan and hookah bearers and every other accompaniment of an East Indian equipage . . ."

Among the most important representations of the East in the museum were the prints by English artists, becoming widely available by the end of the eighteenth century. The first pictures to be displayed in the East India Marine Society Museum were "four copper plate prints, views at Calcutta," donations of Joseph Phippen in 1803. Neither the artist nor the titles were recorded in the museum's register, but the date and the subject make it likely that the views were drawn by Thomas and William Daniell or William Baillie, leading producers of scenes of India for popular consumption. The Daniells and Baillie published views of Calcutta.[46] Most of these views depict the urban scene of British Calcutta, cityscapes featuring Anglo-Indian architecture, peopled by small figures, native and European, going about their business—carrying or riding in palanquins, marching in processions.

William Lander and Thomas Osgood donated another set

Fig. 4.20 *North View of Seringapatam* drawn by Robert Home, engraved by Fittler, published by R. Bowyer, London, and W. Sharp, Madras, 1794. Engraving, 11.7 x 21.1 cm; Courtesy of the Los Angeles County Museum of Art M.73.14.1, Gift of Mr. and Mrs. Edmund O. Wolf. Photograph © 2000 Museum Associates/LACMA.

of prints of Calcutta and sites upriver from the city. These pictures, published in Calcutta by James Moffat between 1800 and 1809, exemplify the serene, distant vistas preferred by British artists and their Western patrons. The majestic new Government House was illustrated in two prints (fig. 4.19). The new Government House had been erected in 1803 by Governor-General Wellesley to provide a palace worthy of a European monarch from which the governor-general of India could rule the ever-growing dominions of the East India Company. Both the views of the Government House and a larger panorama of Calcutta portray the grandeur of the maturing colonial metropolis visited by American mariners. Moffat's other scenes provided museum visitors with glimpses of a Hindu temple dedicated to Lord Shiva on the river's edge; the Dutch trading settlement at Chinsurah; the capital of Mir Kassim at Monghyr (after lower Bengal was lost to the British); ruins of the palace of Sultan Shuja, seat of the Mughal nawab (governor) at Ghazipore; and Benares, seventy-five days upriver from Calcutta in the heartland of India. Visitors to the East

India Marine Society's museum could experience, through the eyes of British artists, many of India's principal sites.

Other prints depicted scenes from the most important events of the 1790s—from the British perspective: the East India Company's wars against Tipu Sultan of Mysore in southern India. A set of six prints portrayed the defeat of Tipu Sultan in 1792. The prints in the museum's collection were published from drawings by Robert Home, who served as the East India Company's official artist during the Third Mysore War (fig. 4.20). The struggle of East India Company forces against Tipu Sultan was reported in the American press. When Lord Cornwallis, lately defeated at Yorktown, led the British victory over Tipu at Seringapatam, Americans' growing sense of supremacy may have been reinforced at the expense of the Mysore army. American forces had defeated the troops under Cornwallis' command. If Cornwallis could defeat Tipu Sultan, the latter's armies, it was concluded, must certainly be inferior to America's. Tipu was forced to surrender his sons as hostages to Cornwallis. Scenes of the surrender were painted by Mather

THE DEPARTURE of the SONS of TIPPOO from the ZENANA

Fig. 4.21 *The Departure of the Sons of Tippoo from the Zenana* by a Chinese painter after a Bartolozzi print based on a painting by Boston-born artist Mather Brown. Reverse painting on glass, 45.1 x 59.7 cm; Peabody Essex Museum E80263, Museum purchase with funds donated anonymously, 1977 (see fig. 1.3).

Brown and prints of the captives after the paintings circulated widely (fig. 4.21). The princes, who remained in Calcutta, became celebrity prisoners. Although no Yankee mariner had visited Seringapatam, the British contest with Tipu Sultan was well known in New England. After news of Tipu's defeat had arrived in America, the *Salem Gazette* of July 31, 1792, devoted half the front page to an article reprinted from *Calcutta Magazine* sketching Tipu's character. A 1794 booklet on the campaigns against Tipu was brought home from Calcutta.[47] New England newspaper accounts were usually reprinted from sources in London, Madras, or Calcutta, but sometimes a report was included based on sources from the French allies of Tipu praising his skills as a general.[48] Tipu's final defeat and death came in 1799, the year of Dudley Pickman's voyage to Madras in the *Belisarius* (chapter 6).

The East India Marine Society's museum also included a few paintings by non-European artists. The portrait of Nusser-

wanjee given by John Dalling in 1803 was the work of a Chinese painter, (probably Spoilum),[49] as was a reverse painting on glass of an eighteenth-century governor of Surat, Nawab Namdar Tegh Khan Bahadur, accompanied by a servant (fig. 4.22). Site of the main British factory in western India until its transfer to Bombay in 1647, Surat was ruled by Mughal governors appointed by the emperors at Delhi until the end of the eighteenth century, when the East India Company took control. In the early years of American trade, Surat was one of the very few ports still under Indian rule. These paintings may have been executed in China based on Indian or Western portraits or, more likely, painted by a Chinese artist working in Surat or Bombay.

Captain Solomon Towne, who donated the picture of the governor of Surat, gave a second painting (fig. I.6). Executed in gouache on paper by an Indian artist probably from Tanjore in southern India, the painting depicts a man and a woman standing face to face. The woman's sari and ornaments reveal her

Fig. 4.22 The Governor of Surat and attendant by a Chinese painter, c. 1790. The inscription in Perso-Arabic and Gujarati reads:
"Nawab Namdar Tegh Beg Khan Bahadur, Year 1206 [1790–91]"; Reverse painting on glass, 64.1 x 43.6 cm;
Peabody Essex Museum E9924, Gift of Captain Solomon Towne before 1821.

southern origins. The man's hat, beads, water pot, and the palm leaf manuscript under his arm signify a Brahmin astrologer or almanac maker. This style of painting was developed by Indian artists for British East India Company patrons and usually employed to depict the varieties of native people, occupations, and architecture. The picture's ethnographic specificity would have been lost on visitors to the East India Marine Society's museum; rather, it would have been appreciated as a depiction of the exotic elegance of native Indians.

Among other early acquisitions from India were three small clay images of the god Balaram from Bengal (see fig. I.3). Two of these were entered in the original register as "Bengal gods"; later a line was drawn through "gods," and "idols" was substituted. The unclad images of Balaram are white, with painted black hair gathered in a topknot, and hands and feet ornamented in red. Images like these were made to be sold in the bazaar, in the potters' quarter, and on the streets at festival times. They were purchased, taken home to be installed in the household shrine, dressed, and ornamented for worship. The production of clay images was tied to the annual cycle of festivals. For the festival's duration, the deity was assumed to be present in the image; at its conclusion, the god departed and the image was ceremonially immersed in a river or pond to return to the mud from which it was made.[50] For New Englanders, the significance of these clay images was, simply, that they were idols, examples of the false gods worshipped by the Gentoos of India. Idols were a perennial in the Society's museum, where they served to remind visitors of the distinction between their Christian nation and those of, they supposed, misguided, doomed heathens across the world.

Other objects on display in the hall were of less weighty import—some associated with navigation, trade, or manufactures. A simple wooden spindle, used by highly skilled women in parts of Bengal during months when the humidity was just right, produced the finest cotton yarns, suitable for weaving the gossamer muslins so esteemed in Empire fashions (see figs. 1.4 and 4.5). Also on display was "A cane from one of the Calcutta pilots," donated by Captain Joseph White, Jr., which served to recall those heroes of navigation on the treacherous Hooghly River from the Bay of Bengal to Calcutta.[51] The pilots, who were British employees of the East India Company, were skilled navigators and essential for the passage up the Hooghly to Calcutta. Every American ship took one on board at the mouth of the river for the difficult and hazardous voyage. Another kind of danger associated with the long and arduous voyages from New England ports to India was encapsulated in "a piece of oak timber, eaten in one voyage to India by ship worms (*teredo navalis*)." Among the most fascinating, and often collected, were the "curious" smoking devices, water pipes known as hubble-bubbles and hookahs, which came in an endless variety of shapes, materials, and decoration, with bowls of plain or decorated glazed pottery and bases made of silver, glass, inlaid metal or coconut, stems of bamboo, or flexible leather tubing covered in velvet or brocade (fig. 4.23; see also fig. I.4).

The museum of the East India Marine Society presented collections from around the world in a way that enhanced Yankee views of their nation's ascendancy in commerce, politics, and morality. Most curiosities in the East India Marine Society's museum emphasized difference—the remarkable, the exotic, the strange—put before the public for visual contemplation. There was almost no information on the indigenous use or meaning of the objects on display; visitors were left to impute whatever further significance they wished. The principal lesson seemed to be that India was an exotic land succumbing to the control of a stronger, more enlightened Western power.

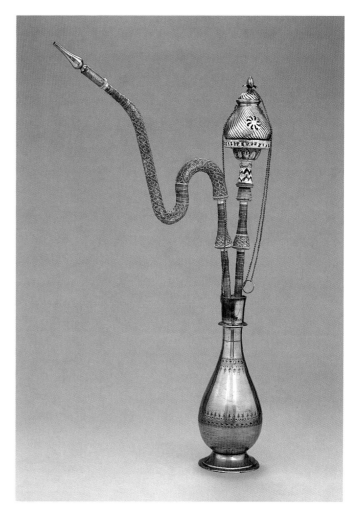

Fig. 4.23 "The instrument used in smoking tobacco in Bengal, vulgarly called hubble-bubble," Calcutta, c. 1810, entry #186 in *The East India Marine Society of Salem* (Salem, Mass., 1821). Silver, bamboo, cotton, ceramic, height 61 cm; Peabody Essex Museum E7385, Gift of Captain Samuel Tucker, c. 1810.

Fig. 5.1 Dudley Leavitt Pickman (1779–1846) by A. Hartwell after a painting by Chester Harding.
Oil on canvas, 90.2 x 72.4 cm; Peabody Essex Museum M352, Gift of William D. Pickman, 1869.

CHAPTER 5

Dudley Leavitt Pickman, Encounter with the East

Almost every native may be considered a beggar . . .

Some of the natives . . . complain . . . that the English are carrying off all the wealth of their country.

When Dudley Leavitt Pickman (fig. 5.1) died in 1846, he was the richest man in Salem, Massachusetts, with an estate worth $1.2 million.[1] Like others of his generation, he had begun his career in commerce, and after the war of 1812 devoted an increasing portion of his energy and resources to industry. Pickman, in family tradition, also pursued a very active civic life. He was elected several times to the Massachusetts legislature, representing Salem in the House and Essex County in the Senate. He was a committed supporter of Unitarianism; its liberal, humanistic tenets seem to have been congenial to many men whose pursuit of maritime trade had given them broad exposure to the world. Pickman's journals of his experiences in Europe, India, and Sumatra manifest a genuine engagement, an effort to make sense of his encounters with far-flung corners of the world. His service to the Salem East India Marine Society, as secretary from 1810 to 1812 and as president from 1817 to 1820, represents not only camaraderie with those who had similar experiences, but a conviction that what they learned should be shared with others.

Dudley Pickman's great-grandfather Benjamin (1708–1773) had moved from Boston to Salem to pursue the West India trade, which he did, very successfully. With his wealth he forged a prominent place for the family in the commercial and civic establishment of the town. The Pickmans lived in one of Salem's finest mansions. Benjamin became an important member of the community, serving as a colonel in the Essex Regiment, as a representative to the General Court of Massachusetts, and as a member of the Governor's Council. Despite his son Benjamin's (1740–1819) eight-year hiatus as a loyalist living in London, the position Benjamin senior built for the family

in Salem was energetically maintained for generations. When President James Monroe came to town in 1817, he was entertained at the home of the younger Benjamin Pickman.[2]

Dudley Pickman finished his formal schooling in his teens and went to work at the Salem Custom House, where his father William—younger brother of Benjamin, Jr.—had been appointed naval officer of the port by President Washington. A few years as a clerk provided young Pickman with a commercial education and, in 1799, John Crowninshield[3] offered him the opportunity to serve as supercargo on a voyage of the ship *Belisarius* to India. Pickman, though scarcely twenty years old, was ready for an opportunity to seek his fortune. The Crowninshields and the Pickmans had engaged in joint ventures since before the War of Independence.[4] Pickman was to be in charge of all the business of trade on the voyage; Captain Samuel Skerry, Jr., would command the ship. Crowninshield directed that the ship stop at Tenerife in the Canary Islands to load wines for India using the firm's credit. But when the *Belisarius* arrived at Tenerife, Pickman found wines extremely scarce. Worse still, no credit was to be had: the English merchant houses Pickman approached had learned of the failure of a New York firm closely associated with the Crowninshield family. The voyage was aborted and the *Belisarius* returned to Salem, where the Crowninshields responded by reloading the ship immediately for a direct voyage to the East Indies. Dudley Pickman was engaged again as supercargo. On December 22, 1799, with Captain Skerry in command, the *Belisarius* set sail for Madras on the Coromandel Coast of India.[5]

The last year of the eighteenth century was a time of momentous change. Just a day after the *Belisarius* weighed

Fig. 5.2 The Apotheosis of Washington by a Chinese painter, c. 1805, after an engraving by John James Barralet published in Philadelphia, January 1802. Washington had achieved an almost godlike status, revered as a military leader, father of the American republic, and a man of estimable character. Reverse painting on glass, 74.3 x 54.6 cm; Peabody Essex Museum E81885, Museum purchase with funds donated anonymously, 1978.

between the Republican party of Thomas Jefferson and the agricultural and laboring classes.

Beyond these political transformations at home, changes were taking place abroad that would powerfully affect the prospects for Yankee shipping. In Europe, just days after the departure of the *Belisarius*, a new constitution endowed Napoleon Bonaparte with dictatorial powers in France. Napoleon made an offer of peace that was rejected, and soon most of Europe was drawn into a conflict that had begun in 1793 and would continue, apart from a brief respite brought by the 1802 Treaty of Amiens, until the final defeat of Napoleon at Waterloo in 1815. For Americans, the opportunities and dangers of neutral trade were never greater.

In India, 1799 was a year of historic triumph for the British. With his father before him, Tipu Sultan of Mysore had frustrated British attempts at control and expansion for more than thirty years. The Fourth Mysore War brought the final defeat of Tipu Sultan, who was killed at his capital Seringapatam in 1799 (fig. 5.3). Southern India was finally secured for the British. Tipu's defeat was taken as the emblem of British ascendancy in India. Scenes of Tipu's death, like those of his sons being taken hostage by Lord Cornwallis in 1792 (see fig. 4.21), were among the most widely printed eighteenth-century depictions of India. Dudley Pickman noted in his 1803–04 journal of the *Derby* (chapter 7) that, as a reward for commanding the British forces against Tipu, Governor-General Wellesley had been given the title of marquis and an annuity of £5,000 sterling.

While Salem and the nation mourned George Washington, the *Belisarius* was sailing into snowy cold gales off Georges Bank. Fortunately, the winds soon shifted northwest and the *Belisarius* made a quick passage to the Cape Verde Islands and reached the equator in twenty-five days. This second voyage of the *Belisarius* to India was a success. The homeward-bound cargo included merchandise (mostly textiles) worth $55,000; 58,000 pounds of pepper; 8,000 pounds of tea; 11,000 pounds of sugar. Duties amounted to $13,492.[7] Pickman had found a satisfactory way to build commercial capital. He sailed again in 1801 in the *Anna* to Sumatra, and the following year in the ketch *Three Sisters* to Havre-de-Grâce.

In 1803, Pickman embarked on his second and last voyage to India, this time as supercargo of the *Derby*, which he owned jointly with his uncle Benjamin and Timothy Williams of

anchor for India, Salem received the news of President George Washington's death. Washington, even in his lifetime, was a hero of mythic proportions, leader of the Revolution and father of the country (fig. 5.2). The entire nation mourned. Everywhere elaborate memorial observances were organized. The *Salem Gazette* was published with thick black borders.[6] In port towns like Salem, where the policies of Washington and his secretary of the treasury Alexander Hamilton favored shipowners and merchants, his loss was felt most grievously, for the national political climate was beginning to shift from a powerful alliance between the propertied class and the Federalist administrations of Washington and Adams, to a new coalition

Boston. The *Derby* was a new ship, built in Salem at the shipyard of Enos Briggs. Benjamin Pickman and Timothy Williams hired Thomas West as master, sent out $70,000 in silver specie, and instructed Pickman and West to proceed to Bourbon (Réunion) or Île de France (Mauritius), both French possessions, for a cargo of cotton and coffee. If that strategy failed, West and Pickman were to continue on to Calcutta. When they reached the islands, they found prices so high that, after purchasing 58 bales of cotton and 76 sacks of cloves, they pressed on to Calcutta to fill out their cargo. There they loaded cotton textiles, raw cotton, sugar, ginger, and copal (a resin used in varnishes). The cargo was sold at Boston for more than $126,000; about two-thirds of the value was in textiles.[8]

With the profits from these voyages, Pickman retired from the sea in his late twenties to devote himself to business ashore. He was a founder of Pickman, Stone, and Silsbee, which specialized in trade with Zanzibar, Sumatra, Java, and the Philippines. The firm was locally renowned for its unwritten partnership agreement and longevity of nearly a century. Pickman's son William and his grandson and namesake, Dudley Leavitt Pickman, followed as principals of the firm. But Pickman's growing business interests extended far beyond commercial shipping and are indicative of the new direction of New England's economy. He invested in companies that developed land and water power for manufacturing in the heartland of the American industrial revolution, the towns of Lowell, Lawrence, and Manchester, founded in the 1820s and '30s. He held shares in cotton and woolen mills, water companies, and railroads. He served as director of several corporations, including the New Market Manufacturing Co., one of many cotton mills to spring up in New England in the second quarter of the nineteenth century. Times were truly changing: cotton textiles had been the most important cargoes for Pickman's India voyages; in his later business concerns, cotton textiles produced locally for domestic consumption and for export were among his most significant enterprises. And, unlike most of his fellow East India traders, Pickman became a supporter of protective tariffs that would curb competition from foreign trade and promote the growth of domestic industries.

During his early years as a supercargo, Pickman sailed on five trading voyages and recorded his experiences of each in a bound journal. In addition to his voyages to India (to Madras, 1799–1800, in the *Belisarius*, and to Calcutta, 1803–04, in the

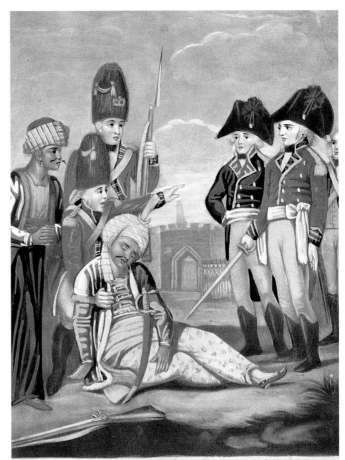

The DEATH of TIPOO SULTAN and SURRENDER of SERINGAPATAM.

Fig. 5.3 *The Death of Tipoo Sultan and Surrender of Seringapatam*, published in London, 1801. Hand-colored mezzotint, 40.6 x 30.5 cm including frame; Peabody Essex Museum M16224, Willard G. Cousins by exchange, 1975.

Derby), the journal contains accounts of the first aborted trip to the East Indies in 1799, the voyages to Sumatra in 1801 and to Havre-de-Grâce in 1802, and a voyage to Naples and Gaeta in 1804–05. Pickman seems to have used these journals as a way to organize what he learned and as a means of sharing his experiences with family, close friends, and business associates. As explained in the preface to his journal of an 1808 trip to Niagara Falls, he kept notes during his travels which were later organized into a narrative: "The following journal . . . [was written] from minutes taken during the journey it describes." All Pickman's accounts of his voyages, bound together in a single journal, were evidently prepared in the same manner: each is written without obvious changes in ink, pen point, or handwriting that would be expected had the entries been made during the voyages. In his Niagara Falls journal, Pickman articulated his relationship to his readers: "Instead of an apology, I shall request the very few persons who may see it to lay it aside as soon as they are convinced it will not repay the trouble of a reading."[9]

In contrast to Carpenter's journal of the *Ruby*, Pickman's accounts were not concerned so much with the business of the voyage as with the places he visited and his impressions of them. His entries cover a wide range of topics. He summarizes the procedures and prospects for trade, but he also describes architecture, politics, and society. His entries were based on what he learned from people he met, personal observations, and information found in books. The style of the journals is almost purely descriptive and contrasts dramatically with extant correspondence to his family. For instance, in a letter written to his young son from Philadelphia years after the voyages to India, Pickman differentiated these genres: "My dear little son, I have sent the history of my travels to your sisters with all the news of this great city—so you must be content with the expression of my good wishes and love for you."[10]

Pickman's journals of India stand out for the effort made not only to record his own experiences but to describe Indian society. To do this, Pickman sometimes incorporated extracts from published sources, including a large section from the entry under "Hindoo" in the 1797 *Encyclopedia Britannica*. At the end of the passage, he compares it with his own observations, noting "this account, as far as my opportunities would allow me to judge, represents faithfully the character of the Hindoos, in which mildness always appeared to me the most striking trait."[11] Since published sources and informants in India were primarily British, Pickman's view of India was significantly shaped by prevailing British perspectives. But Pickman assimilated those views to build an interpretation that is distinctly American.

Certain themes in Pickman's writing resonate with the responses of other American mariners in India. Perhaps the most significant of these was the division of society between the "natives" or "blacks" and the Europeans in the port cities frequented by New England vessels. The largest of these ports, Calcutta and Madras, were founded by the British as commercial centers and each consisted of a fort for trade and security, which was European territory, and a section for the shops and houses of the "native" population. Pickman's descriptions of Madras and Calcutta both begin with the forts: Fort William in

Calcutta and Fort St. George in Madras. For him, these were the central places of the city. The native section in Madras, like that at Pondicherry, was called Black Town. The social hierarchy of the city was based not just on a division between conquerors and subject people, but on a racial division. This structure resonated strongly for Americans who lived in a society in which blacks were enslaved.[12] In Madras, Pickman reported that no "black" was allowed inside the fort in a palanquin. At Tranquebar, he noted: "The whites have a Danish church, and one for the Roman Catholics, where blacks are admitted after the whites have finished their devotions. The blacks (natives) have one of their own color for their preacher who is assisted however by an European clergyman." Racial differences, in the discourse of Pickman's time, were manifested in physical constitution and character. Ideas about the racial foundation of differences between blacks and whites sometimes produced unnoticed contradictions. For example, Pickman claimed that the natives "have little bodily strength." Yet, on a palanquin trip from Tranquebar to Nagore, he recounts that "the same bearers took me the whole distance, thirty-six miles. They went nearly four miles an hour apparently without much fatigue and without suffering at all from the intense heat of a clear sun beating on their almost naked bodies."[13]

Like so many Americans from his time onward, Pickman was astonished and disturbed by the number of beggars. At Tranquebar, he recalled: "There are a great many beggars . . . met here in the streets at all times. Many of them from misfortunes of birth or otherwise are most pitiable objects." In Pickman's New England, people resorted to begging only when desperate (for they risked arrest). In India, on the other hand, begging was a legitimate pursuit for the badly deformed, for religious ascetics, and for anyone unfortunate enough to be without a livelihood. Those who could were expected to provide; giving was considered a duty and a blessing. To Yankee Pickman, however, the widespread practice of begging revealed a defect of Indian character (that is, a racial trait): "There are many beggars in the streets. Almost every native may be considered a beggar; varying their claim however, according to their situation, from plain begging for fanams, to the more delicate request for 'master's favor.'"[14]

While Pickman harshly judged the natives as naturally inferior and subordinate "blacks" who were, by and large, dishonest and unreliable, he was also sharply critical of Europeans, especially the British, in India. He noted the division into classes by which (European) shopkeepers in Madras were considered too lowly to be invited to functions by the governor. For an American from a town like Salem, the division between merchants and shopkeepers seemed absurd. Pickman also noted the irony of a situation in which the supposedly superior British were utterly dependent on "natives" for all their interactions with the indigenous population: "from the lowest menial servants to head dubashes, . . . they have almost the entire direction of their business with the natives." More critically, he observed that most of the British were out to make an immediate fortune to be spent at home and "they pay little regard to the means of accomplishing it. The natives are consequently oppressed and defrauded. Their money is borrowed, without probability or expectation of repaying it . . ." Some of the native merchants "complain, whether with reason I cannot sufficiently judge, that the English are carrying off all the wealth of their country."[15] By contrast, at the Danish port of Tranquebar, Pickman found "such as come from Denmark usually end their days here. This induces a much better treatment to the natives than they experience from the English . . ."[16]

Although Pickman was critical of the British and their conduct in India, European exploitation and dishonesty were attributed to situation, not character. He did not see the dishonesty of natives as parallel to the dishonesty of whites. The latter merely took advantage of a situation to extract the highest profit, as any sensible businessman would do. The native's dishonesty was symptomatic of his natural—that is, racial—character. American ideas about race, which placed white Yankees above "black" Indians, conveniently allowed New England mariners to pursue their commercial advantage, equipped to condemn the shortcomings of "natives," and self-assured enough to ignore their own.

BELISARIUS of SALEM · Benjamin LOVETT COMMANDER

Fig. 6.1 *Belisarius of Salem*, attributed to Guiseppi Fedi, Italy, c. 1797. Dudley Pickman sailed as
supercargo of the *Belisarius*, owned by the Crowninshield family, on the voyage to Madras in 1799.
Watercolor, 41.6 x 62.2 cm; Peabody Essex Museum M5028, Gift of G. S. Silsbee, 1898.

CHAPTER 6

From the Journal of the Belisarius, *1799–1800*

DUDLEY L. PICKMAN

Arrived at Madras after a passage of 111 days from Salem.[1] Distance run per log, this passage, 14,240 miles.

On arriving at Madras, the Government Boat comes along side. The officers come on board and receive such information as is required, respecting the vessel, cargo, passengers, etc. and on their return and report, a boat is sent off. No person is permitted to land before this is done, nor before the ship is brought to the proper anchoring ground, opposite the Custom House. On landing, report is made at the Custom House.

Madras (called by the natives, Chili-patam) is the capital settlement of the English on the Coast of Coromandel. It consists properly of two towns—Fort St. George and the Black Town. In the Fort, which contains a regular built town, are all the offices of government (except the Custom House), the stores of the European merchants, etc. In the Black Town live the natives. All Government orders issue from Fort St. George —and the Europeans generally use the same, instead of Madras.

The Government of the Madras Presidency, as it is called, is vested in the Governor and Council of Fort St. George—subordinate to the Governor General of India, at Calcutta. The latter office is now filled by Lord Mornington,[2] who is considered a man of great talents and energy. Lord Clive[3] is Governor at Madras and spoken of as [a] very weak man. The immediate Government of Madras is vested in a Mayor, Aldermen, etc.

Madras lies along the Coast, and has no harbor. Vessels anchor in the open road, entirely exposed to the weather, at two or three miles distance from shore. It is a place of large trade, which is carried on from hence to all parts of India—to Europe and America. There were 50 to 70 vessels here, loading and unloading, all the time of our stay. Many of them were small, and very few belonged here. The smallest carry on the coasting trade to the small ports on the coast; the larger go to the Persian Gulf, Bengal, China, etc. A very large covered trade is carried on to Manilla, Batavia, Mauritius, etc. under the Danish flag.[4] The neighboring port of Tranquebar, belonging to Denmark, is very useful in this commerce. Rice is brought in large quantities from Bengal, some China goods from Canton, pepper from Sumatra, and European goods and liquors direct from England and Madeira in the [British East India] Company and India ships. The principal export is in piece goods, as Madras, Pulicat, and Ventepollam handkerchiefs,[5] blue guineas,[6] camboys or checks, nicanies or stripes, punjum[7] cloths (white) etc. Pepper, spices, sugar, etc. imported from other parts of India are sometimes re-exported. The finest goods of India are manufactured in the neighborhood of Madras, and exported from thence, such as long cloth,[8] isery [izarees],[9] handkerchiefs of different kinds, and book muslin.[10] Labor and provision for the natives, as rice, are much higher here than in Bengal, and consequently goods of the same description must be also dearer. But in quality the manufactures of Madras far exceed those of Bengal.

Fort St. George is a handsome brick fortification [fig. 6.2]. It appears very strong, but is probably too much extended to make as able a defence as might otherwise be done. It contains a regular built town, containing several houses, many stores, shops etc. besides an English Church, the Government offices, and accommodations for the troops. The buildings [are] of brick, generally lofty and spacious. In the public square, in the middle of the Fort, is a statue of Marquis Cornwallis, lately

Fig. 6.2 *South East View of Fort St. George, Madras* by Thomas and William Daniell after a drawing by Thomas Daniell,
published in *Oriental Scenery*, Series II, plate 7, London, c. 1798. Hand-colored aquatint, 44.5 x 61.6 cm;
Courtesy of the Department of Printing and Graphic Arts, Houghton Library, Harvard College Library.

brought from England. Not being entirely finished it was kept covered while we were here, but was to be opened with [a] great parade in a few days, on the anniversary of the victory gained by that nobleman under the walls of Seringapatam, which produced peace with Tippoo.[11] The public buildings attract no attention from their splendor. No black is permitted to go into the Fort in a palanquin; they must walk in from the gates. All the European merchants have their stores in the Fort. They generally live a few miles from the Fort in the country.

The town outside the Fort, is called the Black Town [fig. 6.3]. The Custom House is kept here, near the beach where all goods are landed and shipped. The natives, with the Armenians and Portuguese, reside here. It is under the same Government with that part within the Fort. It is irregularly built. The streets are narrow and unpaved, many of them dirty, though not very generally so. The habitations of the poorest class of natives are made of mats—are about thirty or forty feet circumference and six or eight feet high—the door three or four feet by two. They cook in them—the smoke going out between the mats. In one of these dwells a whole family. There are but a small proportion who live thus miserably. Many have low one story houses, built of brick and plastered outside. The rich natives have large, handsome houses, with considerable gardens adjoining. One which costs 6,000 pounds sterling was not thought extravagant for a man not in the first class of wealth. The Portuguese and Armenians who live in Black Town, have generally handsome houses, some of them three stories. They are all of brick or stone, and are built as airy as possible. The second story con-

Fig. 6.3 *Part of the Blacktown, Madras* by Thomas and William Daniell after a drawing by Thomas Daniell,
published in *Oriental Scenery*, Series II, Plate 8, London, c. 1798. Hand-colored aquatint, 44.5 x 61.6 cm;
Courtesy of the Department of Printing and Graphic Arts, Houghton Library, Harvard College Library.

tains the drawing and dining rooms. The interior of the houses belonging to the natives is finished in [a] very plain manner, and with but little expense. The few handsome houses to be seen compensate very poorly the ordinary and wretched buildings which are constantly on view. By natives is understood those descended from native parents.

The Portuguese and Armenians, though for several generations resident here, retain their national appellations, and have claimed in some respects, a neutrality in wars undertaken by European nations against that under whose government they live.

The natives are very dark, with coarse black hair, which grows to a considerable length. They are employed by the Europeans in every capacity, from the lowest menial servants, to head dubashes, where they have almost the entire direction of their business with the natives. As writers and accountants, they are very neat and correct. They are employed in all counting houses and public offices, but generally are overseen by an European bookkeeper. The natives are of different casts or religions. The Gentoos[12] do not shave the upper lip and wear a mark on the forehead resembling sealing wax generally a single perpendicular line.[13] The Malabar caste shave the upper lip and daub over the forehead with something resembling blue paint. The Moormen cast have no mark. Besides these, are the Brahmins (or Bramineys—minister cast) who are the highest [fig. 6.4]. They will not touch any, not of their own denomination, without immediately washing themselves entirely after it. There are some Roman Catholics also, and some loose cast, or

Fig. 6.4 Brahmin priest from southern India, after a drawing by Charles Gold, published in London, c. 1806. Hand-colored aquatint, 30.5 x 24.5 cm; Peabody Essex Museum M17707, Gift of John Dominis Holt and Frances Damon Holt, 1978.

whom I knew (belonging to the house with whom I did business) being severely punished one day for a trifling theft. The lower classes are certainly not to be depended on, in any degree. Like the poor of most countries they cannot resist temptation. And even among the richest and most respectable of the natives, as well Brahmins as others, very few are seen in whose honor and integrity great confidence can be placed, or possessing views sufficiently intensive to believe that honesty will bring its own reward and be always found the best policy.

The natives dress very differently according to their ability [fig. 6.5]. The coolies, or laborers, palanquin bearers, and others of the poorest class, go entirely naked except a small cloth round the waist and a small turban on the head. The second class, as writers, etc., wear cotton or coarse muslin to cover themselves entirely, except the head and legs, and turbans of the same—fourteen to twenty-four yards long, bound round the head, some of them neat and handsome. The turban is the most extravagant part of the dress. This class generally wear shoes. Gentlemen usually clothe their servants and bearers in this way. The richest of the natives, as merchants, head dubashes etc., and all who possess property, wear fine muslins and large turbans. They wear shoes, which they throw off on entering a house. None of the natives wear stockings. Their dress is entirely of cotton or muslin, wrapped round them, without being cut to any particular fashion. These observations of course refer entirely to the men. The women, except those of the poorest classes, are never seen in the streets. They confine themselves entirely to their houses. The poor creatures seen in the streets wear course stuff to cover them, but no turbans, shoes or stockings. None of the women wear the first or last.

Marriages are generally made when the parties are very young, by their friends—the ceremony frequently taking place at five or six years old. They generally marry relations. The ceremony continues several days, at great expense, with music, dancing, etc., with fire works at night—according to the ability of the parties. Some of the rich are very extravagant on these occasions. One of the natives told me the marriage of his daughter cost him 8000 pagodas (3200 pounds sterling). Open house is kept during this time. When the parties arrive at proper age, there are new celebrations, but not so general or expensive as

outcasts from the sect to which they belonged. The latter are held in such horror by the Brahmins, that on one occasion, when I wished to enquire out a store in the Black Town, a Brahmin in company refused to ask information, even as interpreter, from one of this description. He spoke to a Gentoo who asked of the loose cast—and finding him acquainted with the object of our search, and that a direct communication was necessary, the Brahmin obliged him to turn his face from him to give the description we needed.

Children are considered of the same cast as their parents. The Brahmins are much more faithful and to be depended on than any other description of the natives, but even these are not worthy of implicit confidence as I found from one of those

Fig 6.5 *Marchand des Perles*, *Musulman*, lithograph by Darondeau, Paris, c. 1810, after a drawing by
Berlanger. Hand-colored lithograph, 20.6 x 14.3 cm; Peabody Essex Museum M17790,
Gift of John Dominis Holt and Frances Damon Holt, 1978.

the first. The women, after marriage, are scarcely seen except by their husbands, to please whom is their great object. They do not go from their own houses—have few children and are very short lived. Some men do not marry till twenty or thirty, and then take wives of five or six whom they have never seen. Second marriages are very rare. No celebrations take place without music and dancing—and in the night, fire works are added. The music is without harmony. The dancing, if so it may be called, performed by girls whose business it is, consists of strange contortions of the face and body, accompanied by the clanking of large rings round their ankles, and horrid shrieking. Their movements are very awkward and clumsy. The fireworks are miserable. Yet all these being to the taste of those, for whose amusement they are exhibited, are very highly enjoyed by them.

The natives live on rice and curry,[14] almost entirely, and of

these they eat great quantities. They eat with their fingers from a leaf. Their curries are extremely hot. They drink water and coconut milk. The lower classes drink spirits when they can get them. They have very little bodily strength. The natives use no pleasure carriages. They ride in palanquins—five or six feet long, three wide and three high—carried by four men, two before and two behind, who bear it on their shoulders by two poles projecting three or four feet from the front and back. The number of bearers usual in the city is six to eight—for long journeys the number is increased, sometimes as far as sixteen. They travel fast and hold out well. Their pay is four fanams, about fifteen cents per day. The journey to Tranquebar, 170 or 180 miles, in a palanquin with sixteen bearers, would take five or six days. Long journeys to the country are undertaken in carts drawn by oxen, who will travel three to four miles an hour

Fig. 6.6 Holyman, after a drawing by Charles Gold, published in London, c. 1806. Hand-colored aquatint, 30.5 x 24.5 cm; Peabody Essex Museum M17708, Gift of John Dominis Holt and Frances Damon Holt, 1978.

their situation, from plain begging for fanams, to the more delicate request for "master's favor."

Of the religious ceremonies I can say but little. While here scarce a day passed in which something of this kind was not done, such as carrying through the streets, images, highly decorated, which they called their gods. Sometimes they were carried on a stage supported on men's shoulders, sometimes in a carriage, and at others on the back of an elephant kept by the church for that purpose. They were always accompanied by music, and large concourses of people, and great respect and obeisance was paid, some even to prostrating their faces in the dust. These ceremonies were sometimes performed in the night, when fire works were added. These, as well as the music and many parts of the ceremony, were very rude. I do not know if their ceremonies are so constant through the year, or if this was a particular season for them.[15] The Moormen have an annual feast, at which they kill a camel. This anniversary happened during our stay, but offered nothing particularly interesting.[16] In one of the processions I saw a fanatic who professed to have devoted himself entirely to god. He was dancing etc. before the image, and applying fire to different parts of his body, apparently without effect. This "the people" considered as proof of approbation and acceptance. I visited a Brahmin (who was head dubash to a house, with which I was intimate) during the celebration of the induction of his son to the Brahmin cast. He kept open house, with dancing, music, etc. as on marriage feasts. The merchant to whom he was dubash was present with his family, and this attention seemed very gratifying to our host, who filled us with garlands of flowers, sprinkled us with rosewater and perfumes, and at parting presented each of us a piece of muslin.

The Portuguese and Armenians born in the country are few in number. They dress and live as the Europeans. The former however, live generally in Black Town, while the Europeans reside in the country, a few miles from the Fort, coming in daily to their business, about 9 a.m. and continuing till 5 p.m. They eat a tiffin or luncheon at twelve or one, dine usually by candle light and, after drinking wine till eight or nine, have tea. The rich live well and at great expense, have a great variety of dishes on table, and drink much wine. Wild fowl, poultry, beef,

on a trot and hold out for a long time. They draw by the forehead, not as with us. Traveling twenty miles a day, they will hold out a journey of five or six hundred miles, and return without difficulty. These cattle have no horns, but are covered with hair. There is another kind with large horns, skins nearly black, and scarcely any hair [water buffalo]. The latter are the largest.

The natives universally chew beetle nut and leaves and chunam [i.e., areca nut, betel leaf, and lime], the former of which gives the teeth and mouth a very red and disagreeable appearance. There are many jugglers here, who call on all newcomers. Their performances very far exceed anything I have before seen, and discover great talent in their occupation. There are many beggars in the streets. Almost every native may be considered a beggar; varying their claim however, according to

Fig. 6.7 Camel by William Daniell, published London, 1807. Engraving, 14.4 x 22.6 cm; Peabody Essex Museum
M17686, Gift of John Dominis Holt and Frances Damon Holt, 1978.

pork, fish, etc. are found here, some of them very good. Of wines, English claret is most fashionable—it comes charged from England as high as sixty-three pounds sterling per dozen, and sells now twelve to fourteen pagodas. Much Madeira also is drunk. All liquors are much adulterated by the shopkeepers and bottlemen. Nothing will sell here, if called under the first quality, but being poor judges, great impositions are practiced. Of fruits, I saw pines [pineapple], oranges and shattucks [large citrus fruit]—none of them equal to those I have seen brought from the West Indies—plantains and other fruits. There are very good grapes brought here from Pondicherry, but they are few in quantity and very dear.

Great numbers of servants are fashionable, a different person being kept for almost every different service. Every gentleman carries his servant, in going to dine. Men are employed entirely, except in fetching water, which is brought a considerable distance by the women. Some excellent servants are found here, but all much inclined to "cheat master." Gentlemen wear white jackets always, when about their business. At other times they dress entirely in European style. The ladies of course, who come from Europe, retain their manners and dress. Some few Europeans have coaches, and many drive buggies or chairs. They are imported from Europe, but can be used only in and near the town, the roads not being suitable. Almost every one has his palanquin. There is no theater, or other public amusement here. Sunday appears totally disregarded by the Europeans as well as natives. Business goes on as usual, and I saw nothing to distinguish this from any other day. The gentlemen who live out from the Fort have gardens, some of which are handsome and very expansive. They all have tanks or ponds, from which to water their gardens in the dry season—without this, their produce would be entirely destroyed.

There are several taverns here, but their charges are enormously high, and it is less reputable to live at them, than to keep house. The Americans whose business brings them to this place, take a house and furnish it, and hire a sufficient number of servants. The expense for a residence of three or four weeks will be considerably less on this establishment, than at a public house. The weather during our stay was pleasant, except when the land wind blew, which was extremely hot. The thermometer stood at about seventy-five to eighty in the shade. No rain fell during our four weeks stay. Sometimes there is no rain for several months, till the rainy season sets in, when they are almost deluged. We saw a few camels here, employed in carrying burthens [fig. 6.7]. Scarcely any birds, except crows, which are very plenty, coming into the house and almost taking things from table. They keep [up] a hideous croaking.

The money of Madras is bank notes, gold coin called pagodas, now very scarce, and silver—rupees and fanams. There is also a small copper coin. The money of account is pagodas, fanams and cash, eighty cash being a fanam [see fig. 3.4]. The exchange of fanams for pagodas is generally forty-four to forty-five, but the merchants keep their books at forty-two for a pagoda, in general, though they differ from one another. A pagoda is reckoned at eight pounds sterling in exchange, and in purchasing English invoices—and is called Star Pagoda to distinguish it from others on the coast. The present exchange of [Spanish or Mexican] dollars, is 165 for 100 pagodas. The Custom House, Boat Office etc. are kept at the beach in the Black Town, and are under the direction of the Master Attendant. There is a Sea Customer, or Collector who receives the duties—a Boat Paymaster, etc. There is also a Board of Trade here. The duties on goods imported in English or American vessels are two and a half percent on the invoice, with an addition of fifteen percent to the amount and five percent on the duties for the Collector's fees. The duties on exports are the same, except the fifteen percent added to the invoice. The invoices are generally made out at reduced prices, though those inward are sworn to. A demand was formerly made of one pagoda per bale, on all goods shipped in American vessels, but as British ships do not pay it, it was resisted and is not now charged.

Ship's boats cannot land here. All goods are loaded and discharged by the boats of the Government, and one of the ship's company should go in each boat to prevent plundering. Boats are had by application to the Master Attendant, and it is seldom more than three or four can be had. They must be paid for at least five trips each, [even] if they do not make so many—but if not detained for lading, they will generally make seven or eight trips each in a day. Caulkers are also supplied by Government, which draws a revenue from all these sources. The boats used in unlading and lading goods, if decked would measure eight or ten tons—are sharp at both ends, entirely open and without masts. No nails are used in building them, but they are sewed with coir. This is rendered necessary from the nature of the beach on which they are to be used. The surf is always rough—sometimes very high, and throws the boats onto the beach with great force and rapidity. When the boat strikes, some of the boatmen jump into the water with a rope which they carry on shore, and with which the boats are hauled as far up, out of the surf, as possible. When the lading is tight casks, they lay the boat in the surf till it has driven the sand from under it sufficiently, when they heave over the boat on its side towards the sea and roll out the casks into the water, and follow them to the shore. The boat is immediately righted. Each boat has eight or ten men, who manage them very well, considering the kind of people. The boats are hauled up entirely out of the surf, and are loaded in this situation, and then pushed off. These are the only kind of passage boats—and it is seldom you can pass off and on without being wet by the surf breaking over you. Besides these are the Catamarans, made of two or three logs, about eight feet long, fastened together by small coir ropes (made from the outside [fiber] of coconut shells) paddled by two men with bamboos. They are used for sending notes and instructions to ships in the road, as also for fishing. They go out several miles.

The merchants of Madras are principally English in the Fort and Portuguese, Armenians and natives in the Blacktown. Of the English Houses, Colt, Baker & Co. do the most business with Americans. Colt, from being a writer in the Company's service, has returned to Europe with a fortune of 200,000 pounds sterling. Baker has an office under the Company, whose legal emolument is 3000 pounds per annum. Mr. Hart, the junior partner, does most of the business of the house. He possesses abilities, and is very attentive, but rather sharp. This, and indeed most of the English houses, is very rich. The House of Harrington, Watts & Co. is considered the first here. Chase, Sewall & Co. are a considerable house. They have an insurance office, but its reputation for liberal and punctual payment in case of loss, is not very high. Roebuck, Abbot & Co. and several others.

In the Blacktown, Satur & D'Monte are undoubtedly first. They are very fair, good men, and much and universally esteemed. They have a very large share of the piece goods business, supplying nearly all the demands of the European houses in the Fort, and most of the Americans who stop here. They also sell to the Armenians, etc. and occasionally ship on their own account. Satur is an Armenian; D'Monte a Portuguese. The latter does all the business of the house, is a good judge of piece goods and very fair, but I did not think highly of his general information or abilities. D'Monte is secretary and almost entire director of an insurance company in which his house is interested. This company has a great reputation for liberality and punctual payment of losses, which gives it a preference in almost all the business of the place. They write generally not over 10,000 pagodas on a risk. The premiums are high and are paid in cash, or by notes on interest. There are some Armenians here, very enterprising, and doing a great deal of business, particularly Gregory Baboom and Mr. Shamier.

Paulem Yagapah Chitty (called by his second name) does a considerable share of the business with Americans. He is a contractor with the East India Company for piece goods and is said to be rich, but we found him much in want of money. He is a Gentoo, and appears a fair man. He cannot give such dispatch, or be so much depended on as D'Monte's house. Paulem Mutiah Chitty, brother to Yagapah and concerned with him, is not so good a man as the other. This is the only native merchant of importance I dealt with. The lower classes have less credit to lose, and are very little to be relied on. "Shopkeepers" are considered of a very inferior grade to merchants, though more respectable in wealth and character than some of those who rank so much higher. Thus the Governor's public invitations to the principal inhabitants of the settlement, includes all the merchants but no shopkeepers. Some of them are rich and do considerable business with Americans. Hope, Reynolds & Griffith (formerly Hope, Card & Co.) are the first, and are very good men. Their store is large and handsome, with commodious go-downs [warehouses] on the lower floor. They purchased several European investments while we remained here—one, extremely well assorted, of 12,000 pounds sterling cost, at sixty-five percent advance. This was considered very high. Waddell, Rannie & Gibson (formerly Waddell, Stuart & Co.) are second, but not so respectable as the former. There are several inferior "shopkeepers." They charge great profits on their goods, but make many bad debts—particularly to the officers, who are frequently unwilling and cannot be compelled to pay.

The Europeans who come to India, do it to make an immediate fortune, to be spent at home. They have, therefore, none of those feelings, which men have who are to close their lives and leave their families on the spot [i.e., men who are making a home for themselves and their descendants]. With an object in view, they pay little regard to the means of accomplishing it. The natives are consequently oppressed and defrauded. Their money is borrowed, without probability or expectation of repaying it—and when the Company's servants are their creditors, they sometimes permit them to oppress in their turns those under them. There are some exceptions to these observations—and to those who form good connections here, it does not appear necessary to resort to fraudulent or improper measures to acquire a competency in a short time. The merchants and others think, however, a very large sum necessary for a fortune. They have large profits on their own business, but will do agency business for five percent. The interest of money is ten to twelve percent. Some of the natives are immensely rich, but they very generally complain, whether with reason I cannot sufficiently judge, that the English are carrying off all the wealth of their country.

Every mercantile house in Madras employs a head dubash, or broker, who is a native and does most of the active business of the house. Some of them are very rich and faithful to their employers, even to joining in any fraud or oppression they may practice on the countrymen of the dubash. One Englishman, on quitting Madras, after adjusting all his business with his dubash, and settling all his concerns with him, gave him as a mark of his confidence and esteem, a real estate renting at 600 pounds sterling per annum. The Americans who trade here find it necessary, also to employ a dubash. There are two only who devote themselves to this business, Vincaty and Villapoy. Neither of them deserves high commendation. The former is more immediately in D'Monte's, the latter in Yagapah's interest. From employing the former, I believe him at least as good as the latter. They require much looking after, and are not to be depended on, having the interest of the merchant from whom they expect future favors at least as much at heart, as that of their immediate employers. It is absolutely necessary to employ a dubash, whose clerks (or conicopolies) attend to receiving, weighing, and shipping goods, etc., which on the part of the merchant is also attended to by natives. The more the whole of them can be overseen, and the less depended on, the better.

The military establishment of the English in India is on a far more respectable footing now, than it has ever before been. The immense territories they have lately acquired, require a great force for their defence.[17] There are about 15,000 Europeans [and?] 60,000 sepoys at present on the India establishment. The Europeans, even in this warm climate, keep up the reputation of the English troops. The sepoys are natives, hired into the service—the privates receiving five rupees per month. They are good soldiers, and when conducted by brave officers and supported by some European troops, will stand as long as any troops whatever. Being accustomed to the climate, they do not suffer from its extreme heat, and march with ease and dispatch at every season of the year. They live almost entirely on rice. They wear short breeches, reaching not so low as the knee, made of white cotton and short cloth coats, with hats. No stockings and generally no shoes. Their dark colored legs, well oiled, form a fine contrast to the white, and at a little distance give them a handsome and very uniform appearance. They exercise and march perfectly well. The commissioned officers are Europeans. The immense expense of the different establishments in India is said to reduce the profits of the Company to less than they were when factories only were established at the different ports, notwithstanding all the taxes and contributions they levy on the inhabitants and the great increase of trade their acquisitions of territory must have brought them. They are also liable continually to new wars, and troops were now marching to the interior in expectation that peace with the Mahrattas[18] would not long continue. The march of the troops occasioned a press of

palanquin bearers for the officers—to carry them through bad roads and in extreme hot weather—six or eight hundred miles, to the scene of action. There is a spacious common in the Black Town, for parading and exercising the troops, of which a large number are generally stationed here. Some of their tents are pitched on the common, where are also two monuments, raised in memory of some of the Company's native servants, now old and defaced.

At Madras, I met very few Americans, and, except in business, formed no acquaintances with the English residents. Of the former, was Captain Cheever, born at Danvers[19] where his relations now live, has been twelve or fifteen years in India, master of a country vessel, has acquired but little property and will probably never return to America. He is deaf and not very intelligent. Mr. Stephen Minot of Boston, lived for several years in Salem with Captain N. West, now trades between Isle of France, and Tranquebar and Madras, probably covering French property, principally prize vessels which he brings back from Mauritius for sale.[20] Mr. Todd, formerly of the house of Todd & Miller, Philadelphia, and Mr. Reid of Philadelphia, who is to return with us to America.

On the whole, Madras has nothing to interest, or to induce a wish to re-visit it. As a place of business, it generally affords the best market for sale of import cargoes of liquors, but has few articles suited for the American market. Money or bills on Bengal can always be had for a return cargo from Calcutta. Having closed out business, we left Madras the 12th May and beat down against the monsoon to Tranquebar, where we arrived the 17th. The ship was light, and a strong current as well as the wind setting against us, prolonged our passage to between five and six days for a distance of 170 miles. We had one disagreeable storm of a few hours attended with most severe thunder and lightning so near us as to be very alarming. We experienced however no accident. Tranquebar is a Danish settlement on the coast of Coromandel, about 160 miles to the southward of Fort St. George.[21] Its limits are very circumscribed, and its appearance very different from that of Madras. The climate cannot be supposed to vary much, yet the few days we passed here were warmer than we had experienced at the former place, and the land and sea breezes much more regular,

Fig. 6.8 *Banyan Tree*, engraving by G. Hollis, London, 1834, after a drawing c. 1800 by William Daniell. The Daniell's views of India were reproduced many times; an earlier print of the banyan tree was in the collection of the East India Marine Society before 1821. Copperplate engraving, 19.1 x 14.6 cm; Peabody Essex Museum M20938, Gift of John Dominis Holt and Frances Damon Holt, 1984.

the former being very hot and sultry, and the latter cool and refreshing. The road of Tranquebar is open and entirely exposed to the weather. Ship's boats do not land. The forms on arriving, the regulations of the boats, etc., are the same as at Madras. Duties in and out [are] two and a half percent.

The fortifications possess no beauty, and, I believe, little strength. There are some European troops here, and some sepoys. The merchants all live in town, and give it a much more pleasant appearance than it could otherwise have. There are many handsome houses in that part where the white inhabitants live, many of whom were born in the country. Such as come from Denmark usually end their days here. This induces a much better treatment to the natives than they experience from the English, who consider themselves merely as "birds of passage." The merchants here do not possess the extensive knowledge and enterprize of English merchants nor have they such exten-

sive connections. The most respectable mercantile house here is that of Harrup and Stevenson. The former died in September 1799, but the firm is still continued. Mr. Stevenson was born in Europe, and appears to be a very fair, good man. Their dubash is Vera Sammy, who is also dubash for the Americans who stop here. He is much more honest and intelligent than either of the Madras dubashes. Rammy Sammy, whom he employs, is not so active as his brother, nor does he possess his other good qualities.

Mr. Hermanson, Second or Lieutenant Governor does business as a merchant—I believe entirely of agency. He is very little a man of business. He has many consignments from Isle of France of prize vessels and goods—probably on French account, but under Danish colors and papers, which are prostituted to every nation that will use them. Mr. Minot whom I saw at Madras is concerned in this kind of business, and is much esteemed here. It is said he wished to marry the daughter of Mr. Hermanson, a most beautiful girl of sixteen, but was thought not sufficiently rich. Beside the above, there are one or two other mercantile houses established here. There is some trade from hence to Europe by individuals as well as by the Company, as also to the different parts of India. This is a small market, yet it will frequently be found worthwhile to stop with an outward cargo, when it can be done without losing much time, particularly if among the cargo is a large quantity of any one article. We saw no Americans here. We put up at the tavern of Mr. Hopff, a Dane—as poor a house as could be wished, yet the best in the place. His charges however are moderate.

The whites have a Danish church, and one for the Roman Catholics, where blacks are admitted after the whites have finished their devotions. The blacks (natives) have one of their own color for their preacher, who is assisted however by an European clergyman. There are very few garden (country) houses out from town. Many respectable families live in Tranquebar, and are on very friendly terms. The young ladies walk frequently in the streets. Among them are *some* very handsome, though not generally so. We went out of the town to "Brothers Garden," belonging to several Moravian Brethren from Germany who have settled here and form a little society of their own. One is a watchmaker, another a cabinet[maker], a third a shoemaker, etc. I met here an immensely fat man said to weigh 500 lbs. Here also I saw a banyan tree [fig. 6.8]. This tree grows up several feet, then branches out horizontally, and from its branches, others drop and take new root in the ground—this extending, if not prevented, it will become very extensive. The one I saw was small, not having more than fifteen or twenty roots. But some, extending in different directions, form of themselves pleasant and extensive arbors. There are a great many beggars of the natives met here in the streets at all times. Many of them from misfortunes of birth or otherwise are most pitiable objects.

Mr. Reid, who had taken passage with us from Madras for America, having business at Nagore and Negapatam, I accompanied him to those places. We set out on May 20, in palanquins, with each twelve bearers. The first part of our journey was by the seaside, on which we observed great multitudes of small crabs. After leaving the shore, there is only a footpath, till you reach Karikal, or Caricaul, five miles from Tranquebar. This place has been taken from the French during the present war. Ginghams of a different kind from any others manufactured on the coast, are made here and known by the name of the place. They are wove white, and painted in stripes, and are much esteemed by the French.

We stopped here at the house of Mr. Grant, English Resident, for passports which are necessary in travelling through any part of the British Dominions in India. He treated us very politely, and appeared a perfect gentleman. A recess in his dining room was partitioned off as a cage for two or three hundred handsome little birds. A considerable number of sepoys are stationed here. Mr. Grant's appeared the only house, of those I saw, calculated for an European, and I understood there were no other white inhabitants in the place than his establishment. From here to Nagore, about eight miles, we passed several ferries, some of them of three or three and a half feet deep our bearers waded through; others we were boated across. That, at Nagore, attracted particular notice from the great number of persons continually passing. The ferry is narrow, and the boat large, carrying fifty or sixty persons—yet it could scarce reach either shore before a return freight was ready, completely to fill it. I observed this, both in going and returning.

We reached Nagore about dusk and then found that Mr. Reid, who engaged to make all the arrangements for our tour, had neglected to engage in it any one who could serve us as an interpreter. We went to visit the "Nagore Pagodas,"[22] which being seen some distance at sea, distinguish this place. They are five in number. The largest is twenty-five or thirty feet square at the base, and for a height of fourteen or fifteen feet, when the second story commences, rather smaller—and so on, for twelve stories, to the top. The stories appear of nearly equal height, and I judge the whole about 170 feet to the top. The remaining four pagodas are much smaller. They are for religious purposes, but having no one with us who spoke English, and no opportunity elsewhere of acquiring the information, I could not learn to what cause was to be ascribed the extraordinary zeal which led to such expensive monuments. Very many of the natives gathered round us, and we soon retired—not however till we had

Fig. 6.9 *Negapatam*, Dutch, 18th century. Engraving, 19 x 28 cm; Peabody Essex Museum
M4514, Gift of Walter Muir Whitehill, 1937.

been forbidden to enter the pagoda with our shoes or boots on our feet. There is an English resident at Nagore, and one or two other Europeans, but to them we had no letters. We afterwards found Tilly, the dubash with whom Mr. Reid's business lies. He spoke French and a few words of English. Nagore formerly belonged to the French.

From hence we proceeded in the evening to Negapatam, five miles from Nagore [fig. 6.9]. This place formerly belonged to the Dutch, but was ceded by them to Great Britain by the Treaty of 1783. Several Dutch families still reside here. Those of that nation I saw spoke of the place and themselves as miserably poor since they changed masters. This is the lowest port on the Coast. It was past nine o'clock when we reached Nega-

patam, where we immediately called on Captain Sopre, the English resident, to whom Mr. Reid had an introduction from Mr. Hermanson at Tranquebar. We found the Captain a perfect brute, extremely cross and ill-natured, and so destitute of hospitality and politeness as not even to offer us a seat in his house. We soon left him and sought for a lodging among the Dutch inhabitants. We found there was no public house, and no prospect of accommodation in any way. One Dutchman who had formerly kept a punch-house offered us a lodging, but on visiting the premises, we found it would not be worth the experiment of seeking repose in his small and very unpleasant apartments. It only remained for us therefore to return to Nagore, for which place we immediately set off. The short time I passed at

DIOMEDIA.

The Albatross.

Fig. 6.10 *The Albatross* by G. Edwards, engraved by J. Pass, published by J. Wilkes, London, 1803. Engraving, 24.5 x 19.7 cm; Peabody Essex Museum NH56.

Negapatam and its being dark prevented my seeing the place or knowing much of it.

Our bearers had now travelled eighteen miles without food and began to complain loudly. Before we were out of Negapatam they set us down at a choultry, and without the least intimation of their designs, left us for the night. Choultries are places built by charitable persons, at different places on the roads, for the accommodation of travellers. Some of them are roofed houses; others merely walls built up three or four feet from the ground. It was in one of the latter description we passed the night, sleeping in our palanquins. There are no public houses on the road, and indeed they would be useless from the extreme poverty of those who pass. Choultries are consid-

ered sacred and no person is known to have been disturbed in one of them. At day break, our bearers returned and took us to Nagore. This is a large town and considerable trade is carried on from hence to different parts of the Coast, Ceylon, and to the other side of the Bay [of Bengal], as Pegu, etc. Having now fasted seventeen hours we inquired for breakfast, but could get only a loaf of bread which the dubash begged from the Resident's House. We were shown to a house kept furnished to let to the captains of country vessels coming here to trade, but had no room assigned us. The captain of a Chittagong[23] vessel, who had an apartment here, soon afterward invited us to breakfast. We accepted and felt grateful for the attention, which was not the less for obliging him to wait till we had drank before he could take his tea—from the scarcity of cups which his establishment afforded.

The day was extremely hot, and after waiting two hours for my bearers who had gone for their breakfast, I was obliged to walk a mile in pursuit of them. Mr. Reid's business requiring his stay longer at Nagore, I set out without him and, after waiting again on Mr. Grant at Karikal, reached Tranquebar after only twenty-four hours absence. In this excursion, the same bearers took me the whole distance, thirty-six miles. They went nearly four miles an hour apparently without much fatigue and without suffering at all from the intense heat of a clear sun beating on their almost naked bodies.

On Mr. Reid's return he informed me that after I left him he was shown to one of the rooms in the house at which we breakfasted, very handsomely furnished, and was provided with everything he could wish, by a native merchant, of whom he purchased some goods. Among other things he was furnished with a mattress covered with silk and muslin sheets. The dubash, Tilly, returned with Mr. Reid to Tranquebar, who spoke highly of his attention, ability and faithfulness.

We left Tranquebar May 25 for Salem. Two days after we saw Ceylon—stood to the south and east and crossed the Equator June 3 in longitude 90 degrees east. To the eastward of Cape Good Hope we caught an albatross which measured ten foot three inches from the extremity of one wing to that of the other; four feet one and a half inches from the beak to the tail; beak seven inches; wing four feet eight inches; neck thirteen and a half inches; foot seven inches long, and seven inches spread on the outer part; outer quill of the wing twenty-one inches [fig. 6.10]. July 6—saw East Coast of Africa. July 12, on Bank Agulhas,[24] in sight of the Cape [of Good Hope], in 45 fathoms water. Caught thirty or forty excellent fish—part of them white and resembling our hake, weighing eight to seventeen pounds each—the others red, from one and a half to eight pounds. Off the Cape, we experienced one or two gales, but on the whole had more favorable weather than we expected, it being the middle of a southern winter. July 27 saw St. Helena. August 5, crossed the Equator in 20 degrees west [longitude] and passed within 60 leagues of the Cape de Verde Islands where we had calms and moderate weather for several days. August 28 passed latitude of Bermuda, 150 leagues east of that island. September 7 saw the south shoal of Nantucket; 10th saw Cape Ann; and September 11 [1800] arrived at Salem having run per log this passage, 13,950 miles.

Fig. 7.1 Calcutta port and vessels by Balthazard Solvyns, 1794. Oil on panel, 67.3 x 121.5 cm;
Peabody Essex Museum M13461, Museum purchase by the Fellows and Friends Fund, 1968.

CHAPTER 7

From the Journal of the Derby, *1803–04*

DUDLEY L. PICKMAN

Dudley Pickman stayed in Salem only a short time after his return from Madras in September 1800. He sailed to Sumatra in 1801 and the next year to Havre-de-Grâce, a voyage that included a long tour of Europe. In 1803, he set out again for India, this time as supercargo of the ship Derby. *Once again he took notes of his experiences and wrote them up in his journal upon his return. En route to India, the* Derby *stopped at Bourbon and Île de France (Mauritius).*

After staying four days here [Île de France], which I spent very pleasantly with Messrs. Merle and Cabot and Mr. Andrew Cabot whom I met here, we sailed February 18 [1804] for Calcutta taking the southern route; judging it too early in the season for the northern passage. The strong westerly winds we experienced near the Equator, in crossing it, induced a belief that we were in error and that had we chosen the other route, we should have saved several days by it. We experienced generally moderate and pleasant weather on our passage, crossed the Equator March 25 in longitude 84 degrees east. April 2 saw the land about Point Gordervare [Godavari].[1] April 4 in the night, run into Balasore Road[2] and anchored, and next morning saw no land, but were fortunate enough to take a pilot at 9 a.m. who got the ship under way, run to the eastward into the middle channel; passed several Indiamen lying in Saugor [Sagar] Road at some distance from us, and at night anchored at Kedgeree [Khijiri]. Next morning April 6 we got under way again at 5 a.m. reached Calcutta where I was happy to find Mr. P. T. Jackson of the ship *Pembroke* of Boston, and Messrs. Ellis and Cabot of the *Asia* of

Beverly.[3] No other Americans in port. On this passage from Isle of France, our distance run per log, 5800 miles.

In going up the river to Calcutta, the first town is Kedgeree, a native village on the left bank about [blank] miles from Calcutta. Two or three Europeans only reside here. Next comes Culpee on the right bank, a place similar to Kedgeree. At Diamond Harbor, the East India Company ships load and unload, as the river above is much shoaler than here. The Company have here an extensive range of stores of one story making a handsome appearance. At Fultah [Falta], thirty miles below Calcutta, is a handsome, well-finished and furnished public house. Vessels coming out against the monsoon are frequently detained here for several days as below here is the most difficult place in the river. This and the pleasure parties from Calcutta support the house, and its owner has already acquired by it a handsome property. The village is small—the river here nearly a mile wide. At Garden Reach, five to eight miles below Calcutta are many handsome houses and fine situations belonging to the gentlemen of Calcutta. The river here is one-half to three-quarters mile wide, and the houses on the banks of the river are very finely situated and extremely pleasant.

Fort William [fig. 7.2] first attracts attention as you approach Calcutta. The fortifications are extensive and considered very handsome. The buildings within the fort are extensive and handsome. It is not so strong as Fort St. George at Madras, but is much less exposed. It is probably sufficiently strong for its situation. I had not opportunity to visit the Fort, as is usually done. It is said well to repay the trouble. This is the British

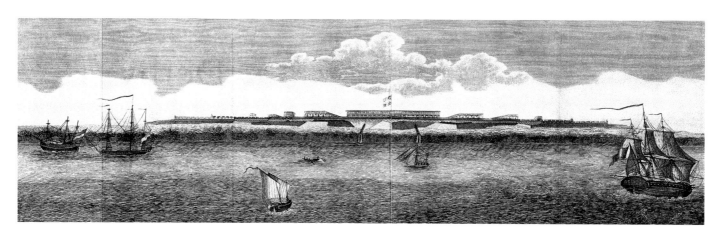

Fig. 7.2 *View of Fort William the Citadel of Calcutta*, c. 1800. Engraving, 21 x 49.5 cm;
Peabody Essex Museum M14556.

headquarters in India, and a considerable garrison is always kept here. The river opposite Calcutta is nearly a mile wide—the approach to the opposite shore being shoal. Vessels carry up seventeen to twenty feet water, according to the situation of the river. The bank on the Calcutta side is very steep, and vessels moor close in shore with four anchors. The pilots for the river can be exceeded by none in the world. They are all Europeans and serve a very long apprenticeship to their business. The river is very difficult as the tides run with great rapidity and strength, and the shoals sometimes shift. In going out against the season, a number of boats are always employed to tow the ship in drifting down.

The rainy season commences in May and continues till September; sometimes raining for several days almost without intermission, and scarcely a day passing without some showers. In July, the river is so full that the freshes[4] begin, but they are not large till August. In this and the next month they are sometimes very strong, so much so that vessels cannot go against the tide, even with fresh favorable winds. Indeed, at these times the pilots will not move their vessels, either up or down. It is then also hazardous lying in the river. The freshes overflow the banks. The tide runs seven or eight miles an hour, down all the time, there being no flood or even still water. In ordinary times the tide runs up five hours and down seven hours. During the freshes vessels have sometimes been detained six weeks at anchor without being able to proceed even a few miles to port. From

October to March is fine, clear, pleasant weather—the finest season at Calcutta; then, to May, growing warm and uncomfortable. During the rains, the weather is very hot and sultry.

Calcutta is situated on the River Hooghly, a branch of the Ganges, and is about 100 miles from the sea, in twenty-three degrees north latitude and eighty-eight degrees east longitude [fig. 7.3]. The English first obtained the Mogul's permission to settle here in 1690. It is now the capital of Bengal and of all British India. In 1756 it was taken by the Nabob Surajah dowla [Siraj-ud-daula], with 70,000 troops and 400 elephants, and 146 English prisoners were confined in the black hole prison during the night of June 20, where 123 died before morning. The next year it was retaken by the English, who have ever since held possession undisturbed. Calcutta is the greatest place of trade in British India. A very extensive business is carried on here with Europe, America and the other parts of India. Here are fine docks for repairing vessels, and shipyards for building. It exports to Europe and the United States piece goods, cotton, sugar, indigo, ginger, etc. From Europe, it imports English goods of every description, liquors, etc. and specie from Europe and the United States. Its trade to other parts of India is very extensive in opium, rice, cotton, sugar, piece goods, etc. Raw cotton was formerly an article of import from Surat to Calcutta. It is now produced in Bengal and exported in very large quantities. Indigo is also an important article of export. The cultivation of both is rapidly increasing. In July and August as the

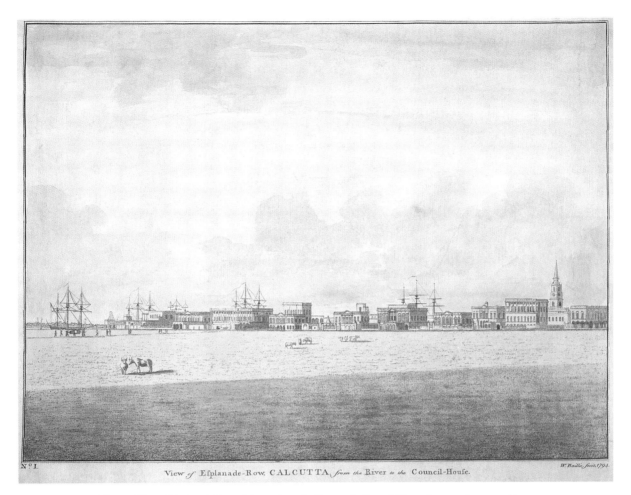

Fig. 7.3 *View of Esplanade Row, Calcutta from the River to the Council House*, drawn and engraved by
William Baillie, published Calcutta, 1794. Hand-colored engraving, 21 x 49.5 cm;
Peabody Essex Museum M15417, Gift of Frances Damon Holt, 1972.

rivers rise, goods come in from the country, and from September to January, is considered the best times to purchase sugar, ginger and piece goods. Many more vessels are here at this, than any other period, and March and April sometimes are found better months for advantageous purchases, than earlier, from an anxiety in holders to push off their goods before new ones come in. The quantities at market are then, however, comparatively small, and a considerable demand would render them scarce and dear.

The Americans in this business have very little to do with the English at Calcutta. They employ native banians, as brokers or agents, and through them make all their purchases. They are paid by the persons of whom the goods are purchased—at least

nominally. Those generally employed are, Ramdulolday [Ramdulal Dey] (who is also banyan to the very respectable English house of Fairlie, Gilmore and Co.) [see fig. 4.7]. He does most of the southern and some of the New England business, is very shrewd and capable, extremely avaricious, and possesses great talents for business. He is considered to be worth three to five millions rupees. Ram Chunder Banorjea, a Brahmin, does some southern and a considerable proportion of the northern business. He is said to be worth five to ten lacs rupees and is a very smooth tongued man. Collisunker [Kalisankar] and Doorgapersaud [Durgaprasad] Ghose do some southern and more northern business. The latter is a shrewd man and industrious when pressed by business [see fig. 11.12]. They are about as rich as Ram Chunder, and I was satisfied with the manner in which they managed the business I entrusted to them.

There are many very respectable English houses here. The principal are Colvins, Bassett and Co., Cockerelle, Trail and Co., Fairlie, Gilmore and Co., and many others. The latter is most known to the Americans, who have frequently had business with them. The merchants have no exchange or place of meeting—their business being done either by written notes, or by the banians, one of whom at least is attached to every mercantile house, and have the entire superintendence and almost direction of everything done. The merchants are frequently indebted to their banians for a considerable proportion of the capital they improve, for which they pay interest—the usual rate of which is twelve percent per annum.

I never could ascertain the number of inhabitants in Calcutta, either of Europeans or natives. The latter, who are certainly very numerous, have been said to amount to 500,000. The former are restricted by their engagement with the Company to Calcutta and ten miles above it, unless by special permission of the Governor General. Their number, exclusive of the military, is small considering this as the headquarters and the immense number of the natives, as well as the business done. The merchants generally employ natives as clerks, except two or three Europeans. The principal streets in which Europeans reside are wide and generally straight—some of them covered with brick dust. During the hot and dry season these streets are kept constantly wet by men employed by the Government for that purpose. This is a great convenience and luxury and adds much to the health, as well as comfort, of the inhabitants. Great attention is now paid to keeping the streets clean, to widen them, when it can be done, and to improve it in every way possible. The city is considered very healthy, except during the rainy season—and even then, with care and prudence, it cannot be considered much otherwise. The streets more particularly inhabited by the natives are narrow, confined and crooked, with some exceptions. More attention is paid now than was formerly to keeping them clean. The houses of the Europeans are generally built of brick and covered with chunam [lime]—of two stories and very extensive, the second story containing all the

apartments of the family. Some of them are very handsome buildings. The rich natives, have houses of brick, covered with tile—generally of but one story. On the outside is a gallery, in which the palanquin bearers, etc. often repose during the day. Within is a court, facing which are the principal apartments, some of which are large, but none elegant. The poorer classes have small and confined houses of one story; most [of] them built of mud or bamboos and covered with thatch.

The Government House at Calcutta [see fig. 4.19], is an extremely large building, more extensive than almost any palace in Europe. Its situation is low, as all the situations in this city are, which prevents its showing to so great advantage as it otherwise would do. It is also painted badly, a dirty cream color. It has a large dome, which appears, however to very little advantage. It was built by the present Governor General—is finished and furnished in a style of great elegance, and must have cost a vast sum of money. It is situated on a large, open square, and several houses were removed which injured its appearance. The ascent to it is by a most noble and elegant flight of steps. It contains offices for the confidential officers of Government, who keep here while the Governor General is in town. It is in every respect a palace, worthy [of] the sovereign of this extensive country, and must give a grand idea of English splendor and magnificence to the natives who are never allowed to depart from their own country.

The Governor General has an elegant seat at Barrackpore, opposite Serampore, fourteen miles above Calcutta. He has two or three elegant yachts, ketch rigged, of 100 tons each to carry him up and down and for great ceremonies, etc. He lives in most splendid style, and probably is not exceeded in pomp and show by any monarch in Europe. This is thought to have a good effect on the natives, impressing them with high ideas of their governors. The present Governor General is the Marquis Wellesley, an Irish peer. He came out [to India as] Lord Mornington, but his very splendid services in [the defeat of] Tipoo Saib [sahib] gained his present title from his sovereign, and an annuity of 5,000 pounds sterling per annum for twenty years from the Company.[5] He possesses uncommon talents and energy, and is eminently qualified for the high station in which he is placed, where, from his distance from home, he must frequently act on the most important affairs without the direction of his superiors. The whole government of British India is in his hands, the Governors of Madras and Bombay being subordinate to him. He is assisted by a Council of four or five members, but may be considered as almost sole monarch of India. He is now preparing for a visit to Delhi, and in a year or two is to return to England. He wears the King's arms on his carriages. He was at his Barrackpore residence during my stay here, so that I had no opportunity of seeing him. During my stay here, an ambassador from Baghdad arrived, and was received with much parade and splendor. The Government vessel which brought him up, as also the Government yacht, were dressed, salutes were fired, the Government officers and an escort of European and native troops with the Governor General's carriage attended and he was received and conducted to his house with much ceremony. He had not an audience as the Governor General was unwell at Barrackpore.

A handsome and very extensive building is erected here by a private concern with the approbation of Government for the Company's civil servants, who hire its apartments. Of the churches the Armenian is the handsomest. It is an elegant building within and without. The new Episcopal Church is the most fashionable as it is frequented by the Court. Its outside is not handsome—its inside I did not see. The "Red Church," also English, is a handsome building inside and out. In summer service commences at the English churches at 9 a.m. and half past seven or eight p.m. The preachers I heard were not first rate. The red church where I went several times, appeared fully attended and the street was filled with carriages and palanquins.

There was formerly a theater here, but it has been discountenanced by the present Governor General as a source of great expense and is now shut up. A gold mohur or sixteen rupees was the price of admittance. Concerts are occasionally given at the same price, and being the only amusement of the kind, are well attended. Some very respectable ladies and gentlemen sing at these concerts. The Esplanade on the bank of the river and leading to the Fort is a pleasant walk. The trees on each side are not yet sufficiently large to make an entire shade, but this is of less consequence as it is not generally visited till near sunset. The walk is covered with brick dust and is kept

Fig. 7.4 *A Palanquin Bearer or Ooria Bearer*, drawn and engraved by Balthazard Solvyns, Calcutta, c. 1800. Hand-colored engraving, 36.8 x 24.8 cm; Peabody Essex Museum M17751, Gift of John Dominis Holt and Frances Damon Holt, 1978.

constantly wet. Yet it is unfashionable and people of the first rank are not seen here. Some European females are seen here, but few however, and those of the lower classes.

The Europeans live here in great style. Every gentleman keeps his palanquin; most of them buggies or one horse chairs; and many of them, carriages. The rich have fine Arab horses many of them superb animals which cost from three to five thousand rupees. Those driven in the Governor General's carriage are perhaps equal to any to be found. The Europeans keep abundance of servants, good tables and very expensive wines. Generally but six bearers form a set for a palanquin. These bearers, of which the number in Calcutta is immense, are mostly from Balasore and that vicinity [i.e., in Orissa] and are so leagued that any injury done to one of them is resented by the whole class and an European sometimes finds it difficult or impossible to get a new set of bearers till he has appeased the wrath of his former ones [fig. 7.4]. The Europeans generally breakfast early, do business from ten to five, eat at twelve or one, and dine at seven or eight, ride out early in the morning, or near sunset in the afternoon. They use very little exercise. The gentlemen wear short jackets while engaged in business, at other times dress in European fashion. The ladies adopt the European fashions carried to their extremes.

As the Europeans come to this country to make fortunes to return to Europe, it is hardly to be expected they should be so mindful of justice in their dealings, or take so much pains to make improvements as they would do if they considered this their abode for life, and the inheritance of their children. They do not generally marry in this country, notwithstanding ladies of beauty, accomplishments and reputation are constantly coming out in pursuit of husbands. The ladies who first came out succeeded in getting good husbands with large settlements. The consequence was that all the ladies who had ambition and enterprise, with friends in India, or could make such, flocked out, creating a supply wholly disproportioned to the demand. Many were obliged to return home unsuccessful or marry much below their expectations and others are waiting better times. Fortunes are not now so rapidly acquired as formerly by the male adventurers and to this no doubt in considerable degree is owing the unfortunate falling off in the prospects of the females. Duelling is very much discountenanced by the present Governor General, who has sent two officers to New South Wales for offending in this respect.

The Armenians, Portuguese, etc. who form a class between the Europeans and natives possess much of the wealth but none of the power and are very little known or thought of here. The Armenian women dress richly; all of them wear camel's hair [i.e., Kashmir] shawls over their heads, falling down at their sides. I saw none of them handsome. They bind up their chins in a manner to give them an unpleasant appearance. The natives, even the extreme rich, in their general appearance make very little show. Their dwellings are not in a style to attract attention and they are forbidden by their religion to eat or drink with Europeans. The rich wear very fine muslin dresses; the poorer classes, coarse; and the lowest have scarcely any covering, merely a cloth wrapped around them. Some of the rich natives spend a great deal of money principally on their holidays or celebrations of great events. They keep palanquins and many servants.

The celebrations of the rich are always [accompanied] by notches [nautches], or dances, performed by dancing girls, feasting their friends and others of their cast, and distributing presents. The dancing girls devote themselves to their profession and are "distinct from any other class, living by their own rules. Their clothes and jewels are considered as implements of their trade and cannot be taken for debt. They may drink spirituous liquors and eat any kind of meat except beef. Their dances are said to resemble those of the ancient bacchanalians represented in some of the ancient paintings and bas reliefs. In some of their dances, they attach gold and silver bells to the rings of the same metals which they wear round their ankles."[6] They also wear rings on their wrists and jewels in their ears and sometimes in their noses. Their motions bear no resemblance to European dancing, but they aim principally at attitudes calculated "to captivate the other sex." Their characters will be easily understood. They have music to which they add occasionally their own voices. They dress gaily and dance without shoes. At a holiday made by Ram Chunder Banorjea, a Brahmin, on the anniversary of the death of his father, he entertained five thousand of his own cast for two or three days, gave two hundred camels hair shawls, besides other articles, to the rich, and money to the poor among his guests expending in all 20,000 rupees on the occasion.

The different castes have many public holidays on which they assemble in prodigious numbers with music and entertainments of different kinds. Flags are carried through the streets followed by crowds of people. At one of these holidays out of the city I saw two very large elephants kept for such occasions by a rajah. Each of them carried six or eight persons on his back. They appeared perfectly docile, walking through the streets surrounded and followed by vast multitudes, carrying temples

Fig. 7.5 *A Nila Payak; The Procession to the Churruck* (Section 12, plate 12), drawn and engraved by
Balthazard Solvyns, Calcutta, c. 1800. Hand-colored engraving, 24.8 x 36.8 cm; Peabody Essex Museum
M15818, Gift of John Dominis Holt and Frances Damon Holt, 1974.

and decorations of every kind and with countenances filled with joy. At another a large tank or pond was over-spread at fifteen or twenty feet high by a large net, was sprinkled with roses, had several temples on boats, and boats also with dancing girls performing on the tank. Here, as on every such occasion, immense numbers were collected to see the show. At such places, we were always treated with perfect civility.

But the most extraordinary circumstances to which I was witness, were the various torments which some of the lower classes voluntarily suffered—voluntary because not imposed and because though encouraged by the priests no compulsion can ever be used. They also take great pains to exhibit themselves on such occasions when they display great pride and exultation. I saw in the streets several exhibitions of this kind [fig. 7.5]. Some cut two gashes in each side of their bodies, about

two inches long, through which on each side they pass a rattan or several strings, twenty or twenty-five feet long. The ends of these are supported by two persons who stop, or move slowly on, while the performer runs backward and forward, the rattans or strings passing through, dancing and exhibiting much self-satisfaction. Others pass a rattan or iron bar, of the size of a large rattan, through their tongues, constantly moving it up and down, passing through the streets. They are all attended by music. A gentleman attached to the Police Office told me that the last year one of the natives substituted for the iron bar a large, venomous snake, holding his head in his hand. While passing through the streets probably much exhausted, the snake suddenly cleared his head from the grasp, entwined himself around the neck of the miserable creature and drew out his tongue. He expired shortly after and the fact was communicated

Fig. 7.6 *View on the Banks of the Ganges with Representation of the Churruck Poojah—A Hindoo Holiday* by James Moffat, Calcutta, c. 1805. Aquatint, 34 x 50.5 cm; Peabody Essex Museum M3103e, Gift of Frances R. Morse, 1927.

to the police of the city. Some of those whom I saw with strings through their sides were boys of fourteen or fifteen years old. They all dress gaily, are of the lowest classes, and generally wrought up by opium.

I had opportunity also to witness the highest feat and that by which most applause is gained—hooking [fig. 7.6]. An upright post is raised, about twenty-five feet from the ground, on top of which a cross piece is placed on a swivel, from one end of which the hooks are suspended and from the other end a rope reaches to the ground by which the cross piece is moved round. There are two hooks passed one on each side about midway [on] the back, twice through the flesh, by which these miserable objects are suspended in the air, twenty feet from the ground and whirled round so rapidly as to bring their bodies in a

perfectly horizontal position, bearing entirely by the flesh so hooked up. This usually continues fifteen or twenty minutes, sometimes longer, yet no sign of suffering is shown—on the contrary great exultation with signs to move round still more rapidly. Three of these machines were erected near to each other and were constantly filled for several hours. There were others in other places. On some former occasions the flesh having broken and suffered the poor wretch to come to the ground, a cotton bandage is now put round them, but in such a manner as to take no part of the weight unless the flesh first breaks. As they wear no covering on their backs, they always afterwards show the marks. And one of them shew [showed] me the marks of six, several times hooking and many times rattan through his sides and tongue. It is surprising that among a people whose religion and manners are so mild as the Hindoos, such customs should exist. They are discountenanced by the English Government who would gladly stop them were not the natives too strongly attached to their ancient habits to render it safe or proper. The same observation will apply to their women burning themselves with their husbands which, though sometimes, is now very seldom practiced.

All religions are tolerated here. Some of the natives have been converted to the Roman Catholic, some are Mahometans [Muhammadans], but the great body are Gentoos or Hindoos, the original religion of the country. The following is principally extracted from an interesting account in the Encyclopedia article, Hindoos, vol. 8.

[*Omitted: excerpt from the* Encyclopedia Britannica, *1797*]

May 12, we left Calcutta drifting down with the tide for four days to the James and Mary's,[7] six or eight miles below Fultah. Afterwards we worked down with the tide which now runs two to two and a half miles an hour, the river being very low. We have now moderate weather instead of the very severe which has been experienced a month past which has detained some vessels and driven back others with loss of cables and anchors. Among these a Danish East India Company ship of 700 tons now waiting till August. May 21 the pilot left us. We

kept on the east side of the bay, had moderate weather and rather favorable winds and on June 10 crossed the Equator in 91 degrees of east longitude. July 13 saw the land about middle points of Natal [i.e., southeast Africa]; the 18th spoke again the ship *India* packet which we saw on our outward passage now returning from Isle of Bourbon [Réunion]. We had now strong west winds which retarded our progress, but were fortunate enough to experience no severe gale or any injury in getting round the Cape Good Hope. August 12 saw Ascension Island and the 18th crossed the Equator in 24 degrees west longitude. September 7 in latitude 31 degrees north were boarded from the French privateer ship *Calibri*, 22 guns, 250 men, from Bordeaux, three months out on a cruise and were detained by her eighteen hours during which time the Frenchmen had possession of our ship and endeavored by threats, promises, etc. to induce our sailors to declare the vessel or cargo "English property." Our crew were all taken out, as also the captain and myself, on board the privateer where we were kept for the night. We were suffered to pass with little injury from the plunder. It was to me a night of extreme anxiety. September 18 we sounded on George's Bank, spoke several vessels outward bound, next day saw Nantucket and the 20th at 6 p.m. anchored in Nantasket road.

Distance this passage by log 14,583 miles. September 21 [1804] we went up to Boston.

Ceylonese Native Canoe

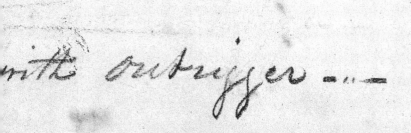

PART III

TRANSFORMATIONS AND NEW ENCOUNTERS

with outrigger ——

Fig. 8.1 *Schooner Independence of New York, Taken by His Britannic Majesty's Brig Rover, March 16th 1813, in the Bay of Biscay*, c. 1813.
Watercolor, 21 x 34.3 cm; Peabody Essex Museum M2695, Museum purchase, 1922.

CHAPTER 8

Transitions

REALIGNMENTS

During the two years following the *Derby*'s return to Salem, U.S. relations with Britain and France continued to worsen. The Jefferson administration, in hopes of making the British realize the importance of their trade with America, decided to withdraw from foreign trade entirely. The total embargo declared by the United States government in 1807 marked the beginning of a new era. Until this time—despite the risks of harassment and capture—American merchantmen prospered while Europe was at war. In the years between Dudley Pickman's voyages as a neutral trader—in the *Belisarius*, 1799–1800, and the *Derby*, 1803–04—and the 1817–18 voyage of William A. Rogers in the *Tartar* to Bombay, recounted in chapter 10, American commerce was transformed and the position of Indian markets definitively altered. The new circumstances were eloquently reflected in the commodities brought home by the *Derby*, which returned to Salem in 1804 with a cargo two-thirds textiles, and the *Tartar*, which entered Boston harbor in 1818 with a cargo of raw cotton for the textile mills.[1] India was no longer a principal supplier of textiles to the world's markets and American industry's appetite for raw materials was growing rapidly.

During the European war, there had been tremendous opportunities for American shipping, far beyond the transport of cargoes to and from American ports. Because scores of European merchantmen were diverted to privateering, and the number that did remain in trade were decimated by enemy attacks, relatively few European vessels were still commercially active. As hostilities continued and the British gained increasing control of the seas, only American merchant vessels persisted, trading as neutrals in ports around the world. Two statistical surveys of U.S. commerce, published after the war in 1817–18, the years of William Rogers' voyage to Bombay in the *Tartar*, assessed the new position of U.S. commerce. In the first of these, Timothy Pitkin, a congressman from Connecticut, wrote "until the commencement of commercial restrictions in December,

1807, and the declaration of war against Great Britain, in 1812, no nation it is believed, had ever increased so rapidly in wealth as the United States."[2] Adam Seybert, congressman from Pennsylvania, stated in his introduction to *Statistical Annals*: "in proportion to our population we ranked as the most commercial nation; in point of value, our trade was only second to that of Great Britain."[3]

Though the war years were a prosperous time for American foreign trade, shipowners, vessels, cargoes, and crews were always at great jeopardy of seizure and confiscation.[4] Measures taken to protect the rights of neutral trade had not been effective. In 1794, the United States had negotiated the Jay Treaty in hopes of reducing British pressure on American shipping, but little changed; searches and seizures, and the impressment of sailors to serve in British vessels, continued. The French, who considered the Jay Treaty a betrayal of U.S. obligations as an ally, increased their harassment of American shipping, precipitating a virtual war in 1797 (see fig. 4.1). Despite French and English interference with shipping, American merchant vessels carried on their global commerce for a decade. Owners and supercargoes followed the course of war closely and gauged its impact on world markets; ships' captains did what they could to elude hostile European naval vessels and privateers. Then, in 1806, a sequence of events began that would fundamentally alter the position of U.S. foreign commerce and transform the trade with India from principally a carrying trade that returned profits and Indian manufactured goods—mostly textiles—to a supplier of raw materials for American industries. Yankee trade with India never regained its former political and economic prominence.

Beginning in 1806, the British government issued a series of Orders in Council proclaiming the intent to blockade all French and allied ports, and recalling all British seamen (even those who had become naturalized citizens of another country). In effect, these orders disallowed neutral trade.[5] The British navy stepped up its practice of detaining American merchant

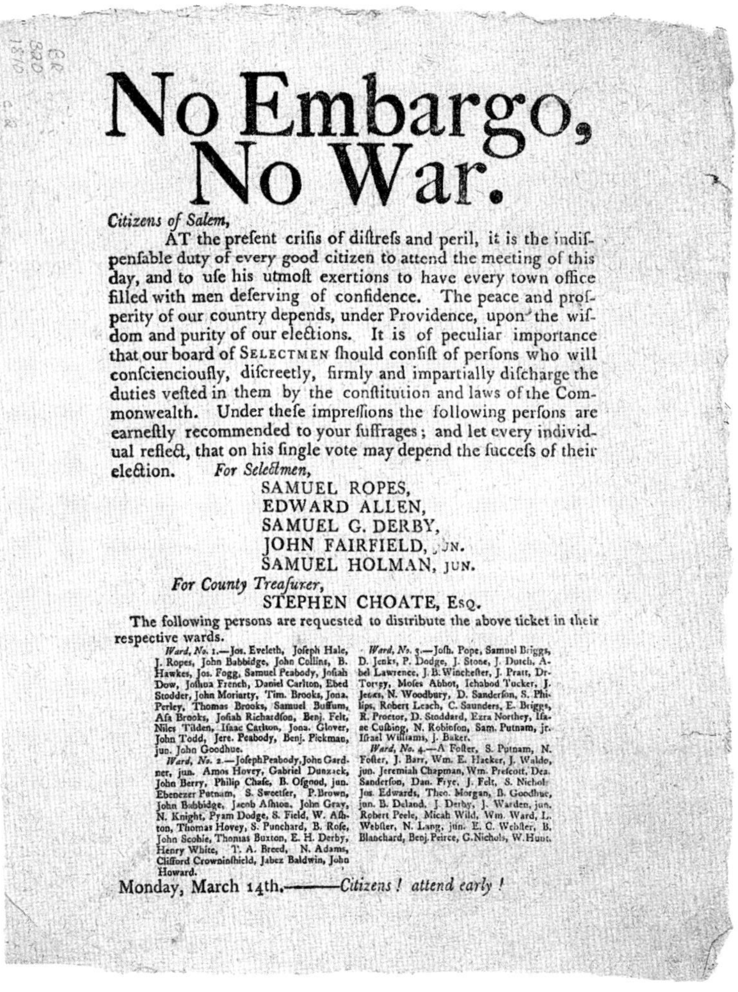

No Embargo, No War.

Citizens of Salem,

AT the prefent crifis of diftrefs and peril, it is the indif-penfable duty of every good citizen to attend the meeting of this day, and to ufe his utmoft exertions to have every town office filled with men deferving of confidence. The peace and prof-perity of our country depends, under Providence, upon the wif-dom and purity of our elections. It is of peculiar importance that our board of SELECTMEN fhould confift of perfons who will confcienciously, difcreetly, firmly and impartially difcharge the duties vefted in them by the conftitution and laws of the Com-monwealth. Under thefe impreffions the following perfons are earneftly recommended to your fuffrages; and let every individ-ual reflect, that on his fingle vote may depend the fuccefs of their election.   *For Selectmen,*

SAMUEL ROPES,
EDWARD ALLEN,
SAMUEL G. DERBY,
JOHN FAIRFIELD, JUN.
SAMUEL HOLMAN, JUN.
For County Treafurer,
STEPHEN CHOATE, ESQ.

The following perfons are requefted to diftribute the above ticket in their refpective wards.

Ward, No. 1.—Jos. Eveleth, Jofeph Hale, J. Ropes, John Babbidge, John Collins, B. Hawkes, Jos. Fogg, Samuel Peabody, Jofiah Dow, Jofhua French, Daniel Carlton, Ebed Stodder, John Moriarty, Tim. Brooks, Jona. Perley, Thomas Brooks, Samuel Buffum, Afa Brooks, Jofiah Richardfon, Benj. Felt, Niles Tilden, Ifaac Cartton, Jona. Glover, John Todd, Jere. Peabody, Benj. Pickman, jun. John Goodhue.
Ward, No. 2.—JofephPeabody,JohnGard-ner, jun. Amos Hovey, Gabriel Dunnack, John Berry, Philip Chafe, B. Ofgood, jun. Ebenezer Putnam, S. Sweetfer, P.Brown, John Babbidge, Jacob Afhton, John Gray, N. Knight, Pram Dodge, S. Field, W. Afh-ton, Thomas Hovey, S. Punchard, B. Rofe, John Scobie, Thomas Buxton, E. H. Derby, Henry White, T. A. Breed, N. Adams, Clifford Crowninfhield, Jabez Baldwin, John Howard.

Ward, No. 3.—Jofh. Pope, Samuel Briggs, D. Jenks, P. Dodge, J. Stone, J. Dutch, A-bel Lawrence, J.B.Winchefter, J. Pratt, Dr-Torrey, Mofes Abbot, Ichabod Tucker, J. Jenes, N. Woodbury, D. Sanderfon, S. Phi-lips, Robert Leach, C. Saunders, E. Briggs, R. Proctor, D. Stoddard, Ezra Northey, Ifa-ac Cufhing, N. Robinfon, Sam. Putnam, jr. Ifrael Williams, J. Baker.
Ward, No. 4.—A Fofter, S. Putnam, N. Fofter, J. Barr, Wm. E. Flatker, J. Waldo, jun. Jeremiah Chapman, Wm. Prefcott, Dea. Sanderfon, Dan. Fry, J. Felt, S. Nichol-Jos. Edwards, Theo. Morgan, B. Goodhue, jun. B. Deland, J. Derby, J. Warden, jun. Robert Peele, Micah Wild, Wm. Ward, I. Webfter, N. Lang, jun. E. C. Webfter, B. Blanchard, Benj.Peirce, C.Nichols, W.Hunt.

Monday, March 14th.————*Citizens! attend early!*

Fig. 8.2 *No Embargo, No War*, broadside addressed to the citizens of Salem urging attendance at a meeting on March 17 (1807) to oppose the embargo on foreign trade. Printed paper, 25.5 x 15.5 cm; Peabody Essex Museum Library.

vessels, pressing seamen into service, and confiscating cargoes and vessels. In response, Napoleon issued decrees from Berlin and Milan declaring that any ship touching a British port or complying with British regulations was liable to capture, and that British goods—regardless of the nationality of their car-rier—were prohibited from entering French ports.

Most Yankee shipowners and commanders were prepared to tolerate these rulings as inconveniences in an otherwise very profitable trade. Accustomed to the precarious position of neu-tral traders among warring nations, merchants and shipowners expected to carry on as they had in the past by accommodating or circumventing the newest restrictions. Most of them were reluctant to jeopardize relations with Great Britain. Not only was Britain America's most important trading partner, London was the financial center where banks facilitated American com-merce by accepting and issuing credit instruments that were recognized around the world. U.S. trade with Asia—especially with India, whose principal ports were British possessions—was heavily dependent on London merchant bankers.[6] For most Yankee shipowners, peaceful relations with Great Britain were a necessity.

President Thomas Jefferson's administration treated the British and French proclamations as threats to national sover-eignty. The immediate motivation had been an especially egre-gious incident: a British warship had fired on an American naval vessel and abducted several sailors. On a wave of public out-rage, the U.S. Congress, at President Jefferson's behest, passed the Embargo Act of 1807 prohibiting all foreign trade. The Jefferson administration represented this action as self-defense necessitated by French and British disregard of American neutrality and sovereign rights. The needs of New England merchants for good relations with England were subordinated to the political imperative that U.S. sovereignty be unambigu-ously acknowledged.

For the Republican administration, the choice was clear. Foreign trade was no longer central to the national vision as it had been for the Federalists. Instead, domestic priorities were paramount—western expansion and an economy built on farm-ing and small-scale manufacturing. The Jefferson administra-tion had initiated a fundamental reorientation of the federal government, devolving power to the states, enlarging the coun-try through the Louisiana Purchase, and encouraging domestic production. Alexander Hamilton, during the presidencies of Washington and Adams, had stabilized and strengthened national finances through policies favoring merchant mariners of the port cities. Duties on foreign goods had been the most important source of federal revenue for building the new nation. Policies born out of Jefferson's vision of the United States as a self-sufficient nation of independent farmers left the interests of shipowners and India traders behind.

The embargo of 1807 was hotly debated. Most merchants and shipowners in foreign trade were resolutely opposed (fig. 8.2). Some, however, supported the embargo. William Gray of Boston, the largest individual shipowner in the United States, believed the embargo necessary to protect American shipping.[7] Members of the Crowninshield family in Salem, who were engaged in lively competition in trade and politics with the Federalist Derby family, held posts in the Republican administration and supported its policy. Because they were deeply engaged in trade with the Continent, especially France, the Crowninshields were less vulnerable to a disruption in commerce with England.[8] Those merchants who supported the embargo hoped that, by suspending access to the U.S. market, it would force the British to realize the importance of its American trade, rescind the restrictions on neutral trade, and stop harassing American vessels and their crews.

The embargo, in effect for fourteen months until March 1809, failed to elicit the anticipated response from the British government. Impressment of seamen from U.S. vessels continued, and Britain's Orders in Council against neutral trade were not repealed. Worse still, the embargo had disastrous effects at home, idling ships and devastating the economies of ports engaged in foreign commerce. Because of its drastic consequences for American shipping and coastal economies, the Jefferson administration repealed the embargo and replaced it with a nonintercourse act that removed trade restrictions— except with England and France. Jefferson's successor, President James Madison, promised to restore trade with France or England if either of those countries withdrew their decrees excluding neutral trade and refrained from interfering with American shipping. But the hostile climate continued, as did the distress at home. After almost a year, in May 1810, the nonintercourse act was replaced by Macon's Bill No. 2, which restored trade but promised to the first power that recognized its neutral rights, that it would stop trading with the other.

Napoleon made such a pledge—though French seizures of American ships continued—and President Madison renewed the prohibition on trade with Britain. British naval vessels continued to stop American ships and take any seamen they claimed were British subjects. In June 1812, the Congress, ready to defend U.S. sovereign rights on the seas and to fight for westward expansion, declared war on Great Britain. The Madison administration's political goal was to secure national sovereignty on the seas and on the western and northern borders, where Anglo-Canadian opposition to U.S. expansion was aided by a Native American alliance. When the war ended after nearly three years, the treaty signed at Ghent in 1815 brought no victory. Prewar boundaries were restored and issues of impressment and the rights of neutral trade remained unresolved. But the urgency of these maritime issues evaporated with Napoleon's defeat and the return of peace in Europe, also in 1815.

The termination of war in Europe had a profound effect on U.S. commerce. With the defeat of Napoleon, peace came to Europe after almost two decades of war. The peace finally ended the lucrative, if risky, opportunities of neutral trade for Yankee merchants. The way was opened for the restoration of European merchant fleets and the reentry of European competition in the trade that Americans had dominated for so long. In India, this new competition had already been set in place in 1813 when, under pressure from its own industrial and mercantile community, the British government ended the East India Company's monopoly on trade with Asia. British private merchants were quick to enter the trade. Thus, in the years between the 1807 embargo and the 1815 peace, the fortunes of American traders and ports altered dramatically. Smaller ports like Salem and Newburyport, which suffered severely from the embargo and war, never recovered their former prominence. More than a few merchants went bankrupt. The peace exacerbated the situation by bringing an end to neutral trade and reinvigorating competition with foreign merchants.

The wartime disruption of foreign trade had other effects on the U.S. economy—effects which transformed the trade with India. The embargo, nonintercourse acts, and the war had protected fledgling American industries from the competition of imported goods. During the war years, the great scarcity of imports—especially manufactures from Britain, Europe, India, and China— increased the market for domestic manufactures and stimulated American industry. The industrial revolution had already begun in the United States during the last decade of the eighteenth century, when cotton mills were set up in New England. In 1788 at Beverly, Massachusetts, a group of investors —including several, like Andrew Cabot and Israel Thorndike, whose capital had been raised in the India trade— established the first mill for carding and spinning cotton (fig. 8.3).[9] The following year, on the outskirts of Providence, Rhode Island, William Almy and Moses Brown teamed up with Samuel Slater to found the first profitable cotton mill. Almy and Brown provided the capital and British-immigrant Slater provided the know-how gained in a long apprenticeship with the latest machinery in England.[10] Their mill produced yarns equal to what was imported from England. The importance of domestic manufactures to national prosperity had been recognized from the beginning of the new republic; President Washington wore a suit of broadcloth made at a newly

Fig. 8.3 *Washington's Visit to the First Cotton Mill, October 30, 1789* by George Elmer Browne, 1897. Browne recreated the celebrated event at the Beverly Cotton Mill in Massachusetts. Ink on paper, 65.3 x 85.1 cm; Peabody Essex Museum 106750.

established woolen mill to his inauguration in 1789.[11] The fast and efficient cotton gin invented by Eli Whitney in 1793 had opened the way for the rapid expansion of the market for cotton produced with slave labor in the South and fueled the growth of yarn and cloth production in the mills of the north. By 1809, there were eighty-seven cotton mills operating in the United States.[12]

Eight years of disrupted trade had reduced competition from imported goods and given domestic manufactures a chance to dominate domestic markets.[13] Timothy Pitkin, in his study of American commerce, enlarged and reissued in 1835, remarked, "American statesmen now [see] the necessity as well as justice of affording some protection to those manufactures."[14] In 1816, Congress enacted a protective tariff. The duty levied on imported cotton textiles priced the inexpensive ones from India right out of the market. According to the law, all textiles costing less than 25 cents a yard were dutiable as if they had cost 25 cents. Pitkin noted: "This minimum price was fixed, for the purpose of excluding entirely from the American market, the low priced Indian cottons, and thereby afford[ing] protection and encouragement both to the American cotton manufactures and the American cotton planter. This duty had the intended

effect, and since that period few India cottons of this description have been brought into the United States."[15]

With the exclusion of most of its textilie manufactures after 1816, India ceased to be an important source of manufactured goods for the American market. The decline of the American market was another blow to India's already struggling cloth producers. British advances in textile production, combined with political control over production and trade in colonized India, had begun to have major effects on yarn and cloth production there. The textiles so admired in the West, especially for their bright, fast colors and vibrant designs, were rapidly being superceded by industrial manufactures. Indian design and technology was imitated, absorbed, and transformed into features of an emerging global textile industry. In the United States, as in Europe, India was reduced from a provider of coveted wares to a source of raw materials. Only a few special textiles remained of commercial significance into the mid-nineteenth century—silk goods, especially middle-market bandanna handkerchiefs, and luxury-market woolen Kashmir shawls.

Between 1807 and 1820, the size and impact of the trade with India was reduced by the combined effect of all these changes: the embargo and war, the protective tariff enacted in the United States, the participation of British private traders, the growth of industrial manufacturing in Great Britain and the United States, and the new opportunities for capital investments in America, which encouraged many shipowners and merchants (including Dudley Pickman, chapters 5–7) to invest trade profits into textile mills, western land, canal construction, banks, and insurance companies. Despite these fundamental changes, more than a few merchants and shipowners, experienced in the India trade and long accustomed to adjusting their strategies to new situations, believed they could continue to prosper in altered circumstances.

PURSUING THE INDIA TRADE IN A CHANGING WORLD—HENRY LEE'S STRATEGIES

From a distance of two hundred years, the industrial and commercial transformation of the United States appears swift and inevitable. At the time, the outcomes of rapid industrial growth and consequent changes in international trade were hardly obvious. For merchants and shipowners operating in uncertain circumstances, turns of events were unpredictable, often precipitated by political and military expediency. In the period of embargo and war, the impediments to trade—blockades, decrees, seizures—and the commercial uncertainties that ensued were a constant hindrance, at times only more or less severe. Shipowners and merchants had to keep up with developments in the wars and the policies of foreign governments that affected their trade—a need made challenging by the fact that news from Asia took six months to reach the United States and even news from Europe often arrived months after events occurred. From the onset of war in Europe, success in neutral trade required tremendous flexibility and constant maneuvering.

Boston merchant Henry Lee (1782–1867) was one of the most tenacious practitioners of the India trade (fig. 8.4). Lee passed up Harvard College, where his brothers had been educated, to join the countinghouse of Marston Watson in Boston as an apprentice. At the time, college was considered optional for someone entering business, and Lee began his business education right out of Phillips Andover Academy. After a few years, Lee was given the opportunity to sail as supercargo on a vessel bound for Calcutta, owned by his brother Joseph and commanded by his brother George.[16] This voyage was the

Fig. 8.4 Henry Lee (1782–1867), c. 1860, after a painting by Gambardella, c. 1840. Engraving, 23 x 16 cm; Courtesy of Henry Lee.

beginning of a lifetime spent in the India trade by a man who was wholly devoted to it and interested in little else. In 1804, Lee entered into a partnership with his brother Joseph.[17] His perspectives on trade, politics, and civilization were conditioned by his singular devotion to commerce.

Henry Lee's views on commerce and politics are an illuminating contrast to those of the Crowninshield family, whose engagement in world affairs was far more cosmopolitan, for example, as represented in Benjamin Crowninshield's account of sati in chapter 1 and his cousin Jacob's memorandum on the India trade discussed in chapter 4, as well as the views of Jacob's brother Benjamin W. cited below. The Crowninshields were interested in the civilizations they encountered in their global trade. They were also nationalists with a devotion to politics that drew them into public office. William Rogers, whose journal of his voyage in the *Tartar* is excerpted in chapter 10, had only a passing interest in the India trade. He went into business with his older brothers hoping to capitalize his law practice from the profits of a few East India voyages. While in India, his attention was captured by the teeming life of Bombay rather than the exigencies of commerce. During his much longer stay in Calcutta, Lee was completely absorbed in business and otherwise oblivious to his surroundings. The range of interests and opinions manifested indicates the breadth of views in the American mercantile community of the early nineteenth century. Henry Lee represented one end of the spectrum and his views contrasted markedly with many other merchants.

In 1807, when the embargo was declared, Henry Lee was in Boston, worried and angry. There had already been a non-importation act in place since April 1806 barring certain British goods from American ports. But it had failed to stop British harassment of U.S. shipping. The British, more intent on their contest with France than concerned with their need for American trade, did not respond as hoped to the Jefferson administration's move and, in late 1806, instituted a virtual blockade of the Continent. When Napoleon responded with a counter-blockade, American shipping was completely stymied. The Jefferson administration then declared the embargo on foreign trade.

The Lee family correspondence reveals the uncertainties and risks of operating in this period of hostilities. Just a week before the embargo went into effect, Henry Lee, always with an eye to the impact of political developments on his business, wrote to a commission merchant in Baltimore about the disposition of the current stock of Indian handkerchiefs, then a principal commodity. Since the bulk of Lee's imported India goods was intended for re-export to Europe, an embargo would not only impede his regular business but would depress the prices of goods, inadvertently creating a glut on the domestic market. Lee foresaw more disastrous consequences of the embargo: "some very rich houses will be ruin'd . . . ," he declared. "I cannot but hope that such a constrain'd situation of things will end either by a relaxation of Decrees on the part of France and England, or by a general peace—till one of those two events occur our trade will be in a dreadful state . . ."[18]

A few months later, in a letter to his New York commission merchant, Lee complained of the perplexing uncertainty of their position and the vexing behavior of his government: ". . . our accounts from Washington are so contradictory that we do not Know what to think of our affairs with England—I believe our government have no wish to settle affairs yet they cannot mean to have a war. I rather think it is their cowardly policy" to avoid Napoleon's retaliation.[19] With his correspondents in Baltimore, he weighed the various possibilities—if their government lifted the embargo, if the French or British rescinded or reduced their blockades.[20] The permutations were complex and the outcomes nearly impossible to predict, though their implications for business were immense.

One of Lee's principal strategies to weather the halt in trade was to seek out new markets. Months after the embargo was declared, when Lee found himself scrambling to find buyers for India goods that could not be re-exported, he contracted with commission merchants in New Orleans, where he had not done business previously.[21] He selected Bengal piece goods that he judged suitable for the New Orleans and West Indian markets, probably cheap cottons to clothe plantation slaves. By early spring 1809, after the embargo had been in effect more than a year without bringing the British to heel, but with dire consequences for the economies of many port towns and their hinterlands, a Federalist-led opposition was coalescing. Political leaders whose fortunes had fallen with the successes of the Jeffersonians regained some of their former position. The Madison administration responded by issuing an act allowing trade—but not with France or Britain. Commerce revived quickly, though the British-owned ports of India remained under interdiction. Lee, always alert to pursuing trade however he could, again turned to new markets, for the first time sending vessels to China.[22]

Despite his best efforts, Lee misjudged the markets and overextended his resources. In 1811, when he was almost thirty years old, his business failed.[23] To set his affairs back on course, Lee elected to serve as supercargo on his cousin Andrew Cabot's brig *Reaper*, on a voyage to London and Calcutta (fig. 8.5). Lee hoped the profits from this voyage would be sufficient to revive his business. He arrived at Calcutta in May of 1812 and learned that a nonintercourse law had been enacted by the administration in Washington, again in hopes of pressuring the British to deal more acceptably with American interests. Lee decided to load the *Reaper* for a return voyage despite the increased risk of capture and the possibility of losing the ship and its cargo. He knew insurance would cover some of the loss, and he judged that taking a chance to bring the owners some return on their investment was worth the risk. Lee remained behind to conclude the business of voyage.[24] The disruption of trade escalated in June 1812, when the United States declared war—though this news would not reach Calcutta for seven months.[25] When Lee learned of it, he despaired that the *Reaper* had been lost to the British. Many more months passed before he found out that the brig and other American ships from Calcutta at sea when war was declared all made it home safely.[26]

Despite the persisting uncertainties of the political situation, Lee, now stranded in Calcutta, continued to hope that the war with England, so detrimental to his business, would soon come to an end. His spirits rose when news arrived that the British Orders in Council which precipitated the American declaration of war had been repealed. He hoped that the conflict might end quickly when the news reached Washington. But the war continued and Lee remained in Calcutta for its duration—until the peace in 1815—trading commodities and serving as an agent for other merchants.[27] Henry Lee's commitment to the Calcutta market deepened as his knowledge of it grew, even though he recognized that more drastic changes were coming, especially in the textile trade. In 1812, writing from Calcutta, Lee predicted what would come to pass in another twenty years: "I never had a favourable opinion of fine cottons from Bengal knowing as I do that they are actually cheaper at Manchester than here, *indeed this country will one day be supplied from England with the finer calicoes* [emphasis in original], at present there are importations of shirtings, the use of which is confined however to Europeans."[28] Lee stayed with the India trade despite its changing character because he knew the markets so well and believed he could, as he had done in the past, modify his strategy to suit the circumstances.

Henry Lee had a low opinion of his country's government. Being stranded by the war lowered it still more. For the sake of commerce and New England's economy, he believed the best course was to secede from the union. Lee had no interest in a national future beyond its impact on his business. Like many other merchants, he believed the federal government's principal responsibility was to support commerce—as it had done in the past under the leadership of Alexander Hamilton. In 1813, he wrote his cousin Patrick T. Jackson that "should the war [continue] God only Knows what may be the consequences, you & all other commercial men largely in trade I suppose will be ruin'd, the only good effect which can result will be the separation of States, & that is quite uncertain. I hope with all my heart

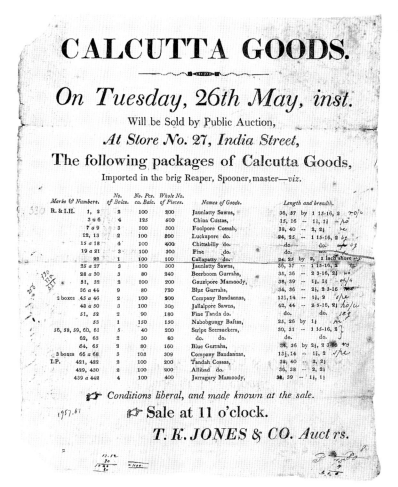

Fig. 8.5 *Calcutta Goods*, broadside for a sale in Boston on May 26, probably 1811. The cargo of textiles is itemized by local names and places of manufacture. The textiles were imported in Andrew Cabot's brig *Reaper*, which returned to Calcutta the following year and made it home safely after the declaration of war in 1812. Printed paper; Peabody Essex Museum Library, Stark Papers.

it may happen . . ."[29] He wrote even more boldly to his wife, "If we were united in New England and New York w'd join us . . . the Western States might have the war to themselves. We must one day or other separate and . . . the sooner it takes place the better."[30] Lee was convinced that national policy had been hijacked by the interests of the southern and western states, a position powerful enough among "commercial men" and others in the north that serious talk of secession persisted throughout the war, culminating in the 1814 Hartford Convention's protest of Republican foreign policy.[31]

But even in the mercantile community, Lee's vision for his country's future was extreme. East India merchants had necessarily developed global perspectives from their experiences in foreign trade, but the positions they took varied widely. Henry Lee evolved an internationalism in which working relations among the business community at home and abroad took precedence over any nationalistic concerns. At the other end of the spectrum were Boston's William Gray and Salem's Crowninshield family who, siding with the Madison administration, accepted the war with Britain as a necessary step to securing U.S. independence and sovereignty. They were committed supporters of a strong nation and concerned about its place in the international community. Others, like young William Rogers, were loyal Federalists, opposed to the war but also ardent nationalists. Rogers had served in the American delegation to France just before the fall of Napoleon—whom he greatly admired. His firsthand experience of French middle-class ascendancy, and his foray into the Asia trade, combined to create and sustain a strong patriotism. Rogers' lively nationalist sensibilities were honed in the journal he kept of the *Tartar*'s voyage to Bombay in 1817–18 (chapter 10), in which he used the sharp contrasts of his Indian experiences to reflect on the distinctive qualities of American identity.

GETTING TO KNOW INDIA—HENRY LEE IN CALCUTTA

Henry Lee stayed in Calcutta for three years, during which he developed his expertise in the commercial life of the city. Lee devoted himself to learning about the sources and production of the textiles he dealt in; he even managed to learn enough Bengali to communicate directly with local merchants, often avoiding the commissions that had to be paid to banians or agency houses. What he learned in these years gave him the background, knowledge, and confidence to pursue the India trade for the rest of his career, until his retirement in the 1840s.

In keeping with his single-minded interest in commerce, Lee's response to his unanticipated long stay in Calcutta was to keep to himself. Apart from his business, Lee stayed in his rented residence and read books. He shared the house with Captain Chardon from New York, owner of the *Union*, which had arrived in September 1812. Lee wrote to his wife about Chardon: "he is acquainted with all the fashionables and is constantly among them—we have no society but I learn from him what is passing in the world."[32] The few Americans around provided some companionship, though he complained of the reserve of a fellow Bostonian, Captain Augustine Heard, per-

haps a projection of his own lack of gregariousness. He wrote regularly to his wife but told her nothing about Calcutta—not what it looked like, or what went on there. He lamented the tediousness of life—"I meet with nothing to describe that can entertain you"[33]—and attributed his isolation in part to the position of Americans as aliens in Calcutta:

> You will hardly believe that a person of my *easy manners* and *insinuating address* should have lived almost a year in this place without making a single acquaintance unless a few persons whom I meet on business. It is true, however, and I should be in the same solitude if I were to remain 10 years. . . . There are two classes of people that make up the English societies—the one composed of Company's servants, as they are called, viz. persons in service of the India Company—military officers and a few merchants. These are the gentry of the place and have among them many respectable persons—live in great style and hold themselves altogether above the common citizens. The other class is made up of merchants, mechanics, shopkeepers, artists, ship masters and adventurers of all sorts, who came out from England to seek what they seldom find—their fortunes. For the most part they are a low-bred and worthless set—their society is had on easy terms—you may be sure I have no inclination . . . to partake of it. . . . The respectable class it is impossible to become acquainted with, without a better introduction than any of our countrymen can obtain, and their habits are such that no man of business could mix with them if he had an opportunity.[34]

The single event Lee recounted with interest was the arrival of the new governor-general, Lord Moira, and the only mention of Indian culture is a translation and digest of Hindu laws sent home to a friend.[35]

In writing about the lack of friendly society in Calcutta, Lee dismissed his banians as being interested only in business: ". . . seeing no one but my banians [Ramdon & Tillock Chunder Bonerjia], who never had, nor ever will have a thought except on business. Were the natives as well informed as they are civil and well bred, one would receive great pleasure from their society, but their opinions are so confined, that I can truly say I never derived half an hour's gratification from any one I have been acquainted with. Nothing can be more uninteresting than their characters."[36] One cannot help but wonder if he did, in fact, understand his banians' preoccupations so well, because they matched his own wholehearted devotion to business. During his years in Calcutta, Lee came to know each of the American banians' particular skills and faults.

> If you buy in the Bazaar you can either employ Ram-shander Mitre or Ram Kissen Day, the former is I believe the best judge of qualities. . . . I am pretty well convinced that no one can serve you or will serve you so well as Ramdon & Goluck [Chunder Day] & Kissen. I am the more convinced of this by comparing the goods
> I purchased through them with all the cargoes shipped since the peace and particularly Dulolls [Ramdulal Dey] and Ruggo Rams which in general are 10% to 15% higher than Ramshander Meties.[37]

He knew that some banians had specialties within the American market: "The southern ships will go to Ramduloll, few to Ruggoo Ram; the Salem and Boston to Ramshander Metie and Duggo Pesaud [probably Durgaprasad Ghose] . . . "[38] In his opinion, Ramdulal Dey—pioneer of the American trade in Calcutta and venerated by many American sea captains and supercargoes—had become too successful; he could demand and receive very high fees for his services. Lee objected not only to Ramdulal's charges, but felt him untrustworthy. He did not agree with his cousin Patrick T. Jackson's great opinion of "Duloll," but wondered if Ramdulal had "changed his character . . ."[39] Lee took his business elsewhere. He shared what he learned with his brother and partner Francis Lee, as well as with others involved in the firm, advising them: "It makes the banians hostile to you when they find their business watched . . ."[40] "Don't confide in anyone, nor make known your intentions to your banians; nor say how long you shall remain in the country to them, or anyone else . . ."[41]

In the conduct of his business, Lee became deeply involved with his banians. Even while he remained aloof from the Anglo-Indian social world, he became ever more enmeshed in Calcutta's commercial life.[42] Based on what he had learned about the American banians, Lee chose to work with Ramdon and Tillock Bonerjia. He knew they needed the business and that they wanted to attract more clients. He reasoned that their own interest would be served in being reliable and economical in their dealings with him. Lee was very satisfied with his choice and recommended his banians to his brother: "by all means

direct your agent to employ Ramdon & Tillock Bonerjia, who are doing my business, it is to them I owe my success in getting so cheap a cargo . . . I mention these things that my banians may have some little credit for their fidelity to me and to your interest."[43]

But the following year, Henry Lee was caught up in a financial disaster. Though the details of what happened are obscure, Ramdon and Tillock Bonerjia speculated with Lee's money and lost; they had overstepped customary limits in managing a client's capital and their gamble failed. Ramdon and Tillock struggled desperately to make amends. To save the situation and their reputations, Ramdon and Tillock had placed their property and families at the mercy of this foreigner from the other side of the world. Henry Lee stuck by his banians in hopes of some restitution, and because condemning them would be tantamount to an indictment of his own judgment in choosing them to begin with. He wrote to his father:

> I have not yet settled my accounts with my banians,
> there will be a loss to us in spite of all I have done, . . .
> I still employ them in conjunction with Ramkissen Day
> and they do my business better than any other banians
> could or would. My misfortune has been in trusting them
> with too much, and their fault, in trading upon my funds
> and spending more freely than they ought to have done.
> I have not found in them any intention whatever to
> defraud me, on the contrary when I was entirely in their
> power, they willingly surrendered themselves and all
> their effects, and are now making every exertion in their
> power to make up my loss. I am much mortified in this
> affair . . .[44]

Despite his carefully maintained aloofness, through this mutual financial disaster, Lee had been drawn into the most intimate of social relations.

On his voyage home in 1815, Lee wrote a letter to his banians, now Ramdon Bonerjia and Goluck Chunder Day. His authoritative tone reveals a paternalism and sense of superiority not present in letters from Boston that predate his Calcutta stay. He wrote: "It is the custom with Banyans to shew their letters to Americans & others. You must never do so with mine. . . . I hope to find from Mr. Burrs letters, that you did my business well, & followed my directions . . . I expect to hear from you by every ship."[45] Financial disaster seems to have combined with Anglo-Indian attitudes toward "natives," absorbed during his

Fig. 8.6 The ordination of five missionaries prior to their departure for India in 1812, c. 1850. Engraving, 35.5 x 50 cm;
Courtesy of the Tabernacle Church, Salem.

three years in Calcutta, to alter Lee's relations with his banians.

Upon his return to Boston, Henry Lee was able to restart his business with the proceeds of his Calcutta years. During a time when the India trade was on the wane, Lee, with the deepened knowledge of business and markets acquired during his extended stay, was one of those few merchants, now concentrated in Boston, who stuck with the India trade in the years after the war. In the decades immediately following peace in Europe and England's peace with the United States, the merchants who stayed with the India trade were men like Henry Lee—including Salem's Joseph Peabody and Bostonian John Stark—who had become so familiar with the commodities and markets that they could continue to make money in a situation no longer favored by neutral trade and absent the principal commodity—cotton textiles—now priced out of profitability.

YANKEES AND HINDOOS

At the same time that Indo-American trade was on the way to becoming the preserve of a few specialized East India merchants, another American involvement with India was beginning. In 1812, just before the war, the first American missionaries embarked for India hoping to bring Christian salvation to millions of "heathen" souls. Late in the year, two American East Indiamen arrived in Calcutta carrying the first American missionaries to take the gospel abroad. Adoniram Judson and Samuel Newell with their wives had embarked from Salem in the brig *Caravan*, Augustine Heard master. The *Caravan*'s owner, Salem merchant Pickering Dodge—according to the Reverend William Bentley—had been urged to offer them passage by Dodge's devout wife.[46] Shortly after their departure, four others, Mr. and Mrs. Samuel Nott, Luther Rice, and Gordon Hall, set sail from Philadelphia in the *Harmony*, Captain Brown commanding.[47] Yankee East India merchants

Fig. 8.7 Rama and Sita with Lakshmana and attendants, Calcutta or Krishnanagar, c. 1815. Clay, cloth, pigments, height 36 x depth 22 x width 44 cm; Peabody Essex Museum E7674f, Gift of Captain Ephraim Emmerton, c. 1815.

Fig. 8.8 "The Pentateuch in the Bengal Language, 4to, Calcutta, 1809," entry #1552 in *The East India Marine Society of Salem* (Salem, Mass., 1821). Printed at the Serampore Mission Press. Peabody Essex Museum Library, Gift of Captain John White, 1809.

Fig. 8.9 "Part of the beard of a Bramin who was shaved on being converted to Christianity," entry #3724 in *The East India Marine Society of Salem*, 2d ed. (Salem, Mass., 1831). The hair, rather than beardlike, seems to be the lock of hair at the back of the head often kept long by Brahmins. Hair; Peabody Essex Museum E8232, acquired before 1831.

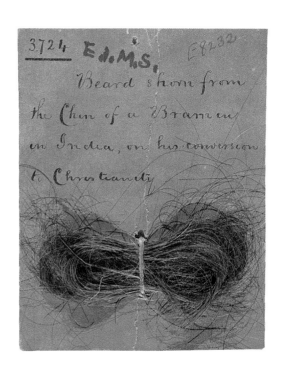

were instrumental to the missionary enterprise, not only providing passage in their vessels but sometimes assisting with mission financial affairs.[48] Despite shifts and realignments in the India trade and its declining position in the national economy, the links to India that came about through commerce expanded.

The five pioneering missionaries, recent graduates of the Andover Theological Seminary, had been ordained just before their departure by Samuel Worcester at the Tabernacle Church in Salem (fig. 8.6). Like most young missionaries, they were not from the port towns of New England but from the farms and villages of the interior, where more orthodox Presbyterian and Congregational parishes flourished. They had attended colleges like Williams and Amherst, where evangelical sentiment was strong.[49]

The American Board of Commissions for Foreign Missions, established in Bradford, Massachusetts, just two years earlier, organized and supported this first foreign mission. They sent Adoniram Judson to England the following year to seek advice from the London Missionary Society, whose activities in India were often reported in New England Christian publications. Periodicals like the *Panoplist*, published in Boston, carried communications from British missions, especially from William Carey and his colleagues at the Baptist Mission established at Serampore, the Danish port just north of Calcutta.[50] The London Missionary Society invited Judson and the other Americans to join them. At first disposed to do so, Judson was dissuaded by the nationalist feelings of the American Board of Commissioners for Foreign Missions, and especially by the terms of the $30,000 donation from Mrs. John Norris of Salem, which provided the financial foundation for the American missionary effort.[51]

The missionary movement gained support in New England as more people adhered to the belief that individual will, rather than predestination, determined the fate of one's soul. Worshippers could attain salvation through their own faith and actions, and they could help others find their way to God. American evangelicals were inspired to direct their efforts abroad by the conviction that millions around the world suffered in ignorance of Christian truth. They were also influenced by the growing stature of the United States—able to hold its own against the British on the seas, second only to Britain in commerce, the paramount power in the Western Hemisphere. Distant peoples and their religions had been brought closer through the experiences of mariners and the exotic curiosities acquired during their voyages. The East India Marine Society's museum in Salem, for example, displayed images of Hindu deities as early as 1801. Originally entered in the museum's register as "gods," their designation was soon changed to "idols" (fig. 8.7).[52] The Society also displayed four volumes of biblical texts in Bengali and Sanskrit recently published by the Baptist Mission in Serampore (fig. 8.8).[53] There was even "part of the beard of a Bramin who was shaved on being converted to Christianity" (fig. 8.9).[54] Many visitors must have viewed these texts and the lock of hair as hopeful indications of the progress of Christianity in India.

But the need to bring Christianity to the world was not seen in the same optimistic light by mariners and merchants as it was by the missionaries themselves. In the same year, 1812, that Henry Lee began his three-year stay in Calcutta, the Judsons, Newells, Notts, Rice, and Hall arrived in Calcutta. Henry Lee wrote to his wife that the missionaries who had come out with Augustine Heard (the Judsons and Newells) were not allowed to remain in the city. The Judsons and Rice, he reported, had become Baptists (they had started out as Congregationalists) so that, Lee believed, the English missionaries in India would accept them. (Judson's memoirs recount a change in their beliefs that occurred during their passage.)[55] In any case, the Judsons and Rice were expelled from India, though they were allowed to stop at Ceylon. Lee learned that Hall, Nott, and the Newells sailed back to Île de France, where Mrs. Newell and their newborn child died.[56]

Lee thought little of the missionaries. Hall and Nott, in Lee's judgment, "appeared . . . to be mad." "All of them seemed ignorant of the world, and extremely ill-informed of the country and the inhabitants which they came to convert. I pitied them most sincerely . . ." Besides, Lee thought their prospects for conversion were dismal. The British East India Company did not want missionaries and the natives of India were beyond reach:

> The Society must abandon their project of Christianizing India—this Government will admit no one, unless they come with the permission of the Court of Directors. . . . As yet few or no converts have been made, perhaps not one respectable native, and it appears to me beyond the reach of human means to change their notions: certainly while they remain as at present in the grossest ignorance

of everything but the particular profession they are engaged in . . .[57]

Five years later, William Rogers encountered some of these missionaries in Bombay and wrote about them in his journal (chapter 10). There he met Gordon Hall and the Notts, who had gone on to Bombay from Calcutta, where Newell, who had been in Ceylon after his wife's death, joined them. Their successful appeals to the governor, Sir Evan Nepean, and the efforts of Charles Grant in London at the East India Company's court of directors, had secured them permission to stay. When Rogers met them, he reported,

> There were at Bombay several American missionaries, among them Mr. Newhall [Newell], the husband of Mrs. H. Newhall [Newell] so famous for her zeal, true or falsely directed I will not say. . . . They appeared personally to be sociable when alone, or rather separate from each other . . . Mr. Newhall [Newell] had a [new] wife brought out to him in the *Saco*, a Miss Philomela Thurston. . . . Their wives were pleasant women, well watched by their husbands, who had the reputation of being a little jealous. They kept schools for the native children, learning them to read the New Testament in Guzerattee [Gujarati], by this means endeavoring to instill into their minds the principles of our faith. But they never have yet made a convert nor will they by the means now used. I think we should do more to honor ourselves and receive greater reward hereafter, should we appropriate the money sent out to India to the purpose of civilization and the promulgation of Christianity among the savages of North America.

Rogers may have been sensing a deeper, more disturbing trouble in the Bombay mission: that same year, Gordon Hall wrote home of the notorious adultery of one, "widely famed in his native land, as something almost transcending human excellence. . . . No thanks to ourselves that we are all whoremasters and rotting with that fatal disease."[58] Rogers may have had reasons to doubt their intellectual and moral qualifications. It was his opinion that Christian missionaries would have better prospects if Westerners behaved in a Christian manner in India, setting an example worth emulating.

The antimissionary views of Rogers and Lee were shared by many in the mercantile community, including Benjamin W. Crowninshield, member of the Crowninshield family firm,

former secretary of the navy, Massachusetts state senator, and member of Congress (fig. 8.10). In 1819, Crowninshield gave a speech during the consideration of a bill for incorporating the Society for Foreign Missions, in which he argued against Christian missionary activity in India, and defended the right of Hindu Indians to be free of such interference. The speech was sharply criticized. C. P. Sumner, who heard it, sympathized with Crowninshield:

> you [drew] a very striking comparison between the manners, the address and the learning of the principal men among the Hindoos, and those whom it was contemplated to send out to *instruct* them. You said that you had spent some considerable time in Indostan, and had become acquainted with the amiable manners of that mild, much misrepresented people, that there were those among them who had examined our religion and were familiar with its doctrine, and who could teach our missionaries the history of their own church; that those people were perfectly satisfied with their own religion and wanted no change; that proselytes to the Christian religion in India could only be expected from those unfortunate beings who had lost their own cast.[59]

Benjamin W. Crowninshield's broad-minded views seem to have been the norm in his family; his unwillingness to pass judgment is reminiscent of his cousin Benjamin (1758–1836), who recorded the astonishingly detailed and unprejudiced account of a sati witnessed in 1789 (chapter 1). The experiences of East India merchants instilled a more complex, sometimes more liberal, view of Hinduism. In contrast to the first missionaries to India, who took the perfection of Christianity and the doomed falseness of Hinduism as axiomatic, mariners, while they certainly shared a belief in the truth of Christianity, differed in their opinions about proselytizing, about the qualifications of the missionaries, about the appropriateness of India as a place for missionary efforts, and about the moral character of Hindus.

In the early nineteenth century, the United States was an emphatically Christian nation, despite the formal separation of church and state, and the rationalism and enlightenment views of some of its founders. Many colonial settlements had been established by immigrants seeking freedom to practice their own brand of Christianity. As long ago as the time of Cotton Mather in the early seventeenth century, some Americans had

Fig. 8.10 Benjamin W. Crowninshield (1772–1851), after a portrait by John Vanderlyn (see also fig. 9.1).
Oil on canvas, 66 x 57.2 cm; Peabody Essex Museum M6704.

viewed India as a land of heathen idol worshippers, its people in desperate need of knowing Christ and hearing the gospel. Perhaps for this reason, too, India was the first foreign destination of American missionaries. The India of "heathen Gentoos" was a foil for shaping American Christians' ideas about their own religiosity and for building a sense of national spiritual and moral superiority. But the varied experiences of Yankee mariners in India introduced difference and complexity into the accepted views, creating a space for varied opinions, permitting some tolerance, and perhaps arousing some curiosity to know more about Indian religion and philosophy. The more liberal opinions, usually associated with the Unitarian movement, were then gaining ground in New England. Salem's Reverend William Bentley, for example, avidly acquired literature and curiosities from the world voyages of his sea captain parishioners, was an enthusiastic student of languages, and had developed a cosmopolitan outlook compatible with his Unitarian faith. He was cited disapprovingly in the orthodox *Panoplist* as saying that "he hoped if the people of our country carry our religion to the Hindoos, they will bring back the morality of India."[60]

Onto this scene came the first voice from India itself. In 1818, the year that Rogers visited India in the *Tartar*, the ideas of the prominent Hindu thinker Rammohun Roy were published in the United States. William Tudor, editor of the *North American Review*, reported with evident interest that a learned influential Hindu had discovered in ancient Sanskrit texts an essential monotheism as well as the rationale for rejecting image worship, and that this Hindu also found an admirable model in some aspects of Christian morality. While Tudor, and many Unitarians who were becoming aware of Rammohun Roy and his ideas, hoped these were a signal that the natives of India might, after all, eventually accept Christianity, the impact that Rammohun Roy had for the next fifteen years—until his death —helped raise interest in India, its religions, and its literatures.

Fig. 9.1 William Augustus Rogers (1792–1821) by John Vanderlyn. William Rogers met Vanderlyn in Paris, where this portrait was painted. Vanderlyn returned to the United States in 1815 and became a successful painter of portraits and panoramas. Oil on canvas; Courtesy of Dorothy Rogers Kaye.

CHAPTER 9

William Augustus Rogers, Republican, Lawyer, and Merchant

A Voyage from the "Freest of All Lands," 1817–18
To see all that was curious[1]

William A. Rogers (1792–1821) was a contemporary of Henry Lee (1782–1867), whose single-minded attention to the India trade, reflected in his business papers and correspondence, so illuminated the period of commercial transformation ushered in by the trade embargo of 1807 (chapter 8). Both men were from prominent New England families and were educated at distinguished boarding schools, Rogers at Governor Dummer Academy and Lee at Phillips Andover Academy. At this point their paths diverged. Henry Lee went directly from Phillips Andover into a countinghouse, where men of business were educated on the job. William Rogers was sent to Harvard College to prepare for the law. Lee's career was sharply focused on building a successful business in the India trade; Rogers, who went on three trading voyages to the East Indies, did so only to finance a law practice which he hoped to set up in Salem. Lee was interested in business and little else; Rogers' journal reflects a lively engagement with global politics, alien ways of life, and the relative merits of governments and civilizations.

William Rogers embarked on his first East Indies voyage on September 9, 1817, sailing as joint supercargo in the *Tartar* from Boston to Bombay. He had been given this opportunity by his older brothers, who were already established shipowners and merchants. His brother Richard commanded the *Tartar*, which was owned by the older Rogers brothers and their brother-in-law Benjamin T. Pickman. For about twenty years, Nathaniel L., Richard S., and John W. Rogers were partners in the India, Zanzibar, and Australia trades as N. L. Rogers & Brothers, becoming one of Salem's most important mercantile firms.[2]

The Rogers' forbears had settled in coastal Massachusetts in the mid-seventeenth century and risen to prominence. An ancestor, John Rogers, served as president of Harvard College in the 1680s. William's own parents were schoolteachers. His father moved to Salem in 1787 to open a classical school. When he died at age thirty-seven leaving a young family, his wife Abigail supported their children by keeping a school for girls. William was the youngest of four sons (a fifth had died in infancy). Because of the family's difficult circumstances, William's three older brothers attended public school and entered the commercial world of countinghouses and merchant shipping as soon as they were old enough, taking advantage of the plentiful business opportunities in Salem and Boston, and of the helping hand given by more prosperous relations.

In his mother's estimation, "Willie" was a very bright and spirited child. Her letters mention playful pranks with young ladies and serious flute lessons, and convey great pride in his academic accomplishments.[3] Mrs. Rogers and her older sons made it possible for William to carry on the family's academic traditions. After boarding school, William attended Harvard College, graduating in 1811 with a class said to be "of great distinction."[4] Mrs. Rogers was very pleased with William's success at Harvard and she wrote to his older brother John, "Mr. Kirkland, the President [of Harvard], speaks very handsomely of your brother's theme [for his final examination], says it is in expression singular in the train of thought and elegant in language." Later, after the examination, she reported: "William got through his exhibition. The President and Professors McKeon and Hedge expressed their highest approbations of his performance, in an interview I had with them after it was over. Their approbation was very pleasant to me."[5]

William was absorbed in politics, at home and abroad, and eager to experience the far-off places his brothers visited so

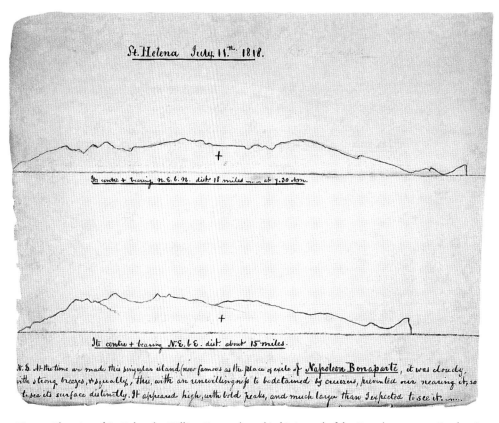

St. Helena July 11.th 1818.

Its centre + bearing N.E. b.N. dist 18 miles ___ at 7.30 Am.

Its centre + bearing N.E. b E. dist. about 15 miles.

N.S. At the time we made this singular island (now famous as the place of exile of Napoleon Bonaparte, it was cloudy, with strong breezes, +squally, this, with an unwillingness to be detained by cruisers, prevented our nearing it; so to see its surface distinctly. It appeared high, with bold peaks, and much larger than I expected to see it.

Fig. 9.2 Elevation of St. Helena by William Rogers, bound in his journal of the *Tartar*'s voyage to Bombay in 1817–18. Rogers was a great admirer of Napoleon and made this sketch of the island where he was imprisoned as the *Tartar* sailed past. Peabody Essex Museum Library.

often on their trading voyages. Letters to them, written when he was still in school, express—with a touch of envy—great interest in their adventures in foreign ports and zestfully report on local political developments.[6] He fumed about the challenges to experienced local Federalist candidates for office and the ignorant ill-prepared "Demos" (Jeffersonian Republicans). But William did not embrace the pro-British views of most Salem Federalists. Like many of his contemporaries at Harvard College, he was decidedly sympathetic toward the French.[7]

In his last year of college, William was issued a passport, in which he is described as five feet eight and one-quarter inches tall with dark hair and eyes and dark complexion. The following year, he was given the opportunity to go to Paris, where he served as a junior member of the U.S. delegation. He had studied French since childhood; in his family, French was considered second only to English. William stayed in Paris until 1815, when an indiscretion with a young lady forced his return home.[8] When Rogers arrived in Paris, Napoleon's power was at its height and the birth of a son seemed to assure succession. He remained through the time when "the world . . . viewed Bona-

parte's power at its zenith,"[9] through Napoleon's exile to Elba and his brief return to power during the Hundred Days, until the battle of Waterloo on June 18, 1815 (fig. 9.2). William deeply admired Napoleon; three years later, in his journal of the *Tartar*'s voyage to Bombay, he extolled Napoleon—on whom "the diadem of France shone with so brilliant a luster." After Waterloo, William visited the battlefield, picked up some relics there, and brought them with him when he returned home,[10] along with many other valuable articles and curiosities,[11] including books, music, seals, and watches. The most significant among these was a copy of the Napoleonic Code, admired by republicans like Rogers as a blueprint for rational government, guaranteeing equality under the law and the right to private property. His admiration for Napoleon was coupled with a strong disapproval of the hypocritical British penchant for supporting monarchies in Europe while destroying ruling dynasties in Asia.

After his sojourn in Paris, William returned to Salem to study law under the Hon. John Pickering—despite nagging doubts about the future this would bring. In 1811, he had written to his brother John, "I hope to do something one of these days and rid myself of dependency. So little prospect is offered to professional men that I wish almost I had gone to sea and by this time might have called my tongue my own."[12] William practiced law in Pickering's office until 1817, when he set up on his own. But his new office was destroyed by fire the day it opened, leaving William to "seek an honorable independency" by entering into commerce with his brothers.[13] His first voyage was on the *Tartar* to Bombay in 1817 (chapter 10). Twenty-five-year-old William Rogers sailed as joint supercargo on his first East India voyage, his ship loaded with masts, spars, and sheathing board from New England forests, materials for building and repairing ships, standard New England export cargoes.

Built in Salem in 1811, the *Tartar* was 400 tons in capacity and 108 feet in length, a typical size for an American East Indiaman. The *Tartar* had two decks, three masts, a square stern, and a figurehead. The ship had been built in one of Salem's busiest shipyards by Enos Briggs, a cousin of James B. Briggs whose own experiences of the India trade are excerpted from his journal in chapter 13. The Briggs shipyard was renowned at the turn of the century for building vessels suited for the East Indies trade.[14] By 1817, the *Tartar* had already had two owners and made at least three voyages. William's older brothers John, Richard, and Nathaniel, together with Benjamin T. Pickman, had purchased the ship from its Boston owners. Richard was to command the *Tartar* on this voyage to Bombay.

When the *Tartar* returned to Boston toward the end of 1818, it was laden with cotton and ginger. Ginger was a perennial commodity in the U.S.-India trade, but raw cotton was new and speculative, intended to compete with southern cotton in supplying the rapidly growing New England mills and to be exported to Great Britain.[15] Cotton-mill machinery was only beginning to be developed that could spin the much shorter fibers of Indian cotton into strong yarn. This cargo of raw cotton also signalled the transformation underway that would make India, once a world leader in the production and export of textiles, into a source of raw materials for cloth manufacture and a consumer of the products of Western mills.

William Rogers kept a journal of his voyage in the *Tartar* (excerpted in chapter 10). Though it was formatted like a shipping log, its content focused not on the course of the voyage or its business, but on William's impressions and experiences.

Journal keeping and letter writing were established practices in the Rogers family. His mother encouraged all her sons to record their experiences. In a letter to John she wrote, "do keep a journal of what you see, hear, who you are introduced to, so that when you have an opportunity of sending to us we may know all that passes with you."[16] William used his journal not only to record what he saw but to incorporate these events and experiences into his view of the world, especially his enthusiastic republicanism, patriotism, and esteem for moral integrity (if sometimes admired in the breach). His journal entries over and again compare his beloved republican America with, on one side, a hypocritical, monarchist, rapacious Great Britain, and on the other, the profoundly alien ways of India. William belonged to the first generation born in a sovereign, independent United States, and he entered the post-Napoleonic world with strong political and ideological views nurtured in Federalist Salem and liberal Harvard College.

As the *Tartar* approached the coast of Ceylon (Sri Lanka), William chastised the British for their conquest of the island. By a treaty signed in 1815, the British had taken possession of Dutch factories around the coast. The interior of the island remained the dominion of the king of Kandy, who was, conveniently for the British, in conflict with many of his nobles. A British army, with the collusion of the opposing parties, succeeded in penetrating the interior and defeating the king's forces. The terms of peace prohibited the king and his entire family from ever again holding power. Rogers condemned the British for their harshness and hypocrisy. Later, when he visited the residence of a deposed Maratha ruler held under house arrest near Bombay, Rogers commented on his pitiful situation, poor treatment, and the broken promises of the British. His sympathetic views of the natives extended to the boatmen, who came out to the ship at Colombo and Cochin with fruits and vegetables to sell. But the kindly disposition vanished in Bombay, perhaps in the face of daily encounters in an alien social world.

On arrival at Bombay, William determined "to see all that was curious." He took in the sights, observed the inhabitants, and learned all he could of local life and customs. He was too engaged in being there to take the time to record everything in his journal, so it was not until he was back on board the *Tartar* for the homeward passage that he composed and recorded what he had learned during his two-and-a-half-week stay in port. A

Fig. 9.3 "A hand, broken from a statue of granite in the temple of the Island of Elephanta, near Bombay," entry #667 in *The East India Marine Society of Salem*, 2d ed. (Salem, Mass., 1831). Granite, height 19 x width 23 cm; Peabody Essex Museum, Gift of Captain Benjamin Lander, 1803.

high point was an expedition to the cave temple on Elephanta Island in Bombay harbor, even in the early nineteenth century a must-see for every Western visitor. The secluded caves were filled with marvelous scenes of Indian gods and goddesses carved out of solid rock. Elephanta was already known in New England. Fragments from the cave temple were on display at the museum of the East India Marine Society in Salem as early as 1803. Several bits of dislodged sculptures, one of which may have been removed from a statue of Shiva, were picked up by visiting New England mariners and donated to the museum (fig. 9.3). There was also a print of the caves, probably from Thomas and William Daniell's publication *Oriental Scenery*.[17] Yankee visitors knew little of the statues' iconography, depicting exploits of the god Shiva, but were awestruck by the enormous monolithic images. That the carved temples appeared abandoned and the island entirely wild, with only a few residents, made the experience exhilarating to a child of the romantic age and reinforced the sense of lost splendor. William Rogers marveled at the artistry of the carving and was enthralled by the mystery of the surroundings. The sculptures at Elephanta, he concluded, with the help of what he had read and heard about

other cave temples, were the "remains of the former grandeur of the eastern world." For Rogers, whatever heights had been reached by Indian civilization were far in the past; the India he encountered had long since been eclipsed by the West and its newest, brightest star, the United States.

William Rogers' journal entries chart his engagement with current thinking about the connections between race, customs, and character. In describing Bombay, he classified its inhabitants as English, Parsi, Portuguese, Armenian, Jew, Hindu, Muhammadan, etc., and portrayed these peoples as distinct nations or castes, ranked by intelligence and other innate qualities. Like Dudley Pickman and many other Yankee mariners, he was struck by the very public presence of beggars and scantily clad laborers. In Yankee eyes, these were unmistakable signs of a debased morality, of weakness of mind and body, of indolence, and of immodesty (perhaps even licentiousness).

Repeatedly Rogers portrays Bombay's Parsis and Hindus as untrustworthy, thieving, and dishonest. Like his contemporaries who frequented these maritime contact zones, he operated entirely within his own moral system and was ill-equipped to do more than apply its standards as best he could. He was certainly unaware that everyone operating in this space justified his behavior as appropriate because it conformed with his own sense of propriety, or as acceptable because the other's expectations or requirements were judged to be nonsensical, unfair, immoral, or simply irrelevant. With no cognizance of the irony, near the end of his account of Bombay, he relates giving a bribe to avoid paying what he considered to be an unfair tax on liquors, and adjusting reported values of goods to compensate for a hefty increase levied on dutiable cargo. Rogers asserted that by "*management* you can get along just as you please"; it seems never to have occurred to him that his own behavior might be dishonest or incorrect.

Just once, for a brief moment, Rogers may have had an experience that transcended the limitations of his New England views. On an outing to the cremation grounds with a friend, he experienced an epiphany—and a good joke on himself: he recognized the fragility of his judgments. The two young men had gone to observe the exotic funeral practices of Hindus, into whose sacred precincts Westerners seemed able to trespass with impunity. Rogers was pulled up sharp when, as they drew close to this repellent yet fascinating scene, they were greeted by one of the "heathen" priests: "We are glad to see you gentlemen, but don't touch the wood." Rogers seemed to recognize at once the priest's civility, tolerance, and religious conviction. For a moment the tables were turned. He and his friend had become the uncivilized, boorish intruders. Most of all, though, Rogers was amused by the instantaneous metamorphosis of this cherished gothic scene. The macabre sensations he delighted in were suddenly swept away by a heathen priest who behaved with impeccable European civility. Any deeper realization of the relativity or ethnocentricity of his own moral judgments fundamentally eluded him.

As Rogers' journal attests, he not only recorded his experiences as a keepsake for himself and to share with family and friends, but used the journal as a receptacle for an abundance of thoughts, opinions, and observations on the "curious." He was confident in his views, in which, as befits a young man of the romantic age, sense and sensibility were thoroughly intermingled. America is praised as "the freest of all lands," a land of fair, honorable, rational, free men. The British are blasted for their "insatiable thirst of territorial expansion." Missionaries are derided as "spies for the filthy love of worldly lucre," and Hindus are condemned for "perform[ing] such tricks before high heaven as would make angels weep." William Rogers found India captivating, and he saw many things that helped him shape and refine his views of the world, and the place of himself and his nation in it.

William's share of the profits from his first voyage must have been enough to make this strategy seem worthwhile, but not so much that he was able to restart his law practice. In 1820, Rogers sailed again on the *Tartar*, this time as sole supercargo on a voyage to Calcutta. Almost as soon as he returned from this voyage, he went out again on the brig *Trexel* to Batavia, taking command for the first time. William Rogers died on this voyage, in a tragic, banal accident at Bangkok, where he was buried. He had taken the brig to Bangkok—an unusual destination for an American vessel—hoping to load a cargo of sugar. One hot, sultry night when the air was thick with mosquitoes, Rogers was invited to stay in the more comfortable accommodations of a nearby floating house occupied by the supercargo of an English schooner. In a letter written to his brothers, the two men left in charge of the voyage described what happened:

> On Wednesday night June 13th at midnight we were hailed from the ship and informed that Captain Rogers had fallen overboard and was probably drowned. [Captain Rogers] on account of the heat having lain on the platform in front of the house had rolled off into the water when the current, which is very rapid here, had, as we supposed, carried him under the house, from which situation he was unable to extricate himself, then sunk to rise no more.[18]

Fig. 10.1 *Tartar Leaving Bombay*, inscribed April, 26, 1818, possibly by William A. Rogers or another member of the *Tartar*'s crew on the 1817–18 voyage. Watercolor, 50.8 x 60.3 cm; Peabody Essex Museum M222, Gift of Daniel B. Lord, 1882.

CHAPTER 10

From the Journal of the Tartar, 1817–18

WILLIAM A. ROGERS

I left Salem at 7 a.m. for Boston, on Tuesday September 9th, 1817 for the purpose of embarking on board the ship *Tartar*, in which I had engaged to perform a voyage to Bombay, Malabar coast, India. Arriving in Boston we found our ship already under way and only waiting us, (R.S.R.[1] was with me). We left India Wharf at 9 a.m. and went on board.

The *Tartar* [fig. 10.1] is a fine coppered ship, 401 tons, and is exceeded in reputation for capacity, strength and good sailing by no ship in Massachusetts. She was built in Salem, in the year 1811 by Mr. Briggs;[2] My brother Richard S. Rogers has command of her. Thomas Hinkely S.M. [second mate] and 1st Officer, Robert Parker 2nd and James Scott 3rd, all of Boston. The crew generally young and apparently healthy, active and quiet men, but I will make no remarks having yet no opportunity to discover their characters.

We are all numbered 21 persons. Ship mounts 8 carriage guns.

In passing down Boston harbor I had an opportunity of witnessing the beauty of the scenery for which the entrance of the port is so justly celebrated. It was a most delightful morning and nothing could have interrupted the enjoyment of the view which would have enriched the imagination of a Vernet[3] but the reflection of parting with these scenes and leaving behind us those whose friendships could add to the happiness of life and without whose sympathies the richest gifts of nature would be prizeless. . . .

[At Thatchers light off Cape Ann] Here I cast one "longing lingering look"[4] to the shores of my native land [fig. 10.3]. And how fortunate was I in the consolatory thought that I left behind me many an anxious friend, who would rejoice at my prosperity or feel an anxiety for one who had left them in pursuit of an honorable independency. How proud were my feelings when I beheld the setting sun covering with his golden mantel the freest "of all lands he shines upon" the land of pure and rational liberty, uncontaminated with licentiousness, and unrestrained by tyranny, the asylum of oppressed humanity, the refuge of itinerant misery.

The night was beautifully placid, the constellations vied with each other to compensate for the loss of the great luminary which had gone to illumine other lands and the western stars

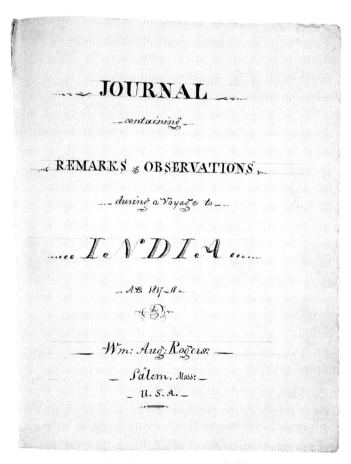

Fig. 10.2 Title page of William A. Rogers' journal of the *Tartar*, 1817–18. Peabody Essex Museum Library.

Fig. 10.3 *Boston Light* by Benjamin Carpenter, in his journal of the *Hercules*, 1793.
The lighthouses along the coast were more than navigational aids, they were deeply felt markers of departure and arrival.
Ink on paper, 10.7 x 19.1 cm; Peabody Essex Museum Library.

shone with heaven's purest light, to guide the oppressed emigrant to the cradle of freedom and the seaworn mariner to the land of his home. Fare well for a time my country, last child of nations, may ages roll on their unwearied courses and find thy sons as wise, as brave, as free and as virtuous as they now are.

[*On September 10, 1817, the second day of the voyage, Rogers began his "Sea account." The following excerpt begins on January 23, 1818, as the ship is approaching Sri Lanka.*]

Tuesday Jany 23 136 days out. Delightful weather. Saw a large bird like a shag [small cormorant], noddies[5] and other birds—5 p.m. saw a large school of fish—like our hard heads[6] which broke the water like breakers. At sunset an appearance in the N.W. like the haze we observe over land. An insect like our devils-needle came on board. By sunset Amp[litude] Var 2° E. by obs[ervation] Star altebaran[7] and moon. Long at 8° 24' 25" to be 82° 39' 45" East. By mer: Alt: of Moon at 12° 22' made our Lat 5° 26' No[rth].

Passed floating wood. At 6 a.m. R.S.R discovered land

from the fore yard.[8] The high lands of Ceylon [Sri Lanka], bearing from N [by?] E to NNW. Distant about 10 leagues from shore. This is the first land I have seen for 135 days! With what pleasure was the distant crags of Adam's Peak[9] observed just [tingeing?] the horizon like a blue cloud. It seemed like my native land. But that land, the loss of the dearest of all friends a son can boast, has deprived me of almost all pleasure when I think of it. After running in for the shore several hours, we neared it so that huts, bays and creeks were discernible.

Many canoes of a singular construction filled with natives nearly naked came off to trade away their fruit. They were honest, intelligent and good natured. Their canoes were furnished with an outrigger to prevent their upsetting [fig. 10.4]. We were boarded by a flag boat from Point de Galle, or Ponta de Galla, more properly, to get a description of our ship [etc?]. The natives appeared very poor indeed, but very honest.

Spoke a dismasted E.I. [East India Company] ship from China for Bombay—about 900 or 1000 tons [see fig. 10.9]. Had experienced a blow off the Nicobar Islands and lost his main top

Fig 10.4 *Ceylonese Native Canoe with Outrigger* by William A. Rogers, in his journal of the *Tartar*, 1817–18. Peabody Essex Museum Library.

mast[10] and mizzen masts[11]—in long 17° 2' 8". Under jury spars.[12] Hove to and offered him assistance, which he declined. She was a fine ship and sailed very fast. In passing along the W. Coast of Ceylon, care should be taken to distinguish the Hooy Mount from Adam's Peak, which although very lofty still may be mistaken for one or other. In passing Colombo in the night we had no opportunity of seeing the town on the coast.

CEYLON SERENDIB SELEN-DIVE[13]

Connected with the description of the productions, inhabitants and appearance of this delightful Indian island, its political history, renders it a subject of peculiar interest and worthy of the attention of every lover of nature and every attentive observer of the progress of that insatiable thirst of territorial expansion, which has marked the conduct of the English since their first settlements in India. And I suspect in no one instance has their rapacity been more strongly exhibited than on this island, within a few years.

In satisfying their thirst for conquest, they have in India passed the barriers of justice and humanity; have created wars, and dictated peace; deposed their rightful sovereigns—or hunting them in their native pingles [settlements] and pursuing them through the fastnesses [strongholds] of their mountains, have reduced them, when at last pent up in their rude fortresses to such extremity, that preferring destruction to submission and death to slavery, their Rajahs and Nawabs in moments of desperation have rushed on the English bayonet or offered themselves the victims of their frenzy at the altar of self-immolation.

While on the continent of Europe they have deluged the greater part with blood, or by insidious intrigue have fomented quarrels between powers whose strength or prosperity she regarded with jealousy, while they have fought the battles of the Bourbons, the champions of <u>legitimate right</u> (mark the words) the <u>knight errants of royal pusillanimity</u>, they have in India by their depositions of their princes contradicted the same principles which they held out as the ground of their attack on the French Emperor—I will not say nation—for it was a war of personality. The diadem of France shone with so brilliant a luster on the brow of Napoleon that while it attracted the admiration of the world, the demon jealousy, companion of guilty fear, pointed it out to England as the meteor which presaged her ruin. Unless she could by her intrigue and by exhibiting a show of virtuous policy, seduce the powers of the continent into a war, which if successful would destroy her rival and strengthen her own power. She pointed out to these legitimates the effects of the French revolution. She held out to them the progress of republican principles. And I have no doubt that the U.S.A., their prosperity and growing greatness, struck terror into their souls. In perspective, they beheld their scepters broken, their thrones and palaces converted to the purposes of liberty and justice and their long and boasted dynasties sinking into oblivion. Yet that day is fast approaching when these infamous practices, this political juggling will be exposed and the influence of fair and honorable policy shall be adopted and man shall be left to exercise that freedom which nature intended should ever be identified with his existence.

The treatment of the King of Candy [Kandy] has led me to these remarks, a monument of baseness, fit to be placed by the side of the tomb of Tippoo Sahib, on the ruined walls of Seringapatam.[14]

The island is situated on the southeast coast of the peninsula of India, on the coast of Coromandel. It extends from 5° 6' to 9° 52' no[rth] lat[itude] and from 79° 43' to 1° 56' east longitude. It is of an oval form; it is nearly connected with the continent by a ridge of sand, mostly dry, about 11 leagues in length, at each end of which is an island called Ramanout or Ramanacer or Ramisseram [Rameswaram] on the west and Manara [Mannar] on the east side. Between these isles and the main are the openings through which the water passes from the Gulph of Manar into Palk's Bay. These openings are but one and a half miles wide and even there at low water have a long ridge of rocks which connect it to the main excepting about 30 yards on which there is from 3 to 5 feet of water.[15]

It is over this sand ridge that the Ceylonese believe our forefather Adam passed on his expulsion from Paradise, and it has the name of Adam's Bridge from that tradition.[16] The delightful fertility of the soil, the luxuriant and spontaneous growth of every plant or fruit which conduces to relieve the wants or gratify the palate, its delightful temperature, led these natives to believe it the Eden of Bliss, the chosen spot of human happiness. On one of the highest mountains called Adam's Peak is an area of about 200 yds square on which is the impression of a man's foot in the rock which they believe to be Adam's.

The earliest authentic history of its settlement is with the arrival of the Portuguese in 1505 or 1506 under Almeyda, who engrossed its trade till the arrival of the Dutch in the middle of the 17th century, when the Portuguese were driven off. The Dutch remained in possession of all the principal ports until in 1796 they surrendered their possessions to the English. They are now sole masters of its seaports and fortresses. On every side the island rises from the sea into lofty mountains, whose summits may be discerned in a clear atmosphere at the distance of 125 miles. They run from N to S. These were formerly divided into petty kingdoms. In the highest range and most inaccessible amidst rock and jungles was the kingdom of Conde Uda,[17] but the petty powers were finally merged in the power of the King of Candy or Kandi, who has finally been conquered, dethroned, and enslaved by the British [fig. 10.5].[18]

These sticklers for hereditary sovereignty and legitimate right have cashiered more Eastern satraps than there are principalities in Europe. In Europe they have acknowledged the founder of a new dynasty, a warrior who held the keys of every fortress on the continent, I can almost say. They have sent one of their greatest politicians and most splendid orators, as an ambassador to his court, and have to all intents acknowledged him as a real legitimate, raised to the throne by the voice of millions of Frenchmen. And after all, when they find him so far advanced in the march of glory that they must be soon overcome, or dwindle into insignificance, then they alter their conduct, proclaim him infidel, because he did not believe their promises, traitor because he did not compromise the interest of his people for his own good, and rebel because his blood, which had not crept through scoundrel legitimacy since the flood, was warm with patriotism and the glory of his country and fired with ambition to "make her the gem and wonder of earth."

I grant that personal aggrandizement may have been an auxiliary to his ambitious views, but point out the statesman and warrior, except our Washington, a man without a shadow of semblance, who has been free from self-interested notions, and then you may call the lone captive of St. Helena an unprincipled hypocrite. Here was persecution for the want of family arms, of crowns and coronets which had rusted on the brows of regal indolence and sensuality, or of coats of armor which had never been put on except at joust at a tournament. It was to rid themselves of royal mendacity of the expensive bills of fare of royal gluttony and in order to support their own impatient and wary kings to establish a principle which should replace on the throne of France a super annuated [?] whose frigid blood like St. [Janarius?] never was warmed except by the touch of religious frenzy.[19]

In India mark the difference. They there have deposed absolute sovereigns who for centuries can boast this famed legitimacy.[20] To aggrandize their national importance, to satisfy the cravings of private avarice and to find employment for their numerous standing forces naval and military, they have enlisted the whole force of religious bigotry and impoverished priesthood. Their missionaries, take them as a body, I consider as a set of licensed religious jugglers, who under the garb of sanctity act as spies for the filthy love of worldly lucre. These last which have been let loose on the continent of India, supported by English bayonets to enforce the mild religion of our Saviour, have called the zealous Mahommedan from his Koran, the Parsee from the altar of the sun, the mild Hindoo from his native, honest and innocent purity[21] and in fact no sect or cast has been freed from these intrusions in search of proselytism. The pure and unsophisticated doctrine of Christianity has never been inculcated, its enlightening consolations have never illuminated their progress. War has opened a road for religious conquest, and after they could boast some outcast for a convert they have made the deluded proselyte ten times more the child of the Devil than before.

This is not the tirade of an enemy to England or Englishmen. I revere their laws, their government and their religion. I boast my descent from a nation yet renowned for acts and arms and for patriotism unequalled by any nation but America. But years have past away since they pursued that honest policy which was the ground work of their present greatness. So long

Fig. 10.5 *Roy de Ceylan*, Paris, c. 1690. Engraving, 15.2 x 15.2 cm; Peabody Essex Museum M17838, Gift of John Dominis Holt and Frances Damon Holt, 1978.

ago indeed that the inscription on the tomb of their honesty has been nearly effaced by the hand of time. In regard to their conduct to the Ceylonese monarch, they held out the ostensible motive of humanity. They pointed out the [?] he committed and the sufferings of his subjects. This apparently was laudable cause for a civilized and enlightened power having forces to make their <u>might right</u>.

A summary view of the dethronement of the king of Candy is as follows. In the year 1814 the Candians, groaning no doubt under the severities of their tyrant, manifested their disposition to rebel in many partial insurrections. The prime

Gen. Brownrigg [?] organized his forces marched Dec 9 against him with 3000 men. After many misfortunes and much ratting,[22] as it is termed, of his nobles, his Kandian majesty surrendered on 14 Feby. He was conveyed to Colombo where he displayed in his conduct all his native ferocity of temper and cruelty of disposition. His name is Wikreme Rajah Sinha. The sentence passed on him is one of the most sweeping forfeitures known in the records of judicial proceedings. Himself and his relations of every affinity were declared enemies and prohibited ever from sharing in the government of Kandi and prohibited even from entering those provinces without a passport from the British governors.

Now here it is appears that a king was cashiered for cruelty to his subjects, for being guilty of every detestable crime and for utter incompetency from his ungovernable ferocity of temper to govern his subjects with propriety. So far very well—very fair for English justice and magnanimity. But mark what follows. Art. 4 in the treaty provides that, the authority of the Kandian provinces be vested in the English governor of Ceylon, or under such native governors of provinces as they may appoint! The governor of Ceylon in this expedition manifested much prudence firmness and moderation. No personal blame rests on him. He received his instructions from home. The British Govt are the agents who break down the proud towers of unalienable legitimacy! Why did not they allow the Kandians another prince of their own choice, then would they have aided humanity not in word or in deed. Little do I believe that human nature has not sufficient energy to govern itself without the aid of extraneous officiousness.

Where were these principles when Joseph Bonaparte was on the throne of Spain, after being obliged to leave his kingdom he then left an opportunity for English influence to exercise itself for the rights of man. They then restored the foolish, superstitious, unprincipled and inquisitional Ferdinand to the throne. When Murat[23] was deposed they restored the crown to a weaker thing. The crown of the young King of Rome was changed to the mitre of a pope and when should I stop enumerating their inconsistencies? I should traverse the continent and in every principality find an example. In Europe no misrule, no tyranny, no licentiousness, no bigotry, no utter incompetency

Fig. 10.6 *The Queen of Candy*, engraved by R. Woodman, 1834, after a drawing by William Daniell. Engraving, 19.1 x 14.6 cm; Peabody Essex Museum M20922, Gift of John Dominis Holt and Frances Damon Holt, 1984.

minister of the King who was governor of a province was summoned to court but refused to attend knowing the temper of his royal master. He immediately offered his services, with those of his province who joined him, to Gen. Brownrigg, who declined them, being premature. His family consisting of his wife & 5 children who were retained as hostages by the King were immediately executed after suffering every evil which cruelty could invent. The Adikar [prime minister] after residing some time at Colombo received the protection of Gen. Brownrigg. The King at this time was revenging himself on his unhappy subjects, and also on the neighboring defenseless British.

in government has been sufficient to destroy the dynasty of a family or break one chain in a million the link of legitimacy. And have not the native princes of the East as high a title to that word as Europeans; are not their ideas as lofty, as noble as those of a Bourbon of France or Spain. Have they in record ever been mendicants without energy or pride and cowards in extremities. The tale of Hyder Aly or Tippu Sultan will contradict it.

To return to the history of the island [Ceylon]. Its fertility is wonderful, being so great that the natives imagine it the Eden of Adam. Cinnamon of the best quality is here in abundance, it is monopolized by the E.I. Company for an annual rent to Government. Ginger, peppers, sugar, cottons and many other valuable articles of traffic are found here. Here is the talipot tree whose leaf can cover 15 persons [fig. 10.7]. Oranges, pineapples, bananas, plantains, etc. etc. in great abundance. The elephant is an inhabitant of Ceylon with most of the wild animals of India. Precious stones of almost every kind are found here. Mines of the most precious metals are found, but not wrought. It is divided into provinces or petty kingdoms of which Candy is the capital. It is now wholly under English Govt. Colombo is the principal settlement—contains 60,000 inhabitants of all casts, nations and languages. It is surrounded by cinnamon gardens and is said to be airy and healthy.

Trincomalay or Trinkoenmala [Trincomalee] on the east side has one of the finest harbors in the E Indies. Most of the other settlements are small and insignificant. This island is separated by the gulf of Manar or Manara from the peninsula. From the fruits we obtained, the honest simplicity of the natives, I do not wonder that here was located the Paradise of the world. Its external appearance was highly beautiful and romantic. The pearls. . . .

January 24. Off Ceylon—Passed Ponta de Galla an English residency formerly Portuguese—has a church with two steeples and a large white house. Rather an insignificant place. 4 p.m. Point de Galle bore N 22° W 4 lea dist. Galmengodde [Ambalangoda?] N 34° W ½ at 10 am Adam's Peak bore NE b[y] E distant 9 lea. from shore—Lat obsd 6° 6' N Long E [blank].

[*Entries on January 25, 26, and part of 27 omitted*]

Fig. 10.7 *The Talipat Tree*, engraved by G. Hollis, London, 1834, after an earlier drawing by William Daniell. Engraving, 19.1 x 14.6 cm; Peabody Essex Museum M20926, Gift of John Dominis Holt and Frances Damon Holt, 1984.

I took sketches of the coast as I passed along. The land of Cape Comorin is very remarkable, being nearly perpendicular and very bold and craggy. The Gaut Mountains [Western Ghats] in the back ground were topped with clouds. Observed spots along the coast of very high colored red sand. On the extreme point of the Cape few trees, a few miles north of it there are very great numbers of cocoa[nut] trees. Many huts peeping through the trees along the shore and numbers of naked natives walking along it[s] burning sands, with no shelter against the burning sun. This coast is in the Kingdom of Travancore which is in alliance with the British. It extends as far as Cochin. Lat obsd 8° 01' Long [blank].

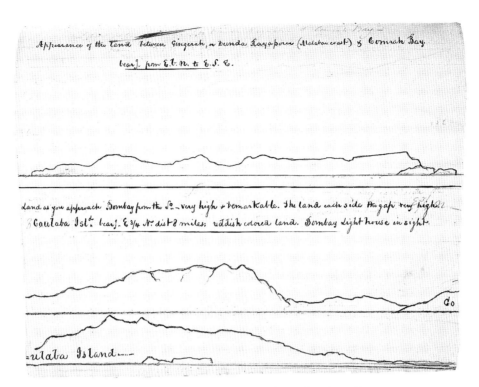

Fig. 10.8 *Appearance of the Land between Gingerah [Janjira] . . .* by William A. Rogers, in his journal of the *Tartar*, 1817–18. Peabody Essex Museum Library.

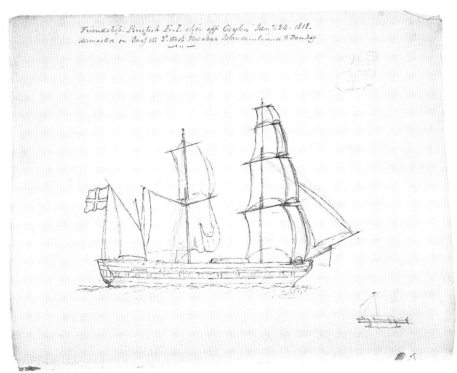

Fig. 10.9 Friendship *English E. I. Ship off Ceylon, Jan 24, 1818* by William A. Rogers, in his journal of the *Tartar*, 1817–18. Peabody Essex Museum Library.

COCHIN *on the Coast of* MALABAR.
Jam. Forbes. 1772.

Fig. 10.10 *Cochin on the Coast of Malabar*, engraved by J. Shury, 1812, after a 1772 drawing by James Forbes.
Engraving, 22.9 x 30.5 cm; Courtesy of the Department of Printing and Graphic Arts, Houghton Library,
Harvard College Library.

Jany 28 Several boats (tonies)[24] alongside with fruit, pigs, eggs, yams, etc. They are Mahommedans—were handsome men, a great deal of sobriety in their countenances, wore their beards and mustachios, unarmed, goodnatured and <u>grateful</u>, which is the greatest of virtues in savage man. After buying many of these articles, I gave one of them a sea biscuit. He immediately offered me cocoa nuts and other fruit. There was one very old man in the boat. They chewed the betel nut and tobacco. Naked excepting a cloth round their middle. They were straight and very well made, but I observed not very strong.[25] They sing together when paddling their tonies. I bought 7 fowls, 4 yams, 3 doz eggs, 2 bunches bananas, 8 cocoanuts for 2 rupees (1 dollar). When pushing off I said <u>salaam</u> (peace) which they understood and all bowed.

Spoke 4 p.m. two coasting brigs from Bombay for Ceylon. 8 a.m. many tonies alongside—bought baskets, yams, limes etc. 3 am in 27 Fath[oms]. The church laid down as so. of Ruttua [Ruttera Point] is to the No. Corrected the directory. Lat obsd 8° 20' no. Long. 76° 50' E. A country ship (Portuguese I suspect) very near us. Tropick birds. . . .

31st Pleasant and moderate. 3 ships and 2 prows [small craft] in sight. 2 pm a ship running down before the wind. 4. spoke her; proved the E I ship *Success* from Bombay for Canton, 5 days out. Reported an American ship going into Bombay as he came out (no doubt the *Malabar*).[26]

Saw Cochin ahead bearing N by E 3 leagues distant [fig. 10.10]. Country very low and level. Soundings very regular. SW current these 24 hours. Cochin, formerly Dutch, has a fort and [bastions?]. They build ships of 200 and 300 tons here. Cochin was formerly Portuguese, then Dutch, now English. In the country of Cochin, pepper is obtained here. It is fortified, has walls 1½ miles in circumference, has 3 gates. Has a church and government house. About 1700 there were 4000 Jews here. In their synagogues, they had their records on copper plates from the time of Nebuchadnezzar to the present day. So they say. Lat. 9° 50' N—Long 75° 39' East.

Feby 1. Passed by [?]. Cranganore [Cranganur]. Chitwa [Chetwai] to Painany [Ponnani]. All the Province of Cochin. Cranganore is a town and fort on this coast. The Dutch sold this to the Rajah of Travancore. But Tippoo Sultan, regant of Mysore, disputing their right to sell it, occasioned a war. Tippoo being opposed to the English, the Nizam of the Deccan and the Mahrattas. Tippoo was obliged to acknowledge the justice of the sale and pay the expenses of the war. It is at the mouth of a river. Stood off and on shore as winds obliged. This is beating to Bombay. Saw several fish like flounders, very white with black tails. Sounded several times in from 12 to 23 fathoms. Several prows in sight. Soundings very regular. Lat. obsd 10° 24' N. Long. 75° 43' E.

Feby. 2 Light breezes. 2 or 3 water snakes passed us. They were 3 or 4 feet long with white rings round them. Look like our adders very much. Swam like eels in horizontal convolutions. Carried their heads out of water. Saw Paniany [Ponnani] bearing N 6 or 7 miles ahead. Many vessels at anchor in the mouth of the river. Formerly a Dutch Factory. Passed Beypore and Tanore [Tanur]. Also Calicut a place of note on this coast. Capital of a country 62 miles square. It produces pepper, ginger, aloes and rice. The trees here are always green. It was subject to Tippoo Sultan, regant of Mysore, but 1792 it was ceded to E I Co.

A woman [of Calicut] may marry a number of husbands, each has her by turns for about 10 days. When pregnant she names the father of her child who supports it. The Zamorin[27] can raise an army of 100,000 men. The city of Calicut contains 6000 houses. This was the first port visited by Europeans. The Portuguese discovering it 1498. An English factory is here. Its proper name is said to be Colicodu meaning cockcrowing.[28] A Mahommedan chief receiving from his sovereign as much land

as could be embraced within distance in which the crowing of a cock could be heard. The inhabitants are Moplays [Mappila].[29] Teak wood was formerly procured here in abundance. The teak tree, is first deprived of all its branches, the trunk cut half through, and incisions made in the bark. It is then left a year to dry. The tree is then cut down and pushed down the river by elephants.

Tippoo in 1789 destroyed Calicut and removed the inhabitants to Nellurca [Nellore?],[30] which place he named Ferrookabad. He banished all foreign agents and merchants, destroyed the pepper plantations, and treated the inhabitants with the greatest cruelty, destroyed the churches, broke through all their established customs. Its inhabitants are stout and industrious, but it is said, great villains. Some beautiful sea-eggs [i.e., sea urchins] passed us with brilliant blue radii. The shore here is covered with cocoanut trees. Lat obsd 11° 04' Long 75° 57' E.

3rd Calms. Tedious navigation. The Gauts rise here very high. They are the Indian Appennino[31] running from Cape Comorin to Surat river in distance of 40 to 70 miles from the sea coast. This stupendous wall has an altitude of 3 or 4000 ft. It[s] great height stop[s] the clouds and in the N.E. and S.W. monsoons, occasion the rainy season on the windward side of the mountains. Saw Sacrifice Rock on Cugnali Island about 3 miles distant. It is I judge ⅛ mile long, very white, (from birds' dung) water very deep by it. It lies 6 miles from shore. Spoke at 9 p.m. British ship from Liverpool for Bombay, 140 days out. Have lost their Captain. Understood her name to be *Duke of Buckingham*. Lat obsd 11° 21' Long. 75° 54' East.

Feby 4 Calms. Passed Cananore or Onore [Cannanore]. Mahe formerly French and Tellicherry, an English place— has a fort and its appearance at about 6 miles distant was very pretty. Saw Mount Dilly or Dilla 8 miles dist. It is a high mountain and may be seen 10 lea[gues] in clear day from sea. Water here full of fish sporting on the [surface], and gulls fishing. Myriads of very small snakes. Lat obsd 11° 56' No. Long 75° 05' East.

5th. Most delightful weather. The navigation of the Malabar Coast in the N.E. Monsoon is unequalled for smoothness of the sea and the steadiness of the [breezes?] whilst the[y] last.

Malabar means Mountaineer.[32] Saw Mount Formoso on our lee beam at 4 p.m. So called for its beautiful appearance. No other land in sight.

8 p.m. about in the Lat of Deklah or Decla; at this place the Malabar coast ends in coasting to the north and Canara [Kanara] begins. 2 ships and several prows in sight, also Mount [Beau?] or Barn Hill very high and bluff, also several small native settlements etc. Passed Mangalore, seaport of some importance on the coast of Canara, with a good road in the SW monsoon. Inhabited by Gentoos and Mahomeddans. The Gentoos on their festivals carry their idols in triumph in a wagon, to the wheels of which are affixed crooked iron hooks, on these they throw themselves and are crushed to pieces. The Portuguese formerly owned and had a church here for black converts. Here is much rice. They have two crops of corn in a year. Pepper, betel, sandal wood, iron and steel are obtained. Lat obsd 13° 03'. Long 74° 18' East.

6th Pleasant and moderate. Barcelore Peak bore at 6 p.m. N.E. dist 12 leagues. 5 am saw the land. Both ships in company. Passed several small native settlements until we came to Barcelore. About 10 lea So of this place are Permeira Rocks, 3 lea from the coast, high as a ships hull out of water and 6 leagues so. of Barcelore entrance are St Mary's Rocks. 2½ lea from shore and may be seen, both St. M and Permin. 3 lea from [?]. Passed these in the night. Next this—Worthy of note is Barcelore, the capital of Canara, first Portuguese, then Dutch, now English. Back of Barcelore, 40 miles NE lies Bednore, capital of [the] province of that name. Passed Pigeon Island about 2 leagues distant at noon. It is a round island covered with small bushes. East of it is a small island called Hog Island. Pigeon Isl. is 4 or 5 lea from the coast—with 2 islets near it easterly. Hog island is 9 miles from it and resembles a sugar loaf. Near Pigeon Island the ship we spoke on the 3d suddenly hove all aback. I judge she must have touched the rocks or lost some poor fellow overboard.

The coast here appears little calculated for cultivation, being very bold, rough and perpendicular—mountains presenting their rocky sides in almost every direction. Saw a large water snake, one of this kind I think would be a great curiosity in America. Lat obsd 13° 55' N. Long 74° 15' East. . . .

Feby 9th Moderate weather, but very pleasant. Both ships in company. Passed Cape Ramas, where the southern boundary of coast of Concan [Konkan] begins. Saw a singular battle between a large turtle and 2 water snakes. They were as large round as my wrist, say 6 inches in circumference. They had entwined themselves around his neck and fins, and over his shell. He appeared in extreme agony. We lowered the boat down but ere it reached him they sunk down. The torture he appeared to suffer and the writhings and apparent strengths of the snakes reminded me "magnas componere parvis"[33] of the wretched Laocoon on the Altar of Neptune.[34] They succeeded in catching a large snake, 3 feet 2 inches long and 5 round. He was very spiteful and bit the wood of the boat and extremely tenacious of life. He had all the vicious appearance of our rattlesnake. We were then 20 miles from shore. His belly was white, tail formed like an eel's, but no fins—forked tongue, and 2 teeth upper and lower. His back was of a black brown and scaly. Many very beautiful white gulls fishing. The snake had two fish 5 inches long in his belly when opened. Ce jour a un heure, le 3 [mate] Mr. S (le meme coquin, mentionne en Dec. 14eme post.) etait demis de sa place pour le present, ayant ete trouve coupable de tels crimes, qui sont preserves d'un caractere le plus vil et abject.[35] Passed [Murmagaon?] Point and St. George Islands. The Gauts mountains seen in the background. Saw Goa at a distance, also Agoada Fort and a romantic convent called Nostra Senhora do Cabo on a high bluff ground surrounded by trees. It looked too lively and picturesque for the prison of immured beauty and youth.

Goa situated on an island divided from the continent by 2 branches of the Mandora is the principal of the Indian Portuguese settlements on the coast [fig. 10.11]. It is the seat of the viceroy and archbishop taken by them in 1510. Its port is one of the best in India, naturally, and it has been much improved by the Portuguese who have guarded it with strong castles and towers with well appointed material for defence. It is 8 miles from the sea on the river Mandora. There is the old and new city, the latter however begins to show marks of decay. It was formerly one of the richest and most flourishing of all the Indian settlements. There are many elegant public structures still remaining, but the[y] remain now but the monuments of what

Engraved by J. Greig.

View of the CITY of GOA, from the River.
Jam. Forbes. 1772.

Fig. 10.11 *View of the City of Goa, from the River*, engraved by J. Greig, 1812, after a 1772 drawing by James Forbes. Engraving, 22.9 x 30.5 cm; Courtesy of the Department of Printing and Graphic Arts, Houghton Library, Harvard College Library.

the city once was. Its decline, I suppose, can easily be accounted for by the diminution of that spirit of enterprize, that persecuting bigotry of its monks and inquisitors which check all enquiry, and the amazing superiority of the British. Its inhabitants are numbered at 20,000, few native Portuguese principally Mestizos. The natives are jet black handsomely featured. Pagans of different nations make up the remainder. The men are represented as proud, jealous and lazy revengeful and poor enough. The women lascivious and skilled in [poisoning?]. Their morals are represented as extremely corrupt.

General Albuquerque gained this important place for the Portuguese. On that occasion he showed great magnanimity—a leading trait in his character—Idalcan [fig. 10.12],[36] its governor, having been dispossessed of his city while [absent?],

marched against Goa with great expedition, obliged Albuquerque to take to his ships. Suffering from the want of provisions he was obliged to send to Cochin for a reinforcement. Idalcan with a native nobleness, which would add a luster to civilized monarchs of later days, offered him assistance in provisions and water, saying he chose to conquer by arms and not by famine. The General refused, saying he could receive no presents from his enemies. He succeeded finally in reducing it. He died in 1515 aged 63. He is represented as just, generous, temperate, and exemplary in private life while his patriotism led him to the love of conquest for the glory of his country. Lat obsd 15° 40' Long. 73° 10' E. . . .

[*Entries for February 10 and 11 omitted*]

12th Moderate enough. Don't know when we shall get to Bombay at this rate. At noon the boat from the *Bombay Merchant*. Came on board. Wanted gunpowder. His conduct to obtain was pitiful. He left Calcutta Jany 4, bound to Muscat [in Oman] and Bassora [Basra, in Iraq]. Informed us that the *Union Cadmus* and *Columbus* were at Calcutta. I hope for the honor of the English flag this man's conduct is not a specimen of their dealings. Remember not to forget to remember his Cooley Rice and Ram Muttar. The strange ship near us must be a Portuguese frigate out of Goa, I suspect, as he is very large and showed his Portuguese flag (and we understood there is one there at anchor when we passed). 2 p.m. should be in next day. Spoke a coaster brig from Bombay informed us the *Malabar* was there. Passed 3 or 4 places of little note [see fig. 10.8]. Lat obsd 17° 02' Long 73° East per chart.

Feby 16th. Moderate. 6 ships in sight. 2:30 p.m. I discovered Coulaba [Kolaba] and Henery and Kenery Islands[37] from F. T. [foretop] yard. 4 pm saw Bombay lighthouse bearing NNE. 7:30 it bore N.E. b[y] E ½ E. 8 miles distant. In running in passed a line of fish stakes 15 ft above the waters edge. Let go kedge [small anchor] for the night. At 8 a.m. got underway. 11:45 H[onourable] C[ompany] Pilot Mr. Greenaway came on board. Stood into the roads. 4 pm anchored.

After a passage of 160 days. Went on shore with R.S.R. Took lodgings with Capt Orne and son[38] in Military Square (ye gods what a square). Visited our merchants Nasserwanjee (Nowrajee and Jahangheer).[39]

17th Stripping ship.

21 Discharging cargo. Arrived *Exeter*, *Lancer*, *Salem*, and *Falcon*, Fairfield Boston.

22 Visited Elephanta.

24 Arrived ship *Saco*, Beckford from Boston. Missionaries on board.

26 Heavy showers.

March 2nd Arrived ship *Horatio* of New York, from Batavia, Bunker master, late Bayley. Had lost captain, 2nd officer and several men. Very sickly at Batavia. Markets dull.

5th Ships copper found to be so bad determined to dock her.

7th Unmoored and stood for Mazagaon [Maheshagrama] Dock, [carries?] to ¾ miles distant and anchored to wait tides. Arrived

Fig. 10.12 *Idalcansi, Re di Guȝarata o Cambaia, Spain,* c. 1790. Engraving, 24.1 x 19.1 cm; Peabody Essex Museum M17697, Gift of John Dominis Holt and Frances Damon Holt, 1978.

Atlas, [*Gisdow?*], from Philadelphia. Last from Sumatra where she got no pepper.

23rd Docked ship. Began to strip off old copper, etc. etc. April 5th Ship finished left dock for Bombay.

8th Began to take in cotton. *Malabar* sailed. (and on 11th the *Horatio*)

19th Sailed *Exeter* and *Falcon*.

22nd Ship full.

Saturday 25th 11 a.m. Pilot Mr. Trotter came on board unmoored. ½ past 2 pm got under weigh and stood out of the roads. 4.30 Pilot left us.

Vide Page—[*A place is left to indicate the number of the page where the voyage continues. At this point Rogers, at sea once again, recounts his experiences at and impressions of Bombay.*]

Fig. 10.13 *Bombay Harbour*, published by John Murray, London, 1786. Engraving, 12.7 x 20.3 cm; Peabody Essex Museum M15599.

BOMBAY

After being at sea 160 days and experiencing every vexation from wind and weather, added to the privations ever attendant on so long a passage, we arrived on the 16th at Bombay where we immediately went on shore, accompanied by Mr. [Josiah] Orne and 2 *dubashes* [fig. 10.13]. We landed at the Custom House Bundar [quay], which is a stone mole[40] projecting about 600 feet—very convenient for landing goods from boats and small craft. Here I was, the moment I landed thrust into a palanquin and carried off to our merchants house whose names were Nowrajee and Jahangheer Nasserwanjee.

In passing from the bundar I was, as may be easily imagined, forcibly struck by the appearance of everything around me. A stranger, the first moment he sees an <u>Indian city</u> is probably more astonished, his curiosity more awakened, perhaps delighted, than it can be in visiting the first European cities.

Although the latter may be decorated with more superb palaces and public buildings, although you find in them much more refinement and luxury, yet they cannot in my opinion excite half the emotion that you feel on first seeing the former. To be placed instantaneously in a crowded city, its houses of a style totally different from any we ever have seen, streets thronged with every cast and kind from the pale European resident to the jet Black Kauffree / Caffie.[41] Thousands of men and women almost naked, others though dressed yet so singularly as to <u>exact</u> attention, from the turban'd Turk to the "sans culottes" coolee—in fact English, Americans, French and Portuguese, Armenians and Jews, Parsees, Gentoos and Mahommedans, each wearing the costume of his nation, displaying its peculiar manners. All this must not only excite our wonder, but raise our admiration at the effect produced by civilization on such an heterogeneous mass composing its population. I am sure that when I entered the city of Paris, so famed for wonders my curiosity was by no means so raised as at Bombay.

While there, about 2 weeks, 10 days, I took occasion to see all that was curious, either as regards the natural curiosities in the neighborhood of the Island, but also endeavored to inform myself as much as possible of the manners, customs and religions of each cast. In so short a time it cannot be expected a person engaged in mercantile pursuits could become thoroughly acquainted with every singularity in the customs of the natives, but what I had an opportunity of seeing I think worth writing for my own future amusement, though to any one else it may appear dull and uninteresting.

BOMBAY called by the natives Moombaee, is an island about 8 miles long and 3 broad and 20 in circumference, in the lat 18° 50' n and 72° 38' east longitude. The entrance to its harbor is easily known by 2 islands Henery and Kenery lying very near it. [*In margin*] There is a handsome lighthouse on old woman's or Coulaba Island. It is 130 ft above the level of the sea. It looks very handsomely on entering the harbor.

In the south west monsoon however, in thick weather, vessels are often obliged to lay off and on several days before they can get in. Great care should be taken not to mistake a bay formed by Malabar Point and Bombay Island called Back Bay for the entrance to the harbor. It is full of rocks and shoals. You can ride with 1000 ships at your anchor in the N E monsoon but in the S.W. a very heavy sea sets in.

The soil of the island is of a reddish color, not very rich though by proper care and daily irrigations, many fruits are raised and some excellent vegetables. It was the dry season when I was in Bombay and there was but one shower for more than four months. This gave the paddy fields and country generally a very parched appearance. Every house has one or more tanks where people are constantly employed watering the grounds. They depend however principally on Salsette for supplies of vegetables etc. Beef, poultry of all sorts, and mutton are plenty and at reasonable prices. Fish are scarce. Mangoes, limes oranges, guavas etc. and excellent grapes are in abundance.

The population is 200,000 on the Island, about 20,000 inside the fort. The rest, principally natives and Pariah Portu-guese[42] live at Black Town, Dungaree, [?], Maheem [Mahim] and Mazagaon. The population in these places is immensely crowded, settlements being made where water is found plenty.

The climate of Bombay is considered very healthy. In the N E monsoon the weather is delightful, especially in December, January, February and March. Then the weather is cool, the sky without a cloud. Regular sea breezes refresh the heat of the day. It requires the rich fancy of Moore[43] to express in words the beauty of the climate. Ships navigating the coast have no fears of squalls or storms. A perpetual serenity of the heavens being the constant appearance. I think, however, owing to the privation of rain and the reflection of the sun on the sands causing great dryness in the air, that the climate must be unfavorable to pulmonary complaints and I observed that coughs were very general. In the rainy season, fevers and liver complaints are frequent as is always the case in India.

Of the city (commonly called the Fort) [it] is surrounded by walls, covered with heavy cannon, I should say 400, commanding access to it in every possible point. It has very fine fosses [canals or moats], well watered. Many of the cannon are in the embrasures of the walls, but the long and uninterrupted possession of the English has suffered the wall in many places to fall and the gun carriages are most of them unfit for service.

The city guard was composed of Portuguese (halfcast) and sepoys—the latter are very fine looking troops, with red coats and short drawers, white reaching half way down the thigh edged with blue, the rest of the leg bare. In line they are beautiful looking troops. I was told they fought extremely well of late. They are drilled by native officers who for some exploit[s] are pensioned and commissioned, but when commissioned English policy will not allow them to enter into actual service. English tactics and drill are used altogether here.

There are three gates: Apollo, Church and Bazar gates, beside two leading through the Custom House to the bundar. These have regular draw bridges and [are] always guarded. No natives are allowed to come in after dark without [a] pass. To Europeans a free pass is always given. The houses are stone covered with choonam [lime], perfectly smooth. The roofs are tiled. The houses have no fire place or chimneys. They have, most of them, verandas. Their internal construction though airy

VIEW OF BOMBAY GREEN.

Fig. 10.14 *View of Bombay Green*, engraved by Charles Heath, 1812, after a 1768 drawing by James Forbes. Engraving, 22.9 x 30.5 cm; Courtesy of the Department of Printing and Graphic Arts, Houghton Library, Harvard College Library.

would but little suit our ideas of cleanliness or convenience. In Bombay they are very close together, so much so that no air circulates in the lower floors.

The streets are very narrow, hard, level and very dirty. The streets are all provided with drains to conduct off the water in the rainy season. In the middle of the city is the green [fig. 10.14], a large open space, covered with every kind of merchandize. You will see here piles of cotton bales, pepper, coffee etc. etc. from 50 to 80 feet high. The public buildings are few. An English (formerly a Portuguese) church is worthy of notice having in the interior some handsome monuments. One of Capt Hardinge, of the Eng. frigate which took the *Piedmontaise*, is beautiful and would not disgrace the walls of Westminster Abbey. The interior of the church is much better than its exterior in appearance. I

attended service but they had such a stupid fellow to preach I did not go but twice. His manner was intolerably unintelligible. His matter—I do not [know?] what as I did not understand him. He was a young man. His colleague read finely, but preached seldom being too old and of ill health at that time.

The Armenians have a church to which I went. It had the appearance of a Catholic church but rather more gewgaw finery. The Portuguese have likewise a church, the Jews a synagogue, the Parsees a temple within the walls. A Scotch Presbyterian church is building which I think will be a handsome edifice. The courthouse is [an] old heavy building, very uncouth. The Governor's house has quite an air of state about it although not very handsome. The Custom House is a large building of common construction.

The screw houses are very large. Here you will see 60 men entirely naked working at an enormous capstan through which the screw passes, screwing cotton. With this enormous power they can raise 1000 tons. Cotton is screwed to the density of wood. A man of feeling can not view this operation without shuddering. I am told they frequently fall dead either from suffocation by the cotton dust, or by the heat. Their pay is about 14 cents per diem. Thousands, however get their daily sustenance by this excessively laborious life. I think steam might be substituted for manual labor and save man this servile degradation and humanity its feelings. They appear however happy and contented.

There are some fine shops here belonging to Europeans. The native bazaar is crowded with shops stuffed full of everything, chiefly kept by Mahommedans and Parsees. Their rule is to ask three times more for an article than they intend taking. This I found invariably a specimen of their honor.

Bombay dock is worthy of notice. There are four docks having two entrances, one large enough for a ship of the line, two for frigates, and one for a sloop of war. Here are built some of the most elegant ships that float the ocean, durable and strong. Fine models and good sailors. They are built of teak wood.

We spoke on the coast bound down, the *Meriden*, 74, bound to Bombay where she was built some 40 years ago. The head builder is Jamsetjee Bomanjee, an old Parsee, of a princely fortune and of the first Parsee family. He is haughty and domineers over the officers of country ships in a lordly style. He is said however to be very shrewd, a capital draftsman and a man of great impartiality. In all Parsee disputes when left to arbitration, which is always the case when both parties are Parsees, he is umpire and woe to the Parsee who should appeal from his award to an English court of justice. He would be out cast and persecuted forever. He generally gives satisfaction however. He is brother of Hermojee or Homanjee Bomanjee of the house of Forbes and Co.

Homanjee is very rich and as haughty as a Persian satrap. Lowjee Castle, which I visited, belongs to him. It is a very large wooden building 3 stories high in the European style. Its entrance is rather imposing. By the door opening to the lower hall are two sepoys cut out of board, painted in the true Lord Dexter style.[44] Indeed if Homanjee had not been so old I should become a believer in the transmigration of souls and persuade myself that his lordship's soul had flown to eastern lands to display the wonders it created on the banks of the Merrimac. There were two immense halls hung round with cheap looking glasses and tawdry pictures which were allowed to ornament the walls of this castle rather from the gold leaf on them than from their worth—generally being nothing but old likeness engravings, sometimes three or four of the same man. In the dancing hall was an orchestra at one end. At the other end red velvet cushions or divans. Here were two lustres [chandeliers] of superb workmanship, richly gilt with as elegant cutglass as I have seen. They were presented to the owner of this place by a party of English merchants who had traded with him very considerably. They were exhibited sometime in London, before they were sent out to Bombay. Cost it is said 1500 Pounds sterling. They were in [the] form of the Roman tripod.

In the larger hall it was that Charles Forbes, known by the name of Prince Charles (now M.P.) gave his balls in opposition to the governor. Homanjee has sons who are likely men. Pertanjee, another brother died three or four years since. He was the richest of the family—owned an immensely valuable landed estate which brought in a very great income. Ruttanjee, another brother is very rich. I mention these men as they are well known in London among the East India merchants and are the first Parsees in the place.

There is a theater at Bombay. The thespian corps is composed of <u>amateurs</u> of the navy, army and company's servants.

Just outside the walls is a large open space of ground called by way of eminence, esplanade. It is rather a shabby place. Here however every evening the *ton* [smart set] of the city show out in carriages and palankeens [palanquins] etc., principally however pedestrians. The equipages of the first inhabitants were rather mean in their appearance. Their horses for speed and points of beauty, though not large, are the finest in the world, being full blooded Arabs. They are extremely well broken and travel very steadily. The natives use them in a little open carriage with very low wheels and drive at a furious rate. They also use what is called a hakray, a little square carriage with a pair of buffalo cows guided by a thong through the nose. They travel very fast. Few natives use palankeens.

Fig. 10.15 *Dancing Snake and Musicians*, engraved by T. Wageman, 1834, after an 1807 drawing by Baron de Montalbert.
Engraving, 22.9 x 30.5 cm; Courtesy of the Department of Printing and Graphic Arts, Houghton Library,
Harvard College Library.

The streets of Bombay are filled with beggars, the most deplorable objects, victims of vice, or wretched survivors of some dreadful accidents or loathsome disease. Sunday is the day they are the most importunate [i.e., demanding]. Their small means of getting any medical assistance gives disease completely an opportunity to show itself in its worst forms.

Jugglers and strolling troubadours are ever to be found. Those who exhibit serpents are very expert [fig. 10.15]. I [saw] one fellow who had a <u>cobra capella</u> ten feet long as big as a man's arm. It was a horrible looking creature. When angry opened its hood and showed great spite, but the sound of his masters lute soon quieted it and rendered it harmless. They pretend its teeth are not extracted, but I know there are none to be seen in the jaws as I persuaded one fellow for a few pice[45] to open it. Dancing bears, monkey[s] and goats generally accompany these fellows.

<u>Dancing girls</u> are very numerous, mostly Moors. They are not handsome, dress very tawdrily, are generally no better than they should be and very fond of money. They are the indispensable part of a <u>nautch</u> or native high-go [drinking spree], dinner or any other party, which the Parsees are very fond of. They have generally two or three [?] men in company. All the guests give them money and they often get very large sums in a night.

The inhabitants of Bombay are English, native Portuguese, half-blooded Portuguese, Armenians, Arab Jews, Mahommeddans, Parsees and Hindoos, some straggling Malays and Chinese. Of these I acquired some interesting facts with regard to their situations, manners and customs, religions etc.

The English are almost all Company servants. <u>Sir Evan Nepean</u> was Governor and General Nightingale Commander-in-Chief. The governor is not very popular, being <u>Parsimon-</u>

Fig. 10.16 *A Mahomedan of Distinction, with a Dervise on his Pilgramage*, engraved by T. Wageman, 1834, after a 1768 drawing by James Forbes. Engraving, 30.5 x 22.9 cm; Courtesy of the Department of Printing and Graphic Arts, Houghton Library, Harvard College Library.

ious (formerly purser in H.M. Navy) and not very fond of shew [show] and parade. (N.B. I saw him at church on Easter Sunday.) Sir R. Austerether [Anstruther] was Recorder. There are a few lawyers here of no great eminence I suspect but by repute great extortioners. There was a little hut called Court of Small Requests, in Military Square, where there was such a "hubbery" and fighting continually that out of curiosity I went in. The sitting justice appeared about 23, each litigant told his story. Hindoos being sworn in by the water of the Ganges and the Parsees by a priest who repeated some passage from their sacred books. After their evidence was finished, he decided the case and they had the liberty of appeal. He was quite civil and was himself highly entertained by their whimsical gestures and apparent madness.

The English here hold the first offices in all the departments. Native Portuguese however (Mr. Newton, e.g.) hold lucrative offices. The half-blood Portuguese are the most miserable, half starved looking objects I ever saw. They are mostly mechanics. The Armenians are a singular race. They are nearly white, wear mustachios, a very singular velvet (black) cap cut in peaks, [resembling?] at a little distance a chapeau de bras. They either dress in white cotton trousers with shirt outside (in appearance) and black sash round the waist or in European coat and pantaloons always retaining however the cap and outside apron in front. They are a money getting, generally rich very quiet class of men. The women are a pale white, rather handsome. Their dress is rich and fanciful. They wear a square cap covered with golden ornaments with a veil gold-sprigged hung easily behind the head half length down. They are very domestic and modest as I understood.

The Jews are from Arabia and the neighborhood of the Persian Gulf. They are generally rich, wear camels hair shawl turbans, long surtouts [robes]. They have the real Jew physiognomy. They black their eyelids with the mixture I suspect that is mentioned in the Old Testament. Their women when passing are entirely covered by a cloth so you cannot see their faces. I lived in the neighborhood of two or three families during the festival of the new moon, a circumcision, or any such merry making matter, they kept up all night and continual howlings singing, and praying, not much to their own edification or our comfort. They wear a string of beads which they are always fingering when making bargains.

Moormen or Mahometans [Muhammadans] are numerous [fig. 10.16]. They are shopkeepers and watermen—very clever at bargains. Zealous Moslemites—you will see them on the esplanade at sunset performing their religious prostrations and praying very earnestly. Some are very handsome men and quite well informed and communicative. One with whom I conversed made no hesitation of conversing of his prophet and expressed his opinions of Jesus Christ whom he considered as a very great man, endowed with supernatural powers and of vast capacity of mind as regards the knowledge of mankind, but by no means the messiah. It was on the humble, forgiving and philanthropic Mahomet [Muhammad], this honor was conferred. I never saw a Mahommedan woman.

The Parsees [fig. 10.17], who rank next to the English in point of intelligence and respectability, are a race of men sui generis, entirely distinct from every other on the face of the earth, I believe. Of their history and the course of their settlement in India I obtained some information. (To Shapoorjee Soorabjee I am principally indebted for verbal account of his cast and their emigration.) The account he gave me is much the same as that given by the dastoors [dasturs], or doctors of civil and ecclesiastical law. It is as follows.

After the promulgation of the Mahomedan religion in Arabia, and its subsequent diffusion in Persia, the ancestors of these Indo-Parsees, retired to the mountains and lived in exile until the overthrow of the Persian monarchy in the death of Yezdeguid.[46] Despairing of ever again returning to their homes or enjoying their religion and tired of exile, they wandered towards the port of Hormuz or Ormuz,[47] governed at that time by a descendant of the Persian royal family. After 15 years tarry here and gaining a little knowledge of ship building and navigation, they quitted Ormuz and sailed for Dieu or Diu another Island on the north side of the entrance of the Gulph of Cambay. Here they stayed 19 years, but being disgusted for some cause, not probably affording sufficient field for their industrious habits, the greater part left it and came to Seyjan (Commonly called St. John) on the Guzeratte [Gujarat] coast, a place from [which] a Rajah, who then possessed considerable power took his title.[48] After some little hesitation, he allowed some of the crew to land selecting the most intelligent. Those who understood business and were acquainted with the Persian religious and civil institutions were conducted to him. The Rajah questioned them very particularly of their history, etc. They answered in the Sanskrit in 15 verses which detailed their faith and customs. They pleased the mind of the Rajah and he answered them in another verse, making 16, which are all carefully preserved by the dustoors [dasturs, priests] in a little book.

After stipulating that they should disarm and wear the Indian dress (then wearing the Persian) that they should abstain from eating cows' flesh or rabbit, that they should be publicly married and use the native Guzerattee [Gujarati] language, he suffered them to land.

After some hundred years, they lighted up an Atish Beharain or sacred fire.[49] Growing discontented some again emigrated to Nowsaree, Veirow, Occlicar,[50] Broach and Cambay. Their establishments at Surat and Bombay are of later date. And the exercise of conscience and the liberty [of] worshipping according to their own ideas has tended greatly to promote their increase.

PARSEES at BOMBAY.
Jam. Forbes 1769.

Fig. 10.17 *Parsees at Bombay*, engraved by T. Wageman, 1834, after a 1769 drawing by James Forbes.
Engraving, 30.5 x 22.9 cm; Courtesy of the Department of Printing and Graphic Arts, Houghton Library,
Harvard College Library.

At Seyjan when the Rajah was threatened by Mahmood Begra, Prince of Ahmedabad, they fought (1400 in all) with great fury for their protectors and defeated the invader, but a numerous army returned and subdued them in turn and compelled them to pay tribute. Since that time they have lived on the west coast of India, the Parsee men sometimes going voyage to China as agents and sometimes to Europe. The Parsee females never quit settlements where there are priests and holy fires etc.

The following is the translation of the fifteen verses from the Sanskrit which was spoken by them on their visiting the Rajah and the 16th is his answer and solemn invocation for their prosperity, etc. [*Passage omitted*]

The Parsees do not practice inhumation; their burial places have divisions into which families place their deceased relatives, exposed to the sun. Here they rest till the sun and air has completely destroyed the flesh etc. and then the bones are thrown into an ossuary in the middle of each division. None but priests and two men provided expressly are allowed to enter the walls of their cemetery. One custom of which I was well informed by themselves as being a fact—I learnt that a few minutes before a dying friend leaves the world, he is taken from the bed, laid on the bare floor and suffered to die alone as no one dare touch him and should any touch the clothes of the dead, his clothes would be destroyed and his person must undergo a purification. This unfeelingness to the dearest of our friends in a dying hour is horrible.

The dead are placed on a bier as soon as the breath is out of the body (if sunshine) and a dog set to watch it to guard it and to keep off the spirits of the air, of the existence of which they are firm believers. They have the greatest aversion and express great horror at the idea of handling a dead dog or crow or even the dearest of their friends.

Their women are very modest and chaste, always covered. They are domestic and sensible. The cast is divided into mobids [mubid, priests] and behdeen [behdin, laymen]. The former are the priests' order and the latter the laity. A mobid man may marry a behdeen female, but not vice versa. They admit converts into their cast. They betroth their children at 3 or 4 years of age. Widowers must marry widows. A woman under 40 years may marry again. They marry with public solemnization between 4 and 9 years of age. Our merchants had a boy and a girl both married, about 7 years old.

They pay very little attention to literature. Some pretend to a knowledge of Sanskrit, but money making absorbs every other inclination and closes every avenue to mental improve[ment].

Molna Ferozh is the most learned of the Parsees and their high priest.[51] He has a great revenue—every Parsee on the death of a friend or relation making him valuable presents. Many of the poorer people take up money on interest to give to the priests.

Most strangers are pleased with their characters, but I found too much dishonesty in the reputed intelligence in business, too much self interest in their good nature and too much licentiousness in their private characters, to entitle them to indiscriminate confidence. The poor are thievish to an extreme. The[y] give suppers, drink Parsee brandy and wine in abundance. I was at one at our merchants' country seat. There were 40 or 50 at table and they sat till broad day light. There was a procession of food and wines and great hospitality. Our merchants gave the Americans and French assigned to them a grand

nautch—equal to a 4th July dinner, and something like it. They have a very fine country house with fine gardens and tank.

Our merchants were the sons of Nasserwanjee Monackjee [Nusserwanjee Maneckjee Wadia] a man who sustained a most estimable character [see fig. 4.4]. He did all the American business at Bombay. His sons are his successors in the establishment and bid fair to get all the American business. They are clever and honest. But the natives have none [of] that method which is necessary in transacting business. Their names were Nowrojee and Jahanjhier Nasserwanjee. The Parsee son always takes the given name of his father for a surname. Their boys have a very serious, sedate air and look nearly as old as their fathers. They begin the art of bargaining as soon as they quit the cradle almost.

In their religion there are certainly many points of faith which inculcate the purest doctrines of benevolence and very many practice the most extensive charity. Their idea of the supreme being is very definite and they worship with apparent zeal and sincerity. You will see hundreds of them worshipping at the setting of the sun on the esplanade and by the sea shore. They believe in aerial spirits and believe dogs can see them and that their howling indicates their approach.

Their houses are not cleanly generally suffering dogs and goats, crows and kites, etc. etc. to prowl about in every direction. There are vast many dogs belonging to them in Bombay although in April annually hundreds are killed off by order of government.

The Hindoos, native inhabitants of the country, are next worthy of being mentioned. They are by far the most numerous being 9/10ths of the inhabitants of the Island. They are composed of Bra[h]mins, Banians, shopkeepers and mechanics, watermen and cooleys. Their history is too well known for me to attempt to give it. They are here Maharattahs [Marathas], very warlike and high spirited and differ essentially in their physical organization from those who inhabit the banks of the Ganges.

There are many of them employed in the Company's service as writers, called Purvoos.[52] They write English very well and are generally sensible men. Their religion is the most disgusting and at the same time the most degrading to the human mind that can be imagined. It unites every thing frivolous and horrible, childish and cruel, with the most disgusting lewdness and superstitious bigotry. It is near the temples dedicated to Maha Deva or Maha Deo that you will behold objects and witness scenes which degrades below the most abject of creation, that lofty supremacy of mind, which entitles man to that rank his God assigned him and makes us shudder with the idea that man endowed with reason and blessed with the prospect of immortality should so sport with his hopes and make a ship wreck of every quality of goodness and religion.

I was at Bombay during the Huli or Hooley festival, which takes place in the month of March about the full of the moon.[53] It is at these celebrations they perform such tricks before high heaven as would make angels weep. It begins by the suspension of all business and every occupation; everything gives way to debauchery and drunkenness. They build large fires in the streets (and some I saw in the Fort of Bombay) of their towns into which they throw some offering either sandal wood or coconuts and the oil and flowers. They howl and dance round them repeating the most obscene expressions accompanied with the lewdest gestures. Their fires are very large and have sometimes destroyed whole villages.

Their origin is founded on the following fact according to tradition. Ibrahim (Abraham) had a most lovely daughter who was beloved by [a] chief of another cast, thought inferior to her own and her friends did all in their power to prevent the connexion, but he carried her away finally by stratagem, aided by her own love for him. Her tribe watched an opportunity and got possession of her person. To gratify their revenge they sacrificed her on the funeral pile. After the flames had ascended in every direction and they expected the object of their malice had been consumed, they were struck with astonishment and horror to behold her more beautiful then ever, sitting unhurt amidst the flames. She then ascended in a cloud to heaven. They became struck with remorse at their cruelty and to appease her injured husband whom they had excited to war against them and to immortalize her name, they instituted this festival. They even to this day throw images of females into the fire. This is the story—how much grounds for belief of its traditional truth I know not.

About 2 miles from Bombay are many temples, but one in particular which I visited during the days and nights of the festival, I mention particularly. It was a very large temple dedicated to Maha Deo in front of a very large tank—finely stoned and filled with water. It covered an area of 800 feet square. Its water was dirty stagnant, indeed had a most offensive stench, yet they wash in it, from religious notions of its efficacy. Round its banks are thousands constantly praying.

The temple is a long building with 3 outer apartments each provided with a recess behind. It has a long veranda in front, under which are three images of most horribly grotesque appearance. Their countenances are besmeared with oil and red paint. These are the images of two dogs in stone which they worship, expressing great terror. Numerous bells are constantly ringing, tom-toms (a kind of drum) beating, which together with the scenery, their fires, howling and singing, almost tempted me to believe myself at the portals of the infernal regions. Indeed a heathen poet might have found ample materièl and abundance of dramatis personae for a representation of Hades.

They use in their rites a red or [cake?] colored powder which [they] throw over each other and which gives them a most singular appearance. By throwing it on a stone or piece of wood, the substance becomes a deity and they fall down and worship it.

The women are as lewd as the men. One custom of which I was an eyewitness would have disgraced the most debauched devotees of the Roman P. . . . s.[54] After 3 days spent in this round of drunkenness, debauching and bonfires and processions etc. etc., exhausted nature gives way and they end the whole by a grand feast.

Round the temple of Mahadeo, are many devotees. I saw one measuring his distance from the temple by prostrations, lay flat and reaching out with his hands. Then rising and prostrating again. So doing for a half mile. One was a good natured crazy fellow who set upon a stone in a particular posture many years. Another was sitting before a very hot fire, under a burning sun, throwing ashes on himself. A third had held his left arm up perpendicularly so many years that it had withered and was immoveable. His hand was clenched and the fingers were like horn. His nails 2 inches in length and grew into the hand. One at a temple at Malabar point had held his hands clasped together till the nails had perforated the hand.

This is a faint picture of the reality. No words of detestation can express any impression at beholding these objects. Yet they are tolerated. And in all their ceremonies never interrupted by the English. A shrewd Parsee told me it was good policy in them to keep in the dark this vast portion of the population. With a little information they have sense and courage enough to become troublesome subjects.

They do not bury their dead, but being remote from the Ganges they burn them all on the seashore just after dark. I once witnessed (with McGalway of the *Horatio*)[55] a scene which would have made Ann Radcliffe[56] stark mad with delight, it was so horribly interesting. On the sea shore of Back Bay we were just returning from a ride, when the horses being tired, we gave rein to the servant and walked ahead. It was not midnight, but the time answered very well, it being quite dark except when the half formed moon just showed her silver light in fitful gleams thru' apertures in the nubilous drapery which over spread the circumambient canopy of heaven!!!! It served but to render more beautifully horrible the surrounding scenery.

Before us lay the guarded ramparts of the Fort. The echo of the sentinel's challenge on the drawbridge would (if his voice could have been heard a mile or two farther) have struck the ear like the solemn warning of some ghostly seer. On our right was the roaring and rushing like the noise of distant cataracts, of the waters of Back Bay, over its sepulchral shoals and rocks. On our left three cemeteries crowded the poor remains of what once was life, served to enrich the scene, and give it that unity always requisite to a finished piece.

Behind a scene far more distressing. It is [sic] very sight made my poor feet ache worse than the Pilgrim who travelled to Loretto with peas in his shoes—it was—our horse and buggy stuck fast in the sand. By a due application of the os. humerii to [the] axis we cleared it from its immersion and moved on to a light a few paces ahead. Here was before us jet black Bra[h]mins dressed in white robes, muttering prayers (perhaps enchantment no knowing, gentle reader) over the crisped body of some poor Gentoo. Round them were several other corpses to be burnt when their turn came. As we advanced they ceased their prayers and viewing us with a fixed stare, seemed to be brooding some diabolical scheme of mischief to reward our intrusion

and punish our curiosity. As we advanced toward the burning pile and McG's boldness leaning him to approximate too near the sacred wood, judge our sensations, when our minds must have been so wrought up by the scene of horror and our imagination bewitched by the ideas produced by them; judge our surprise to hear ourselves addressed in perfectly good English, "We are glad to see you gentlemen, but don't touch the wood." There was a transition for you from sublime to bathos, from perturbation to quiet that would have honored the versatile talents of Whitefield.[57]

After seeing 2 burnt we went homeward. I have seen a funeral procession with the corpse on a bier carried with flowers, some with roses in their mouths and even the cheeks painted—the whole preceded by men playing on tom toms and carrying old flags and every species of fine raggery they could pick up. Their marriages are performed in public with processions, etc.

Their dress is extremely simple generally turban, jacket, and waistcloth being their whole wardrobe. The cooleys or koolees [laborers] are nearly naked having only a cloth six inches wide round the middle; but what is a little singular you will often see round the arms and ankles and waist of both men and women of the poorest cast, solid silver chains and sometimes gold. These are preserved with religious care, being heirlooms I suppose, although the wearer be naked and half starved.

The women have a shawl around the waist, a kind of stays to support the breasts, nearly naked—large gold ring in the left nostril. They carry heavy burdens on the head. They are however generally very chaste. The men carry very heavy burdens.

The palankeen bearers are generally strong and healthy but [be]come stiff in the joints from the speed with which they travel. It is impossible for an European or American to endure the sun. Palankeens are absolutely indispensable to preserve the health. It is however very disagreeable to hear them pant when on the way. You have a mussaul[58] boy who carries the chittery or umbrella.

On the whole, taking in view every point of character as far as belongs to Bombay and its environs, I think the Hindoos a low, cheating, brutal race, but a short remove from the brute creatures. I hope however the day is yet soon to arrive when

Fig. 10.18 *Part of the Interior of the Elephanta*, drawn and engraved by Thomas and William Daniell, 1800.
Hand-colored aquatint, 48.2 x 64.8 cm; Peabody Essex Museum M17860, Gift of John Dominis Holt and Frances Damon Holt, 1978.

the example of Christians, influenced only [in] their conduct by the principles of the religion they profess, this advancement in the arts of life and its comforts, will induce these deluded and degraded people to embrace the Doctrine which, insures the pleasures of this life and the immortal honors of the next. It is only by example that conversion can be here effected. By exhibiting the superiority of our advantages, by instilling the gentleness, the principles of Christian morality and by showing how happily and usefully we can live among each other and presenting to their native enthusiasm of mind, pictures of real happiness, the effect of our love for each other, by using such means the Christian world may soon boast of an addition of millions.

But such are not the examples set them by the English in India, (I will not single out the English; it has been the case throughout the world). Rapacity, thirst for conquest and the worst evils of war have followed their entrance into their settlements. Their public officers have been tyrants, their individuals extortioners. They have overrun the peninsula of Hindoostan and extermination has been the order of the day until an offending Rajah, who dared to assert his rights to independence and the government of his territories, should suffer captivity and dethronement. The English, unable to force their officers to a general battle, have carried on a war of [?], harassing the unoffending and innocent, and on the other hand, the natives pushed to extremity and infuriated with despair have burnt their towns and put to the sword the inhabitants, to prevent them assisting the British or to reward them for having consented to become subjects to them. Yet the day will come "decreed by Fate" when these enormities shall be revenged with tenfold vengeance on the heads of their oppressors. That there are humane and honorable men among the English officers it were absurd to deny, but I have understood, and I believe it, that they are generally men who cannot get an honest livelihood at home and come out here to seek their fortunes.

At Bombay there were two chiefs who had been, one in close confinement for five years (a [?] and a man of extraordinary courage and ferocity) the other a Mahrattah Nabob, named Ayar who had been in surveillance and his father before him for 20 years. They received per agreement 10,000 Rs per month each when first taken, but the Company have continued reducing their pension till now it is only 2000 per annum. The father died five years since, the son resides in their country seat, which is about four miles from the Fort. He lives, although a state prisoner, a miserably poor life. He formerly never appeared without his guards, but now unable to pay them, he never shows himself. And all this treatment, for what? For nothing but because his father was [an] immensely rich and powerful Nawaub and did not choose to suffer the impositions of these invaders. They built a most beautiful tank by their house. You descend a flight of 100 stone steps of hewn granite at both ends; the sides are perpendicular of the same stone. It has a great deal of water at all times in it. 400 ft. long and 250 feet broad.

Soon after my arrival at Bombay I visited with some friends the cavern at Elephanta, which has so justly excited the curiosity of every visitant at Bombay. We started in the morning at an early hour and after about four miles row landed at Butchers Island, about half way; it is a very pretty place, with barracks used as a depot for men who are out of service, while a man-of-war is in dock, etc. There is a most remarkable banyan tree here whose [fibrils?] have grown and spread at a great distance so that some are as large as the parent tree which is at least thirty feet in diameter. We left this place and pursued our route to the island, soon landed. The natives came off and carried us on their shoulders to land. We ascended a very steep hill and came to the entrance of the cave in front of which a gate is erected to prevent the entrance of any one without leave from the serjeant. Indeed such has been the mutilations committed here on the figures that the regulations at Bombay require a pass; but we supplied its want by the offering of some liquor etc. which soon opened his gates and drowned his wits. He was so glad to get brandy, that we got little local information from him although he had lived here 25 years. He had a very neat little house here and appeared quite happy.

On first entering the cave you are struck with the imposing grandeur created by the extent of the Hall as well as the gigantic magnitude of the figures [fig. 10.18]. In front are four mossy pillars (one much broken by the superstitious Portuguese who, when they first came here, believed it the residence of devils) of bases about ¼ their height square. The body of the pillar round, fluted and exceeding well cut, their capitals well designed overhanging the pillar. Their diameter is about 4 feet. They continue 7 in depth through the hall. At the farther or upper end of the hall you are struck with the profusion of figures cut in high relief, exhibiting as numerous a collection of gods and goddesses, he and she devils, saints and heroes as ever existed in Heathen mythology. They are very naturally carved; their positions easy and majestic, so naturally done are some that I could almost believe the grey rock was alive.

In the centre of all these figures, in a niche with a recess behind it, are the figures of their supreme deity. They are busts of about 18 feet from the crown to the lower part of the breasts—joined in one body below [fig. 10.19]. The middle head is that of <u>Brahma</u>, or the <u>creative</u> attribute of deity, on the left is that of <u>Vishnoo</u> or the <u>preserving</u> and on the right you find that of <u>Siva</u> or the <u>destroying</u>. These are the 3 attributes of their god. <u>Brahma</u>'s face is represented full with a look of dignity and composure. His head and neck covered profusely with ornaments. <u>Vishnoo</u>'s is in profile with a look of kindness and expressing a complacent regard. It is richly decorated. One hand bears a lotus flower, the other a pomegranate. On [one] of his wrists is a ring as worn at the day by the Hindoos. <u>Siva</u>, on the contrary frowns with a terrible countenance in profile, with a projecting forehead, staring eyes and pouting lips firmly closed. Snakes supply the place of hair and a human skull

Interior View of the principal Excavated TEMPLE on the Island of ELEPHANTA.

Fig 10.19 *Interior View of the principal Excavated Temple on the Island of Elephanta*, engraved by J. Greig, 1812,
after a 1771 drawing by James Forbes. Engraving, 22.9 x 30.5 cm; Courtesy of the Department of Printing and Graphic Arts,
Houghton Library, Harvard College Library.

covers his head. One hand grips the head of a monstrous cobra de capella, the other, one of a smaller size. His who[le?] appearance does ample justice to their ideas of him and is calculated to excite terror and amazement. From the crown of the head to the chin is 6 feet, without the cap which is six feet more.

Behind this figure is a hollow recess large enough to contain a person of full size. Its access at first is not seen. It is imagined it was for the purpose of letting some one of the priests in to give the figures the appearance of sending forth voices. On the left of the great hall you find a large open room provided with two recesses whose floors are cut lower than the others. Here are multitudes of figures cut in the walls. I imagine they must have been bathes for those employed in the service of the temple. Over the door leading to it is a well defined Grecian border. On the right is a square closet with four doors detached from the wall, containing nothing but a large square stone—this about 15 feet square and reaches to the roof, the stone inside is 10 feet square, all cut from the solid rock. I think it must be the grave of some saint.

By it in a large niche on the right is a monstrous figure 17 feet high representing power. It has seven arms, some of which, though gigantic and subject to the inconvenience of placing them with ease, would not disgrace the chisel of Canova.[59] One arm particularly, with a drawn sword, was exquisitely cut. By this is [an] open square uncovered leading to an aperture in the ground about ten feet wide and three and a half feet high. Here you find cold and limpid water. Various are the conjectures with regard to this place. Where its out let is, or whence it is supplied with water being at the summit of [a] very high, rocky and dry hill. I got down on my hands and knees and went in five or six feet, but the sergeant cautioned me to go no farther as many who had gone in had never returned. He said the natives believed the devil took them off, but he thought the air was so dead it produced suffocation, or that they might have fallen into the water. He said he had himself sounded in 20 and 35 fathoms of water 15 feet from its mouth when this only a [foot?]. I hallooed very loud and its echoes were reverberated by a thous[and?] different apartments apparently. There is a tradition that a canoe once went in and paddled out the other side of the island. Certain it is, that is a strange looking place, and I think I should be perfectly willing not to proceed farther than ten feet into it.

There are over many of the figures, inscriptions in a language no person has been yet able to understand. This cave was no doubt a place devoted to the religious worship of the Gentoos. Even at these times they visit it in great numbers on certain days of the year. They show great fear and reverence when in it. But their excessive ignorance of history or tradition, prevents any information being derived from them.

There is about ½ mile from the cave the mutilated remains of the stone elephant; its head is broken off, and body much injured. There are on Salsette (about 15 miles from the fort) Island, many caves more spacious than that of Elephanta, but none which will be comparison with it for elegance of design and excellence of workmanship. At Carli [Karli] in the Gaut Mountains is one of a most stupendous magnitude and wonderful execution. All the monuments of the arts seem to prove that at some earlier period than our knowledge of Asia extends, its inhabitants were skilled in the arts and sciences. We have certain proofs of the science of the Arabians and we have seen them dwindle by degrees to ignorance and become degraded to barbarians. The rise and fall of nations, the most interesting subject for the reflection of the historian and philosopher, can be sometimes traced by these remains of ancient greatness.

Their gigantic structures and solid materials seem to bid defiance to the shocks of the natural world and stand on the page of time as marks of the different stages of the civilization and improvement of man. Such are the caverns of Elephanta, Carli and Salsette existing remains of the former grandeur of the eastern world, whose inhabitants at their construction perhaps could boast of as great advancement in refinement as ourselves and who when the continent of Europe, was a host of barbarians, and when America was unknown except to her own savage children, enjoyed the comforts and luxuries of life and derived from the knowledge of the arts and sciences, means to arrive at that height of improve[ment] which introducing luxury produced their decline.

There were at Bombay several American missionaries, among them Mr. Newhall [Newell] the husband of Mrs. H. Newhall [Newell] so famous for her zeal, true or falsely directed I will not say, and for her book. They appeared personally to be sociable when alone, or rather separate from each other, but the appearance of one of the fraternity served to elongate their [phizez?] astonishingly. Mr. Newhall [Newell] had a wife brought out to him in the *Saco*, a Miss Philomela Thurston.[60] This is quite in the Indo-English style, the residents here often sending to England for partners and their friends send them out such as they think would suit best. They are engaged in a translation of the New Testament into Guzerattee. Their wives were pleasant women, well watched by their husbands, who had the reputation of being a little jealous.

They kept schools for the native children, learning them to read the New Testament in Guzerattee, by this means endeavoring to instill into their minds the principles of our faith. But they never have yet made a convert nor will they by the means now used. I think we should do more honor to ourselves and receive greater reward hereafter, should we appropriate the money sent out to India to the purpose of civilization and the promulgation of Christianity among the savages of North America. In the words of Phillips "God bless such itinerant humanity" for it needs a blessing enough.

The small towns on the island are crowded with thousands in little huts covered with mats. They sit in front of them and idle [a]way a greater part of the day. Mazagaon is quite a pretty place being higher land than the rest of the island and many very elegant country seats are on it.

The commercial regulations at Bombay are by no means perplexing to foreigners. You are obliged to take a pilot inward and outward. You are to present your papers to the Custom Master, who sends them to the Gov. You are to make out the manifest of your cargo with a valuation of it <u>on oath</u>, to which valuation they add 60 percent—a custom which must have arisen from the impression that the Government had been defrauded by those who visit the port and to indemnify themselves in future against such frauds they have unjustly and indiscriminately saddled it on everyone who comes here. But Yankees can always take off enough to square the account. On this you pay 4½ percent government duty and an excise or town duty which is on particular articles, and varies in its amount. On liquors it is very high. On cordials I paid 24 Rs per dozen. It almost amounts to a prohibition. However by a little <u>management</u> a man gets along easily. I sent the officer who permits to pass all the merchandize landed, a few cordials, and by some unaccountable mistake, the greater part were entered as cider and so the good people of Bombay got cordials smuggled into them instead of the cider. You must get permits to land and embark every kind of goods, but by <u>management</u> you can get along just as you please.

Mr. Newton, one particular pass officer, was half English and Portuguese. I suspect. He had a chichee [Eurasian] wife. His daughter played very elegantly on the piano. If I go that way again I must remember my <u>promise</u> to carry some new tunes. He was very polite to us and invited us to his house often. He lived very genteelly and comfortably. You generally can get to sea by two days after you are loaded. This detention is necessary for the examination of your papers by the Government.

THE MAHRATTA WAR—[*blank space*]

Your household in Bombay consists of Parsee servants mostly. They are the cook and his mate, pantry man, comprador or market man, body servant, sepoy or porter, 4 hummauls[61] or palankeen bearers and a mussaul or umbrella carrier. So you generally have 8 or 10 servants at your heels. Their pay is small but they expect gratuities when you go, which they call cherry merry. Ships often keep a dingay boat [skiff], it is very convenient being safe and large and saves your own boats which the worms would soon destroy.

I have thus endeavored to give a little sketch of Bombay but I never was so rejoiced as when our ship's topsails loosed to leave a place where no affections bound me, no interest could connect me.

PART IV

THE DOLDRUMS

Fig. 11.1 Joseph Peabody (1757–1844) by Charles Osgood. Oil on canvas, 135.9 x 104.8 cm;
Peabody Essex Museum M369, Gift of George and Francis Peabody, 1848.

CHAPTER II

Decline of the Trade

THE TRADE TRANSFORMED

Many factors contributed to the decline of U.S. trade with India after the War of 1812. First and foremost was peace itself, which deprived Americans of their special position as neutrals in a world at war. Losing the commercial advantage of neutrality was exacerbated in the India trade by new competition from British private merchants, who were permitted by the 1813 East India Company charter to enter the India trade.

At home, a revolution in transportation and manufacturing was transforming the nation's commerce. First canals, then railroads, propelled the consolidation of shipping at strategically located ports. The port of New York grew at such a rate that it soon outstripped other northern ports and became the undisputed center of U.S. foreign trade.[1] Before the War of 1812, New England ports had roughly equaled New York and Philadelphia in customs duties. In 1825, New York's import tax revenues were triple those of Massachusetts and Philadelphia, each bringing $5 to $6 million.[2] In the late 1820s, New York's Erie Canal and the regular service established across the Atlantic consolidated New York's position. By the 1830s, Boston, having taken the lead in the Baltic, Levant, and India trades, remained New York's only serious competition in foreign trade. In these new circumstances, smaller ports like Salem, Providence, and Newburyport were never able to recover from the commercial disruptions brought on by embargo and war.

At the same time that commerce was being transformed by developments in transportation, industry was rapidly expanding. Wartime isolation had stimulated manufacturing, especially the production of staple textiles that had been the heart of the India trade. American industrialists pressed for new tariffs to protect their up-and-coming textile mills from foreign competition. When Congress obligingly enacted a duty on imported textiles in 1816, the increase to the cost of inexpensive Indian cottons succeeded in pricing them out of the market. Industrial production proceeded apace and by the early 1840s, as Henry

Lee had predicted during his wartime sojourn in Calcutta, New England mill-made cottons had not only replaced Indian products on the domestic market, but were fast becoming a viable commodity for export to India. In 1846, for example, more than $5,000 worth of printed cottons were shipped to India in the *Chilo*, William Nott, master and supercargo. As a consummate irony, included in the shipment was a case of imitation Madras handkerchiefs, made in New England mills.[3]

The alteration in both the magnitude and significance of the trade was dramatic. Between 1801 and 1805, the time of Dudley Pickman's voyages to Madras and Calcutta, imports from India averaged $3.5 million out of a total foreign trade of about $75 million (about 5 percent), figures that do not reflect the considerable returns from the carrying trade during the war years.[4] Jacob Crowninshield had written in his 1806 memorandum to James Madison that annually thirty to fifty ships went to Calcutta. Through the 1820s, an average of fourteen ships each year landed there.[5] In the late 1820s, the value of imports from India hovered around a half-million dollars per year, less than one percent of the total. By the time of James B. Briggs' 1832 voyage in the *Apthorp* (chapter 13), East Indian imports had risen to $2.5 million, still only about 2.5 percent of all imports. Through the 1830s and '40s, imports from India continued to fluctuate markedly, between highs of over $3 million in 1837, for example, and lows of little more than half a million in 1838.[6]

Changes in the extent of the trade were accompanied by the transformation of its substance and significance. The 1820s and '30s presented a sharp contrast with the heyday of neutral trade. Industrial production and high tariffs had removed manufactured products—chiefly textiles—from the center of the trade, replacing these with "gruff goods," raw materials—indigo, saltpeter, and hides—intended for American manufactures. Once dominated by admirable and useful cotton and silk goods, the commodities now imported had little Indian identity, and whatever there might have been vanished entirely in the transformation of raw materials into finished goods—dyed textiles, gunpowder, shoes, and boots. Once the preserve of nationally prominent merchants, the India trade progressively became the specialty of New Englanders, operating principally from the port of Boston, whose commercial interests were no longer at the center of the nation's economic and political development.[7]

Changes in U. S. trade with India were part of a worldwide shift. The rapid rise of industrial manufactures in Europe and the United States, supported by protective tariffs, weakened the world market for Indian products. Inexpensive Indian hand-loomed cottons, once a global staple, lost ground to Western manufactures.[8] While the presence of Indian textiles diminished in world markets, their designs and color schemes were copied and adapted. British and French manufacturers had begun to copy dyeing techniques and decorative patterns in the eighteenth century. Industrialization accelerated the process and in the nineteenth century Indian textiles had become thoroughly globalized. Silk bandanna handkerchiefs, for example, a mainstay of Indo-U.S. trade, by the 1830s could be of Indian, British, or Chinese fabric, printed in Bengal, Manchester, or Philadelphia.[9] Fine cottons, muslin or mulmul, though no longer as fashionable as before the War of 1812, were still in demand, though now a specialty of both Scotland and Bengal. A book on haberdashery and hosiery published in 1833 noted that the chief markets for English muslins were America and the West Indies.[10] Kashmir shawls, a luxury accessory for women since the turn of the century, remained so until the 1870s. At a cost of two to three hundred pounds sterling, Indian shawls were the privilege of the well-to-do and were often special ordered one or two at a time. Increasingly in the nineteenth century, Indian shawls, already a blend of Chinese, European, and Indian design, competed with imitations made in Scotland and France.[11]

The Indian market was also being transformed—opened to private traders, filled with the products of industrial production in the West, and increasingly subject to British control over agriculture, manufactures, and commerce. In the late 1820s, for example, reverberations were felt from the depressed economy of Great Britain. British trade with its greatest port, Calcutta, declined precipitously and the piece-goods trade continued its slide. With the rapid expansion of printing and dyeing in Europe and America, British and Indian capital in Bengal turned increasingly to indigo cultivation and manufacture as the demand for it increased. When James B. Briggs arrived in the *Apthorp* in 1833 (chapter 13), the commercial turmoil he found

had been caused by upheavals in British-controlled indigo production. In the late 1820s, indigo crop failures and the decline of indigo prices in London precipitated disaster for British Indian and Bengali investments in indigo. After struggling toward stability, the gravity of the situation became inescapable when in 1833 the leading private British firm, Palmer and Co., failed—the fortunes of other agency houses and East India Company employees foundering in its wake.[12]

YANKEE PERSEVERANCE IN THE INDIA TRADE

During these difficult years, American trade with India became both more limited and more intensely concentrated at Calcutta, now India's key port for foreign trade. Madras exports to the U.S. were hardly one percent of Calcutta's, and Bombay's trade was insignificant.[13] In 1833, for example, Calcutta exported about $1 million to the United States, carried in 17 American vessels; in 1804, 29 ships had brought out nearly $3 million in goods.[14] Among those who persevered and succeeded in these new circumstances was Henry Lee, who wrote a letter to his wife from Calcutta during the War of 1812, foreshadowing his choice:

> our friends will have some proofs of the advantages an experienced agent has over those who are less acquainted with this trade. . . . It would be very singular, if, after I have devoted 18 years to this trade, and during that time been the largest importer and one of the greatest dealers in Bengal goods of every description, I should not be confident in my abilities to carry it on with uncommon advantages.[15]

During his years in Calcutta, Henry Lee had become a specialist in Calcutta commodities. On his return to Boston as a sedentary merchant, he remained loyal to the India trade until his retirement in the 1840s.

For Lee and the others who chose to continue, the trade was a challenge in such altered conditions. For several years after his return, Henry Lee maintained his old buying and selling practices, even though he knew that the markets had fundamentally changed. Competition from British traders made India goods often cheaper to import from London than to buy in India.[16] Spain's prohibition on the slave trade, enacted between 1817 and 1820, also affected the market for low-priced cottons. But Lee expected to find new outlets for the coarse cotton goods

Fig. 11.2 *Ship* George by Edmund Stone. The *George* made twenty-one voyages to Calcutta between 1815 and 1837.
Watercolor, 30.5 x 41.3 cm; Peabody Essex Museum M1970.

and broken indigo that had sold so well in the past.[17] In 1821, business was in such poor condition that Lee, as he had a decade earlier, elected to go to India himself, as supercargo of the brig *Palmer* belonging to his brother Joseph. The voyage was a success and Lee's affairs remained on an even keel. In later years he concentrated on investments in cargoes shipped on vessels owned by others and, with his son Henry, Jr., who joined his countinghouse in 1838, on chartering vessels to load for Calcutta and Rio.

Despite the decline of Salem and other smaller ports, some of their merchants continued to prosper, frequently landing their ships at Boston or New York. Joseph Peabody (1757–1844) (fig. 11.1), Salem's leading merchant, was one of these.[18] Reared on a New England farm, Peabody went to sea at nineteen and rose through the ranks, taking command of his first vessel on a voyage to Jamaica at the close of the Revolutionary War. Peabody's first venture in the Asia trade was to Batavia in

1795.[19] After the 1816 tariff and the increasing emphasis on industrialization and western expansion, Peabody was among those who mastered the India trade. Peabody vessels were renowned for sailing to India with unprecedented regularity. Most famous was the *George*, which made twenty-one voyages to Calcutta, between 1815 and 1837 (fig. 11.2).[20] Scores of young New Englanders experienced India in Peabody's employ. Many rose in their profession: forty-five crew members of the *George* became masters; twenty, chief mates; and six, second mates.[21] James B. Briggs, master and supercargo of the *Apthorp*, was one of these, serving as supercargo on two voyages of the *George* to Calcutta, in 1831 and 1836.[22] The *George* was so well known in Calcutta that on one of its last voyages, banians in the American trade presented a complete set of silk signals and colors to the ship.[23]

Fig. 11.3 *Bunwah Coolies Carrying the Plant to the Vat* (above); *Packing the Vats* (below), from *A Treatise of the Process and Manufacture of Fine Indigo* by William Osborne, printed at the Indian Lithographic Press, Calcutta, 1832, by W. Holland. Peabody Essex Museum Library.

GRUFF GOODS FOR BURGEONING INDUSTRIES

The homeward cargo of Briggs' *Apthorp* was typical of this period of retrenched trade: industry oriented yet attentive to a range of potential demands—chiefly indigo, hides, and saltpeter, but also including shellac, gum copal, senna, camphor, nutmegs, mace, twine, gunny bags, silk goods, and ginger. A few years later, in 1836, Charles Currier, acting as an agent for David Pingree in Salem, wrote to his family in Hopkinton, New

Hampshire, from Calcutta describing commodities he was purchasing for shipment to Boston: "about one thousand pieces of blue baftahs a kind of coarse cloth suitable for the South American markets and as many pieces of blue gurrahs and the same number of checks all of which are cloths for the same markets, a few silk choppa handkerchiefs, goat skins, buffalo hides and cow hides, ginger, chillies (a kind of pepper), gum arabic etc. all of which I have purchased, and some other kind of goods I am in treaty for such as coffee, linseed, indigo, ivory, shellac, lac dye, and various kinds of drugs etc."[24]

Before the development of synthetic dyestuffs in the mid-nineteenth century, indigo was the most widely used dye. As industrialized textile production progressed in the West, the market for indigo expanded and the British in India made indigo cultivation and manufacture into a major export industry. By 1805, when the British textile industry was well established but before the U.S. textile industry had taken off, the number-one export from Bengal was indigo; nothing else came close in value.[25] While indigo had been grown in northern and western India, its intensive production was a European initiative. Farmers were maneuvered into cultivating indigo while British and Indian entrepreneurs set up factories for processing it (fig. 11.3). By 1830, there were about 700 indigo factories in Bengal and Bihar.[26] Ironically, a stimulus for its development was the inaccessibility of indigo from the southern United States during the Revolutionary War years, and the subsequent replacement of indigo by cotton as a commercial crop. In the United States, the demand for indigo increased as the textile industry grew. In the 1820s and '30s, after the decline in the U.S. market for Indian textiles, indigo replaced piece goods as the leading import, and remained an important component of India cargoes until its displacement by synthetic dyes in the later nineteenth century. Rhode Island was the center of calico printing and a major consumer of imported indigo.[27] In 1827, Philadelphia, where there was also an extensive printing and dyeing industry, used $228,000 worth of indigo.[28] During the 1820s, half a million dollars' worth of indigo was imported each year; by 1860 annual importation had doubled.[29]

The demand for other raw materials also increased with the expansion of American industry. In New England, where shoe manufacture grew from cottage industry to factory production, hides were in great demand. During the 1830s, about 3.5 million pairs of shoes and boots annually were exported in

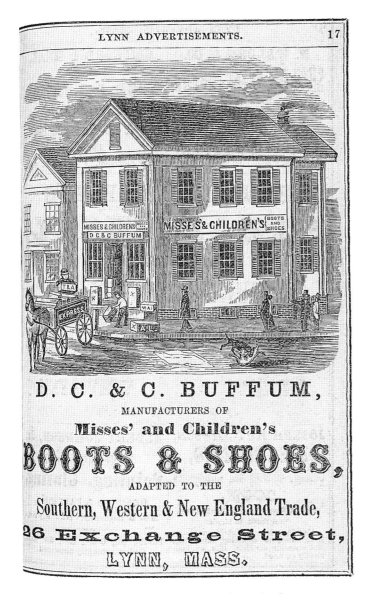

Fig. 11.4 "D. C. & C. Buffum, Manufacturers of Misses' and Childrens' Boots & Shoes," advertisement in *The Lynn Directory*, edited by George Adams, 1854. Peabody Essex Museum Library.

Fig. 11.5 Frederic Tudor (1783–1864), the ice king, c. 1860. Photograph, 26.5 x 21.5 cm; Courtesy of Baker Library, Harvard Business School.

Boston vessels to the south.[30] Lynn, located between Salem and Boston, became the foremost shoe and boot producer in the United States (fig. 11.4). In 1831, Lynn's total output of shoes was more than a million-and-a-half pairs valued at $200 million.[31] To supply the shoemakers, hides were brought from far-flung sources, including South America and India. Calcutta was an important source of goatskins, as well as water-buffalo and cattle hides.

After indigo, hides and saltpeter were the most valuable commodities imported from Calcutta in this period. Saltpeter (potassium nitrate), also known as niter, was imported from Calcutta for the manufacture of gunpowder. The Dupont factory in Wilmington, Delaware, led in production, and gunpowder became a major U.S. manufacture. As the United States expanded westward, gunpowder was in demand not only for firearms and military supply, but also as an explosive for building roads, railroad beds, and canals, and for mining and quarrying granite.[32]

Yankee merchants continued to find more to import from India than to export there; the balance of trade remained in favor of British India. But in 1833, one of the most unlikely export cargoes imaginable was carried up the Hooghly in the ship *Tuscany* from Boston. Although it had little effect on the balance of trade, for the first time Americans had found a domestic export highly valued in British India: ice. After a four-month journey around the Cape of Good Hope, the *Tuscany*, Captain Little of Newburyport master, brought sixty cords of ice to Calcutta.[33] Frederic Tudor (fig. 11.5), the Yankee entre-

Fig. 11.6 Standing cup, Hamilton and Company, Calcutta, 1833. Inscribed: *Presented by Lord William Bentinck Governor General and Commander in Chief India/ to Mr. Rogers of Boston/ in Acknowledgement of the Spirit and enterprize which/ projected and successfully executed the first/ attempt to import a cargo of American Ice into Calcutta/ Nov. 22, 1833.* Repoussé gilded silver, height 26.7 cm; Peabody Essex Museum E75104.AB, Gift of Miss Anne P. Halliday, 1986.

preneur who invented the long-distance ice trade, had devised a way to insulate ice so that it could survive the four-month voyage to the tropics:

> The space allotted for the ice will admit about 60 cords to be put on board, fitted first with a sheathing of boards one inch from the skin of the vessel, then six inches straw [on] the bottom, 6 inches hay stuffed and rammed in the

sides, then one foot boards or lumber on the bottom, then a foot deep straw on the sides and bulkheads, one foot thick of dry straw rammed in hard—boarded under the beams, and a foot of straw or perhaps 10 inches all dry and connecting with the straw of the bulk heads and side so as to make an unbroken stratum on top and sides and bottom.[34]

On January 31, 1834, Tudor recorded in his diary, "I have news of the safe arrival at Calcutta of the *Tuscany* with her cargo of ice and the good order it was calculated to arrive in— that is the loss of one third."[35] The cargo was received with great excitement:

> How many Calcutta tables glittered that morning with lumps of ice! The butter dishes were filled; the goblets of water were converted into miniature Arctic seas with ice-bergs floating on the surface. All business was suspended until noon, that people might rush about to pay each other congratulatory visits, and devise means for perpet-uating the ice-supply. . . . Mr. Tudor was so pleased with the success of his first venture, that he thenceforth kept the principal towns in the three presidencies well sup-plied. I believe that 1500 tons of fresh-water lake ice of America are now consumed in India. In the hospitals it is invaluable.[36]

This unique accomplishment was welcomed by the British authorities, and the occasion was honored by Governor-General Bentinck, who presented an inscribed silver-gilt cup to William C. Rogers, supercargo of the *Tuscany*, for having successfully landed the first shipment of American ice in India (fig. 11.6). British residents of Calcutta, Madras, and Bombay quickly mobilized to construct icehouses to store the American treasure. With the ice from time to time came apples, butter, hams, and other delicacies for the Anglo-Indian table. Like the wines and naval stores Americans brought, the ice and the food-stuffs that accompanied it were almost exclusively for use by British residents, and the value was relatively small.[37] But the market was so stable that Tudor became another regular in the U.S.-India trade—with some competition from other Boston firms—maintaining a constant supply at Calcutta, Madras, and Bombay for more than thirty years (fig. 11.7).

Fig. 11.7 *Madras Ice House—South View*, signed Just Gants[?], Madras, 1858. Watercolor, 35.6 x 57.2 cm; Courtesy of Baker Library, Harvard Business School.

A MUSEUM OF THE EAST INDIES

The business of men like Henry Lee, Joseph Peabody, and Frederic Tudor maintained a steady connection between New England and India that carried in its wake an encounter transcending commerce. Hundreds more young New Englanders had firsthand experiences of India and returned with stories, souvenirs, books, and pictures. Many Yankee captains and supercargoes were regulars in Calcutta.

Despite the reduction and alteration of trade after 1820, American interest in India continued to grow. Nowhere is the irony more apparent than in Salem, Massachusetts. Just as the town's days as a major seaport were coming to a close, the Salem East India Marine Society, which had been acquiring "artificial and natural curiosities" principally from Asia and the Pacific since 1799, elected to build a hall to house its collection, now more than 4,000 objects. The museum was already recognized as one of the country's most important. From 1804 to 1824, the Society occupied rooms in the Salem Bank Building.

In 1818, the *North American Review*, the *Atlantic Monthly* of the time, included a short article on the East India Marine Society and its "Museum or Cabinet of Curiosities," which included "several dresses and costumes of the East Indians, the Chinese, Javanese and other nations; some good pictures and engravings, and several ships built and rigged in the most exact and perfect manner as models of real ships. The Museum," it was noted, "is open every day in the year, except Sundays, and is accessible to all persons without any expense. The only requisite necessary is an introduction by some member of the Society."[38]

By 1820, the East India Marine Society's proprietors observed, "the elegant arrangement which had been made in the Museum . . . had been considerably broken in upon by the great accumulation of articles . . . [which] had been stowed away wherever a spot could be found to place them." To remedy the situation, the Society engaged Dr. Seth Bass to rearrange the collection, grouping "things of a similar nature" and preparing a catalogue for publication.[39] Bass was the first of several superintendents who were doctors of medicine,

Fig. 11.8 Exterior of East India Marine Hall, at the death of President Ulysses Grant, 1877. Photograph, 23.5 x 19.1 cm; Peabody Essex Museum, Gift of John Robinson.

evidently considered suitable as men of learning and science. After just a few years, new donations crowded and compromised Dr. Bass's fine arrangement.

In 1824, the Society decided to build anew, engaging Thomas W. Sumner, a Boston housewright and contemporary of Charles Bullfinch, Asher Benjamin, and Alexander Parris. The building, with its granite facade designed in late Federal style, was the grandest in the town. *East India Marine Hall* was carved into the stone above the row of tall, elegant, arched windows on the second story (fig. 11.8). The ground floor provided offices for the Asiatic Bank and the Oriental Insurance Office. The second floor of the building was a large single room—the Society's meeting place and the exhibition space for its collection. The dedication of the East India Marine Hall in October 1825 was attended by the President of the United States, John Quincy Adams. The *Salem Register* of October 17, 1825 reported:

> This Hall, over 100 feet in length and 40 in breadth, is
> as chaste and beautiful a specimen of architecture as our

country can exhibit, and filled as it is by the rare and curious productions of nature and art from the four quarters of the globe, forms a cabinet unrivalled in this, and excelled perhaps by few in any country. On this occasion, the Society was honored with the company of THE PRESIDENT OF THE UNITED STATES, and many other distinguished guests.[40]

President Adams had been elected earlier that year by the House of Representatives after the poll in the electoral college had produced no clear winner. Despite being the son of John Adams and a member of New England's aristocracy, he was not a popular man with New England's merchants. He had supported the trade embargo in 1807 and war in 1812, both of which had done great damage to shipping and had been vigorously opposed by most of Salem's leading citizens. Nevertheless, the presence of the President at the dedication of the Society's new hall was testimony to its importance and to the stature of Salem and its citizens, even in the face of the seaport's obvious wane and declining political influence.

British travel writer Anne Royall, who visited soon after the new museum opened, recommended it: "The collection is one of the richest in the United States, and worthy the attention of all lovers and friends of science."[41] Settled in its new grand building, the museum's reputation continued to grow, as did its collection. In 1838, Dr. Henry Wheatland, the museum's fifth superintendent, reported to the Society on his thorough overhaul of the exhibits in which everything was cleaned and rearranged. Wheatland grouped "such articles as bore a resemblance to each other or were used for the same purpose in the economy of life by the different nations, such as the cooking utensils, shoes, hats, warlike instruments, etc. etc. The natural productions are in a like manner brought together, such as the corals, specimens of the woods, fruits, fishes, reptiles, etc."[42] In this arrangement, objects from the same place were separated and distributed according to their functions. By choosing to group together "like" things, visitors were encouraged to comprehend curiosities by contrasting exotic forms with familiar ones, grouping the new and strange into existing categories to be compared, evaluated, and ranked with similar products from different parts of the world (figs. 11.9–10).

The museum—its stature and its contents—was a powerful presence in the community, and its exhibits made lasting, deep impressions. Caroline Howard King, who grew up in

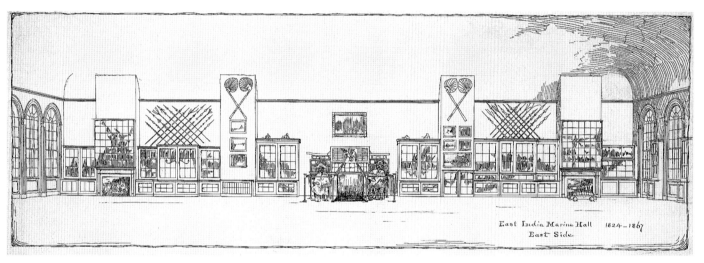

Figs. 11.9–10 *East India Marine Hall, 1824–1867* by James H. Emmerton, 1879. Above: *West Side*, showing the circle of figures including those donated by James Briggs (see figs. 11.11 and 12.2) and the portrait statue of Raj Kissen Mitter, seated on a chair at the right (see fig. 14.5). Below: *East Side*, showing the seated portrait statues, with Rajinder Dutt at left (see fig. 14.9) and Durgaprasad Ghose at right (see fig. 11.12). Behind them, installed above the stairwell, is the East India Marine Society's palanquin (see fig. 4.18). The drawings were based on the recollections of Dr. Henry Wheatland and on actual measurements of the room, its furnishings, and the objects displayed. Ink on paper, each 15.2 x 44.5 cm; Peabody Essex Museum M503A (*West Side*) and M503C (*East Side*).

Salem in the 1830s, remembered the museum of her childhood as a place of fascination:

> it was an experience for an imaginative child, to step
> from the prosaic streets of a New England town, into that
> atmosphere redolent with perfumes from the East, warm
> and fragrant and silent, with a touch of the dear old
> Arabian Nights about it. From the moment I set my foot
> in that beautiful old hall, and greeted and was greeted by
> the solemn group of Orientals, who draped in Eastern
> stuffs and camel's hair shawls stood opposite the entrance
> . . . the hours were full of enchantment. . . .[43]

The "group of Orientals" who so intrigued Caroline King were the first things visitors encountered as they entered the second-story hall from the stair at one side. Six of these were life size, modeled in clay, and had been presented to the museum by Captain James B. Briggs of the *Apthorp* (chapters 12 and 13). There were two coolies or palanquin bearers (fig. 11.11; see also fig. 12.2); a sircar (clerk), "accurately coloured and clothed"; "a Juggler, playing with a Spectacle Snake"; and two fakirs, or mendicants. Briggs' donation also included a seventh figure, one that indicates the changing climate in which Calcutta's artists worked. It was a copy of a classical Greek statue, catalogued as

Fig. 11.11 Cooley, life size, "by a distinguished native artist of Calcutta," attributed to Kashinath Pal, Krishnanagar, entry #2695 in *The East India Marine Society of Salem*, 2d ed. (Salem, Mass., 1831), c. 1823. Clay over straw, pigments, and cloth, height 71 cm; Peabody Essex Museum E9924, Gift of Captain James B. Briggs, 1823 (see also fig. 12.2).

Fig. 11.12 Durgaprasad Ghose, life size, attributed to Sri Ram Pal, Krishnanagar, c. 1837. Clay, straw, pigments, cloth, height (seated, life size) 119 cm; Peabody Essex Museum 9937, possibly given by Durgaprasad Ghose, c. 1837.

a "model, executed by the same hand [as the previous six], of a Greek antique statue of the boy extracting a thorn." Briggs commented that these models were "copied from nature by a distinguished native artist of Calcutta."[44] In 1823, when Briggs was master of the 271-ton ship *Emerald* to Calcutta, he acquired the seven fragile figures, appropriating space in the hold of his ship that could have been used for commodities. Briggs' massive donation to the museum contrasts sharply with his terse port journal of the brig *Apthorp* at Calcutta in 1833 (chapter 13), which records only the business of loading, unloading, and repairing the vessel, and nothing of his experiences in port.

The models of East Indians, prominently placed in the center of the hall, also included a portrait mannequin of Nusserwanjee Maneckjee Wadia made in Salem to display the Parsi clothing he had given to the museum, and the seated portrait of Durgaprasad Ghose (fig. 11.12). In later years, these were joined by two more life-size seated clay portraits of Bengali banians, also brought from Calcutta (see figs. 14.5 and 14.9). In addition to these life-size figures, there were more than thirty smaller clay figurines, admired for their detailed and realistic portrayals, displayed in the glass-fronted cabinets lining the walls of the East India Marine Society's museum. The full-size

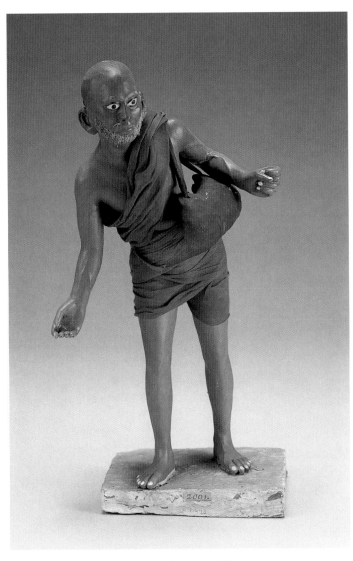

Fig. 11.13 Bheesty (water carrier), Calcutta or Krishnanagar, c. 1825. Clay, pigments, cloth, height 38 cm; Peabody Essex Museum E7643, Gift of Samuel Barton, 1825.

naturalistic depictions, they collaborated with their British, American, and Indian patrons to produce portraits and illustrations of Calcutta's social types, a virtual inventory of Indian society from the foreigners' perspective. Unlike most other objects in the East India Marine Society's collection, the clay figures were actually made for display, specially constructed representations made by Indian artists to depict their society for foreigners. The characters resonated with the experiences of American merchant mariners in India, the banians with whom they worked, and the plethora of servants required for their business and living arrangements, as well as the public entertainers and strange-looking religious ascetics encountered in their travels in the city and countryside.

In the early 1820s, seventeen-year-old Samuel Barton had presented three clay figurines to the East India Marine Society's museum, probably purchased on his first voyage to Calcutta: a "Brahmin pilgrim," a "*sircar* or scrivener" (native clerk), and a "*bheesty* or water carrier" (fig. 11.13). In 1834, when Barton was again in Calcutta, he acquired a set of twenty-one clay figures that had been specially commissioned. The order had been placed in 1833 at Calcutta by W. H. Allen, second mate on Joseph Peabody's ship *George* and donated to the museum the following year by Barton, then the *George*'s supercargo. A copy of the contract made with Goundhun Ghose reads:

> Sreesu Kistnoju—Protool Kurtah[46]—To the High
> Dignity subject W. H. Allen Esq.—I Sri Goundhun
> Ghose do hereby bind myself unto the said W. H. Allen
> Esq. to make an agreement with him that at his arrival in
> Calcutta on the next voyage I will supply him several
> sorts of idols at the bazaar price. In case I cannot do so as
> I make in this agreement, I shall be guilty towards the
> said W. H. Allen Esq.—dated 7th July 1833—

A note on the surviving copy of the contract indicates that "the above relates to twenty-one figures in clay model illustrating some of the Castes, Devotees, Costumes, occupations etc. of the Hindoos of Calcutta."[47]

On this visit, Barton rented house number 228, Old China Bazaar, for Rs.140 per month. The usual retinue of servants kept to run the house consisted of two sets of palanquin bearers, a khansama (house-steward), a "boy" or personal servant, a butler or waiting servant, a doorkeeper, a sweeper, and a bheesty (water carrier).[48] Charles Currier, writing home to his family in New Hampshire five years later, described a similar household

figures and the small models that depicted Indians of different occupations and religious sects were the largest group of curiosities from India. Except for two standing statues that had been made in Salem to display costumes brought from India, all of these figures were made of sun-dried clay, painted with earth pigments in a tamarind-glue binder, finished with fiber hair, and dressed in cloth garments. This work was the specialty of potter-sculptors from Krishnanagar, a small town about fifty miles upriver from Calcutta.[45] The clay modelers of Krishnanagar were of the potter caste, makers of utilitarian clay vessels and of images of Hindu deities for use in seasonal festivals. In their

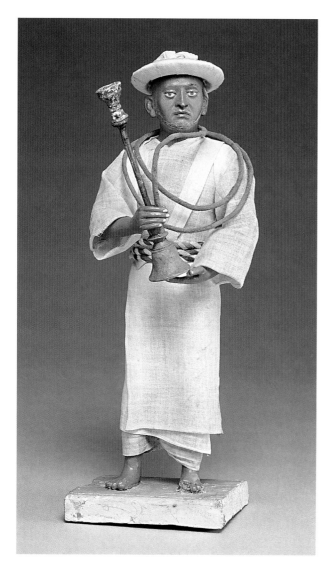

counterclockwise from upper left:

Fig. 11.14 Hookah-bearer, Calcutta or Krishnanagar, c. 1833. Clay, pigments, cloth, height 34 cm; Peabody Essex Museum E7654, Gift of Samuel Barton, 1833.

Fig. 11.15 Syce (groom), Calcutta or Krishnanagar, c. 1833. Clay, pigments, cloth, height 29 cm; Peabody Essex Museum E7649, Gift of Samuel Barton, 1833.

Fig. 11.16 "A Banian or Merchant of the Upper Caste," Calcutta, 1833, entry #4471 in *The East India Marine Society of Salem*, 3d ed., supplement (Salem, Mass., 1837). Clay, cloth, pigment, height 36 cm; Peabody Essex Museum E7678, Gift of Samuel Barton, 1833.

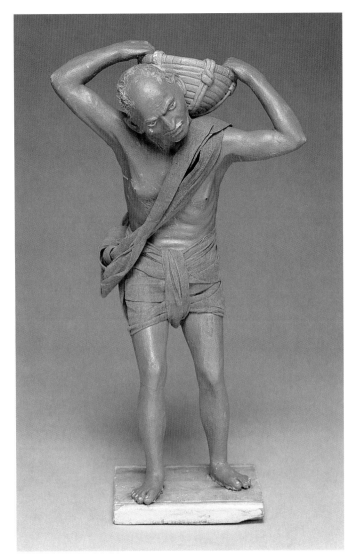

Fig. 11.17 Porter, Calcutta or Krishnanagar, c. 1833. Clay, pigments, cloth, height 33 cm; Peabody Essex Museum E7645, Gift of Samuel Barton, 1833.

Fig. 11.18 Brick and mortar bearer, Calcutta or Krishnanagar, c. 1833. Clay, pigments, cloth, height 35 cm; Peabody Essex Museum E7647, Gift of Samuel Barton, 1833.

staff: "Our servants consists of one head man (or native title khansumer) he purchases all our daily provisions and superintends all concerns about the house, one cook, one butler, one mater or sweeper, two boys to wait upon the table, two bearers or servants to go [on] errands and have the charge of our sleeping rooms and wearing apparel, all our servants are males no females about our establishment. . . ."[49]

Several figurines in the set donated to the museum represent household servants: a bheesty; two figurines of hookah-bearers, "his sole business to prepare the hooker" (fig. 11.14); a syce, or groom, one of whom was assigned to each horse kept by the master (fig. 11.15); and a "female of low caste," perhaps a sweeper, the only female servant ever connected to such a

household, whose job was to remove refuse, including human waste. Samuel Barton's world as supercargo of the George at Calcutta was also illustrated among the figurines by two "banian[s] or merchant[s] of the upper caste" (fig. 11.16); a serang or stevedore, head of a team of coolies like those who loaded and unloaded ships; a "coolie . . . porter" (fig. 11.17); a "brick and mortar bearer" (fig. 11.18); and a "hackery or truck-car and driver," which transported cargoes between godowns and the wharfs.[50]

Figures of entertainers, dancers and musicians, and religious devotees represented exotic India. Most American merchants in Calcutta attended public religious festivals when they had the chance. By the 1840s, many were invited to the homes

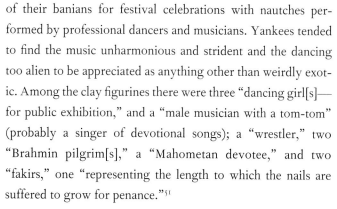

Fig. 11.19 Jagaddhatri, c. 1815. Clay, pigment, cloth, height 43.5 cm; Peabody Essex Museum E7673, Gift of Captain Ephraim Emmerton, c. 1815.

Fig. 11.20 Parvati and Ganesha with Shiva, attended by Kartikeya, Nandi, and Bhringhi, c. 1815. Clay, pigment, cloth, height 43.5 x width 40.5 x depth 33 cm; Peabody Essex Museum E7675f, Gift of Captain Ephraim Emmerton, c. 1815.

of their banians for festival celebrations with nautches performed by professional dancers and musicians. Yankees tended to find the music unharmonious and strident and the dancing too alien to be appreciated as anything other than weirdly exotic. Among the clay figurines there were three "dancing girl[s]—for public exhibition," and a "male musician with a tom-tom" (probably a singer of devotional songs); a "wrestler," two "Brahmin pilgrim[s]," a "Mahometan devotee," and two "fakirs," one "representing the length to which the nails are suffered to grow for penance."[51]

The figures that had been chosen by Sri Goundhun Ghose were illustrative of the constellation of servants, religious devotees, and entertainers familiar to Americans in Calcutta. They represented what Ghose, and the unidentified clay modeler with whom he placed the order, believed foreigners would want as souvenirs. The sculptor's subjects had distinctive costumes, ornaments, or equipment that made their identities obvious to any informed observer: the bheesty had his animal skin for

carrying water; the hookah-bearer, his water pipe; the syce (groom), his horse. When they were commissioned to represent characters and scenes of native life by British and foreign patrons, Indian artists, painters as well as image makers, made those visual distinctions into insignia of identity, much like the weapons and other symbols depicted in images of gods and royalty that were their traditional subjects.[52]

Figurines of native types continued to be popular souvenirs throughout the nineteenth century, and several other places, including Poona and Lucknow, made them a specialty. In 1864, John Cole of the ship *Gem of the Ocean* wrote to his wife from Calcutta about some items he was sending to her: "the things in the box are not of much value, but I know you will be pleased to have them, there is two sets of wooden toys, one for Hattie and one for Dick's little girl, there is also a dozen of plaster images showing the way the natives look and how they dress, also a worked skirt for Hattie, and two collars and cuffs for your self. . . ."[53]

Besides the naturalistic figures depicting "native types," there was a small group of "Bengalese idols," also modeled by Bengali potter-sculptors using the same techniques, but executed in a more abstract traditional style. These were already on display in the East India Marine Society's museum at the time of Barton and Allen's gift; they had been donated around 1815 by Captain Ephraim Emmerton, who was a regular on Joseph Peabody's *George* and other Calcutta-bound vessels. Among these was a small painted image of Jagannatha, "Lord of the World," whose worship is centered at the great temple complex in Puri, Orissa (see fig. 16.27). The others in the group were an image of Jagaddhatri, a local form of the widely venerated goddess Durga which gained favor in early-nineteenth-century Bengal,[54] depicted as a yellow-skinned goddess in red garments on her lion mount above the vanquished elephant-demon (fig. 11.19); a composite of the righteous King Rama enthroned with his devoted wife Sita and accompanied by his loyal brother Lakshmana and attendants, probably made for worship on Rama's birthday, the day on which Bengali merchants usually began their year's accounts (see fig. 8.7);[55] and an image of the goddess Parvati enthroned, holding her infant son Ganesha, accompanied by her consort Shiva and an attendant carrying her other son Kartikeya (fig. 11.20). The intensely rich cultural significance of these images vanished completely in the East India Marine Society's museum, where visitors knew almost nothing about who these deities were and how they were worshipped. Perhaps the donor, Captain Emmerton, who had made several voyages to India, or some other experienced members of the Society, were able to provide some explanation to the curious. But it is likely that visitors found the designation "idol" sufficiently informative.

The standard American view of Hindu practice was epitomized in the 1833 donation by Captain Joseph Webb of

> two Hooks, used by the Hindoos for the purpose of
> transfixing and suspending the natives before the public
> to recover their caste when lost by some misdemeanor or
> for penance. In 1832 these identical hooks were inserted
> in the flesh, below the ribs, and the individual hoisted to
> the public gaze in Calcutta, as witnessed by the donor
> of them to the museum. (fig. 11.21)[56]

This description, one of a handful more than a few words in length, portrays the hooks as instruments of punishment, rather than a means for demonstrating the strength and depth of

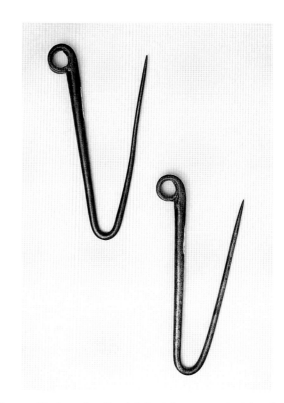

Fig. 11.21 Hooks used at Charak Puja, Calcutta, 1832. Steel, length 12 cm; Peabody Essex Museum E7391, Gift of Captain Joseph Webb, 1833.

religious devotion. Hook-swinging was part of the annual Charak Puja, which took place during the festival for Shiva at the end of the Hindu year. Dudley Pickman, whose account of the festivities in 1804 is reproduced in chapter 7, noted the tremendous zeal of the participants. Hook-swinging, like sati (the ritual suicide of a woman on her husband's funeral pyre), simultaneously fascinated and horrified the many American mariners who had the opportunity to witness it. In Western eyes, hook-swinging and sati were the most savage of Hindu practices. For the British rulers of India, these became emblems of Hindu barbarity, providing what they believed was a powerful moral rationale for British conquest (figs. 11.22–23). Sati was outlawed by the East India Company in 1829.

New Englanders studying the religious objects from India on display in East India Marine Hall could feel comfortably affirmed in their convictions of moral and cultural supremacy, innocently unaware that their understanding was superficial or distorted. Charles Currier, writing home to New Hampshire from Calcutta in 1836, gave his views on the delusion of Hindu idolators:

> from the little I can learn from English Gentlemen here I
> should think our missionaries stood in very good repute

Figs. 11.22–23 Silver-gilt snuffbox with a scene of hook-swinging on one side (left) and sati on the other (right), China, c. 1830, after engravings by Balthazard Solvyns. Condensed on this small snuffbox, which would have fit in the hand of an Anglo-Indian, are two practices that the British believed provided moral justification for the conquest of India. Repoussé gilded silver, height 2 x width 7.3 x depth 6 cm; Peabody Essex Museum E85229, Museum purchase with funds donated by Mr. and Mrs. Richard Vietor, 1996.

in India. The superstition of the natives of Bengal is beyond conception. They eat no meat. The servant that waits upon the table will not on any account black your shoes or assist in dressing; every servant must have his own work and no more. This is a part of their religion and if a man break it they loose their cast, to gain which they would be obliged to hook themselves in the back and swing on poles in the air and endure some other painful performance such as their priest might prescribe.[57]

The East India Marine Society's collection, housed in its refined and imposing building, projected a view of the East emphasizing its exotic, "heathen" character. At the same time, this imposing collection cast distinction on the accomplishments of the Society's members. The *New York Journal of Commerce* reported in 1833: "Has the reader ever visited the Salem East India Museum? We have many a time and we do not hesitate to say that to us it is the most interesting Museum we have ever entered. It affords a fine illustration of the enterprise, science and taste of the Salem ship masters . . ." About a decade later, a traveler from England wrote: "The Museum is a large and lofty building . . . it makes an imposing appearance. . . . I made several visits…, and was on each occasion abundantly gratified. The articles are well arranged, and kept in excellent order, and there is never so great a crowd of visitors as to prevent the careful and uninterrupted examination of any article . . ." Following a lengthy description of the contents of the museum, he concluded: "Such is the singular mixture and variety of curiosities

in the Salem Museum . . . it cannot fail, therefore, to furnish abundant information and amusement to visitors of all classes, from the venerable navigator and hydrographer to the holiday pupil, as there is as much to entertain as to inform."[58]

The museum was a monument to American enterprise. It was also a last stand of the maritime Yankee aristocracy against its fading power and importance. During this period, mercantile New England was increasingly out of step with the nation. Andrew Jackson had just been elected to a second term as president in 1832, and the country continued moving toward populist democracy and western expansion and away from the Yankee mercantile and professional elite. Soon after his reelection, President Jackson and Vice President Van Buren came to Salem while on a national tour. They stopped at East India Marine Hall to see the museum and signed the visitors' register. Local sentiment toward the intrusion was dramatically expressed by the daring prank of two little girls. One of them, Caroline Howard King, whose fond memories of the museum were recounted above, described the deed in her memoirs:

> We felt that our beloved Museum would be desecrated
> by his presence and hoped that the group of stately orien-
> tals opposite the door, would rise up in a body and forbid
> his entrance . . . [The next day] we went to inscribe our
> valuable autographs in the visitor's book . . . [and saw]
> scrawled across the page in large straggling characters
> the hated name of Andrew Jackson and beneath it
> Martin Van Buren. This was too much, and thoughts of

vengeance filled our little souls . . . [W]e returned . . . armed with weapons to achieve our fell purpose . . . We watched our opportunity . . . we whipped out our scissors, and in a moment a gaping blank stood where the offensive signatures had been.[59]

GLIMMERINGS OF RAPPROCHEMENT: RAJA RAMMOHUN ROY AND AMERICA

Those Americans who were inclined to look beyond the curious appearance of objects displayed in the East India Marine Society's museum or brought home as gifts or souvenirs, could read accounts by American and European sojourners. Mostly these were the work of missionaries or functionaries of the East India Company's colonial bureaucracy. In America, missionary publications were a ready source of information and opinion about India. Journals such as the *Panoplist*, published in Boston, carried columns by British missionaries in India. Americans like the pioneer missionary Samuel Nott, whose "A Sermon on the Idolatry of the Hindus" was printed in Norwich, Connecticut, in 1817, were eager to communicate with their own people and garner their support. Occasional book-length memoirs also appeared, including William Ramsey's *Journal of a Missionary Tour in India*, published in Philadelphia in 1836. European publications were also available; the French Jesuit Abbé Dubois' *Description of the Character, Manners, and Customs of the People of India* was translated and published in Philadelphia in 1818 and noted in *North American Review* in 1819. Such sources encouraged Americans to look at India through the filter of their Christian convictions and offered no incentive to understand the significance of Indian curiosities or practices in their cultural context.

A small space for such considerations was, however, slowly opening up. Already, many New Englanders had moved away from Puritan beliefs in predestination, to admit worshippers' will to believe and their God's inclination to forgive sinners, positions that fueled evangelical aspirations. They could bring enlightenment to "heathens," show them the truth of Christian belief, and God would accept them. In New England, especially, there was growing controversy between liberal and conservative congregations about the nature of God and the Trinity. Differing views of God's relationship with humankind were accompanied by differences of opinion about the prospects for Christian proselytizing, and the character of Hinduism. The more liberal view was expressed in the writing of the Crowninshield cousins—Benjamin in his description of sati in 1789 (chapter 1) and Benjamin W. remarking on the role of missionaries in 1817 (chapter 8). Henry Lee and William Rogers harbored misgivings about missionaries almost as strong as their judgment of Hinduism (chapter 8). In New England, where the India trade had flourished for so long, the ground was especially fertile for the development of a range and variety of views, for a deeper engagement with Indian civilization.

It was among Unitarians, a recently founded liberal sect, that the consideration of Asian religions progressed beyond the superficial. In New England's Congregational churches, Unitarianism had been developing gradually as part of a growing belief in individual moral responsibility. In Salem, for example, the Rogers and Crowninshield families, parishioners of Reverend William Bentley, followed him to Unitarianism.[60] Joseph Priestly, a leading British Unitarian minister (and discoverer of oxygen), emigrated to Philadelphia to escape detractors and join other members of his family. In 1799, he published *Comparison of the Institutions of Moses with Those of the Hindus and Other Ancient Nations*.[61] The movement came to prominence in New England when, in 1805, a Unitarian became professor of divinity at Harvard University.[62] New England, perhaps because of its concentration of cosmopolitan merchants and mariners with their wide-ranging experiences of the world, was becoming the center of this liberal Christian movement.

At the same time that Unitarianism was gaining adherents in America, Rammohun Roy (1772–1833) (fig. 11.24), acclaimed as "the father of modern India," was developing a reformed Hinduism in Calcutta. His views, drawn from the ancient Sanskrit Vedas and influenced by Islamic and Christian theology, had a distinctly Unitarian flavor. Rammohun Roy was part of the same social class in Bengal as the banians who specialized in the American trade. These men, from high-ranking families, had made fortunes in the new British Calcutta, and had mastered English. Some of them were well read in Western literature, science, and theology.

In 1818, the year of William A. Rogers' voyage to Bombay in the *Tartar*, Rammohun Roy's ideas had been introduced to America by William Tudor, son of a leading Boston merchant, brother of Frederic Tudor, the "ice king," and Harvard-educated editor of the prestigious *North American Review*.

Fig. 11.24 Rammohun Roy (1772–1833) by Rembrandt Peale, 1833. Oil on canvas, 73 x 60.3 cm; Peabody Essex Museum 137982, Museum purchase with funds donated anonymously, 1999.

William Tudor based his article "Theology of the Hindus, as Taught by Ram Mohun Roy" on copies of Roy's translations of the Upanishads and his *Defense of Hindoo Theism*.[63] Although there is no record of how Rammohun Roy's writings first reached Boston, it is most likely they were brought directly from Calcutta on Boston vessels. Translations of Sanskrit texts and works on Indian civilization were becoming more readily available in the 1820s, published principally in London and Calcutta, and were brought to America from both places.

During the 1820s, interest steadily grew in Rammohun Roy's writings on religious and social reform. American Unitarians, especially, found him a kindred spirit who professed belief in one god (rather than a Christian trinity or a Hindu 330 million). At least half the religious journals published in the United States in the 1820s made some reference to him.[64] It was above all his essay "The Precepts of Jesus," published in 1820, in which he endorsed the teachings of Christ, that captured the attention of New England's rapidly growing liberal movement. In 1823, *The Christian Disciple and Theological Review* published "The Writings of Rammohun Roy,"[65] based on sixteen works in the author's possession.[66] In 1825, William Cullen Bryant reviewed Roy's *The Precepts of Jesus* in the *New York Review*.[67]

Roy's second book, *Vindication of the Incarnation of the Deity*, was excerpted from a publication brought from Calcutta and reviewed in the *Salem Courier* in 1828 (September 17).[68] Roy corresponded with many American friends, including David Reed, editor of the *Christian Register*, Joseph Tuckerman, a Unitarian clergyman, and Rev. Henry Ware.[69] The Unitarian movement emphasized Christ's moral teachings and the unitary character of god. Similarly the Brahmo Samaj, founded by Rammohun Roy, emphasized the monism of Vedantic Hinduism, rejecting both polytheism and image worship. The Brahmo Samaj, though it did not accept Christ as god, incorporated Christian morality. New England Unitarians and Bengali Brahmos found in each others' views echoes of their own positions, fueling and bolstering them in their convictions, and allowing each to transcend local orthodoxies through transcultural ties.

Rammohun Roy was the first contemporary Indian intellectual to gain serious attention in America. He was the first to conceive of British and Americans as an audience and, primarily because of the Unitarian's predisposition to his views, he succeeded in reaching them. He was particularly interested in America, and had hoped to visit there in the spring of 1834: "America, with its freedom from religious practices and prejudices, was to him the symbol of everything that India was not."[70] His work, through publication and commentary in the United States, created the first sensation of profound commonality between Americans and this alien, exotic culture. Undoubtedly a large part of his appeal was that he seemed to be Christian, or nearly so, in his ideas about religion. Many Yankees saw hope for the progress of Christianity in India. But American Unitarians also found a similarity between Rammohun Roy's views and their own that corroborated their ideas and encouraged the prospect of a worldwide Unitarian movement.

Rammohun Roy had become so well known that in 1833, when the Philadelphia artist Rembrandt Peale was in London and had the opportunity to meet him, Peale not only went out of his way to do so, but also invited Rammohun Roy to sit for his portrait. Roy, now Raja Rammohun Roy, had arrived in England as the titled ambassador from the Mughal emperor to represent the demands of Indians for equal treatment under East India Company rule. The American artist and the Bengali intellectual and reformer apparently found in each other kindred spirits, perhaps because of their shared position as outsiders in England and their ambivalent feelings toward English society and culture. Peale's sensitive and striking portrait of Roy attests to their relationship. The following year, when Peale returned to the United States, the portrait was exhibited at the Boston Athenaeum. The Athenaeum purchased it in 1837 and exhibited it from time to time for a community in which Rammohun Roy was well known and esteemed, the first "native" of India to gain a respectful audience in America. The impact of Rammohun Roy in America paved the way for the serious consideration of Sanskrit literature and Hindu philosophy that influenced the Transcendentalists and led to the blossoming of American literature at mid-century.[71] The movement toward a more serious engagement with Asian religions and philosophies had begun.

Fig. 12.1 James B. Briggs (1790–1857), c. 1820. Oil on canvas, 68.7 x 50.8 cm; Peabody Essex Museum M379, Gift of Miss Mary Ellen Briggs, 1885.

CHAPTER 12

James B. Briggs, Commander

James B. Briggs (fig. 12.1) was born in 1790 at Scituate, Massachusetts, into a family wedded to the sea. He was named for his sea-captain grandfather. When he was a boy, his father Elijah, who had apprenticed as a shipwright, moved his young family to Salem to join the thriving shipyard of his cousin Enos Briggs. Elias Hasket Derby, Salem's doyen of the East Indies trade, had brought Enos Briggs from Plymouth especially to make vessels for voyages to Asia. The Briggs yard had already established its reputation building vessels for the East Indies trade. The ship *Tartar*, on which William A. Rogers sailed to Bombay in 1817 (chapter 10), had been built there in 1811. When Enos died in 1819, Elijah took over the shipyard and continued to build vessels for the Asia trade, while his son James was making his mark as a captain and supercargo of East Indiamen.

William Rogers and James B. Briggs were contemporaries, but they found their way to the same calling from different sections of New England society. Rogers came from a family of educated professionals, Briggs from skilled artisans, but both were lured by the promise of fortunes to be made in ocean-borne commerce. Rogers had abandoned, temporarily, a career in the law in order to acquire "an honorable independency." Briggs, whose father placed him in the countinghouse of one of Salem's leading merchants, John Forrester, learned the business of trade and capitalized on early opportunities to escape the sedentary life of a clerk for the adventures of a master and supercargo of voyages that took him around the world. Briggs, like Benjamin Carpenter (chapter 3), remained a mariner, retiring from the sea only when he was nearly fifty. His career spanned the 1820s and '30s, a time when New England towns like Waltham and Lowell, just miles inland from the ports of Salem and Boston, were leading the industrialization of the United States.

No records survive of Briggs' early voyages, but a group of account books and shipping logs kept when he was in his thirties and forties are ample evidence of a very active career as a master and supercargo of trading voyages to Asia, South America, and Europe. There is documentation for eleven voyages in the 1820s and '30s and indications of several more. In those years, Briggs continued to work for John Forrester, in whose countinghouse he had learned about commerce. He commanded Forrester's ships, the *Emerald* and *Two Brothers*, on at least five voyages in the 1820s, three of which took him to Calcutta. In the 1830s, there were four more voyages to Calcutta on ships belonging to Forrester, Joseph Peabody, and to the Boston firm Gould, Goddard, and Gould.[1]

With each voyage taking at least nine months, during these two decades Briggs spent more time at sea and in foreign ports than he did at home. Despite his long voyages, Briggs built a home life. In 1821, he married Mary Hosmer. He was thirty-one and she twenty-four. During the next decade, Mary bore him three children: Mary Ellen, James Cabot, and William. The household also included Mary's widowed mother and unmarried sister, a congenial arrangement for the women, given Briggs' lengthy absences. The house itself belonged to Mary's mother, who left it to her when she died. Mary in turn bequeathed it to her daughter Mary Ellen.[2]

Briggs maintained other strong ties to Salem. He belonged to the Salem Marine Society and the Essex Lodge of the Masons, both organizations supported by Salem's mercantile and professional men. In 1821, the year of his marriage, he joined the East India Marine Society, the town's exclusive fraternity of masters and supercargoes in the Asia trade. For the Society's museum, he collected samples of metallic ores, copper, iron, and silver from Elba, Chile, and Peru, as well as bird skins, including a European buzzard and a pilgrim falcon. He also donated a medallion of Carl John, king of Sweden. In 1823, when he commanded the *Emerald* to Calcutta, he acquired seven life-size clay figures for the museum, allotting them cargo space that could have been used for something that would bring a return (fig. 12.2; see also fig. 11.11). Like many of his fellow East India captains, he was devoted to the Society and its mission to share what they learned of the world with people at home. The

Fig. 12.2 Cooley or palanquin bearer, life size, "by a distinguished native artist of Calcutta," c. 1823, entry #2696 in *The East India Marine Society of Salem*, 2d ed. (Salem, Mass., 1831). Clay with straw core, pigments, and cloth, 78.5 cm; Peabody Essex Museum E9922, Gift of Captain James B. Briggs, 1823 (see also fig. 11.11).

statues of East Indians presented by Briggs were placed in the center of East India Marine Hall where, for many decades, they remained prominent reminders of the ties created through commerce between New England and Calcutta.

When Briggs finally retired from the sea, his well-established position among Salem's mercantile class provided him with a smooth entry into the commercial life of the town. From 1843 until about 1855, he served as president of the Essex Insurance Company, which underwrote maritime ventures. The company's charter lapsed in 1855, perhaps because of Briggs' increasingly poor health. He died two years later. He was remembered as a man bred to the sea:

> For many years he was one of our most accomplished
> and trusted shipmasters and factors in the commerce with
> East Indies and China. When he relinquished this pursuit
> he was elected president of the Essex Insurance Company
> and continued to discharge with fidelity and success the

duties of this office till the expiration of the company's charter...He was a gentleman well known and highly esteemed in this community. He was an amiable, upright, honorable man; a man of quick sensibilities and a cheerful and happy temper; a pleasant companion, a lover of children, unselfish, prompt in deeds of kindness and charity and a good neighbor.[3]

In 1832–33, James Briggs was master and supercargo of the brig *Apthorp* on a voyage to Calcutta. The *Apthorp*'s return cargo is listed at the end of Briggs' journal and exemplifies the transformation in the trade that had taken place during the past decade. The *Apthorp* was loaded with "2649 bags salt petre, 274 cases shellac, 256 bundles twine, 756 bundles rattans, 43 chests indigo, 98 cases and 5 packs silk goods, 60 bales G.S. cow hides, 137 loose cow hides and 325 loose buffalo hides, 54 bales senna leaves, 717 bags ginger root (444 [started?]), 89 bales gunny bags (22,250) and 11,250 loose [total] 33,500, 36 bales goat skins, 100 bags cloves, 1 box sago, 1 box preserved ginger root, [and] 2 bales cotton piece goods." The new array of commodities purchased at Calcutta were known collectively as "gruff goods," and consisted of raw materials required for the rapidly growing industries at home.

The port journal Briggs kept during his stay in Calcutta, excerpted in chapter 13, is an extension of a shipping log, with its typically terse entries recording wind and weather, latitudes and longitudes.[4] Sea logs normally ceased while a vessel was in port, but Briggs' situation was not ordinary. He arrived in Calcutta on March 13, 1833. The *Apthorp* stayed in port for two months, from March 15 to May 14, in the intense, sultry heat of summer. On March 23, Briggs wrote to the *Apthorp*'s owners, in a letter reproduced with the journal, to inform them of his arrival and to warn them of the poor market conditions he found there and the brig's need for extensive repairs. The *Apthorp* was in no condition for the long voyage home. The bends, the thick planks on the side of the vessel, were dangerously open and would require careful caulking. Moreover, many of the crew had fallen ill, so Briggs would have to hire lascars (local sailors) to do most of the work. In a letter to Mackay and Coolidge of Boston, who had an interest in the voyage, and another to Gould on April 26, Briggs explained the necessity of staying longer than planned: "my crew have been more or less off duty ever since we arrived. One I was obliged to discharge—Geo Harris as he was completely worn out—have shipped another in his room. We have now two sick. The cook is in the hospital. It is now very sickly; 300 die daily in Calcutta. I have been a little unwell but am much indebted to Mr. Bacon for advice and assistance in my business . . ."

Still more discouraging, a crop failure in 1831 had produced speculation in indigo the following year, and when the harvest was abundant in the next two years prices declined and the British agency houses collapsed.[5] The decline meant that bills of exchange could not be converted to cash for purchases. Briggs complained that everyone had to act as his own banker. The turmoil in the indigo market created great fluctuations in supply. When Briggs arrived, there was very little indigo available for purchase. The East India Company had taken the best, and what little was left was of very poor quality. The fate of New England's merchant marine and industries was ever more closely globally entangled with the banking industry in Britain and the credit it could provide, and with the indigo planters, European and Indian, and farmers who raised the crops in eastern India.

Briggs knew he would have to stay in Calcutta considerably longer than expected and that he would be held accountable. Dismal market conditions dimmed his hopes for a successful voyage. He kept his port journal to maintain a record for the owners of what transpired each day, and his efforts on behalf of their interests. Each entry is begun as in a shipping log, noting the day's weather, continuing with cargoes discharged and loaded, activities of hired laborers and crew in preparing the brig for sea, and punctuated with reports of illness, drunkenness, and desertion. Each short entry plainly reflects the tedious, laborious, repetitive day-to-day routine of a Yankee East Indiaman at Calcutta.

Figs. 13.1–5 (above and on following pages) Five-part panorama of the waterfront in and around Calcutta, c. 1830.
Watercolor, all height 64.4, width 92.7–100.3 cm. Peabody Essex Museum M11151.1–5, Museum purchase 1962.
1: Native and European vessels with Anglo-Indian country houses in the background; 2: Native and European vessels;
3: Native and European vessels with Government House and nearby buildings in the background; 4: Native and European vessels
with part of Fort William in the background at left; and 5: Native and European vessels with a pontoon bridge.

CHAPTER 13

From the Journal of the Apthorp, 1833

JAMES B. BRIGGS

Thursday March 14 1833
Commences with light airs and calm. At four a.m. weighed from Garden Reach and proceeded towards Calcutta. At 7 arrived abreast of the moorings, secured the Harbourmaster and hauled to the Company's moorings. Moored ship with the bower and stream chains. Employed the remainder of the day in chaining [securing] ship, unbinding sails, sending topgal't and royal yards down, etc. End with fine weather. [*In margin*] NNE (winds); 130 days from Boston.

Friday March 15th
Pleasant weather with light southerly winds. Employed at sundry work about the ship. Discharged what cargo we had on board per cargo book. Cleared the hole for discharging ballast etc. 11 lascars [sailors] and one serang [foreman] came on board to assist discharging ballast . . . ½ day—

Saturday, March 16th—1833
Pleasant weather and calm. Employed discharging ballast, stowing provisions and water, and getting ready to receive cargo. Discharged 2 lighter[1] loads ballast. 11 lascars and serang on board . . . Ends pleasant. Broached Bbl [barrel] Pork. [*In margin*] George Harris, Seaman on shore without liberty.

Sunday March 17th 1833
Pleasant with strong southerly winds. Part of the ships company on shore on liberty. Delivered 3 barrels beef to the ship *Dover*.[2] [*In margin*] 11 lascars, 1 serang.

Monday March 18th
Pleasant weather. Employed discharging ballast. Delivered 17 boat loads. Received 100 mats for dunnage and 100 bamboos. 11 lascars and 1 serang on board. Ends hot, sultry weather.

Tuesday March 19th, 1833
Commences pleasant. Employed at sundry work about the ship. 11 lascars and serang on board. [*In margin*] Received 2 boats **A**[3] no. 1; 150 bags saltpetre.

Wednesday March 20th
Pleasant, hot sultry weather. Employed at sundry work about the ship. Sent down yards and masts. Received 4 boats, 380 bags salt petre. 11 lascars and 1 serang on board. 16 caulkers and a master to work, caulking the outside of the ship. Ends fresh breezes. [*In margin*] Received 4 boats; 380 bags.

Thursday March 21 1833
Pleasant weather. Busily employed. Discharged 10 lighter loads ballast. Received 3 d[itt]o [lighter loads] salt-petre. Part of the ships company at work on the yards. 11 lascars and 1 serang on board. Also 16 caulkers and one foreman—1 man off duty says sick. [*In margin*] Received 3 boats; 273 bags.

Friday March 22 1833
Pleasant weather with light winds. Employed discharging ballast etc., and taking in saltpetre. Received 100 bamboos. 16 caulkers and foreman to work caulking the ship outside. 11 lascars and serang on board assisting to discharging ballast etc. Delivered three barrels mess beef & 6 barrels flour. [*In margin*] Received 2 boats; 145 bags saltpetre.

Saturday March 23 1833
Pleasant weather. Employed about the rigging and receiving cargo. 15 caulkers and one foreman caulking outside; 11 lascars, 1 serang on board. . . . Ends pleasant. [*In margin*] Received 3 boats; 324 bags saltpetre.

[*Following is Briggs' letter written on this day to the* Apthorp*'s owners informing them of the alarming state of the markets in Calcutta:*][4]

Calcutta March 23 1833

Messrs Nathaniel Goddard, B.A. Gould, G. A. Goddard

Gentlemen:

I avail myself of the present opportunity by the *Dover* to inform you of the safe arrival here of your Brig *Apthorp* on the 13th—126 days to the pilot.[5] We had a very pleasant passage, but I am sorry to inform you we have arrived here in a very bad time. Business is uncommonly dull at present; owing to extensive failures among which are some of the principal English houses, Alexander's and Mackintosh's. Others are expected.[6] In consequence all confidence in money transaction is entirely destroyed. Every one now is obliged to be his own banker. Cash is very scarce. I am afraid we shall find some difficulty in selling bills for cash. We might negotiate them at any time by taking their indigo, such as it is, at their own prices, but this will not answer. The crop is said to be 130,000 m[aun]ds and is all brought in. About one half of all the best indigo was taken by the Company early in the season from the insolvent houses at prices about 10 to 15 rupees advance on the last year's prices. It has since risen 10 to 15 more. There is at present very little in Calcutta. None of first quality—of second quality about 40 chests has been offered without any rejection at 140/—third quality 110 @ 125—the very worst sorts, broken, mixed, hard and burnt indigo, which last year was sold as low as @ 90 now sells for 100 to 120.

Am at a loss to know what to do. Cannot think it for your interest to take much indigo under present circumstances. The principal part is held by speculators. Have an idea we must purchase at any price and I expect to pick up some small lots in the bazaar that may answer and shall take the rest of your funds in gruff goods, some silks. W. Austin returns with a great part of his funds. He and all have almost gleaned the place of every box of indigo worth taking. Shellac is high. None of first quality: [?] in market [an indistinct insert here about a purchase of bazaar shellac at 6/8][7] Mirzapore orange which was last year 30/ now selling 36 @ [i.e., to] 38/; 2nd qty [quality] 31 @ 33. Beerboom orange 33@ 34. Salt Petre:

Godenore 7/4 @ 7/00;

Gazipore 7/8 @ 7/8;

Chopra 6/4 @ 6/14;

Mirzapore 5/12 @ 6/8;

Caunpore 5/8 @ 6/.

Have bought about 1000 bags @ 6/3, @ 7/. Senna 7/8 to 8. Gum Copal 33/34. Camphor 56/. Nutmegs 3 sicca rupees per seer. Mace 6 ditto. Twine 10/ per bazaar maund. [Munjut?] 4/8 @ 5/. Cowhides—Patna green salted 20 @ 22; Patna green dry 12 @ 13; Gazipore Green salted 25 @ 26; Hashkally-Hashally 11 @ 12. Gum Copal 33 @ 34. Twine 8 @ 10; Gunny [bags] single 6/8 @ 7/12.

Madras goat skins 23/. Patna 18 . 19; Cawnpore 21. 22/ Spanish dollars 210/. Sovereigns 10/8. American dollars 206. 8. Five frank pieces [12 pence?] Have sold yours at 192/8. Exchanges have sold. £ of your bills at 2/. We have commenced loading; have on board 800 bags salt petre good fair quality; Cow hides and goat skins are so much cheaper than last year, I think it well to exceed your order for these articles. Shellac so much higher shall not take so much.

Silk goods:[8]

Sup: Possakee choppas		140 @ 155
Possakee	d[itt]o	125 . 135
Chullum	do	112 .115
Medium sup. choppas		105 @ 110
Nim possakee	do	90 @ 95
Chullum	do	75
Sup: Possakee bandannas		142 @ 152
Possakee	do	127 @ 133
Chullum	do	114 @ 117
Large fine choppas		84 @ 85
Serampore " ditto		134 @ 140
" nim	ditto	120 @ 125
" fine mid n	do	100 @ 102
" 2nd	do	92 @ 93

Small choppas now in market. Some expected. Have purchased about 1000 bags salt pctre @ 6/3 @ 7. 300 bags ginger at 6/8. Shall wait a few days before we purchase any shellac in hopes to get it lower. 10,000 goat skins at 23/. 200 buffalo hides for dunnage @ 10/.

Shall continue to purchase as good lots may offer of either of the above and expect to find some small lots of indigo in the bazaar. Am in hopes to get away in one month. Part of our crew are sick and we are obliged to hire lascars. We find the brig's bends are very open and shall have them caulked. This is an expense I did not calculate on but it is absolutely necessary. I assure you gentlemen I shall be as economical as possible. I am here at present under very discouraging prospects, but shall act with prudence and use every exertion in my power to promote your interest. No freight to be obtained. Mr. A[ustin] has taken a few tons but very low.

Sunday March 24th 1833
Pleasant weather. Light winds from the souther[ly?]. Part of the crew on shore on liberty. Ends pleasant. 11 lascars and serang employed scraping. [*In margin*] Ship *Dover* employed down the river.

Monday March 25 1833
Cloudy weather. Employed discharging ballast and at work about the rigging. George Wheeler did not return until 10 AM this morning, and stayed on board about half an hour, without going to his duty, after giving very insulting language went again in the boat, and returned on shore without orders from me. Ends pleasant. [*In margin*] George Harris deserted the ship. 16 Caulkers and one foreman on board; 11 lascars and serang on board.

Tuesday March 26th 1833
Pleasant weather with fine breezes from NNW. George Wheeler returned on board at 10 a.m. Employed about the rigging, scraping the sides and receiving cargo on board. 16 caulkers and one foreman, on board. Finished caulking today. 11 lascars and serang on board. Ends pleasant. [*In margin*] Received 4 boats, 286 bags saltpetre; 100 bamboos.

Wednesday March 27th 1833
Pleasant, with fine cool breezes. Employed about the rigging, scraping outside, sent topmasts up. 11 lascars and 1 serang on board. No cargo today.

Thursday March 28 1833
Pleasant weather. Employed about the rigging. Stowing saltpetre etc. No cargo today. 11 lascars, 1 serang.

Friday March 29th
Fine weather, very hot and sultry. Employed about the rigging paying,[9] bends,[10] filling water etc. etc. 11 lascars, 1 serang on board.

Saturday March 30th
Fine weather, fresh breezes from WNW. Employed about the rigging. Sent topmasts and topgallant masts up and lower and topsail yards etc.[11] 11 lascars and one serang on board. No cargo today. Ends pleasant.

Sunday March 31st 1833
Pleasant weather. 10 lascars and serang on board. Ends as above.

Monday April 1st 1833
As usual pleasant. Fresh westerly winds. Employed about the rigging. Same number of lascars on board. Ends with fine weather. [*In margin*] Received one boat load saltpetre, 107 bags.

Tuesday April 2nd 1833
Fresh breezes from the westward and pleasant. Employed about the rigging and receiving cargo. 11 lascars and serang on board. Carpenter sick. Ends fresh breezes. [*In margin*] Received 131 bags saltpetre; 230 d[itt]o ginger; 10 bales gunnies; 20 bundles, 50 each, gunnies.

Wednesday April 3 1833
Fresh breezes from the southward. Employed tarring rigging, receiving cargo, etc.. 11 lascars and serang on board. Carpenter off duty, sick. Ends fresh breezes. [*In margin*] Received 92 bags ginger; 35 bundles twine; 408 bags saltpetre.

Thursday April 4th 1833
Fresh breezes from the SSW and pleasant. Set up lower and topmast rigging. 11 lascars & serang on board. Carpenter remains sick. Ends fresh breezes. [*In margin*] Received 187 bags saltpetre; 20 bales gunnies.

Friday April 5th 1833
Strong breezes from SSW and fair weather. Employed about

Fig. 13.2

the rigging. Ends fresh breezes. Carpenter remains sick. 11 lascars and serang on board.

Saturday April 6th 1833
Strong breezes and pleasant. Employed painting masts and yards. Stowing saltpetre and receiving cargo. 11 lascars and serang on board. Ends fresh breezes. [*In margin*] Received A 100 bundles twine; 224 bags saltpetre.

Sunday April 7th 1833
Light winds and fine weather. Part of the crew on shore on liberty. Carpenter still remains sick.

Monday April 8th 1833
Strong breezes from the SSW and hot sultry weather. Employed

about the rigging etc. and receiving cargo. Same number of lascars on board. Finished taking in all the saltpetre, making in all 2649 Bags. Received 114 bags ginger in old bags; 65 bundles rattans; 34 bags saltpetre.

Tuesday April 9th 1833
As usual fresh breezes and hot weather. Employed painting outside and receiving cargo. 2 men off duty sick; same number of lascars on board. Ends fresh breezes from SSW. [*In margin*] Received 77 cases shellac; 4 bales hides; 27 bales goat skins; 10 bundles each containing 20 loose cow hides; 50 bundles containing 2500 gunny bags.

Wednesday April 10th 1833
Commences strong breezes and pleasant. Ships company stow-

Fig. 13.3

ing cargo and sundry work about the ship. All the lascars on shore it being Holy-day.[12] No cargo to day.

Thursday April 11th 1833
Fresh SSW gales and pleasant. Ships company employed stowing cargo. All the lascars on shore.

Friday April 12th 1833
Commences pleasant fine weather. Employed stowing cargo, taking up the planks between decks etc. Ends with strong squalls. [*In margin*] Wind-SSW. Discharged all the lascars tonight.

Saturday April 13 1833
Commences pleasant. Ships company variously employed. Carpenter still remains sick. Employed part of the day varnish-

ing decks. Latter part of the day heavy squalls with, thunder, lightning and rain. No cargo today. [*In margin*] Winds all around the compass.

Sunday April 14th 1833
All these twenty four hours squally with rain at intervals. Carpenter remains off-duty, sick.

Monday April 15th 1833
This day pleasant weather with fresh winds from SSW. Employed about the rigging, repairing sails, and sundry work about the ship. 2 men off duty sick.

Tuesday April 16th 1833
Pleasant throughout the day. Employed at sundry work about

Fig. 13.4

the ship and taking in cargo. 2 men sick. Ends pleasant. 3 Bengali carpenters at work fixing new scuppers.[13] [*In margin*] Received 181 bags ginger; 100 bags cloves; 30 bundles twine; 20 bundles gunny bags (1000); 15 bales cowhides; 43 boxes indigo.

Wednesday April 17th 1833
This day fresh breezes from SSW and pleasant. Employed at sundry work about the ship and taking in cargo. Received 33 boxes shellac.

Thursday April 18th 1833
Commences pleasant weather. Ships company variously employed. Broached barrel beef. Ends with fine weather. Received 91 bundles twine; 30 bundles gunnies (1500); 100 bundles rattans (1500).

Friday April 19th 1833
Fresh breezes and squally weather. Employed at sundry work about the ship, repairing sails, and taking in cargo. Carpenter employed caulking the hatches, etc. Ends fresh breezes. [*In margin*] Received 35 boxes shellac; 5 bundles hides.

Saturday April 20 1833
This day moderate winds from SSW and fine weather. Ships company variously employed about the ship, repairing sails and receiving cargo. Ends with fine weather. [*In margin*] Received 4 bales goat skins; 4 bales hides; 50 bags ginger (old); 15 bundles containing 150 hides.

Fig. 13.5

Sunday April 21 1833
Pleasant weather with light winds. All the ships company on board.

Monday April 22 1833
All this day very hot sultry weather. Employed about the ship examining the bread and variously employed. Cook and one man off duty sick. Broached [?] of bread. I started it in the bread room. [*In margin*] Received 224 boxes shellac; 200 bundles rattan.

Tuesday April 23 1833
Pleasant weather with gentle breezes. Employed repairing sails and other necessary work about the ship. Two men off duty sick. Ends pleasant. 3 carpenters on board fitting new whelps to the windlass.[14] [*In margin*] Received 30 bales of gunnies.

Wednesday April 24 1833
Pleasant but very hot sultry weather. Employed repairing sails etc. 2 men off duty sick. Cook went to the hospital today sick. 3 carpenters to work on the windlass. Ends as above. Received 54 bales senna; 200 bundles rattans.

Thursday April 25 1833
Hot sultry weather. Employed at sundry work about the ship. The ship *United States*, Capt. Webb sailed today.[15]

Friday April 26 1833
This day pleasant, but very hot and sultry. Employed repairing sails and other necessary work about the ship. Received 11 boxes shellac; 9 bales gunnies; 50 bags ginger loose; 2 hundred bundles rattans.

Saturday April 27 1833
First part pleasant, hot sultry weather. Latter part of the day squally.

Sunday April 28 1833
All this day pleasant and clear. Part of the crew on shore on liberty.

Monday April 29 1833
Pleasant weather with fresh breezes from SSW. Employed at sundry work and taking in cargo. Ends pleasant. Delivered 2 pipes navy and 3 barrels pilot bread [ship biscuit]. [*In margin*] Received 25 boxes shellac; 40 bundles gunnies containing 2000; 1 box sago; 5 bales goat skins.

Tuesday April 30 1833
Pleasant fresh breezes from SSW. William Wardwell deserted the ship this day. Ends pleasant.

Wednesday May 1 1833
Commences pleasant with strong winds. Employed binding sails and other work about the ship. William Wardwell was delivered on board by the police officer. Ends pleasant.

Thursday May 2nd 1833
All this day fresh breezes from SSW and very hot weather. Employed setting up rigging and receiving cargo on board. William Wardwell deserted the ship again during the night. [*In margin*] Received 93 boxes and 4 parcels of silk goods; 15 bales cow hides; 20 bales of gunnies; CH[16] 5 boxes freight.

Friday May 3 1833
Strong breezes and pleasant. Employed about the ship and taking in cargo. Ends pleasant. Eli Ring sent to hospital sick. [*In margin*] Received 22 boxes shellac; 50 bundles containing 2500 gunnies.

Saturday May 4 1833
As usual fresh winds from SSW and very hot weather. Employed in receiving and stowing cargo. George Cole seaman came on board in place of Eli Ring, who was sent to the hospital sick. Ends pleasant. Ship *Corvo* Captain Towne arrived today from Boston.[17] [*In margin*] Received 11 bales cowhides; **BBS** 2 bales

blue goods—freight. Broached 1 barrel pork and 1 barrel beef.

Sunday May 5 1833
Fresh breezes and fine weather. Ends the same.

Monday May 6 1833
First part of the day moderate winds with heavy rain. Employed about the ship and taking in cargo. The cook returned on board today from the hospital. Ends pleasant. [*In margin*] Received 53 boxes shellac; 2 bales cowhides; 14 loose hides; 1 muster box indigo.

Tuesday May 7 1833
Commences pleasant. Loosed sails today. Employed getting ready to drop down river. Clearing ship etc. Finished stowing cargo. Carpenter employed caulking the hatches. Received on board the stock etc. [*In margin*] Received 15 bundles loose gunnies.

Wednesday May 8 1833
Commences pleasant fine weather. At 5 AM the Harbour Master came on board, unmoored the ship from the H.[onourable] C.[ompany] moorings and dropped out. At half past five the pilot came on board. Employed working ship down river. At 12 the tide change came too. At 5 weighed—and came too for the night. [*In margin*] 12 meridian anchored; 5 weighed; 7 anchored.

Thursday May 9 1833
Commenced moderate and pleasant. At daylight weighed and worked ship down. English ship in company. At 5 PM weighed and dropped down. At ½ past 7 anchored for the night. [?] to 30 f[athoms] on the chain. Furled sails at 8 PM. Sit the watch. Squally appearance in NW. 11 ½ AM anchored 6 fathoms; 5:30 weighed; 7:30 anchored.

Friday May 10 1833
Commences pleasant with fine weather. At daylight weighed and proceeded down river. 10 AM anchored above the James and Marys.[18] At 5 PM weighed and worked down. At 7 anchored.

Remarks on Saturday May 11
Commences fresh breezes. Squally appearances. At 4:30 weighed and worked ship down river. At 7 passed the James and Mary's.

At 9 AM passed Diamond Harbor. 11:30 anchored; furled sails. Ends fresh breezes from SSW.

Remarks on Sunday May 12
Commences with light winds and fine weather. At 4:30 weighed and worked ship down river. At 1 PM came too abreast of Mud Point. At 5 PM weighed again and at 7:30 PM anchored in 5 fathoms. Furled sails. Ends pleasant.

Monday May 13 1833
Commences light winds. At 5 AM got under way and proceeded down river. At 9 AM passed Kedgree [Khijiri]. At 1 PM came to anchor in 52 fathoms, about half way between Kedgree and Saugor [Sagar]. At 6 weighed again and worked down until 10 PM. Anchored in 5/s fathoms. Saugor point NNW 5 to 6 miles.

Remarks on Tuesday May 14 1833
Commences light winds. At 4:30 weighed and worked down the eastern channels. At 11 PM saw the light vessel. At 12 midnight had a fresh squall from NW [cleared?] all up. At 6 AM the pilot left us. Light vessel bearing NNW 4 miles. Lat 21.03 N; Long 88.25 E. Lat at noon 20.54 N; Long at noon 88.37 E. [*In margin*] SA [sea account] commences Wednesday May 15, 1833.

[*Soon after the* Apthorp *reached Boston, Briggs wrote to his banians in Calcutta to let them know he was too ill to come on the next voyage and that they should expect Henry Bridges in his place.*]

Boston, October 24, 1833
Baboos Ramtonoo Ghose, Madden Mohun Bose and Co.

Gentlemen,
I am happy to inform you of my safe arrival at this place in the *Apthorp* 134 days passage. We got home one day before the *United States* and shall make a decent voyage. I am not very well in health and Capt. Henry Bridges is now master and supercargo of the *Apthorp*. I have recommended him to your house and have no doubt you will use every exertion on your parts to procure him a cargo in every respect good and as cheap as you would if I were in the vessel. I have told him that I place the utmost confidence in you and hope you will be very attentive this voyage as I have recommended you to the owners of the *Apthorp* who will probably have 2 or 3 vessels every year. You must do your best this time or they will blame me. I shall probably come and see you again next year in the season for indigo.

I found all your accounts correct except the 200 half buffalo hides which you charged me 10/ per corge of 20 pieces. It is a mistake as they were half hides. The price was 5/ per corge of 20 pieces or 10/ per corge of 40 pieces. On these you have overcharged me 50 sicca rupees which [I] have been obliged to pay the owners. Also in the disbursements 10 yards silk for flag 10, ditto 3; tailor for making flag 3.4; sicca rupees 13.7. This flag you made me a present and I was surprised to see it charged to me. Have no doubt it was a mistake of the house sircars. I have therefore given Capt. Bridges an order on you for Rs 63 . . . 7 on my account which balances all our accounts of the *Apthorp* voyage 1833.

PART V

REVIVAL

Fig. 14.1 *Government House* by Charles D'Oyly, Dickinson and Co., lithographers, London, 1848.
Government House was the residence of the governor-general and the seat of the British empire in India. Lithograph, 31.6 x 54.5 cm;
Peabody Essex Museum M3104.1, Gift of Frances R. Morse, 1927.

CHAPTER 14

Gruff Goods, Transcendentalism, and the Bhagavad Gita

THE UNITED STATES AND INDIA IN THE 1850S

By mid-century, both the United States and British India had fulfilled their continental ambitions. In 1853, the Gadsen purchase, a strip of land in the southwestern United States acquired for $10 million from Mexico, completed the shape of the United States. In India, under Governor-General Dalhousie (1848–56), policies were instituted that enabled the British to achieve full control of the subcontinent. Rajas could be deposed for misrule or indebtedness, and kingdoms without direct heirs could be absorbed into British India—bypassing the established practice of adoption. In this way, realms of previously "allied" princes became British territory.

During these years, both the United States and British India experienced the effects of industrial development. Transportation and communication infrastructures—railroads, telegraph, and postal service—were rapidly extended. In the early 1850s, Governor-General Dalhousie opened the first rail and telegraph lines, and established uniform postal rates in British India. In 1850, a telegraph line was opened from Calcutta downriver to Diamond Harbor.[1] Meanwhile, in the United States, railway lines nearly tripled to more than 30,000 miles.[2] The first telegraph line, between Baltimore and Washington, became operational in 1844.[3] In the United States, the goal was to make the vast "empty" continent available for settlement and to integrate it into the national economy. In India, the goal was different: to create a viable market for British enterprise and manufactures, to move raw materials to ports, and, especially after the 1857 rebellion, to strengthen communications and make the densely populated subcontinent easier to control.

The expansionist policies of British India and the United States were each set against a background of tensions that would explode in the years following the *Rockall*'s 1854 voyage to Calcutta (chapter 16). The debate over the extension of slav-

ery into the new western territories was the central political issue in the United States. Attempts to arbitrate Northern and Southern interests by controlling the territories into which slavery could be extended failed to resolve the conflict, and in 1861 the situation escalated into civil war. In India, British intervention in royal succession through the policy of lapse and the removal of rajas for "misrule" alienated many client kings. In 1856, the annexation of the kingdom of Oudh, together with the arrogant disregard of the sensibilities of Indian sepoys, who were horrified at being issued cartridges reputedly greased with the fat of cows and pigs, galvanized resistance into insurrection. The conflict lasted from the middle of 1857 until late 1858, when the British regained control. Both the American Civil War and the Rebellion of 1857 (or Mutiny, as it became known in the West) ended with affirmations of existing power relations, of the industrial North over the agricultural South in the United States, and of the government of British India over rebellious native rulers and soldiers.

INDO-U.S. TRADE: NEW COMMODITIES AND REVIVAL

In the late 1840s, after two decades of languishing, Indo-U.S. trade began to grow again. Hides, indigo, and saltpeter remained important commodities, but two new products suddenly became prominent on cargo lists: linseed, from which oil was extracted for use in the manufacture of paint and varnish, and jute, in the form of yarn, twine, cloth, and "gunny" bags, in ever increasing demand for the packing and transport of bulk commodities.[4] Commerce and navigation reports, published by the U.S. Department of the Treasury, did not even list linseed among the commodities imported from India until the 1840s. By 1854, the year of the *Rockall*'s voyage (chapter 16), the value of imported linseed jumped to almost $900,000, exceeded only by saltpeter and jute (including jute products) each at about

$1 million, and followed closely by hides. These commodities together accounted for about $4 million of the $5.5 million in goods imported in that year, about 2 percent of total imports.[5]

Both of the new commodities, linseed and jute, were being actively developed for export by the British in Bengal during the last half of the nineteenth century. The halt in trade between Britain and Russia during the Crimean War (1854–56) was an added stimulus, encouraging entrepreneurs in Calcutta to supply the needs for these commodities by further increasing jute and linseed production as substitutes for their Russian counterparts. In 1831, for example, almost all the linseed imported into Britain for oil was purchased from Russia (2.2 out of 2.8 million bushels);[6] by the late nineteenth century, nearly all of it was from Bengal. In the United States, the market for linseed as a component of paint and varnish was growing rapidly, and importers turned to Calcutta for provisions. During the 1850s and '60s, machinery developed to grind pigments in oil made it practical to produce ready-to-use colors. At the same time, containers were designed and fabricated suitable for transporting prepared paints. For the first time, ready-made paints became widely available and the demand escalated with the building boom that accompanied the doubling of the U.S. population between 1860 and 1890.[7]

Until mid-century, jute had also been insignificant as an export, though it was grown in northeastern India for local use. Between 1840 and 1855, the amount of jute exported from Bengal increased tenfold and its value thirty times.[8] The United States was a leading market. By the turn of the century, jute had become the fourth largest export of India, and Calcutta surpassed Dundee, Scotland, as the principal place for its manufacture.[9] In the United States, cloth woven of jute fiber was in increasing demand as a cheap, strong material for baling cotton in the South and for bagging corn and other crops as commercial agriculture rapidly expanded westward. With the introduction of the steel plow and the reaper in the 1840s and '50s, grain production took off. In the 1840s, the corn harvest nearly doubled (from 377 million bushels in 1839 to 600 million in 1849). In the 1850s, the wheat output grew 75 percent.[10] These abundant harvests needed to be poured into sacks for transport cross country and shipment abroad. Most jute was imported into the U.S. ready to use, but there were a few factories for producing cloth and twine—four in 1890.[11] Jute factories tended to concentrate around Boston, since it was the leading port of entry for

Indian commodities. Colonel Francis Peabody, son of Joseph Peabody, whose ship *George* had made annual voyages to Calcutta for more than twenty years, built processing facilities for linseed oil and cake, rice, and gunny cloth near Tudor's Wharf, where ice was loaded for Madras, Bombay, and Calcutta. Peabody also built a linseed oil and jute factory near his hometown, Salem.[12]

While linseed and jute imports boomed, Indian cotton and silk textiles, once the heart of the trade, declined still further. Modest quantities were imported—in 1854, silk cloth worth $32,000, and Kashmir shawls, still the most luxurious wrap an American woman could own (fig. 14.2). A market, if only a small one, for silk handkerchiefs also survived. In 1848, S. H. Bullard ordered 500 large tie-dyed bandannas, each case of 50 to contain 20 yellow, 15 red, 10 chocolate, and 5 blue. Bullard also asked for 500 large choppas (printed handkerchiefs); 500 medium (30 inches square); and 250 each of 28- and 29-inch squares. Most luxury textiles were so expensive that they were ordered by the piece. In 1844, for example, Miss Flagg ordered two square Kashmir shawls with black fields; one of these, expected to cost Rs.200 ($100), was to be almost two yards square, with a narrow border and palm leaves in the corners. H. H. Crocker, at the same time, ordered a square shawl, "the most handsome available," expecting to pay Rs. 300 ($150). Other textiles were also special ordered. Mr. Linzee, in 1846, ordered two silk "pollamposies" (i.e., palampores, bedcovers). He wanted salmon-colored grounds with a house in the center, measuring 3.5 by 3 yards. Mr. Linzee also ordered Cossimbazar plaid silk for two dresses, three pieces of seersucker (along with engravings, views of Calcutta).[13] This diminished demand for Indian textiles was all that survived; it was economically trivial, and concentrated on Indian specialties like bandanna and choppa handkerchiefs, and luxury goods, especially Kashmir shawls and silks. None of the old staple cotton goods were included; those had long since been priced out of the market by tariffs and superceded by American manufactures. It was the gruff goods—linseed, gunny, saltpeter, hides, and indigo—that made the trade profitable for Americans and fueled the growth of trade at mid-century. As it had from the outset, the balance of trade remained firmly in favor of British India. In 1854, the year of the *Rockall*'s voyage, cargoes worth about half a million dollars were shipped from the United States, and American vessels brought home almost $5.5 million worth of Indian goods.

Fig. 14.2 Kashmir shawl, c. 1855. Wool and silk, embroidery, 170.2 x 155 cm;
Peabody Essex Museum 128449, Courtesy of Mrs. Benjamin D. Shreve.

As the India trade revived, Boston maintained its leading position. Between 1856 and 1860, when New York had far outpaced other American ports in foreign trade, Boston's trade with India was more than twice New York's: "averaging 61 ships of 67,000 tons against 31 ships of 26,000 tons for New York."[14] In 1857, a particularly busy year, "ninety-six out of the hundred and twelve vessels that loaded at Calcutta for the United States, landed their cargoes at Boston, earning an average freight of twenty-thousand dollars."[15] That year, 6 million pieces of gunny were shipped to Boston.[16]

By mid-century, the makeup of exports from the United States to India had also altered profoundly. Manufactured textiles had become a fixture of export cargoes. In 1854, nearly half the value of U.S. exports to India was in cotton textiles.[17] Jeans and drills, light and heavy twilled cottons, the same class of utilitarian fabrics that U.S. vessels once brought from India, were now manufactured in New England mills, and figured prominently in cargo manifests. Ice, the ingenious development of the

doldrum years, continued to be a major export, comprising nearly one-fifth the total exports of 1854.[18] Although U.S. manufactured goods, including glassware and clocks, as well as cotton textiles, had increased markedly, there was still demand for the typical North American products that had long been fixtures of the trade. In 1858, the outward-bound cargo of the Boston ship *Indian*, W. H. Averill master, carried tobacco, flour, and naval stores, including pilot bread, tar, turpentine, boards, and planks. Treasure, in the form of silver specie, once indispensable for purchasing goods, was of little importance. Most of the trade was financed through bills of exchange on London banks, and some by Bengali banians who extended credit to their Yankee clients.

BOSTON BRAHMINS AND CALCUTTA BANIANS

By mid-century, Indo-U.S. trade settled at Boston and Calcutta, where there was a heightened sense of familiarity, a new ease to the encounter. Prominent members of the elite in both cities

Fig. 14.3 Raj Kissen Mitter (1811–1872), Calcutta, c. 1845.
Watercolor on ivory, 12.1 x 9.5 cm; Peabody Essex Museum
M9109, Gift of the Bostonian Society, 1957.

Fig. 14.4 Rajinder Dutt (1818–1889), Calcutta, c. 1850.
Watercolor on ivory, 14.6 x 9.5 cm; Peabody Essex Museum
M5027, Gift of William Norton Bullard, 1941.

shared long-established connections. In coastal New England, the East Indies had given not only wealth to those who succeeded at it, but great distinction as well. The East Indies trade (embracing the China, Manila, and Java trades as well as that of British India), Samuel Eliot Morison has observed,

> enjoyed a greater prestige than any branch of Boston commerce. . . . An "East-India merchant," in ante-bellum Boston, possessed social kudos to which no cotton millionaire could pretend unless previously initiated through Federalist commerce. To have an office on India Wharf, Boston, or to live in the India Row that comprised the fine old square-built houses of many a seaport town, conferred distinction.[19]

The East Indies was so firmly instated in New England that when Oliver Wendell Holmes dubbed the elite of Boston "brahmins" in his 1859 serial *The Professor's Story*,[20] the appellation struck a cord and became standard usage. The imported Indian term seemed to suit the prominence, exclusivity, endogamous practices—and in the late nineteenth century, progressively racialist thinking—of Boston's elite, and to spice their collective identity with a hint of exoticism.

By the 1840s, family firms whose connections to India spanned two or three generations included the Cabots and the Lees, with their ties to Newburyport, Beverly, and Boston; the Mackays and Coolidges of Boston; and the Rogerses, Peabodys, Stones, Pickmans, and Silsbees in Salem and Boston.

Besides the principals of such firms, there were the hundreds of men who had taken part in the trade as mariners or merchants, some of them logging the equivalent of years of residence in Calcutta. When nineteen-year-old Edwin Blood, whose account of his 1854 voyage in the *Rockall* is excerpted in chapter 16, arrived there to find seven fellow townsmen, he commented in his journal: "At present Newburyport is well represented in Calcutta . . . men and women, seven in all"—from a town of barely ten thousand. By the 1840s, Calcutta was as familiar a place in maritime New England as many of the cities of Europe. The ships that sailed there and the men who voyaged in them continued to be the principal conduits for encounters between India and the United States.

Like the East India merchants in Boston, the banians in Calcutta who specialized in the American market belonged to their region's elite. Most were Kayasthas or Brahmins whose more traditional callings, as administrators, priests, and teachers, required the kind of education and language study that suited them for positions as translators and business agents in colonial Calcutta. Many such families had succeeded as middlemen for the East India Company or for British private merchants; and some had prospered by concentrating on the needs of American merchant mariners stopping at Calcutta. These banians were prominent among the *bhadralok*, Calcutta's gentry. By mid-century, some of them had moved far beyond functional proficiency in English and knowledge of the local markets and East India Company regulations; they had become conversant in European literature, philosophy, religion, and science. The British administration of Bengal, during Governor-General Bentinck's term in the 1830s, had begun to advocate the Westernization of the elite to create a class better equipped to assist colonial rule.

The American connections that Calcutta banians established through their businesses also provided them with instructive experiences outside the colonial hierarchy of Anglo-Indian life. Americans, though perceived as kin to the British racially and linguistically, were plainly outsiders. They were not accepted socially by the elite whom they considered their peers. Their home market had distinctive requirements and as merchants they operated independently, without the power of the East India Company behind them.

Two of the banians most active at mid-century in the American trade were Raj Kissen Mitter (figs. 14.3 and 14.5; see also

Fig. 14.5 Raj Kissen Mitter (1811–1872), attributed to Sri Ram Pal, c. 1840. This photograph, c. 1940, shows Raj Kissen's portrait with its original chair and hookah. Clay, straw, pigments, cloth, cane-seated wood chair, metal hookah base with silk-wrapped leather tube, height of seated statue 122 cm; Peabody Essex Museum E9935, Gift of John A. Parker, 1840.

fig. 16.6) and Rajinder Dutt (figs. 14.4 and 14.9),[21] kinsmen of Ramdulal Dey, the American market pioneer who had risen from a childhood as a poor relation to become one of Calcutta's richest and most prominent men. The Mitters were *kulin* Kayastha, the caste's highest rank. Raj Kissen's father Radha Kissen had married Ramdulal Dey's daughter, a match that advanced Dey's position in Bengali society. The Mitter family, not surprisingly given their status, were social and religious conservatives who affirmed their place in Bengali society by sponsoring large public rituals and financing the construction

Fig. 14.6 Mughal rulers, from left: Emperor Bahadur Shah (r. 1719–48), Emperor Alamgir (r. 1754–60), and
Nawab Asaf ud Daula of Oudh [Avadh] (r. 1775–97). Opaque watercolor, each 16.5 x 12.7 cm;
Peabody Essex Museum, from left, E82704.5, E82704.7, E82704.13, Gift of Baboo Hulloohun Bhose, 1846.

and maintenance of temples. Rajinder Dutt, also a Kayastha, though not of the kulin rank, married a granddaughter of Ramdulal Dey. Rajinder's family fortune had been made by his grandfather, Akrur Dutt, a banian for the East India Company. Rajinder received a Western-style education just as it was becoming fashionable to do so among the liberal, cosmopolitan section of the elite. Rajinder Dutt and Raj Kissen Mitter represented contrasting sites in the social and political spectrum of nineteenth-century Bengal. Raj Kissen Mitter's conservative orientation toward traditional values—temple building and the acquisition of *zamindaris* (landed estates)—differed sharply from Rajinder Dutt's interests in new medical developments (especially the introduction of homeopathy), in social reforms permitting young widows to be remarried and encouraging education for girls, and in new sectors of the economy such as steam navigation and mechanized textile production.[22]

Despite their social, religious, and political differences, both Raj Kissen Mitter and Rajinder Dutt enjoyed close relationships with their American clients. Their relationships with Americans and their interest in the connections between Yankee and Bengali society prompted both of them to take advantage of a local specialty in the visual arts. Each had a life-size likeness made in clay, seated on fashionable Anglo-Indian chairs and dressed in proper Bengali style—Mitter was portrayed complete with his hookah (fig. 14.5). The portraits were probably the work of Sri Ram Pal, at the time the most renowned of the potter-sculptors who worked in the recently developed naturalistic style. Both statues were specially commissioned and presented to American clients, to be brought to the United States. The statues, intended for public display as an amusing and educational representation of Bengali society for Americans to enjoy, were installed in the congenial environment of the East India Marine Society's museum.

Raj Kissen Mitter gave his likeness to John Parker, a Boston-based client, in 1840. A handwritten card accompanied the portrait: "I remain, Dear Sir, Your very faithful Servant—Raj Kissen Mitter." In 1848, Dutt gave his portrait to T. A. Neal, who was in the India trade with his father, David Neal. The Neals and the Dutts had developed a friendship that spanned at least three generations. In an undated letter, Rajinder Dutt conveys his pleasure that Neal's daughter planned to write to him. "Tell her that she must come out to India and see her black grandpa and also tell her that when she sees me that I promise to give her some Indian ornaments which our ladies take a pride in wearing." Rajinder also promised "to send . . . a daguerreotype likeness of the members of our family [?], of course our male members. I will not be able to persuade the females to sit for their likenesses."[23]

In the East India Marine Society's museum, Dutt and Mitter's statues joined those of Durgaprasad Ghose and

Nusserwanjee Maneckjee Wadia, and the life-size clay models of characters from Calcutta society. Around the same time, in 1846, another of Calcutta's banians for the American trade, Baboo Hulloohun Bhose, made a contribution to the representation of Indian civilization in America. Bhose donated a set of sixteen miniatures depicting rulers of the Mughal dynasty, which still, if in name only, ruled at Delhi. The portraits included Timur Shah, who founded the dynasty in 1398; Babur Shah, who established its power in India in the early sixteenth century; Akbar and Jahangir, who ruled at its height, as well as kings of eighteenth-century successor states in Mysore, Oudh, and Afghanistan. The portraits, in gouache on paper, seem to have been meant by the donor as a visual history lesson of Indian India (rather than British India) for American viewers (fig. 14.6).

THE MITTERS

According to family tradition, Mitter forebears settled in the area that would become Calcutta shortly before the city was founded in 1690. Radha Kissen (1770–1842) (fig. 14.7), who married Ramdulal Dey's daughter, had five sons. One of them, Raj Kissen (1811–1872), flourished as an agent for the American trade. He was the banian for the *Rockall*'s voyage in 1854. Records indicate that the firm of Raj Kissen and Radha Kissen Mitter was inaugurated on March 15, 1839, and that Raj Kissen, an astute businessman with an entrepreneurial spirit, led it successfully for twenty-five years. Apart from his own skills as a businessman, Raj Kissen may have benefited from the gradual retirement of his uncles, the sons of Ramdulal Dey, who left the business to manage the family property and live as landed gentry, a lifestyle to which the elite of Bengal traditionally aspired. Traditional aspiration prevailed twenty-five years later, in 1864, when Raj Kissen and his only son Amar Kissen closed their office so that Amar could devote full attention to the family's properties in Calcutta and their estates in the 24 Parganas south of the city.[24]

Although Raj Kissen was raised in an aristocratic, orthodox household, his father elected to provide him with a Western-style education at Hindu College to prepare him to move in the Anglo-Indian world. Raj Kissen's mastery of English and acquaintance with Western ways enabled him to manage the cultural divide and form close friendships with a number of his American clients. In addition to the Neals, who

Fig. 14.7 Radha Kissen Mitter (1770–1842), Calcutta, c. 1840. Presented by Radha Kissen to his client E. Rollins Morse of Boston. Watercolor on ivory, 15.2 x 11.4 cm; Peabody Essex Museum 123191, Gift of the estate of John T. Morse, 1931.

brought home Raj Kissen's portrait in clay, other families included in this transcultural circle were the Mackays, the Coolidges, and the Morses, all of Boston. Unitarian, republican New Englander R. C. Mackay and Raj Kissen formed a special bond.[25] Mackay made fourteen voyages to Calcutta; his sons, Francis Lodge and George H., both served as supercargoes. When they were in Calcutta, the Mackays stayed at 55 Radhabazar, the Mitter residence, built in 1809. Mackay and Mitter exchanged portraits. Radha Kissen Mitter presented young George Mackay with a ring to be kept until it could be given to his wife. Mitter, in turn, was presented with a silver tankard from George's father, inscribed "R.C.M to R.K.M." A photograph of Raj Kissen Mitter was also given to the Mackay family (fig. 16.6). Mackay's partner J. T. Coolidge was given a portrait of Raj Kissen painted on ivory in the new fashion, "accompanied by a cane" as an expression of gratitude for "the numerous and extensive acts of kindness which I and my family have experienced from your house. . . . I shall not forget them for as long as I live."[26] Portraits in oil on canvas by the Bengali artist H. C. Roy, painted in 1901 after likenesses of R. C. Mackay and J. T. Coolidge in the family's possession, were displayed in the main hall of the Mitter residence and remained there well into the twentieth century. As late as 1919, the families were still in correspondence. The Mitters also presented portraits to other Yankee business associates, including E. S. Coffin and John T. Morse.[27]

The social concerns of Radha Kissen and his sons, like those of his father-in-law Ramdulal Dey, centered on traditional community and religious life. Radha Kissen, whose family was of the highest (kulin) rank, was the more conservative. A strict supporter of orthodoxy, he joined the Dharma Sabha founded in 1830 to defend Hindu traditions and resist British interference with religious practices. His father-in-law, Ramdulal Dey, who had risen from humble origins through an astute ability to parlay financial success into social precedence, used his wealth and power to gain stature for his family and close associates. Father- and son-in-law came into conflict when Ramdulal used his influence to help reinstate a family friend ostracized for flouting Kayastha standards of behavior. His orthodox son-in-law Radha Kissen was deeply offended by Ramdulal's deliberate manipulations of caste rites and procedures. Ramdulal Dey's liberal, reformist biographer, writing in the 1860s, represents Radha Kissen Mitter as narrow-minded (perhaps, "orthodox"), poorly educated (perhaps, un-Westernized), and unprepossessing.[28] Ramdulal, in turn, has been represented by his detractors as a schemer and social climber who married his daughters into socially prominent families and used his wealth to achieve preeminence in Kayastha society. Whichever interpretation was favored, liberal or conservative, it seems likely that serving as commercial agents for outsider Americans merchants brought wealth that became a new source of rivalry within the community and fostered a sense of autonomy that emboldened some to defend, manipulate, or reform their own social situation.

RAJINDER DUTT

The first book by an Indian describing his culture for an American public was written by Philip Gangooly and published in Boston in 1860. One section of his book, *Life and Religion of the Hindoos*, describes the annual round of Hindu festivals. On Rash Jatra, the birthday of Krishna, the author noted: "In Calcutta, a rich family is widely known for the display of statuary, pictures, and ornamental works, on the *Rash*. Every American merchant engaged in the Calcutta trade knows that family of which Baboo Rajendro Narain Dutto is the head."[29]

At Rajinder Dutt's death in 1889, an obituary appeared in the *New York Nation* and was reprinted September 24, 1889 in the *Statesman*, Calcutta:

> Out of the host of Americans who, during the last half century have visited Calcutta, there must be a good number among the living, to whom mention of the name of Babu Rajinder Dutt will revive the memory of a man that no one knew but to esteem. . . . To be equally respected by his own countrymen and by foreigners is seldom the fortune of a native of India, but such was his fortune . . . He was of medium height, lithe of figure, purely Caucasian as to feature and rather dark for a Bengalee of good family . . . he would, but for his complexion and dress have been indistinguishable in most essentials from the typical American.

Dutt's American eulogist conferred what he certainly felt was a great compliment—that only the indelible fact of race distinguished Rajinder Dutt from an American.

Among Calcutta's banians, Rajinder Dutt (1818–1889) stands apart for the relationships he established with Americans. He was a new kind of Bengali. His grandfather Akrur Dutt had made his fortune working with the East India Company in the decades after the Battle of Plassey (1757), and understood prosperity to be linked with the British presence. Rajinder was educated at Drummond's Academy and Hindu College, elite institutions where well-born Bengalis of his generation could receive Western educations. Rajinder continued his studies at the Medical College, and though he withdrew after three years to join the family business, he persevered in his medical studies, eventually becoming a pioneer practitioner of homeopathy in Calcutta. Rajinder remained throughout his life deeply attracted to and well read in Western literature, science, and theology.

Besides imparting Western learning, the schools Rajinder attended had become, in the decade before his arrival, scenes of energetic challenges to conventional Hindu social and religious life led by the iconoclastic Young Bengal movement. Rajinder was encouraged to think in new ways about his own society and the British presence. According to his biographer and kinsman

Fig. 14.8 Gajalakshmi, lustrated by elephants and accompanied by cows of plenty, Jaipur, c. 1850.
The image of the goddess of wealth and good fortune was a fitting gift from a commercial agent to a museum established by
East India traders. Painted marble, main figure height 25.5 x width 25 cm, cows of plenty each height 12 x width 11.5 cm;
Peabody Essex Museum, Gift of Rajinder Dutt, 1850.

Haradhan Dutt, Rajinder was "deeply impressed with [Young Bengal's] progressive thoughts and spirit of enquiry" and their determination to change practices they thought repressive.[30] Rajinder became an active proponent of education for girls and remarriage of widows, a reform whose urgency struck home when one of his daughters became a widow at the age of twelve, condemned to remain unmarried for the rest of her life.

Rajinder read widely, avidly acquired books, and kept these available for others to use. The *New York Nation* obituary noted: "Even before he was thirty, his Library was by far the largest and the most valuable of any private person in Calcutta, and it went on growing to the last. . . . " At his death, the collection was considered the equal of the Calcutta Public Library. Dutt planned to print a catalogue and sought assistance in acquiring the works of Edgar Allan Poe, N. P. Willis, J. R. Lowell, James H. Perkins, publications on the aboriginal monuments of New York state, and even *The Book of Home Beauty* by Mrs. Kirkland.[31]

As a doctor of homeopathy, Rajinder treated the lowly and the exalted. His patients included the Tagores of Jorasanko[32]

and Radhakanta Deb's family at Shobhabazar, as well as visiting royalty, like the Maharani of Jaipur, and the great religious leader Sri Ramakrishna, founder of the movement that became the International Society for Krishna Consciousness. No one was charged a fee. One year, when the Jaipur royal family was resident for the social season and the Maharani fell ill, Rajinder was called in to treat her. In gratitude, and in lieu of payment, Dutt was sent a large collection of Jaipur marble figures. One of these he later presented to the East India Marine Society's museum, an image of Gajalakshmi, the goddess of wealth and prosperity—a truly fitting gift from a merchant to a society of merchants (fig. 14.8). In 1847, his reputation as a pioneer of homeopathy led to his name being submitted for an honorary degree in medicine at Harvard University.[33]

Given the family's connection with the East India Company, his Western education, and his intellectual bent, it is no wonder that Rajinder Dutt's interest in his American clients went beyond business connections and personal friendships to broader social, cultural, and political concerns. In 1853, Dutt met Charles Eliot Norton, a young Bostonian intellectual who had come to Calcutta as a supercargo for his brother-in-law's firm (Bullard and Lee, successor to the business of Henry Lee). Norton, the Harvard-educated son of prominent theologian Andrews Norton, had eagerly taken the opportunity to earn money and travel to the East. His real calling would lead him in a very different direction: Charles Eliot Norton is best remembered for founding the discipline of art history in America as a professor at Harvard.

In contrast to Dutt, Norton held rather conservative views. He believed firmly in the Greco-Roman foundation of art and his influence was instrumental in keeping Indian and Asian art from receiving serious attention in America until the end of the nineteenth century.[34] His estimation of Asians, despite his admiration for Rajinder Dutt as an individual, was not complimentary. When Norton published his views in the prestigious *North American Review*, Dutt responded: "I was sorry to find that you have been doing an injustice to the Hindus in accusing them of wanting benevolence." Hindus "possess as much of this virtue as any nation in the face of the globe. . . ."[35] Despite Norton's bias, the two maintained a lively intellectual fellowship through letters written during the 1850s. In these letters, Rajinder speaks of his own engagement with the issues of the day. In one he recounted how he explained to a large crowd of Hindus that water, contrary to the Vedic scriptures, was not a primitive element, but a compound of two gases, and that therefore the Vedas, in which water was considered a primal element, could not be revealed truth. Rajinder commented: "Chemistry and geology . . . will surely prove more effectual than all the theological discourses . . ." On the same grounds he also enjoyed challenging his Christian interlocutors, noting in another letter to Norton that the Christian concept of a six-day creation was impossible: "geology has assailed that point and with irrefutable arguments. . . ."[36]

Rajinder's concerns were social and political as well as theological and scientific. Though hardly rebellious, he advocated reforms. Besides working for widow remarriage, he helped found a school for girls. He also railed against the prohibition on travel across the oceans, which—because he was unwilling to risk ostracism—had prevented him and his sons from visiting Britain and America. He knew change would not come easily, and that ". . . no innovations can be effected without suffering the consequences of excommunication and the concomitant pains. . . ." But he reasoned that "as our number is daily increasing, the Hindus of the old school are becoming more and more tolerant not from any conviction of the absurdity of their views but because they have no help and cannot restrain the torrent of . . . thoughts. . . ."[37]

In the political arena, Rajinder was a strong proponent of equal rights for his countrymen. In the early 1850s, the government of Bengal attempted to extend the jurisdiction of their courts from the natives of Bengal to include resident Europeans, a move against which British citizens protested vigorously. Dutt commented: "For my part, I wish government would frame a code of laws applicable to all nations without respect to colour or creed."[38] Later on, Rajinder Dutt was a supporter of the British Indian Society, which his uncle helped found, and of the Indian National Congress.

In America, Dutt was renowned for his hospitality to sojourning merchants, who were regularly invited to his house for celebrations of major Hindu festivals.[39] To accommodate the objections of some local Christian clergy to their parishioners' presence at Hindu rituals, Rajinder usually asked his European and American friends to "a separate entertainment [on] the fourth night to protect them from their ministers."[40] Because of Dutt's special regard, Charles Eliot Norton was invited to festivities at the Dutt house on both Jagaddhatri Puja and Rash Jatra in 1849, attending at times usually reserved for family and Hindu participants.[41] For Rash Jatra, a celebration for Lord Krishna, the Dutt family was renowned "for the display of statuary, pictures, and ornamental works. . . ."[42] In a letter to Norton, Dutt described figures he commissioned in 1852: characters from Shakespeare and Scott, heroes of the French Revolution, even George Washington. He reported to Norton that the festival

> went off with great eclat. . . . We had the usual decorations with several improvements and additions. Several new figures were made amongst which we had Washington from the engraving which you had kindly sent to me, but the likeness I am sorry to say was not a good one. The masons however had succeeded in making several faithful representations of French characters who have been active in the late French Revolution.[43]

Rajinder Dutt was a master of the Calcutta tradition that celebrates religious festivals with deep devotion to god, and with public entertainments intended to amuse and edify (fig. 14.9). The displays of secular statuary he commissioned deftly promot-

Fig. 14.9 Rajinder Dutt (1818–1889), attributed to Sri Ram Pal,
c. 1848. Clay, straw, pigments, cloth, height (seated) 122 cm;
Peabody Essex Museum E9936, Gift of T. A. Neal, 1848.

ed the European literature he esteemed and inoffensively projected what could have been interpreted as seditious political
views—views that certainly drew sustenance from his association with republican Yankees from an erstwhile British colony.

INDIA AND THE NEW ENGLAND LITERATI

In America, the intellectual and literary dynamism of the 1840s
and '50s, long celebrated as a maturing of American identity,
was centered in New England, at Boston, Cambridge, and Concord.[44] Deep within this movement was the first serious intellectual engagement with the religions and philosophies of India.
Though the quality of their understanding and appreciation has
been a perennial topic of debate, there is no question that
American intellectuals were reading Indian sources and using
these in essays, poetry, and fiction.[45] Ralph Waldo Emerson's
aunt, Mary Moody Emerson, introduced him to Rammohun

Roy's writings and to Sanskrit works translated by others.[46]
Among Emerson's favorites were the *Bhagavad Gita*, the
Puranas, and the Upanishads.[47] Emerson's concept of the Over-
Soul, which "absorbed man in an all-enfolding Divinity,"[48]
resonated with his readings in those works where he found congenial ideas, including the notion that individual souls and God
are one. Emerson encouraged others to read Indian literature
and philosophy. At his urging, John Greenleaf Whittier read
the *Bhagavad Gita*. His neighbor, Henry David Thoreau, discovered Sanskrit literature in Emerson's library, where he read
William Jones' translation of the *Laws of Manu* in 1841.[49] But
Thoreau's favorite text was the *Bhagavad Gita*, of which he
wrote: "The reader is nowhere raised into and sustained in a
higher, purer, or rarer region of thought than in the *Bhagavad
Geeta*."[50] Years later, Thoreau remarked that his acquaintance
with the religious writings of the Hindus, Chinese, and Persians
was more intimate than with the Old Testament.[51] When
Thoreau died, his library of more than forty volumes of Indian
works in translation was passed on to Emerson.[52] Herman
Melville also partook of the widespread presence of ancient
Indian literature and civilization among the writers of the
period. Tracing the history of whale imagery in *Moby Dick*,
Melville cited "the famous cavern-pagoda of Elephanta, in
India" as the earliest depiction of a whale, noting that all the
"trades and pursuits"

> were pre-figured ages before any of them actually came
> into being. No wonder then, that in some sort our noble
> profession of whaling should have been there shadowed
> forth. The Hindoo whale referred to . . . depicting the
> incarnation of Vishnu in the form of Leviathan, learnedly
> known as the Matse Avatar. But though this sculpture is
> half man and half whale, so as to only give the tail of the
> latter, yet that small section of him is all wrong.[53]

Several factors converged to produce this engagement
with Indian literature. For more than fifty years, New England
merchant vessels had been bringing books from Calcutta and
London, as well as curiosities from all the ports they visited in
India. For decades, American missionaries, having established
themselves in India, had been sharing their views of "heathen"
life in sermons, books, and magazines. Though the missionaries
left little room for any appreciation of alien civilizations, they
succeeded in broadening American awareness of India and creating an arena in which different views of the character and

ICE CUTTING AT SPY POND, WEST CAMBRIDGE, MASS.

Fig. 14.10 *Ice Cutting at Spy Pond* (West Cambridge, Mass.),
woodcut from *Gleason's Pictorial Drawing-Room Companion*, Boston, 1854.

merits of Indians could be expressed. Especially in New England, where the more liberal Unitarian movement flourished—often supported by the seafaring cosmopolitans of port towns—the way for an engagement with Indian literature and philosophy had been prepared by the impact of Rammohun Roy's writings on Hindu unitarianism. Many of the Transcendentalists, who had been associated with the Unitarian movement, found the way open, inviting a genuine engagement with alien philosophies of the East.

In 1842, when the first organization dedicated to scholarship on the East, the American Oriental Society, was established, its founding president, John Pickering of Salem, acknowledged in his inaugural address the debt to the mariners and missionaries who had cultivated an awareness of the East. Salem-born Bostonian Pickering (who had taught law to William A. Rogers; see chapter 9) noted that the society's purpose, "the cultivation of learning in the Asiatic, African, and Polynesian languages,"[54] had been pioneered by American missionaries, who had learned exotic languages to translate the Bible. Pickering also acknowledged the instrumental role

played by American merchants, whose "extended commerce—the second in the world— . . . affords . . . an intercourse with the people of every habitable spot of the globe."[55] Pickering cited the Salem East India Marine Society, in his home town, "whose intelligent members are constantly enriching it with rare and valuable articles from distant countries."[56]

The connection between Indo-U.S. commerce and the mid-century engagement in Indian thought did not escape the New England literati. Henry David Thoreau understood that New England's commerce with the East helped create a milieu in which the translations of Hindu scriptures found an audience. In a well-known passage from *Walden*, after he had been watching Irish laborers cutting and hauling ice on the pond, he wrote of the attraction of Hindu scriptures and of the connection for New Englanders between this literature and commerce (fig. 14.10):

> Thus it appears that the sweltering inhabitants of
> Charleston and New Orleans, of Madras and Bombay
> and Calcutta, drink at my well. In the morning I bathe
> my intellect in the stupendous and cosmogonal philoso-

phy of the Bhagvat-Geeta, since whose composition years of the gods have elapsed, and in comparison with which our modern world and its literature seem puny and trivial; and I doubt if that philosophy is not to be referred to a previous state of existence, so remote is its sublimity from our conceptions. I lay down the book and go to my well for water, and lo! there I meet the servant of the Bramin, priest of Brahma and Vishnu and Indra, who still sits in his temple on the Ganges reading the Vedas, or dwells at the foot of a tree with his crust and water jug. I meet his servant come to draw water for his master, and our buckets as it were grate together in the same well. The pure Walden water is mingled with the sacred water of the Ganges.[57]

The creative involvement with Indian thought and religion present in the work of Emerson, Thoreau, and their circle, was limited in its reach. Their contemporary Charles Eliot Norton had found nothing in Indian civilization to esteem. Acquaintance and friendship did not necessarily yield a deepening intellectual rapprochement. The engagement with India often reverted to a familiar form, arising from a firmly established sense of superiority. Even the Unitarian movement succumbed in the 1850s, abandoning its earlier opposition to proselytizing and taking up missionary work. In 1853, the first American Unitarian pastor traveled to India. Charles Brooks, born in Salem in 1813 and educated at Harvard College and Divinity School, set sail for Madras on the *Piscataqua*, which carried a cargo of ice and three missionary families returning to their stations. Brooks was succeeded in 1855 by Charles Dall, who began a thirty-one-year ministry at Calcutta. Born in Baltimore in 1816, Dall had moved to Boston as a child and attended Boston Latin School, completing his education at Harvard College and Divinity School. Dall and his American Unitarian supporters had high hopes for conversions in India that were never realized.

During his first year in Calcutta, Charles Dall met Rajinder Dutt, whom he considered a "'pioneer' in the Unitarian cause" for his willingness to come to the Unitarian church and support it financially.[58] But Dutt was no more interested in conversion than Rammohun Roy had been. For the Bengali reform movement—from Rammohun Roy to the Young Bengals and including Rajinder Dutt—Dall and the American Unitarians provided a realm outside the Anglo-Indian power structure from which social reform, political participation, and status in the Anglo-Indian world could be examined. Dall's rejection by the European English-speaking community in Calcutta only enhanced the role of American Unitarianism in creating a new space for independent thought.[59] Throughout these years of Indo-U.S. commerce, the opportunity for connections with men who were like the British and yet clearly distinct, who represented a republican polity, an erstwhile British colony, who were usually cordial, sometimes became friends, and occasionally engaged in serious intellectual debate, gave quarter to some early strivings for self-determination and equality in India.

Fig. 15.1 *View of Newburyport (from Salisbury)* by Fitz-Hugh Lane after a sketch by A. Conant, Lane & Scotts Lithographers, Boston, c. 1846. Lithograph, 39.4 x 63.5 cm; Peabody Essex Museum M9511, Gift of the Bostonian Society, 1957.

CHAPTER 15

Edwin Blood, Supercargo's Clerk

Nineteen-year-old Edwin Blood embarked for Calcutta aboard the *Rockall* in January 1854. The document registering him as an American seaman describes him as five feet six-and-a-half inches tall with dark hair, dark complexion, and dark eyes. He was engaged as supercargo's clerk for the voyage.[1] Edwin never went to sea again; the voyage was intended not as the beginning of a career but as a finale to his formal education, a means of building his physical stamina and character, and an opportunity to become acquainted with the world beyond New England—an experience that would provide sound preparation for a young man intending to follow his father in commerce.

Edwin's father James was a self-made man whose own father had died when he was only nine years old. James had made his way from rural poverty in Hollis, New Hampshire, via Salem, Boston, and Vermont, to Newburyport, where he prospered, eventually becoming one of the town's wealthiest citizens.[2] The scope of James Blood's business interests reflected the economy of mid-century Newburyport, a port town at the mouth of the Merrimac River with a population approaching 10,000 in 1850 (fig. 15.1). Newburyport had been a flourishing center of shipping and shipbuilding in the eighteenth century, but its port-centered economy never recovered from the foreign trade embargo of 1807 and the war with England that followed. With the great successes of the textile factories upriver at Lowell and Lawrence, the propertied class that James became part of in the middle of the nineteenth century had turned most of its attention to manufacturing, and to the expanding financial and transportation infrastructure. James Blood owned factories, including an iron foundry and a machine shop on Merrimac Street across from the docks that had once dominated the economy of the town, and he was a director of the Ocean Bank.[3] But Blood also invested in the port's surviving maritime industries; he was a shipowner with his own wharf, and he was the appointed collector of customs during the administrations of presidents Buchanan and Pierce.

As a wealthy and prominent citizen, James Blood stood apart from his Newburyport peers, the vast majority of whom were conservative Whigs, heirs to the once powerful Federalists of coastal New England. James remained faithful to the Democratic party of his rural youth, which elected him to represent the town in the state legislature in the 1840s. His Democratic affiliation was connected to a deeply held liberalism. Having been raised a Congregationalist in Hollis, New Hampshire, he later joined its Unitarian offshoot, which privileged rationality and individual morality over faith and predestination. These convictions also drew his strong support to public education in Newburyport, where he served on the town's school committee.

As a father and a liberal, James Blood was deeply involved in the development and education of his son Edwin. In 1845, when Edwin was nine years old, the renowned phrenologist Lorenzo A. Fowler visited Newburyport. James arranged for Edwin to be examined. Phrenology had become immensely popular; the Boston area was its North American center. Like Unitarianism and Transcendentalism, phrenology suited the humanistic temper of the times, valuing individual capacities—morality, spirituality, and character—over a more restricted view of human potential as the preordained consequence of God's laws. Lorenzo Fowler and his brother Orson had both been raised to be preachers, but after Orson heard Dr. Johann Spruzheim lecture in Boston, he was attracted by this new science that disavowed the New England Calvinist belief in the innate sinfulness of man and instead declared that each individual was endowed with variable qualities, some good, some bad, which could be "read" in the shape of a person's head. Orson Fowler soon learned that these views were eagerly sought and there was a good living to be made in the practice of phrenology.

One of phrenology's most popular applications was the assessment of children, to reveal their aptitudes and help chart suitable futures.[4] When Lorenzo examined Edwin Blood in 1845, he submitted a long, detailed appraisal, reporting that the lad's brain is too large and too active for the strength of his system, and what he needs more than any other thing is physical culture—stamina and hardihood of constitution—capability for enduring hardships and the rough and tumble consequent upon a life of action in the business scenes of this world. He should not be tender of himself nor exercise his mental at the expense of his physical nature, but should accustom himself to endure fatigue from application and exercise of his muscles by labor.[5]

Edwin's voyage on the *Rockall* ten years later fulfilled Fowler's recommendation that physical culture be an integral part of his preparation for a career in business. Edwin's spirited intellect, which Fowler interpreted as the output of an overactive brain, is amply displayed in his journal of the voyage to Calcutta (chapter 16).

In 1854, with his father's encouragement, Edwin Blood "made arrangements with the firm of Gray and Morse, No. 44 Oriental Wharf, to go out to Calcutta in their employ in the capacity of supercargo's clerk. . . . So now behold me embarked on board the good ship *Rockall* still fast to the wharf in Boston ready for an early start."[6] The *Rockall* was a full-rigged ship of 644 tons owned by a group of Bostonians.[7] Years later, on learning of the death of the *Rockall*'s captain, Blood wrote of the ship and its captain in a letter:

> She was a fine ship of her class with oak-timbers, planking, ceiling and decks; staunch and safe; but a dull sailer. We were over six months on the homeward passage from Calcutta for Boston and the best day's run she made in the whole voyage was 234 miles in 24 hours and this scudding under bare poles. She was built at Medford for the father of Epes Sargent (long the editor of the *Boston Transcript*). Capt. Martin sailed in her on her first voyage as cabin-boy, was brought up in her from the age of ten years and worked up through all the grades till he finally commanded her. He was a good navigator, careful and sage and of untiring energy and vigilance.[8]

Edwin's preparation for the journey doubtless included books about India, which by the 1850s were becoming readily available, including translations of Sanskrit works, histories, and travelers accounts.[9] He had surely seen some of the published views of India by British artists, and probably visited the museum of the East India Marine Society in Salem. But a great deal of what he learned about India was imbibed during the long months of the voyage when there was little else to do. For Edwin, life on board the *Rockall* centered on the companionship of Captain Martin, the officers, and two passengers, Benjamin F. Farnham and G. H. Greenleaf. Farnham, already an experienced India hand who later became consul at Bombay, and Greenleaf, who was to stay on in business at Calcutta, relentlessly edified young Edwin with tales of Calcutta. The effect was not as intended. Edwin was so weary of their chatter that he wrote: "And so I hated Calcutta before I had seen it . . ." Though inevitably influenced by what he had heard and read, Edwin's experience of Calcutta was intensely personal and self-conscious. He constructed his own encounter with the East and composed it in his journal on the long voyage home.

Edwin intended his journal of the *Rockall*'s voyage, as he states at the outset, "to give a true picture of life as it is," including "the noticeable features of the mode of traffic and trade." Although he wrote for his own satisfaction ("for no eye but my own"), he had in mind an eventual publication, perhaps a book in the travel genre so popular in the last half of the nineteenth century, describing his narrative as "merely the nucleus of a subject to be here after extended and elaborated." He was anxious about the logic of its composition and organization: "The manner in which I am 'reeling off my yarn' may appear without order or connection," but, he rationalized, "I am not striving for an elaborate treatise of my subject but merely presenting 'Life in the East' as it appeared to me." His concern reveals the seriousness of a project which often comes across as lighthearted.

Edwin Blood's voyage up the Hooghly to Calcutta took place as the era of steam transportation and electronic communication was opening, and a little more than a decade before the Suez Canal (1869) would revolutionize transportation between East and West. At the mouth of the river, on Sagar Island, a magnetic telegraph installed in 1851 conveyed the news of the *Rockall*'s arrival to Calcutta fifty miles upriver.[10] At Sagar, Mr. Farnham boarded a steamer for the trip up the river, but the rest of the passengers and crew made their way as always, under sail guided by an East India Company pilot—a treacherous journey whose terrors are vividly captured in Edwin's narrative.

The Calcutta Edwin experienced and described in his journal is less alien than in earlier accounts, though still unmistakably exotic. By mid-century, the British were at the zenith of

Fig. 15.2 *General View of Calcutta* by Charles D'Oyly, Dickinson and Co., lithographers, London, 1848. Lithograph, 31.6 x 54.5 cm; Peabody Essex Museum M3104.11, Gift of Frances R. Morse, 1927.

their mastery of India (before the "Mutiny" of 1857 instilled an indelible unease); the subcontinent was firmly in their control and their sense of moral supremacy secure. Calcutta was their place, the paramount city of British India, a large cosmopolitan center of nearly half a million people.[11] As much a British city as an Indian one, it had a familiar feel to American visitors (fig. 15.2). Besides, after seventy years of trade, Calcutta was well known in New England's ports: so many ships and mariners had been there, so much had been brought home. In the 1850s, after a nearly two-decade slump, American trade with India had begun to boom again.

When Edwin arrived at Calcutta, among the seven Newburyporters he found in residence there was a Miss Dole, about whom he remarked: "The last time I had seen Miss Dole before meeting her in Calcutta was a year ago last winter when I collected some of the girls in a coach for one of the Merrimack soirees . . . Little I then dreamed that I should next meet . . . [her] on the banks of the Ganges." For Edwin, Calcutta was a place both intriguingly exotic and reassuringly familiar. Edwin's spirited exploration of the city reflected an ease with its

Anglo-Indian character and an orientation rooted in his upbringing, which supported an intensely individual subjectivity. In his journal, he strove for a sense of immediacy, drawing his "reader" into the scenes described: "I cannot perhaps convey a better idea of the appearance of Calcutta by lamplight than by taking the reader upon an imaginary stroll . . ." In contrast to the other journal keepers, Edwin Blood seems to have been intent on going beyond the description of life in the East to capture the texture of his experiences.

Despite his distinctive orientation, Edwin Blood responded to what he saw in much the same way his predecessors had. Like them, the scanty clothing of the natives took on moral significance, though Edwin was also comfortable taking a closer look. On a festival day, when many people had gone to the river to bathe, Edwin observed: "nearly in a nude state . . . many beautiful female forms, young and handsome." Like his predecessors, Blood was also inclined to attribute differences he experienced between himself and "natives" to race, from the unchangeable working habits of coolie laborers to the inability of aspiring young Bengalis to bring off their imitations of

Fig. 15.3 Sitting room in the Calcutta home of John Atkinson, Calcutta, c. 1860. Atkinson, a merchant from Newburyport, Massachusetts, doing business in Calcutta, is mentioned in Edwin Blood's journal of the *Rockall*. Photograph, 15 x 10 cm; Courtesy of New England Historic Genealogical Society, Boston, Massachusetts.

fashionable European behavior. Similarly, he shared the common Yankee Christian response to Hindu practices: "I do not wonder that you laugh in looking at little stumpy goggle eyed, no armed Juggernaut, which you can buy for a curiosity for a few rupees, and wonder at the same time how blinded man may become by superstition . . ." Yet, as with so many of his fellow mariners, there was an ambivalence about the representatives of his own faith that left a space for doubt: ". . . but I fear that all

the good these preachers in general do the nation as far as morals are concerned is more than counter balanced by examples of their fellow countrymen." Blood went even further; perhaps his liberal Unitarian background enabled him to see his own culture exoticized:

> [our own countrymen] would scoff at the idea that anybody could go to Heaven or to any other place except the lowest depths of Hell unless they swallowed whole, and without winking, the entire creed of the Episcopal church,—kept all the fasts, abstained from meat and ate fish Fridays and pancakes at Shrovetide, and did many other things which would appear equally ridiculous to the Hindoos, as do many of their religious observances to us. . . . So where is the difference; we have our traditions and they have theirs; we have a bible, and they their Vedas; . . . Let us then beware while we censure bigotry in others we do not ourselves fall into the same error.

This ability to see his situation from different angles, limited though it was, also allowed him to experience a profound human fellowship in the kindness of a linseed godown sircar named Ram Rutton who befriended him: ". . . among the pleasantest recollections I have of my sojourn in the Far East, is that, this poor old clerk, Hindoo and heathen that he was, of a different religion and race,—[and myself of] a race that despise and ill treat his countrymen, befriended me in a manner that would do infinite credit to the most exemplary professor of the Christian Faith!"

On his return from Calcutta, Edwin Blood settled down to mercantile pursuits in Newburyport. In 1856, he joined A. L. Merrill wholesale grocers as a junior partner. A few months later, the business, which probably belonged to the family of his sister's husband Benjamin L. Merrill, became entirely his when its proprietors went west. Edwin also served as treasurer of the Essex Hat Factory. His commercial interests continued to grow, extending beyond Newburyport to the region's most important market at Boston, where he wholesaled flour. Like his father, Edwin remained active in the social and intellectual life of his hometown. In a diary kept intermittently before his marriage, Edwin recorded dancing "wildly enough with Hattie Plummer," playing whist, and debating. In 1857, just three years after his return from Calcutta, he was elected curator of the Lyceum, which brought to town some of the most popular lecturers in the country. That same year, he was a founder of the Mechanics Library Association, intended to promote useful knowledge "and more especially for the instruction and improvement of young men engaged in mechanical pursuits."[12] Edwin's literary bent, so evident in his journal, also found expression in a poetical political satire *The Washiad* printed privately in 1858, which lambasted efforts to oust his father from the customhouse and decried his own unsuccessful efforts to gain a government appointment.

Edwin affirmed the family's social position among Newburyport's elite by marrying Mary Elizabeth Simpson in 1861. Mary was the daughter of Captain John Simpson, a stalwart of the town's upper stratum whose fortunes had been made in shipping, member of the Newburyport Marine Society, and for many years superintendent of the maritime museum. Though Edwin Blood's New England had become the nation's industrial center, shipping, especially the East India trade, was becoming firmly ensconced as an emblem of the region's glorious past.

Fig. 16.1 Calcutta from the banks of the Hooghly by C. J. Martin, 1852. Incribed on the back:
"Painted by C. J. Martin for John W. Linzee, Calcutta, June 1852." Linzee was an American merchant residing in Calcutta.
Oil on canvas, 38 x 62.2 cm; Peabody Essex Museum, Gift of Charles H. Taylor, 1932.

CHAPTER 16

From the Journal of the Rockall, *1854*

EDWIN BLOOD

After 117 days' passage, the Rockall *had reached the mouth of the Hooghly, where it would take on an East India Company pilot to navigate the ship during the difficult passage upriver to Calcutta* (fig. 16.1).

(117) Monday, May 29th . . . At sunrise we hoisted the Union Jack at the fore & in reply the pilot brig telegraphed "Steer N.E. by E. for a pilot." At 5:30 discovered a sail bearing down from this last named direction. She proved on near approach to be another pilot brig. She sent a pilot on board . . . of us to say "The Captain's compliments" & that he had no pilot, the last one having just left. We eagerly gathered round this fellow, (all except Farnham, who shut himself up in his stateroom in disgust) to learn the news but he could give us none. The boat that brought him was manned by 8 Lascars or native sailors. They were of a dark copper color with straight black hair & beautiful teeth [fig. 16.2]. They were not overburdened with clothing, being bare headed, with a loosely fitting jacket and pants rolled lightly up to the body exposing their bare legs the whole length. After stopping on board about 15 minutes they returned on board the pilot brig, after giving us the information that the ship on the weather beam was the clipper *Gem of the Ocean* of Boston.[1] He also pointed out another pilot brig ahead.

At 7.30 a fight on the top g'ant forecastle between the carpenter & "Bob." At 10 A.M. the pilot brig answered our signal, & at 11.30 a pilot came on board in a launch manned with 10 oars & rowed by Lascars. He brings a servant & leadsman with him. The leadsman is an English boy, the servant a native Bengalee. He is dressed in large flowing pants a loose frock & skull cap; all white. He waits upon the pilot fanning him when he desires it etc. etc. The pilot is an Englishman & a true specimen of John Bull. He brought Calcutta papers up to the 26th of May. The first thing that struck my eye in taking up one was the declaration of war against the Russians[2] by Queen Victoria dated the 28th of March at Westminster—the next item an advertisement headed "Dr. Townsend's Sarsaparilla"! Light wind till 9 A.M. then becalmed all the rest of the day. This afternoon Mr. Greenleaf was sketching the pilot brig & gathered in a picturesque group around him was the burly form of the pilot & the slight form of the leadsman contrasting strangely with the bronzed & roughened features of our second mate & the swarthy countenance of the Asiatic. The barometer is still very low & as night closed in the weather looked very threatening. Anchored at 10 P.M. Weighed anchor again at 12. Terrible hot; Temp. 91. Sharks, water snakes & plenty of land insects about us all day. Baited & fished for a shark this P.M. but though he would come up repeatedly & smell of the bait he would not take it.

(118) Tuesday, May 30th—Anchored at 1 A.M. but got under way again shortly after. Anchored again at 8 A.M. & again got under way at 11 A.M. Anchored at 9 P.M. Dead becalmed all day. The thermometer stands at 94° in the cabin & must be at 100 in the shade on deck. The water glares like molten glass around us. There are two men on the sick list, & all hands having worked night & day for the last 48 hours are much exhausted by the terrible heat and are unfit for duty. Still they work on hoping for a happier time. At 9 P.M. we are about 50 miles from Saugor [Sagar] Island at the mouth of the Ganges. The night looks black & threatening; an inky thunder cloud broods upon the horizon seaward; while the lightning never leaves the heavens. And with all this we have the consolation of knowing that if a gale comes on (of which there is every probability) our fate is inevitable, the ship must go to pieces & we must give our bones to whiten amid the shoals & quick-sands of the "Sand Heads."

Fig. 16.2 *Lascar* [sailor], Calcutta, c. 1850, from an album owned by
Thomas Wigglesworth, Jr. (1814–1907), a Bostonian who did business
in Calcutta between 1841 and 1853. Painting on mica, 13.3 x 9.2 cm;
Peabody Essex Museum E82002.33, Gift of S. Dillon Ripley in honor
of Evelyn Bartlett, 1986.

One year ago to day I made the following entry in a "Diary" of
my life experience, "Heigho! I wish I was at sea, dancing over
the bright & sparkling waters!" etc. Well here I am rolling on a
miserable ground swell more than ten thousand miles away from
the spot where those words were written with every possibility
of not "surviving" many hours! Do I regret my choice? No!! At
11 P.M. a terrible shower of rain with lightning. Temp. 94°

(119) Wednesday, May 31st—Weighed anchor at 1 A.M. & got
under way with a light wind, which soon died away, leaving us
becalmed. Passed the middle (formerly the outer) light ship
about 3 A.M. The channel is now buoyed out from here to the
inner light ship & from there to Saugor. Since my last writing
I have stood face to face with "the silent warrior, in sombre
harness mailed, Dreaded of man & surnamed 'the destroyer.'"
At 8 A.M. the pilot upon the springing up of a light breeze determined to try a channel bounded upon both sides by dangerous
reefs, knowing that if the wind failed or hauled to the Eastward
while in the pass we must go on shore without a possibility of
saving the ship or a single life on board, (as he by way of con-
soling us!) informed us. When we were about half way through,
it suddenly fell calm & we commenced slowly drifting sideways
upon the reef where the breakers were running masthead high!
Our fate seemed now decided and there appeared but a brief
half hour between us and Eternity!

All hands were gathered upon deck & a death silence
reigned over the ship. The Captain stood leaning against the
mizzen shrouds with firmly set teeth & with as little motion as
though he had already passed the "valley of the shadow," the
pilot was running about wringing his hands & crying "O! we
are very unfortunate men!" "Blow! for God's sake blow!" & G
was leaning over the rail his face as white as chalk; while Farnham in vain endeavored to whistle & looked terribly "blue
about the gills." The second mate, after damning his soul to hell
at least two hundred times a day during the passage now that
there existed a strong probability of its going there in a very few
minutes did not at all appear to relish the idea; for his eyes were
sunken his cheeks haggard & his whole countenance looked
ghastly yellow. In fact all the colors of the rainbow were represented by the countenances of those on board. I have never
known before that fear affects the color of the face in different
shades according to its intensity; but as such appears to be the
fact why could not the degree of fear be thereby determined?
The first mate, Mr. Wilcox (who is a New Hampshire boy & a
noble fellow) was the only one who appeared himself. He was
walking in the waist with his sou'wester tipped on one side of
his head coolly smoking his pipe!

As for myself, when the wind first died away & I found

myself drifting into the jaws of death, I felt a dread sinking sensation about the heart, as if it had suddenly turned to lead in my bosom, but it was gone in a moment & I felt perfectly calm & busied my thoughts for a few minutes in thinking of what my friends at home were about at that time. Having decided that they were comfortably turned in & were sleeping in happy, unconsciousness of all earthly things, I joined the mate in his walking & conversing with him on the modern advancement in ship building & other indifferent subjects, awaited our doom.

We were now fast approaching the reef. In a few minutes more all would be over. I took my place with the mate on the larboard[3] rail watching the ship's progress to destruction. We were very near! Five minutes more & we should be among the breakers! There was a puff of wind! Every eye was raised to the "fly," or wind vane. It was fluttering! Another & another puff! There is a chance yet! "Brace round the yards with a will, cheerly!" shouted the pilot. The men sprang to their stations. One moment of suspense then the breeze freshened & we were safe! This was about 9.30 A.M. at 11.30 we made Saugor Island, the first land we have seen since we left Boston just 4 months ago.

Though for the present safe we were not out of all danger as it was necessary for us to gain about 20 miles farther to get into sufficient depth of water at low ebb for anchorage. It is however useless to lengthen the account. At noon Saugor light bore N.N.E. distant 15 miles. With a light wind we slowly stemmed the ebb and gained upon it. At 5 P.M. we passed the "Anchor Buoy" shortly after the New York clipper ship *Sky Lark* and Boston ship *Josephus* outward bound & waiting for a fair wind who showed their flags in answer to ours as we passed them. At sunset we anchored in Saugor Roads off the light. Saugor is a large island situated between two mouths of the Ganges. It is covered with jungle & uninhabited save by the light keeper & his attendants. His bungalow is plainly visible from the deck. There is a magnetic telegraph here for the purpose of telegraphing the names of the vessels as they arrive, to Calcutta, in the same way they are telegraphed from Sandy Hook to New York. Thus after tossing upon the bosom of old ocean for four long months, this still & quiet evening finds us at anchor in smooth water gazing upon the muddy waters of the Ganges & the rich luxuriance of tropical vegetation.

Fig. 16.3 Postman, Calcutta or Krishnanagar, c. 1870. Clay, pigments, cloth, leather, height 26 cm; Peabody Essex Museum E44837, Gift of Henry Peabody and Co., 1968.

[*Entries omitted for June 1, 2, and 3, when the* Rockall *passes two outward-bound Boston vessels, the clipper ship* Malay,[4] *and the barque* Lyman.[5]]

(123) Sunday, June 4th—Once more pleasant & very hot. At 11.30 A.M. weighed anchor & at 12 M. were fairly underway with a strong breeze from the S.W. Passing thro' Lloyds' channel with only two feet of water between the bottom of our keel & the bottom of the river we arrived off Cowcolly [Geonkhali]

Light at 1.30 P.M. Here we passed a boat full of natives who gracefully threw a flowing cloth over their nakedness as we swept past them, supposing perhaps that we had ladies on board. Directly after passing this boat we hove to for the Kedgeree [Khijiri] dock or post boat to board. This contained the best specimens of the Bengali race we had yet seen, tall, straight & well formed with no clothing but a piece of cotton cloth wound loosely about the middle.[6] After some considerable difficulty for we were going very fast the boat came along side & the postman with his tiger skin letter bag strapped over one shoulder clambered nimbly over the side sprang upon the quarter deck, & making a low salaam to those of us there assembled, spread his letters before us [fig. 16.3].

These consisted mostly of circulars from ship chandlers for ship captains etc. but some there were real letters worn by much handling & some years old addressed to those who never might receive them. One particularly I noticed in a mourning envelope addressed to a young man (I know it must be a young man) in a woman's delicate hand & post marked in some rural town of merrie & old England. What a tale of sorrow & disappointment might be there with connected! Short time however was allowed for such reflections for the letters were soon hustled over & after finding one for the pilot & one for the Captain they were thrust unceremoniously into the letter bag & the boat left us, & squaring away the main yard we again swept on.

At 1:45 we passed Diamond Harbor where there is another telegraph station & directly entered upon a new region. The two banks of the river now approached other to within two miles and from the deck & from the tops presented a magnificent spectacle, for miles & miles & miles as far as the eye could reach was one extended grove of the mango, date, lemon, pineapple, cocoa-nut all loaded with fruit & surrounded by a jungle undergrowth of the wildest luxuriance of tropical vegetation peeping out from which in strong contrast to the surrounding green were the white monuments or pilot beacons. Once we saw a pagoda rearing its tall head above the surrounding village of mud huts. At 4 PM we were at Hooghly Point. Here is the most dangerous pass of the river there being here a dangerous bank in the mid channel known as "The James & Mary's" upheaved by the confluence of the Roopmerain [Rup-

narayan?] river with the Hooghly but we passed safely by & dropped anchor at night fall 6 miles above Fulta [Falta] (where there was formerly an English Hotel now in ruins) & about 30 from Calcutta. Just after anchoring we were struck by a tremendous thunder squall which caused us to drag anchor for a short distance, but we finally fetched up a short distance from the bank by paying out more chain.

(124) Monday, June 5th—Got under way at 6 A.M. with a light but fair breeze. As we passed slowly up the river several boats boarded us bringing fish, fruit etc. Our own "dingy" (which the Capt. engaged & sent off before I turned out) brought off some milk which we drank in our tea & which made me sick. The scenes as they now opened before us presented more & more of human life etc. [As] we advanced, large boats with rounded & high sterns & curiously fastened with small clamps of iron swept by us & beside these many smaller canoes with their naked crews. After breakfast ascended with Mr. Greenleaf into the mizzen top to look around us. The prospect was delightful. On every side as far as the eye could reach was one extended plain spotted with jungle & magnificent trees, from amid which here & there peeped out a mud village of the natives. Busier & busier grew the scene as we advanced both upon the river & on its banks. Women with burthens were seen walking beneath the magnificent trees, bathing in the river or watching herds of goats upon the banks. At 9 A.M. we passed Budge Budge, where there are extensive factories. At 12 we entered Garden Reach, upon one side of which are the Company's Gardens & on the other the villas of the English residents [fig. 16.4]. At 1 P.M. we rounded the bend at the end of Garden Reach & a great commercial city throbbing with life & activity lay before us. At 1:45 P.M. four months & 4 days from the wharf at Boston, we dropped anchor off Calcutta.

Life in the East—First Experiences, On Shore—June 5th, 1854—At 3 P.M. on the first day of February, after getting fairly clearly off the land [from Boston] five persons seated themselves at the table spread for dinner on board the *Rockall*. These were Capt. Martin, Farnham, Greenleaf, Mr. Wilcox & myself. Although we were entire strangers to one another, never having met till that morning when we stood on the ships quarter deck

Fig. 16.4 *Garden Reach* by Charles D'Oyly, Dickinson and Co., lithographers, London, 1848. Lithograph, 31.6 x 54.5 cm; Peabody Essex Museum M3104.3, Gift of Frances R. Morse, 1927.

still having introduced ourselves over a tumbler of brandy and water when passing down the harbor we now began to feel slightly acquainted, & so while we continued to satisfy our appetites, introduced the "feast of reason & the flow of soul." I had made a few commonplace remarks & had been followed by Mr. Greenleaf, when, elevating his head to allow the downward passage of a huge mouthful of victuals, Farnham broke forth on the subject of "Calcutta." Thus introduced, the "city of palaces" continued to be the topic of conversation till the mud hook dropped this morning into the waters of the Hooghly off the mooted subject of our hopes & fears, conjectures & speculations during the outward passage. And so I hated Calcutta before I had seen it & how could it be otherwise? Imagine all ye who have never sailed upon blue water of being regaled till you were gorged to satiety, with one subject of conversation & then for weeks afterward have it forced into unwilling ears. Such was my

position & I have walked the decks, by day & night, thro' storm and beneath a broiling sun to escape the horrid din kept up between Farnham & Greenleaf about the way of life in the place of our destination. In the morning, afternoon or evening at our meals, the card table or on deck it was all the same: one continued clatter of questions from Greenleaf & answers from Farnham, deduced from the observation of a narrow mind thro' a limited vision in a terribly opaque skull. Thus it will be seen that I must have been pretty well posted in the manners & customs of the Hindoos upon arrival, after hearing the subject handled, twisted & turned during the four months passage & so it was I knew what to expect, I expected & my expectations were not realized.

The starboard anchor had not rested five minutes on the bed of the river, before Capt. Martin, Greenleaf & myself, dressed in our best clothes (and not very good) were over the

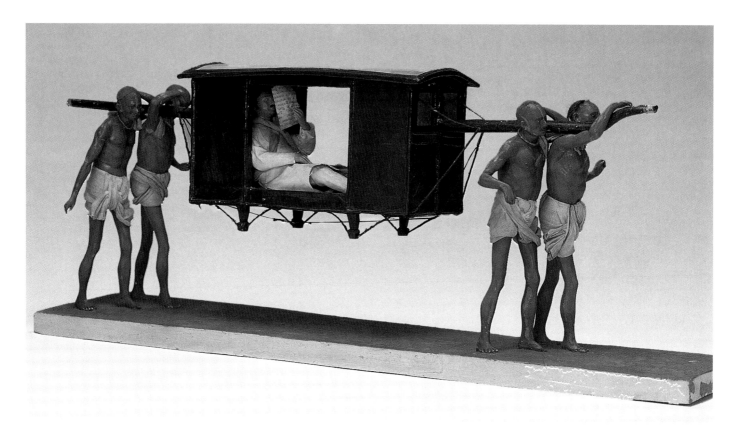

Fig. 16.5 Palanquin, with Western passenger and native bearers, Calcutta or Krishnanagar, c. 1870.
Clay, wood, pigment, cloth, height 11 x width 58 cm; Peabody Essex Museum E44862, Gift of Henry Peabody and Co., 1968.

side, in the dingy & off for the shore. The first impression that struck us as we looked back to the ship was the fine appearance she made upon the water, but our attention was soon called to the scene before us. Forcing her way among a crowd of similar craft that lay along the bank our dingy touched the beach. Capt. Martin stepped forward, was taken on the backs of two of the dingy wallahs & carried over the intervening space of mud to terra firma. Greenleaf & myself followed the "old man's" example by grinning like a porpoise while carried aloft but I assumed the position with all the dignity of an old East Indian. After a transit of about a rod in this manner I was placed on my feet at Police Ghaut [Ghat][7] & stood for the first time on Asiatic soil. There was an immediate rush about us of a crowd of natives with demonic yells of "palkee sahib"! & palanquin clashed with palanquin as the bearers, rushed to the charge to get a job. At last however we were seated & having obtained from the harbor master the place of residence of the Supercargo, squared

away for 110 Radha Bazaar. Nothing could exceed the delight of the artistic Greenleaf at finding himself actually in a palanquin; to be stretched out in an easy position in a carpeted box & borne on the shoulders of four men was the realisation of his happiest dream of Oriental luxuriance [fig. 16.5]. This said he to me as we suddenly turned a corner & as we were going side by side, this is the far famed "Tank Square." "Yes, groaned I " & "I hear the name for the thousandth time; don't mention it."

We were indeed in "Tank Square." A large tank, of which there are many about Calcutta to supply the inhabitants with water, lay before us fringed with a beautiful flower garden, and issuing in a steady stream from the gate ways that led to it were hundreds of water carriers carrying on their backs & shoulders their skins and pots of water, & they could be seen along the street as far as the eye could reach, mingling with a motley crowd of men & women bearing burdens on their heads, bullock carts of bamboo & rope, palanquins & carriages. Hotly glared the sun upon the flat roofs & from the white walls of the houses along the street, but still onward pressed our sturdy bearers, the perspiration streaming from every pore, on through the great thoroughfares, by ways & narrow lanes, till suddenly passing beneath the arched gate way of a castelled mansion they halted in the "compound" of my new home.

On Shore—As we stepped from our palanquins we were received by a Hindoo in the full dress of the country, who made a low salaam & bade us follow him. This we did & carrying us up a long flight of stairs & leaving us standing in a large hall he disappeared. The scene now before us was purely Oriental; Hindoo servants, in flowing pants & robes & turbans of the purest white were hurrying to & fro. Just before us on a lounge lay the Supercargo at full length & standing over him was a servant plying a huge fan. We remained standing perhaps two & one half minutes, when Farnham appeared, packed Greenleaf off without ceremony to the office of Foster, Rogers & Co., his final destination, & handed me some letters from Newburyport which had been waiting my arrival & which were, as can be imagined, as the oasis in the desert, the first glimpse of Mecca to the pilgrim Mussalman, or the cry of "Land Ho!" to the tempest tossed & ocean wearied mariner.

Having seen Greenleaf fairly off, Farnham introduced me to the office. This was a large cool room opening upon the veranda containing two desks over which a punkha or large fan pendant from the ceiling was hung, and at work at the punkha string was another Hindoo servant. While reading my letters a fine looking middle aged native entered, addressed Farnham in perfect English this person I at once knew to be the Baboo Rajkissen & thus I introduced him [fig. 16.6].

I had just time to finish my letters when dinner was announced & we proceeded to the dining room. There were five of us at the table, these were F. F. Rollins the supercargo, Capt Martin, Farnham, Mr. Linsee [Linzee] the head of an American house & myself [see fig. 16.19]. I will not stop to comment upon the variety or richness of the dishes laid before us; suffice it to say that the table as a whole is such as is not seen in America. Behind the Supercargo stood the Kunsemar [khansama; fig. 16.7] or supplier of the table with folded arms, & behind every guest also a servant all dressed in the purest white flowing

Fig. 16.6 Raj Kissen Mitter (1811–1872), Calcutta, c. 1860. Photograph published in *Other Merchants and Sea Captains of Old Boston* (Boston: State Street Trust Company, 1919), from an original that belonged to George Mackay. (See also figs. 14.3 and 14.5.)

pants, robes and turbans, while overhead, & moved by a string passing out of the room was a huge punkha keeping in continual motion an artificial & highly acceptable breeze. An occasional glance at Farnham convinced me that he did not suffer the transition from on shipboard to onshore to affect his appetite, nor to confess the truth did I; but I gulped down the good things set before me, notwithstanding half a dozen Asiatics were staring me in the face, with considerable gusto.

PREPARATIONS FOR DOMESTICATING—After dinner, which occupied about an hour in eating, I was introduced to the room which was to be mine during my stop here. It opened upon the veranda & had two windows overlooking the street. In one corner stood a huge bed stead, with its white bed & the made his appearance & reported that the baggage was all packed, but on account of the rain he could not bring it up before tomorrow morning.

With reading my letters & looking over the news in the newspapers to gather what had occurred in the world during the passage the hours wore away till supper time. This was about half past 7 PM, at the supper table the same company was present as at dinner. About 9 o'clock a servant appeared in my room & making a low salaam seated himself on the floor; and when shortly after I commenced undressing he motioned me into a chair & performed the operation for me, carefully folding up the clothes & putting them away. Finally he washed & wiped my feet, brushed the mosquitos from the curtains & when I had located myself in bed closed them, made a low salaam, and spreading a strip of white cloth upon the veranda in front of the door, stretched himself out to sleep.

June 6th—My first night on shore was by no means an easy one. Sleep did not vouchsafe to visit my pillow, but through the long hours of the first & middle watches I turned & tossed over the wide area of my bed. Towards morning I fell into a doze but it was broken by uneasy dreams & frightful visions. Sometimes I heard the waves roaring round me & the hoarse voice of the officer of the watch calling "all hands on deck," & then I was voyaging upon a single plank which immersed itself beneath every wave nearly wrenching me from my hold; and then suddenly I lay stretched at ease in an Elysian grove with Hindoo servants fanning me & ministering to my wants. Once more the scene changed & me thought that I was in the midst of a parched & burning desert, nothing but hot sand around & a glowing sky & burning sun above me. I lay stretched & bound upon the blue roof of a palanquin, whose bearers were pressing forward, singing a low chant. I could not turn, though the sun was burning into my eyes & broiling my very brain; & thus I thought hours and hours of agony went by.

The perspiration which at first started & poured down my brow & body, seemed long since dried up; all the corporeal fluids were exhausted; the skin was parched & shriveled & the hair crisped, when suddenly there came a blast as if from Heaven across my brow. I knew there must be water near & I

Fig. 16.7 Khansama (butler), Calcutta, c. 1850. The original owner of the painting was Captain John Martin, probably the same Captain Martin who commanded the *Rockall* in 1854. Painting on mica, 14.2 x 11 cm; Peabody Essex Museum E82703.6, Gift of Mr. and Mrs. Richard L. Nichols and Family, 1978.

whole was surrounded by mosquito curtains, in another a bureau & in a third a wash stand & various other articles of chamber furniture scattered about, all these however were quickly arranged & the room made ready for my use.

After examining my room & the bathing room connected with it, finding that it was desirable to have my baggage on shore, I left the house under the guardianship of a sircar or native clerk. Comfortably reclining in a palanquin, I passed through the same streets as a few hours before with the sircar walking beside me answering such questions as I asked him. Arriving at the Ice House[8] I stopped, and writing an order for my baggage to the steward dispatched the sircar while I returned to the house. After waiting for some time my factotum tried to rise; but my bonds held fast. I shrieked & yelled in agony. I cursed God & man till my parched throat refused farther utterance & the tongue swollen & blackened hung from my gasping mouth! O! It was horrible! Blast succeeded blast of the cooling breeze, till suddenly the bearers plunged with the palanquin into the waters. Ye Gods! the delicious sensation that came over me, as the waves closed around me; it would repay for years of torture. I knew that I must die, but I blest God for his mercies & was content to thus yield up life. I felt myself sinking & with one last glance upward in which I caught sight of a dusky face with a white turban bending over me I went down.

A convulsive shudder & a start and I sat upright in bed. The broad day light was streaming thro' the window blinds & there at my bed side was the dusky face & the white turban of my dream attached to my Hindoo servant of the night before, who was swinging a huge fan over me. My night clothes and the sheets under me were wet with perspiration and my mouth parched and dry, explaining the heat agony, while the cool breeze of the punker solved the mystery of the blasts from the cooling waters.

"Bring me a glass of water," were the first words I uttered. The Asiatic made no reply, but gazed at me with such a look of bewilderment and distress that I could not help laughing. "A glass of water," I repeated mildly. "Nag junta, sahib" [I don't understand, sahib], he answered with the same bewildered look as before, I now began to comprehend that the English was not the vernacular in Hindoostan, and suddenly recollecting the little Hindoostanee I had learned from the pilot's servant in coming up the river, I gave utterance as best I might to, "Bruf pawnee lao!" [bring ice water]. With this he turned quick as thought and with the words, "Heumjentah sahib" [I understand, sahib] and a flourish that would have eclipsed any pigeon wing of an Ellser or Taglaoni[9] in their palmiest days, cleared the room at a bound. He soon returned his countenance all alight with smiles, (there was nothing of the grin about him) bringing a huge tumbler of water, in which was floating and clinking musically against the glass, a large piece of Wenham[10] ice [fig. 16.8]. Without pausing to think of the "prickly heat," from which I had suffered since our advent in the Bay of Bengal, and which troubles all new comers to India, and in fact old res-

Fig. 16.8 Servant with tumbler of water, Calcutta, c. 1850, from an album owned by Thomas Wigglesworth, Jr. (1814–1907), a Bostonian who did business in Calcutta between 1841 and 1853. Painting on mica, 13.3 x 9.2 cm; Peabody Essex Museum E82002.39, Gift of S. Dillon Ripley in honor of Evelyn Bartlett, 1986.

idents more or less, and which is thrown into action by suddenly heating or cooling the system, I drank off a large draught, but repented of my temerity before the first drop had reached the abdominal region. For now I was in a real agony, nearly as bad as the torture of my dream. Shooting fires pervaded every portion of my body as if needles charged with electricity were thrust deep into the flesh. I rolled over upon the bed, broke down the mosquito curtain and came down upon the floor, but here was no relief and I jumped up and danced round the room fanned till I was well cooled and then arose, and took a bath in which my servant was of much assistance as the bathing tubs in common use are huge earthen bowls known as "Kedgeree pots" from their place of manufacture. They measure about 4 feet in diameter across the top and about 2 feet across the bottom, and of course do not admit of a reclining posture, consequently some one to scrub you is a great luxury, especially as it saves exertion on your part. Duly scrubbed wiped and my joints cracked I returned from the bathing to my sleeping room where my feet were washed in the manner of the night before and my servant proceeded to dress me, which operation occupied about an hour.

We breakfasted at 9 and breakfast over the business of the day began. My things arriving from the *Rockall*, I proceeded to put my things to right and in an hours time all was arranged. My shore clothes were packed neatly away; my sea clothes made into a bundle for the washerman; my books and papers spread upon the tables and with my sea chest standing near the head of my bed the room began to look quite home like [fig. 16.9].

During these operations of domesticating I secured two servants according to the custom of the country as the one I had last night belonged to the supercargo and was only loaned me till I could procure one of my own. These two servants are know respectively by the general names of bearer [fig. 16.10], and my kipmegar [kitmutgar] or boy [fig. 16.11]. The duties of the first are those of a body servant or such as were performed by the servant spoken of above; while those of the latter are to wait upon you at the table and run errands. The former was of the old original Hindu religion; the latter (as are all kipmegars in India) was a Mussalman. I engaged these servants on the recommendation of Mr. Farnham and they set to work with alacrity in putting away my clothing blacking up my shoes etc.; while the perspiration streamed from them in working as it did from me in a merely superintending and looking on.

In the performing of these duties of righting up, the hours of daylight gradually wore away. The day was very hot, unrelieved by any showers as the rainy season had not yet fairly set in, and the disappearance of the sun below the horizon brought little relief, for the air was still hot and oppressive and the perspiration still ran freely, "Braf pawnee lao"! was about the extent of my orders for this day as I had not yet learnt any other

Fig. 16.9 Bedroom in the Calcutta home of Newburyport merchant John Atkinson, Calcutta, c. 1860. Photograph, 15 x 10 cm; Courtesy of New England Historic Genealogical Society, Boston, Massachusetts.

on one foot, fell over a chair, up again and round upon the other foot till I dropped exhausted upon the bed with the perspiration streaming from my face; and all this time, my servant had stood in an easy position with folded arms looking on with an imperturbable cast of countenance as if he witnessed such pranks every day.

The paroxysm, (which is never of long duration) soon passed over and lying at full length, I allowed myself to be

Fig. 16.10 *Bearer*, Calcutta, c. 1865. Originally owned by Charles H. Greenleaf, who was in Asia in the late 1860s. A G. H. Greenleaf was a passenger on the *Rockall* in 1854. Painting on mica, 13.3 x 9 cm; Peabody Essex Museum E27601, Gift of Katie D. Holt, 1985.

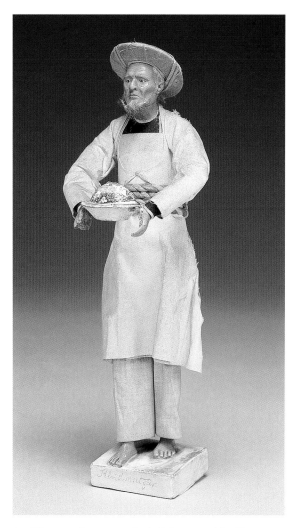

Fig. 16.11 Kitmutgar (server or waiter), Calcutta, c. 1860. Clay, cloth, pigment, height 25 cm; Peabody Essex Museum E44832, Gift of Henry Peabody and Co., 1968.

household phrases; but I spent a part of the evening in enquiring of my bearer the Hindoostanee names of the various articles of clothing I had given into his charge, and of my kipmegar the names of table furniture, and noting down such of those as I thought would be of use to me.

June 7th—*Looking about Me and Hindoo Style of Dress*—My second night on shore brought me several hours of quiet sleep. By daylight in the morning I was stirring and without stopping for a bath sallied out for a walk. Following along the only streets I had yet been through I found my way to the river.

Perhaps the strongest proof presented to [a] stranger landing in India that he is in a strange land, is the nearly nude condition of the natives. This he first observes to be the case among the boatmen on the river, but he is more forcibly struck with the fact on shore. Here all classes nearly are, what would be called in Broadway or Washington Street entirely naked. Their only clothing consists of a piece of cotton cloth wound about the middle of the body all other portions are entirely naked [fig. 16.12]. This however, strictly speaking, is true of only the laboring classes, for during business hour the merchants, clerks have the upper portions covered, as do the servants while on duty;

Fig 16.12 *Cooley*, Calcutta, c. 1850, from an album owned by Bostonian Thomas Wigglesworth, Jr. (1814–1907). Painting on mica, 13.3 x 9.2 cm; Peabody Essex Museum E82002.49, Gift of S. Dillon Ripley in honor of Evelyn Bartlett, 1986.

Fig. 16.13 *Mussulman Native of Hindustan*, Calcutta, c. 1850, from an album owned by Thomas Wigglesworth, Jr. (1814–1907). Painting on mica, 13.3 x 9.2 cm; Peabody Essex Museum E82002.37, Gift of S. Dillon Ripley in honor of Evelyn Bartlett, 1986.

but if you will follow any of these home when the labors of the day are over and you will find all classes, from the rich Baboo worth his 5 lacs of Rupees to the poorest cooly in the same style of dress. It is easy to be seen that they are not at home in the upper garments, and especially in shoes and stockings. Call a servant suddenly and he comes to you half naked, putting on his jacket or robe, as the case may be.

For there are two distinct styles of dress in India; one as adopted by the followers of the old religion or Brahmanism, and the other worn by the disciples of Mahomet [Muhammad]. The first, I now speak of the full dress, consists of a peculiar turban upon the head, a loose jacket of white cloth coming to the hips and then about the waist [see fig. 16.10]. Another strip of cloth is wound in several turns, allowed to drop down in a fold over each leg below the knee, and the end is then passed between the thighs and fastened by tucking in behind; this is a very graceful costume and very gracefully worn by a graceful people. The costume of the Hindoo Musselmen resembles closely that of the Turks. It consists of a Turban, a long robe fastened in front, and flowing pants [fig. 16.13]. There are slight modifications of both these styles of dress but I write of them as one would see hundreds in a day in the streets of Calcutta. The dress of the labor-

Fig. 16.14 *Bengalee Hindu Woman*, Calcutta, c. 1850, from an album owned by Thomas Wigglesworth, Jr. (1814–1907). Painting on mica, 13.3 x 9.2 cm; Peabody Essex Museum E82002.40, Gift of S. Dillon Ripley in honor of Evelyn Bartlett, 1986.

ing women consists of a long strip of cloth wound about the body or drooping over the legs as above described, but instead of the jacket over the shoulders they simply wear a piece of long cloth about the neck, which being brought forward by the hands conceals the breast [fig. 16.14]. Thus if an European lady here, has the chance of studying the male physiology in a state of unadorned nature, so on the other hand, can the gentleman fresh from the countries where clothes are worn, see exhibited around him more natural female charms, than he could, even at a fancy ball at Newport or Saratoga.

Such was the subject that filled my mind as I made my way through the already busy streets on the morning of which I write.

It was about 5 o'clock, that I stood upon the bank of the river at one of the numerous *ghauts* or landing places, with which the Calcutta bank abounds. It was a busy scene before me; extending up and down the river in a line as far at the eye could reach was one range of vessel masts, moored along the shore, and farther out, swinging at anchor in the stream were many more vessels waiting for a berth in the moorings to be vacated. Close before me were many of the small dingys and the larger craft with the rude gear and in the rude style of many centuries ago, with their crews, who always live on board, cooking their breakfasts on deck in rude earthen utensils, while upon the opposite shore, across the rapid current of the muddy waters before me, were the docks of the E.I. [East India] Company and beyond them, stretching away to the point where earth meets sky, was the dark, green luxuriance of tropical vegetation.[11]

Section IV—*Business Life in Calcutta in 1854*—Connected with the office, to which I was introduced the first day of my arrival, in an adjoining room was the office of the native clerks connected with our establishment. Here about 12 or 15 Hindoos seated…a la turc upon the floor before boxes about a foot high serving as desks, followed their avocations of bookkeepers, cashier, and clerks for various departments and duties. It was here that I received various instructions from the head sircar after returning from my walk mentioned in the last section, preparatory to my entering at once upon the duties which I had been sent to execute. After listening to all this worthy individual had to say, I left the office in a *garee*, a carriage peculiar to India, drawn by a span of horses and in company with Farnham and a native merchant, Doyle by name, and a nephew of our Banian proceeded to a linseed bazaar, into which I was introduced after riding about two miles, up the bank of the river, by Farnham, who had enlivened the way by a learned disquisition, of which I had not heard one word except the introduction, which was something about "Calcutta business," having long before learned the value of his ideas upon that subject. Hauling up the vehicle in the main street we proceeded through a narrow lane upon one side of which a drain filled with putrid water and dead vermin; among which I noticed several enormous rats, we entered the bazaar which was nothing more than a huge store house filled with huge piles of bags of linseed.

Immediately upon our arrival, the coolies of which there were about 30 in number, commenced the operation of "making up the pile," that is in opening the bags and pouring their contents upon the floor. As this was done a "muster" a sample from each bag was handed Farnham that he might receive or reject it. After a considerable pile had thus accumulated of acceptable seed, and a grand flourish of grandiloquent remarks from Farnham, he and Doyle left me to my fate.

I was "monarch of all I surveyed," for the time a least: that is I was "supreme boss" over about 30 coolies and two or three sircars, who were to work under my direction. As soon as the skirt of Farnham's coat had disappeared round the corner of the lane I gave the word to proceed and having seen the scale balanced my coolies began weighing. The bags which were of double gunny were filled by baskets and a muster of each bag was passed to me that I might learn of the quality from the judgement of the sircar beside me who had been a long time in this department of the business. This sircar Ram Rutton by name was quite an old man and he as well as myself kept an account of the weights as they were declared by the weighman after the style, ek [one], teen [three], sartaro [seventeen] and then in the same sing-song tone the English one hundred, 2 quarters, seventeen pounds. The sircars account was kept in Bengalee and mine of course in English, and at every ten bags we summed up and compared the results. The scale was erected in a shed outside the main building and was one of the old fashioned English scales with the beam balanced in the middle and was hung on a tripod of bamboos.

The shed in which we were located afforded but little protection from the sun which poured terribly hot upon its earthen roof and heated to an intensity almost unbearable the air confined in the narrow yard about us. We had just got fairly under way and I was in a comfortable state of perspiration when a sircar arrived from the office, bringing me a letter which had laid over in the Post Office since the arrival of the last mail owing to an informality in the direction. Finding it was from an old friend in Boston I gave the word to [heartumrow?] to my band of coolies, and seated on a broken down bamboo chair surrounded by an eager crowd of gazers of nearly naked men and half naked women, with my white dress stained with sweat and linseed dust and the perspiration literally dropping from my fingers' ends I read the epistle penned two months before within the cool and comfortable precincts of a Boston counting room.

Farnham upon leaving had promised to send me tiffin (or luncheon) at one o'clock, but one o'clock came and two and three and brought no Kipnegar. Six hours in that hot and tainted atmosphere had not passed without their effect on me; I was weak, weary and faint and cursed Farnham who was probably amusing himself at the house, brushing his whiskers, while I was suffering from want of drink and food. At last Ram Rutton noticing that I was very faint dispatched a cooley after some fruit, who soon returned with a quantity of mangoes, bananas and a nondescript looking fruit which I took from its appearance to be a green melon. I finished in a very few minutes two large mangoes, five or six bananas and then turned to the nondescript; but it was as hard as a rock. "Why" said I to the sircar,"you do not expect me to eat this." He laughed, and muttering "milic" motioned for me to drink, at the same time taking out a piece of rind which had been cut from one end. I did not wait for a second invitation, but putting the aperture to my lips, raised my face to heaven, and swallowed about a pint of a delicious beverage at a single draught. This was a green cocoa nut the milk of which at a particular stage of ripeness is a peculiar richness.

About 4 P.M. we had weighed about 300 bags of seed and closed the lot at this bazaar. While the sircar and myself were summing up our last account my kipmegar, sweating with his walk of two miles under the hot sun, made his appearance with the tiffin. I did not however stop now to eat, but packing up my papers and taking a glass of ice-water prepared to leave for home. There was now wanting a mode of conveyance which for some time was not to be had, but as I was on the point of setting out on foot (which would have probably been the last of my walks as subsequent experience has proved to me) an old sircar made his appearance with a "rack a down," or an old broken down garee, with a span of horses, of the bunch-of-bones-covered-with-skin order attached by a rope yarn harness. Into this turn-out the sircar and myself got while my servant perched himself on top with the coachman and off we started for Radha Bazaar, the iron work of our carriage musically jingling on the way. Finding that my companion was inclined to be communicative I entered into conversation with him and he gave me much desirable information of the places of interest we passed on the road. He pointed out in succession the burning ghaut where the Hindoo dead are burned, the dead house where the sick are brought to die; a Hindoo temple; the house of a Hindoo nabob and the mint of the Hon[ourable] E. I. Company. And finally upon my asking him about a horrible looking image standing against a tree by the road side, he answered, "That is God Almighty." My only reply was "do tell."

Arriving in Old China Bazaar we found it thronged with soldiers of Her Majesty's 98th infantry, who were out shopping with their wives; Chinese; and mendicants, & such was the press as we neared the house that we were obliged to haul up some distance from the gate. Springing out I attempted to make my way on foot, but had not progressed ten steps before I was confronted by a horrible looking object in the shape of a man who displayed a hand which, altho the fact may appear incredible to one who has never been in the east, was swollen fully as large as the bottom of a common sized chair! Uttering an exclamation of horror I tried to pass him, but he still kept before me asking for "buckshish" [donation]. As soon as I had recovered my senses which had been somewhat disturbed by the apparition, I bethought me of the remedy for such a nuisance and flung a rupee at him, the only money I chanced to have about me.

But the wretch saw his advantage and still continued to persecute me for "deucerer" [alms]. Had he been a common man I should have knocked him down, or "tried to," but the loathsome object that he was I dared not touch him. But at length the sircar came to my assistance and with a "jow jow" [go, go] that rang in my ears for some minutes afterward protected my retreat inside the gate—the Rubicon, no beggar dares to pass. But here a sight almost as disgusting as that which I had just left outside, confronted me, and this was the crew of the *Rockall*, who had come up to the house to get paid off, who were all drunk and who were amusing themselves with a general knockdown. One known by the synonym of "Scottie" upon the outward passage lay hors d'combat upon a ladder on one side of the yard horribly bruised, with the blood streaming from his nose and mouth, and all the others were bleeding more or less, but still fighting. I was sorry to find in this interesting company old Burrows the second mate, of whom, "shell back" and "bring eye" that he was I had a better opinion. But there he was comfortably "tight" with a black hat on one side of his head presenting a most comical appearance. As soon as these worthies perceived me they raised a shout of Mr. B and rushed forward to shake hands and it was with considerable difficulty that I prevented Burrows from embracing me; but I finally escaped and made good my way into the house.

Wearied with my exertions through the day and sickened by the loathsome sights thro which I had just passed I threw my account book on the desk, and myself into a chair almost fainting. Here I was quickly disrobed by my servants and plunged into a tepid bath, which at once revived me. Once more dressed I sent for the old sircar who had befriended me and attempted to reward him. But he would accept nothing; although I am happy to add that I found many opportunities of repaying his kindness during my stay in Calcutta. When connected with those at work under my direction, he experienced many an easy day and many a good hour's "caulking" on a gunny bale by my permission.

To a fireside adventurer all this may seem a very slight matter, but any one who has felt himself "a stranger in a strange land" will appreciate my feelings. I love to record such proofs of the fact that the world is not so bad as many would have us believe it,—that human nature is not totally depraved, but, when uncontaminated by contact with the world there is a principle of good will from man to his fellow man, springing spontaneously from the "life within."

Such kindness as that of the old sircar for me is not soon forgotten: it sinks deep into the heart. And now, among the pleasantest recollections I have of my sojourn in the Far East, is that, this poor old clerk, Hindoo and heathen that he was, of a different religion and race,—[and I of] a race that despise and ill treat his countrymen, befriended me in a manner that would do infinite credit to the most exemplary professor of the Christian Faith![12]

A Hide Bazaar and Its Peculiarities—The next article on the list to saltpetre to be attended to in making up the cargo was the hides of the buffalo, cow, and the skins of the goat. The bazaar for these was in altogether a different quarter of the city where there were less ditches and filth. Here I had a new set of sircars to get acquainted with and here also the mode of procedure was somewhat different from that to which I had become accustomed while engaged on the saltpetre and linseed.

The main person to be depended upon in the hide bazaar is the hide cooley who, from long experience in handling, can tell at a glance the quality of the hide or skin. There is also an under sircar to take a rough account as they are received. From the bazaar the hides or skins are sent to the screw house and there screwed into bales of different sizes according to the kind.

It was as soon as I recovered sufficiently from my sickness that I made my appearance in Terretta Bazaar, at the godown where the hides were being received. Farnham had given me certain instructions, and I listened to others more to the purpose from an open mouthed sleepy sircar, and others still from the hide cooley, till I had learned to judge of the quality tolerably well. The over-hauling then commenced and I took my stand by the pile so as to catch a sight of every hide as it was thrown over and say "reject" or "take."

The hide cooley was a "brick." Long and thin with an apple shaped head upon a long crane like neck, he was anything but the counterpart of the renowned Wauter Van Twiller, who measured 4 ft. 7 inches in height and 7 ft. 4 inches in circumference. He was by no means melancholic or taciturn, but commenced upon me the first hour of our acquaintance to enquire of the circumstances of the various firms for whom he had selected hides that had been shipped to Boston and being satisfied upon this point he proceeded to interrogate me upon the uses of the hides after their arrival at their place of destination and finally upon the subject of what kind of a place America was "any how." I answered all his questions to the best of my ability, interpreting to myself his broken English and making as intelligible as possible my replies. Nor was he by any means ungrateful for all this, but made me many offers of service, which however I did not accept.

After we had been steadily at work for about an hour, he

asking questions and I answering and listening to such comments as the sircar was pleased to make in very good English but in a tone of voice that sounded as if he had a broken jaw; he perceiving a watch chain attached to my pants asked the time and upon my replying "igara ghuntee" [eleven o'clock] he dropped the hide he had half picked up and "evaporated." "Where the devil has he gone to" I asked of the sircar, thoroughly vexed at his leaving. "To pray, cooley gone to pray" replied my gawky friend. I know that it was towards the close of the month "Rammesin" [Ramadan] during which all recollected Musselmen fast from sunrise till after sunset, & knowing that all the coolies were devout Mohamedans, I seated myself to wait patiently his returned from the Mosque, deliberating in the meanwhile the greater devotedness of the followers of Mahomet and even the followers of Brahm[a], to their religious ceremonies than many Christians.

In about an hour the cooley returned and after a comfortable smoke of the "hubble bubble" at which the sircar had been tugging during his absence, we resumed our labor. About 2 P.M. he again enquired the time and again left for the Mosque and again about 4 o'clock, making a serious interruption of business. The number of times for daily prayer prescribed by the Koran is five and these are very strictly observed by the devout Mohamedans. Some, however, from the nature of their daily occupations being unable to attend during the day make up by unusual devoutness in the morning and evening. I shall have occasion hereafter to speak upon the subjects of the Mosques and I shall then refer more particularly to Islamic rites and ceremonies.

Day succeeded day and one differed not much from another in the receiving of hides. One afternoon the owner of the godown or the hide merchant came in where I was receiving. He was the finest looking Musselman I saw while in the East. He was tall, stout and good looking with a very benevolent cast of countenance, and was dressed with the tight fitting skull cap, the flowing robe and pants common to all Hindoo Mohamedans. He shook hands with me and treated me very politely although he could not speak English. He also referred to my watch and finding it was prayer time left for the Mosque.

One afternoon when we had nearly finished receiving, the

Fig. 16.15 *Custom House* by Charles D'Oyly, Dickinson and Co., lithographers, London, 1848. Lithograph, 31.6 x 54.5 cm; Peabody Essex Museum M3104.4, Gift of Frances R. Morse, 1927.

cooly left for the Mosque a little earlier than usual and the other coolies took advantage of his absence for a "caulking" spell. Most of them were asleep and the sircar was smoking his "hubble-bubble" when Farnham made his appearance. Before he reached the door he began with "Where in H__l are you all" and as he entered and saw how matters stood, he appealed to the coolies with his foot and shook the sircar. "This is a great go anyhow" murmured the great man as he viewed contemptuously the small pile of hides selected "what have ye been about all day?"

I now stepped forward and explained the matter, "Ah," said he, "I was not aware you were present; but as to this praying it is all gas, and I shall put a stop to his going off every few minutes." At this instant the hide cooley entered and Farnham after recommending a fiat from the Almighty to condemn his soul to the infernal regions, said, "not go to mosque any more,

no more pray." The cooley did not understand and Farnham who always spoke in broken English to the natives repeated more slowly his injunction. Still the cooley did not comprehend and it finally had to be interpreted by the sircar, who during the time had been looking on in opened mouthed wonder. When he fully understood nothing could exceed the contempt with which he regarded Farnham drawing himself up to his full height and folding his arms upon his breast he said "Humjentah sahib," I pray. Farnham now attempted to stir them up to work; but the sircar smoked out his "hubble-bubble" and the cooley smoked out his and they then began under the direction of Farnham, but he could make nothing out of them by storming, a fact that I had learned sometime before, and he finally left in high dudgeon.

I have merely introduced this anecdote to illustrate a characteristic of the race. They will do as much and no more and no amount of bullying will drive them. They may in particular

Fig. 16.16 *Sepoy*, Calcutta, c. 1850, from an album owned by
Bostonian Thomas Wigglesworth, Jr. (1814–1907). Painting on mica,
13.3 x 9.2 cm; Peabody Essex Museum E82002.3, Gift of S. Dillon
Ripley in honor of Evelyn Bartlett, 1986.

instances when in fear of personal injury move a little faster
before your face but you will be the loser in the end.[13]

The Custom House [fig. 16.15]—As an export duty is chargeable
on all goods carried out of India, articles of merchandise must
be cleared and shipped from the Custom House. It is here that
the hides, and gunnies are weighed and measured and the final
account taken of them and many a long hour have I spent in
taking weights from the scale beam or measure from the
calipers, beneath a burning sun. But the long hours grew into
long days and the days into weeks and this duty was finally at

end. There only now remained for me the duties of the counting room. But as these are the same the Christian world over it
is needless for me to particularize.

The Custom House at Calcutta is a large and handsome
building situated on one of the principal streets and the bank of
the river. It is surrounded by a high wall and has connected with
it extensive grounds and store houses which indeed are necessary for the immense amount of goods passing through it. All its
ingress and outlet are guarded by a sepoy armed cap-a-pie [fig.
16.16], and the main gateways of the yard are high and arched.
The internal arrangements of this establishment differ but little
from others of the kind elsewhere. A preventive officer is put on
board every vessel arriving who sees that nothing but what has
been properly cleared from the shore authorities be put on
board. The effects of a passenger, however, if he takes the trouble to get a pass are exempt from examination. There is no elud-
ing the revenue laws, for they are so connected with the pilot
service that no pilot can be obtained till everything is straight at
the Custom House, and attempting to leave Calcutta without a
pilot would be equivalent to signing a man's own death warrant.

Thus in a few hastily written sketches I have endeavored
to give some idea of "Business Life" in the East, but I would
state in conclusion that the writing is for no eye but my own,—
is not considered as finished, but merely the nucleus of a subject
to be here after extended and elaborated.

Domestic Life—The manner in which I am "reeling off my
yarn" may appear without order or connection and I am aware
it is by no means logical, but it must be remembered that I am
not striving for an elaborate treatise of my subject but merely
presenting "Life in the East" as it appeared to me. And yet one
would naturally suppose that the order of this appearance would
be domestic, before business life. But our natural suppositions
often mislead and they do so in the present case, for long before
I had an opportunity to examine the workings of the domestic
economy I was deeply engaged in the mission on which I was
sent. And here is another reason why business life should be first
treated upon, being the primary object of the voyage, it of
course, received my attention first, while the other subjects
of observation were matters of second consideration.

Fig. 16.17 *Chowringhee* by Charles D'Oyly, Dickinson and Co., lithographers, London, 1848. Lithograph, 31.6 x 54.5 cm; Peabody Essex Museum M3104.25, Gift of Frances R. Morse, 1927.

Calcutta is a large city containing all told a population of more than 800,000. Of this number, judging from a rough estimate as I have no statistics by me, there may be 10,000 English. In our old geographies the English portion of the town is spoken of as Chowringee, as upon a street of that name the English residents were formerly almost exclusively located [fig. 16.17]. But with the rapid increase of the Calcutta trade within the last few years they have spread for a long distance from this locality. The English town is still however distinct, not that it is inhabited by English exclusively, for here are to be found the representatives of almost every commercial nation as well as the richer natives; but it is distinguished by its style of architecture; it is in fact as Margette tells us, a "city of palaces." This style of architecture is purely Hindoo, the intercourse of nearly three centuries with Western nations have produced no innovation in this respect. As Alexander or Semeramis[14] found it; it is to be seen by the adventurer today. Nor is this strange, for the Hindoos, as with all Far Eastern nations are no friends to progress. They are in fact genuine old fogies, believing "As it was, even so it is, and so it ever shall be." And again those who

have come among them have been unable to produce anything, any better or even so well adapted to the climate, as the native style of building.

The houses are of brick covered with *chunam* or a thick coating of plaster, presenting a smooth surface which, being kept whitewashed, presents the appearance, when a short distance, of marble [fig. 16.18]. They are very large in extent; the basement in most cases in the city is used as store rooms, but in country houses is finished into a hall open at the two ends. The first (or as it would be called with us, the second story) is the place of residence; this has on two sides a veranda and is divided into halls, dining rooms, and sleeping apartments as the fancy of the occupier may suggest. The rooms are very lofty, being generally about eighteen feet from floor to ceiling, but they are often much higher, and the division walls between them as well as the outside wall is four feet in thickness. The floors also are very thick, being of brick resting on wooden rafters. The story above the first, and there are often four, is finished in the same general manner, veranda above veranda, the floor of the one being supported by pillars from the one

Fig. 16.18 The Calcutta home of John Atkinson of Newburyport (Mass.), Calcutta, c. 1860.
Photograph, 18.2 x 26 cm; Courtesy of New England Historic Genealogical Society, Boston, Massachusetts.

below; and room above room giving in many instances as many as forty large apartments in a single house. The windows are protected by venetian blind and by a light glass shutter. The roof, as in all Eastern countries, is perfectly flat, surrounded by a low wall through which are apertures for the escape of water. No provision is made for fire with fire places or chimneys; the cooking is done in a separate building, which with various others used as store rooms or lodging places for the servants stables etc., surround the yard forming an inaccessible wall with the opening of a single gate which is closed at night and strictly guarded by two *dewans* night and day. The appearance of all these houses are some what castellated with their open verandas, the flat battlement roofs and high walls, and their narrow arched gateways, and could in fact, garrisoned with a full force, hold an enemy at bay for some time with their thick walls and the advantages otherwise afforded to repel an attack. That this in fact was not taken into consideration by the

original builders after this model, we have no proof. Most likely in fact it was, for India was ever disturbed by [internecine?] warfare during the times of the Great Moghul and the Rajah chiefs.

Our House—"Our House" was situated in Old China Bazaar, or Radha Bazaar, as it was commonly called, about a half mile from the river and about a quarter from the Government House. It was small for a Calcutta House, containing only, besides the store rooms of the basement, 8 apartments on the second floor. These were a large hall, the dining room, two offices and the sleeping rooms. My room was next the office and looked out upon the street. This room and the offices were in a wing of the main house, the two verandas being connected. Beneath the veranda of the main portion of the building, which was merely supported by pillars and so entirely open, were the stairs leading to the great hall and to the offices. The pair leading to the hall were long broad and winding, built of wood, inlaid in diamond shaped pieces, but those to the office were of stout and substantial timber.

You entered the gate, the *derwan* of which arose and saluted you as you passed, upon your left were the cook houses, the stables and the lodging houses for the servants, all enclosing a very small space for a yard, while directly before you were the entrances to the godowns and the stairs above mentioned. Pushing up the main flight you entered the large hall, just beyond which and connected with it by three doors was the dining room in the centre of which, and running nearly the whole length, was [swung?] a huge punkha [fig. 16.19]. Upon the four walls about 8 feet from the floor were fastened lamps of a curious fashion being in the shape of a large wine glass with a small vase inside containing cocoa nut oil, the most commonly used substance for illumination in India. This room was handsomely furnished with 3 large sofas, a large mahogany dining table etc. etc. etc. There were three rooms and one large window opening out of it, one room occupied by the supercargo, one by Captain Martin and one by B. F. F. My own room, as I have before remarked, was in another part of the house.

But enough of such a cursed description, which is harrowing up my soul and causing my brain to turn as I sit writing this terrible hot day in the Bay of Bengal, Lat 8 degrees N Long. (as I copy it from the Captain's slate which he [has] before me) 91 degrees—18' E. (Aug. 30th) Homeward Bound.[15]

There were about 30 servants connected with our domestic establishment. These were the *kunsemar* or supplier of the table, *kipmegars*, bearers, cooks, *punkha-wallahs*, *derwans* and *maters* [sweepers]. All these are rendered necessary by the difference of caste in the natives. No Hindoo will touch food cooked by an inferior caste, so all the cooks, *kunsemars* and *kipmegars* are Mussalmen. The bearers will wash and dress you, but as they are of a comparatively high caste they will perform no more menial office. *Maters* therefore are employed to do the sweeping up, keeping the rooms clean etc.

Kipmegars & Breakfast— At the table the *kipmegar* stands behind his master, and the *kansemar* behind the head of the house, so at our table there were five servants in attendance.

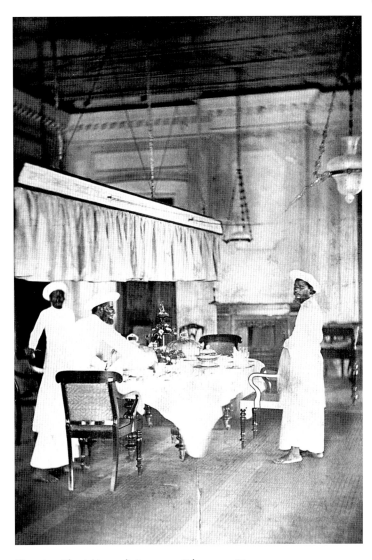

Fig. 16.19 The Atkinson dining room, Calcutta, c. 1860. Photograph, 15 x 10 cm; Courtesy New England Historic Genealogical Society, Boston, Massachusetts.

Each *kipmegar* attends immediately upon the wants of his master and when not employed stands with his arms folded.[16]

A Newburyport Boy—There was one old fellow who dined with us quite often, a captain of one of the steam boats running up the Ganges, by the name of Wheeler who would entertain us with accounts of the most unheard of adventures which all his auditory were aware were lies made up out of whole cloth for the occasion; but as the old fellow was rather amusing no one attempted to interrupt him or contradict his marvelous tales.

Fig. 16.20 John Atkinson of Newburyport and Calcutta, c. 1855. Photograph, 12 x 9 cm; Courtesy of New England Historic Genealogical Society, Boston, Massachusetts.

This worthy, hearing I was from Newburyport, called upon me privately one day and informed me that he was from Newburyport also, and this I had no reason to doubt as he appeared perfectly acquainted with the localities and with many of the old families in that "ancient town." He informed me that he had come out to Calcutta about 20 years ago in a Boston ship, had there left her and entered upon the E. I. Company's service in one of their country ships and after many hard struggles rose to the command, and, upon the line of steamers being placed upon the Ganges, he was offered a Captain's berth which he gladly accepted as the salary is 3600 Rs per year with every opportunity to make a fortune in the way of trade between the far up country and the sea board in the course of a few years. He is now about forty years old and he told me that in a few years more he hoped to have amassed a sufficient competency to enable him to return to his native country. His mother is still

living in Roxbury. Altogether he was a good old fellow and looked as if living in India agreed with him and although he would occasionally tell a story that it would require a considerable stretch of imagination to believe, yet these stories never had the least tendency to harm any one, while his perfect good nature and the indomitable energy, the indefatigable industry and the sterling worth which had forced a way through all the obstacles in the path of an aspirant for favors from the E.I. Company, entitled him to hearty respect and I was happy to own him as a fellow townsman.

A Bridal Call—The hour after dinner is the time which the bachelors generally appropriate to calling upon one another, and among those who presented themselves at our house during my sojourn there, were three more Newburyport boys. These were John Atkinson [fig. 16.20; see also figs. 16.9, 16.18–19], now the head of a flourishing business house, James Adams late U.S. Consul at Singapore, and lastly Frank Wills, then lately arrived with his sister and Miss Dole in the ship *Hippogriffe*. The two first I did not see and should not have met the latter had he not dispatched Farnham to my room where I had retired with a message that he desired to see me.

A strange meeting was ours. The last time I had seen him was the day before I left Newburyport, in a fancy team with Patsy Titcomb skimming along Pleasant Street and now we clasped each others hands, our feet upon Asiatic soil and our heads shaved; (or his shaved and covered with a huge wig and the hair upon my own remarkably short.) Then we were wrapped in heavy overcoats to protect us from the cold, now we were in white linen and beneath a huge punkha and still perspiring with the intense heat. Mr. Wills received me very politely and cordially pressed me to come down to the house "any time."

I might as well here state that I accepted the invitation and called at No. 8 Banks Hall street, July (Friday) 28th four days before I left Calcutta, The party from Newburyport had arrived but about 3 weeks before and Miss Dole immediately upon arrival (July 4th) had been married to George Wills, brother to Frank, and the head of the house of Augustine, Wills and Co. I chose, of course, for my call the fashionable hour which is about noon. Arriving at the gate and after a preliminary cursing to the coachman for not rounding up in good shape, I descended and entered the gate, and handed my card to the derwan to carry up. I waited in the lower entry till his return, and amused myself in studying the various pictures of Hindoo deities upon the walls. In one corner stood the derwans bed over which was a formidable display of clubs and swords, which I looked at attentively during the long absence of the derwan. I began to grow impatient fearing that my standing dickey would melt down. I thought of the trouble I had been in fixing up and now perhaps they would not be "at home." I was in full dress, shoes polished up to the highest degree as only my bearer could polish them; white socks, ditto pants, ditto vest with a wide black watch guard; a straw colored grass cloth neck hdkf, standing collar; a heavy imperial [beard] and moustache, and all this was topped with a slouched hat of felt covered with white silk.

The reason for wearing this last was as follows. When I left my room I had upon one side of my head a handsome white beaver hat, but getting into the yard, I felt what I supposed to be perspiration streaming down my face "How very warm it is," I remarked to myself as I removed my hat to wipe my forehead. Imagine my horror to find it a perfect nest of white ants who had bored it in several places. Throwing it from me I had roared out for my other hat; my "every day one" and upon its being produced off I came.

All this and much more I reviewed while waiting in the entry for the return of the derwan and I was just beginning to think seriously of "evaporating" when he made his appearance and motioned for me to go "up," which I did two long flights of stairs when I was met by a bearer who piloted me up a third into the drawing room. I had just time enough to observe that it was very handsomely furnished, after I was comfortably seated, when Mrs. and Miss Wills entered.

Newburyport Girls in the East—She came immediately forward, that is the prettiest one, gave her name as Mrs. Wills, and introduced her companion. We now all seated ourselves and a desultory conversation, such as is usual on such occasions, ensued. She gave me some particulars of the passage out which it seems was very unpleasant on account of the drunkenness of the cap-

tain, and the summary of the latest Newburyport news; about somebody's engagement and about a May Fair at the City Hall etc. etc. After a stop of about 15 minutes I arose to take my departure; told them that I left homeward bound next Tuesday; upon which they requested me to call and see their folks and tell them how pleasantly they are situated, which I of course promised, and I finally made my exit, congratulating myself that all had gone off so well and that in my passage down the three flight of stairs I had not broken my neck.

Arrived home again I threw myself upon a sofa roared for boy, bearer, and punkha wallah to undress me and cool me off. Besides Mr. and Mrs. G. Wills there is but one American <u>family</u> now in Calcutta and this is that of Mr. Charles Bayley, head of the house of Foster and Rogers the firm by the way where Greenleaf is established as clerk. It was at Bayleys that Miss Dole remained till she changed into Mrs. Wills. But Mrs. Wills informed me that Frank goes home to bring out his wife in about four months, and as the brother of C. Bayley was soon expected out with <u>his</u>, they would have soon quite a society by themselves. Mr. and Mrs. Wills are soon to leave their present residence for a house in Elysian Row close by Mr. Bayley. and so gather all into one community.

At present Newburyport is well represented in Calcutta by those already mentioned, Frank Adams, and John Atkinson, making when I was there men and women 7 in all. The last time I had seen Miss Dole before meeting her in Calcutta was a year ago last winter when I collected some of the girls in a coach for one of the Merrimack soirees at the request of E. Griffen. Miss Wills I saw at the last Thanksgiving ball when I mistook her for some one I had engaged to dance with and upon my rushing up to her, a most ridiculously ludicrous scene ensued. Little I then dreamed that I should next meet those who figured in them on the banks of the Ganges. Into what strange kaleidoscope combinations do the fortunes of our lives bring us.

The Strand—The office hours of Calcutta business life extend by universal consent only from 10 A.M. to 4 P.M., of course a very foolish arrangement as this comprises the hottest part of the day. Yet still some time for recreation must be allowed, and it is perhaps after all questionable whether it may not be

Fig. 16.21 *Derby Day at Calcutta*, c. 1840. Oil on canvas, 49.5 x 95.5 cm; Courtesy of the Estate of Margaret Pope Parker.

pleasanter to work through the heat within doors, and enjoy the cool hours of twilight in the open air. At any rate this is the opinion of "the residents" and they act upon it accordingly. From 6 P.M. "the Strand," a public drive, a sort of Hyde Park, is alive with the fashionable Calcutta world. Everybody rides, in something from a hackry to a barouche. Every thing is in the true Anglo-Indian style, the ease and comfort of the one with the luxury and display of the other. The turn-outs are most of them very elegant, and mostly barouches and buggies (or chaises) with richly dressed coachmen and outriders. The horses are walked slowly , the tops of the carriages are turned down showing in full dress the inmates; the ladies of course in white dresses and white kids with their poodles and fans and the men with hats off "taking it cooly" [fig. 16.21].

Officers of the army and of the navy, and of the civil service improve this hour in a drive with their wives and children, and for miles the Strand is alive with the brave, the gay and fair. The English and whites however do not monopolise the Strand;

the native nabobs, Armenians and Jews are to be seen there also, and some of them with such an attempt at display as to excite the derision of the beholder. I have often seen a Hindoo merchant in a splendid barouche, drawn by a span of beautiful horses, attended by 8 or 10 servants clinging to the carriage wherever a hold was to be had. The Armenians, Jews and Parsees mostly content themselves with a simple horse and buggy, but this in very good style. Altogether it is a strange scene witnessed every pleasant evening upon the Strand. The rich turn outs and the English in their gay white dresses; the fat old nabobs with their many attendants, the red turbaned merchants and the tall black capped Parsees, and the long-bearded, sharp-featured piercing eyed Jews.

Lord Dalhousie[17]

Lord Dalhousie is no common man. During the life time of the Duke of Wellington it was the policy of the English government to send such men as governors to India as were recommended by him and pushed forward by his influence, and these were invariably some of his old companions in arms,—very good men no doubt, brave soldiers, skillful generals, but they had grown old in the service, their energies had been wasted in the peninsula and at the Cape, and they were unfitted for the active duties of the cabinet and of the civil government. Since the days of Warren Hastings the administration of India, with single exception of the years of the incumbency of Lord Bentinck, has savored strongly of the drum stick and court martial, and conquest has been its end and object. Thus it is, that for the two and a half centuries that England has held dominion in Hindoostan that there has been rather a retrograde than a progressive movement in her social institutions. But the old foggy times have passed away and, with accession of Lord Dalhousie,[18] a brighter and a happier day has dawned upon India. Nor were the early days of his administration marked by any favorable auspices. He found the government involved in the Rangoon war,[19] and a black cloud of sedition gathering in the Northwest.[20] These difficulties he has overcome, or rather turned them to advantages for in his hands they have been the means of the important additions of the North West Provinces and extensive possessions in Birmah [Burma] to the British India Empire, and, for the first time for many years the Army of India is a peace establishment. But it is not upon these achievements, great though they may be, that his fame rests. To him belongs the high honor of introducing many and great internal improvements. Under his paternal care the genius of steam is working the mighty revolution of civilisation, and the shrill neighing of the iron horse even now startles the tiger from his lair in the jungles of Bengal. Soon extensive lines of railway, canal, and telegraph will traverse the length and breadth of this vast fertile region, and almost annihilate the distance between the salubrious vallies of the Punjab and the burning and yet productive plains of the Deccan. And thus will the different portions of the empire be more firmly bound together and to the mother country; thus will all classes in India be greatly benefited, as surely as these great motors have always benefited the masses of the people; and finally thus will the Indian revenue be greatly augmented eventually. It is the genius of one man that has seen these results so desirable, and traced out the causes by which

they might be obtained, and the same genius is now practically urging on the causes to the results, after conquering long and bitter opposition by steadily and strongly putting his own shoulder to the wheel! Thus has India become a field of glory to Dalhousie and these are the achievements which will cause his name to be cherished in Eastern history when even those of Clive and Napier[21] shall be forgotten!

After Supper Life[22]—We generally mustered all hands returned from the Strand, about 8 P.M.; at this hour accordingly tea was brought on, which being finished and cleared away the kipmegars left for the night. A game of whist sometimes succeeded if the four of us felt disposed to stop indoors, or we passed an hour in spinning yarns beneath the cool breeze of the punkha in our night dress and then turned in.

One great <u>desideratum</u> in Calcutta is some place of public amusement for the evening. Strange as it may appear in a city as large and as luxurious as this there is nothing of the kind; no theatres, no concerts, no lectures no anything by which a stranger can help kill the hours between tea and bed time.[23]

An evening stroll—At a later hour the scene is changed. The lights are extinguished and the merchants without troubling themselves to close the establishments, throw themselves upon the floor or upon a bamboo bedstead in the open street and thus pass the night. Some even sleep upon the naked ground and the pedestrian now needs to keep a wary eye about him lest he stumbles over some sleep-wrapped Hindoo.

I cannot perhaps convey a better idea of the appearance of Calcutta by lamplight than by taking the reader upon an imaginary stroll through the most noticeable localities, and acting merely as a guide, point out to him, as far as my time, space and ability will allow the more remarkable features of the scene as they present themselves in succession before us.

It is of course a sultry and oppressive evening, so throw off your vest, and put on with me this light felt hat covered with silk, made on purpose for evening wear, turn up the bottoms of your white pants, and if you feel the slightest trembling of fear at the thought that you are in a strange and <u>heathen</u> land, here take this Colt's revolver, it is charged to the muzzle, and we will sally forth. We are in the yard; come take my arm and we native men and women hurrying along in crowds, and inter-mingled among them we see an occasional solider and sailor; but who is this that approaches us at a lazy pace clad in a shirt like robe with a red turban, and a red sash about the waist, swinging a formidable looking club, why only a "chowkeedar" or native policeman [fig. 16.22], but let us push on, for we are in a suspicious locality and are beginning to attract attention. The buildings upon both sides of us are grog shops, and in some a violin and in others a drum and fife are "discoursing sweet music" to charm in the passer by. Here is the "Albion," here the "Columbian," and here the "New York," and they are all insti-tutions of the same class. The various flags fluttering over our heads are the ensigns of various nations, and are merely dis-played to attract attention. It is indeed from this superabun-dance of bunting always flung out to the wind here that this thoroughfare is named. Ah! here is a drunken brawl, and now we hear a continued roar of bacchanalian shouts and laughter. Let us turn the corner.

Cossitollah—This is Coolotollah (street) and here are the bazaars upon the both sides, and the stifled hum of business alone assails our ears. We will examine the first shop, as it appears to be a fair specimen of its class. It is a fruit stand and the whole establish-ment is comprised in this little room, not more than eight feet square, which is however so filled up with fruit that there is scarcely room for the vendor to sit even compressed as he is into a small space. Look, what a variety; it will give you some idea of the fruitfulness of the East, and if you will ask the merchant he will tell you that it was all plucked fresh this morning.

Do you smile at my calling him a <u>merchant</u>? Why that fel-low, although his whole clothing consists of a piece of cotton cloth wound about his middle, may be the possessor of a lac [100,000] of rupees; this is the last place in the world to judge of a man by his appearances. But observe, here are fine apples, mangoes, mangosteens, cocoa nuts, custard apples, limes, pom-meloes [a large orange], figs, plums, and peaches, and while we are eyeing them see how contentedly the proprietor sits smok-ing his hubble-bubble and eyeing us. Yet do not think we shall get off so; he only waits for us to make a selection; if we attempt to start away without purchasing he will raise a terrible clatter

Fig. 16.22 *Mussulman Cho-ke-dah (Constable)*, Calcutta, c. 1860, from an album owned by Bostonian Thomas Wigglesworth, Jr. (1814–1907). Painting on mica, 13.3 x 9.2 cm; Peabody Essex Museum E82002.7, Gift of S. Dillon Ripley in honor of Evelyn Bartlett, 1986.

will push forward. At "<u>carput bunkero</u>," the *derwan* (or door keeper) makes a low salaam, the huge gate swings open before us and we are in the street.

Flag Street—"Muddy"! do you say; "O, yes a little but never mind we shall see more by and by." This is Radha Bazaar, and as it belongs to the English portion of the town, that is, as its patrons are mostly English, the bazaars are now closed and it is enveloped in darkness. Here we will turn this way into Flag Street, where there is something of an illumination. All these houses that you see before you are sailor boarding houses, and as we approach nearer we shall hear the noise of drunken carousal. Notice now what a strange scene is before us, see the about our ears.—Do you say, "buy a few annas worth to prevent this?" O! Yes, certainly if you wish to amuse yourself by throwing it into the ditch, but you must not think of eating any, unless you intend to violate a fundamental rule of East India life, for fruit is never eaten here by an old stager, except in the early part of the day, at any rate not at so late an hour as this.

Come let us go. There, you see although we have not moved ten steps, that this vendor of fruit was not wedged into his stall as tightly as you imagined and as in fact, as he appeared to be, for he has dodged out quickly by a side passage, and is now saluting us with a copious discharge of, "buy some sar [sir], very nice fruit, buy some sar, buy some sar!" Ha! ha! ha! has he got hold of your coattail? Well no! no! don't strike him! I merely turn towards him and make the motion of a blow, with the exclamation of,—"Jow your soor[n?]!" and he is off.

Here is a nut bazaar, and among the collection you see peanuts and the beetle nut, You smile at finding the first here and ask perhaps how the price compares with that of the same article at home, and if it has "riz" lately, but you will be still more interested in the second when I tell you, (if you have not learned it in your school geography) that it takes the place of tobacco among the Hindoos and is even more extensively used among them than is the "weed" with us. All classes, ages and sexes use it, from the boy or girl of 3 years to the old man or woman of 70, from the cooley and mater, up through all the 29 lower, the 4 higher, casts even to the Brahmin. There is nothing peculiar in it as it lies before us, but you will observe that it closely resembles a nutmeg. The only preparation it undergoes for use is to be cracked into small pieces, and enveloped in a little paste of *chunam* [lime], and a piece of plantain leaf [sic, betel leaf], and this little bundle of compounds is put into the mouth whole, in chewing it leaves a bright red stain upon the lips and teeth, with an odor rather unpleasant.

At the corner opposite is a vendor of it in the last mentioned form, and these you will meet every few paces through the length and breadth of Calcutta. This whole establishment consists of a desk shaped box containing his stock and implements of trade, consisting of a little heap of cracked beetle nut, a few strips of plantain leaf, and a little pot of chunam or damp plaster, and in the use of these he is very dexterous. He first

Fig. 16.23 Woman selling betel nut preparations, c. 1860, from an album owned by Bostonian Thomas Wigglesworth, Jr. (1814–1907). Painting on mica, 13.3 x 9.2 cm; Peabody Essex Museum E82002.12, Gift of S. Dillon Ripley in honor of Evelyn Bartlett, 1986.

takes a piece of the beetle, places it upon the strip of plantain, dashes a little chunam over it with a wooden spoon, gives the edges a peculiar turn and lays [to] one side a neatly made little triangular shaped bundle ready for the mouth of anyone disposed to purchase. If you have a mind to taste this nut step forward and buy a few bundles. You do so by paying four times as much for it as a cooley would, and find that it is bitter but by no means unpleasant to the palate [fig. 16.23].

I see your eyes are fixed on the next stall of the bazaar, so let us move on. These large rolls of a gummy black looking substance is the Hindoos substitute for smoking tobacco and is to be found in the hubble-bubble of the servant and the

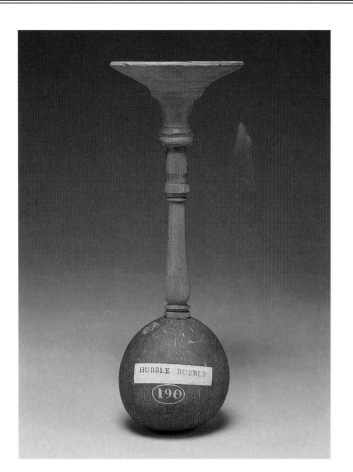

Fig. 16.24 *Hubble Bubble*, Calcutta, c. 1800. Coconut and earthenware, height 34 cm; Peabody Essex Museum E8122, Gift of George Pierce, 1803.

hookah of the nabob. Like the beetle its use is universal among all classes and ages, and both sexes. This dirty looking stuff is made of molasses, chunam, and of what else I am as ignorant as yourself; for of the many natives I have asked for a synthesis, they have all given me a different list of component parts, with the exception of the two named. It is however nauseating in the extreme and none but natives can use it. If you wished to purchase you have but to name the quantity the knife divides a piece which being thrown upon the scales is always of the exact weight, a fact which leads to the suspicion of unfair play.

Hubble-bubbles, Hookahs & Islam—Here too in this same stall are plenty of hubble-bubbles, you will observe that they are nothing more than the shell of a small cocoa nut scraped and polished with an upright stem, upon the end of which is and earthen cup or bowl [fig. 16.24]. This bowl contains the sub-

stance to be smoked and the fire; the shell is filled with water through which the smoke is drawn by placing the mouth at a hole upon the side, and it is from the peculiar noise which this operation produces that it derives its name. The hookah [see figs. 1.4 and 4.23] differs from the hubble-bubble, only in a being more elaborate exposition of the same principle. Instead of the cocoa nut shell it is furnished with a metallic vase, from which rises, upon one side a slim tube supporting the bowl for the tobacco and fire, and from the other a flexible stem varying in length from four to fifteen feet according to the fancy of the owner. This stem is generally wrought with party colored silk and silver thread and is terminated by a silver mouth piece. The use of the hookah is probably not nearly so injurious as that of the common pipe or cigar, from the fact that as the smoke passes through water it must be purified of its oily vapor and thoroughly cooled before it enters the mouth, and is consequently at once rid of two of its most hurtful properties.

While here let us notice the light which you will perceive is furnished by an apparatus consisting of a section of cocoa nut shell supported by a long wire. The shell is filled with oil also of this—to the Hindoo—valuable nut, and a strip of cotton rag laid upon one side serves as a wick. This is the simple lamp which the native portion of the inhabitants use, throughout India.

We pass on. This is the "New Mosque," and it is the hour of evening prayer, and here we have an opportunity to witness Mussulmen at their devotions. The building is large and elegant of the usual materials, the roof being surmounted by many domes and gilded minarets [fig. 16.25]. Upon one side externally is a row of large lamps which light up a strange scene in the yard adjoining. Here congregated and fixed with military precision in rank and file, clad in white robes with bare feet and heads are at least 500 devout followers of the Prophet of Mecca. Like well trained soldiers they stand shoulder to shoulder fixed and immovable: but it is only for a minute; now with a simultaneous movement every head is bowed, now they drop upon their knees, and now fall prostrate with their foreheads against the ground. Together they rise to again and again bow, kneel and fall, ever looking towards Mecca. Here is a laborious devotion for you and this is the fifth time since day break that the Muezzin from the minaret has called, "Come to prayer." It is now the

Fig. 16.25 *Mosque aux Environs de Calcutta*, by Lauvergne, V. Adam lithographer, published by Bichebois, Paris, c. 1840.
Colored lithograph, 19 x 26.7 cm; Peabody Essex Museum M17804, Gift of John Dominis Holt and Frances Damon Holt, 1978.

month Ramazan [Ramadan], during which all Mohomedans are particularly devout, fasting during the day, tasting not even of a drop of water while the sun is in the sky, from one new moon to another. After this is the feast of Barain, when eating and drinking to extreme will be the order of the day. Islamism was planted in Hindoostan by Mohmud[24] in the 11th century who established the dynasty of the Great Mogul; Genghis Khan also visited this country in the 15th [sic, 13th] century. In returning home from the mosque at this time, many of the worshippers before us will prostrate themselves at every few steps and pray devoutly. "What! in the mud?" do you ask. "O! Yes, I reply, certainly, even in their clean white robes they bow till their foreheads rest in the liquid ooze that is growing deeper and deeper beneath our feet."

Opposite us is a blacksmith's shop and you will observe that the only light is that of the fire and of the red hot iron, which furnishes enough for them to work by. "Tired, hot!" you exclaim. Why, yes it is rather warm, but there is no rest for the weary sole of the foot here; the mud is growing worse; however we will pause for an instant and look around us. In the interest of our examinations you have not perhaps noticed that we are but two of a vast crowd. Cast your eye before us now and observe the throng, Hindoos, men and women, bearing burthens and pots of water upon their heads; sircars in white robes, coolies in a near approach to the state of nudity, females with not a superabundance of clothing, and with many of the charms which in a colder climate are hidden, fully displayed; red turbaned merchants from the far up country, and the uniformed chowkeedars with their red sashes, brass plates, and heavy clubs mingle together in a gay and wild confusion. And the wildness of the scene is increased by the uncertain and flickering light which flashes over the white dresses and dusky forms from the

Fig. 16.26 *Hindoo Mat (Temple) in the Chitpore Bazaar* by Charles D'Oyly, Dickinson and Co., lithographers, London, 1848. Lithograph, 31.6 x 54.5 cm; Peabody Essex Museum M3104.22, Gift of Frances R. Morse, 1927.

cocoa nut torches of the bazaars. These bazaars as we now look at them present in general the same appearance, differing only in the article exposed for sale; the arrangement of all is the same; a little room 6 or 8 feet square, open in front, with the proprietor in the middle with his wares spread before and upon all sides of him. He, the owner of the establishment sits with the air of a philosopher smoking the eternal <u>hubble bubble</u> pausing occasionally to trim his light.

A Portuguese Wedding—But hullo! look here! what think you is this coming round the corner preceded by a band of music? It surely resembles a Yankee torchlight procession; let us approach and examine. It is a Portuguese wedding. The figure on horse back covered with a pink veil from head to foot is the bride; the palanquin close behind contains the bridegroom, and those about the newly married pair leading the horse and bearing torches, are their friends conducting them to the bridal couch, where we may hope that they will consummate the nuptials, so enough of this and let us get clear of this cursed band consisting of three kettle drums and three fifes played by red coated sweating Portuguese, whose noise combined with the shouting of the crowd bearing the torches is enough to drive one mad.

The Portuguese were the first Europeans that visited India by the way of the Cape of Good Hope; they discovered the passage of the Cape in 1497 and planted a colony at Calicut on the Malabar Coast the same year. Their possessions in Hindoostan, once extensive have now dwindled to the comparatively insignificant districts of Goa and Diu, in the vicinity of their first settlement. Those of this race in Calcutta are shown by their color to be by no means of a pure breed: they are employed mostly as clerks and writers in the screw houses and public offices. Their pedigree is probably to be traced through several generations of Hindoo mothers; and it is for this reason that they are here known as Coir Portuguese; in appearance they are by no means pleasing and they retain but little more than the dress and religion of their progenitors.

In giving you this slight sketch I have brought you back over a portion of the way and we now stand upon Chitpore Road [fig. 16.26]. This is a greater thoroughfare than the street we have just left as you may see by the crowd that throngs its length as far as the eye can reach. But it is getting late and the bazaars are for the most part closed for the night, and so here a new phase of life in the East is presented to us.

Move cautiously now, for deep ditches border upon both sides of the way filled with the foulest filth, while I ask you to look aloft to the second story of the houses here, which you will observe to be of a much better class than those we have before seen. These for the most part are finished in front with balconies one above the other, and connected with doors, or rather by blinds to the interior apartments. Upon these balconies, bestowed in every comfortable position, with fans and punkhas, resting from the fatigues of the day are the owners or vendors of the bazaars beneath. The slight glimpses we can obtain of the inner rooms show them to be neatly and even at times elegantly finished, and furnished; that is in the native style. If you will glance again you will perceive that the slight steps before the doors of the bazaar are covered with sleeping forms, and here at our side upon a bamboo cot, placed exactly over the ditch, repose two Hindoos, inhaling the foul miasma of the filth beneath them, which is sowing in their systems the seeds of death. Is it any wonder that the world scourging cholera, was brought forth in India, if such, as in fact it is, is the mode of life of hundreds of thousands of the natives?[25]

Here is one stall or shop not yet closed; let us see who it is that still keeps a vigil for customers. It is a seller of images, and in his collection are the household gods of the Hindoos. They are mostly however Juggernaths, (or Juggernauts) [Jagannatha] and Vishnus, varying in size from three to 8 inches in height [fig. 16.27]. The Juggernaths are facsimiles of the great up country Juggernauts, the Moluch of the East, and the Vishnus are modeled from some large idol of the temples, and by the way

Fig. 16.27 Jagannatha, Calcutta, c. 1815. Clay, height 18 cm; Peabody Essex Museum E7626, Gift of Ephraim Emmerton, c. 1815.

farther up the street where we are now standing are two temples containing splendid idols of Brahma and Vishnu. What a display is here before us, hundreds of these smaller copies, of the images, that are held in reverence and adoration by millions of human beings! I do not wonder that you laugh in looking at little stumpy goggle eyed, no armed Juggernaut, which you can buy for a curiosity for a few rupees, and wonder at the same time how blinded man may become by superstition, bent and ludicrous and ugly as his appearance is, sixty millions of our fellow creatures bow down to and worship him as a god.[26] The great original is located in the province of Orissa, and it is of him that you have read or heard from some missionary, the account, how yearly, when he is brought out upon his car, mad devotees immolate themselves gladly, before him, expecting thus to gain an easy admittance to future happiness. The English by their early treaties with the natives covenanted not to interfere with their religious customs, but still they have done much and the missionaries have to put a stop to this outrageous practice; but the evil still lurks and that to a greater extent than is believed in the United States or England, and how can it be otherwise while idol worship yet continues. Besides these images of which I have been speaking you notice several little balls, which you perhaps suppose to be marbles for the amusement of the Bengali children at the approaching holidays; but if so you are mistaken; these little spheres are also worshipped as deities![27]

We move again. There is no crowd now and the street before us is almost deserted, save by the sleepers and the white clad "chowkeedars" who pursue their lonely beats in silence. A low, soft, mournful song hummed by some Hindoo, lulling himself to rest upon his damp and filthy couch, occasionally meets the ear, but otherwise an unbroken silence is stealing over this vast metropolis.

A Remnant of the Old Days—More lights! they are torches in the distance. Another Portuguese wedding? Ah! No! Here is indeed something worth seeing, so let us pause. The crowd approaches; first come two natives in full dress bearing torches; then follows a litter of the most luxurious description borne upon the shoulders of four men and containing a young boy of 12 or 13 years clad in garment sparkling with gold. His long black curling hair also sparkling with this precious metal droops from beneath a richly wrought cap upon his shoulders, and over his left shoulder is thrown a costly and beautiful fabric of the vale of Cashmere. Following this are two more torches and then comes a plain black palanquin closely shut and veiled; a dozen or more natives bearing torches, closes the pageant. You stand gazing in astonishment and ask, "Is it some bright vision!" I answer No! "They have gone to be married! gone to swear a peace! gone to be friends!" You look incredulous, but such is indeed the case.

It is the Indian custom to marry children very young; or you may call it a betrothal at the age of 7 or 8.[28] The veiled palanquin contained the young bride probably not more than 7 years old. This custom of marrying young is common in all Oriental and in all tropical nations where the sun's torrid heat brings man to a state of ripeness much earlier than in the higher latitudes, and makes those that are children with us heads of families. Yet after all this early perfection of the procreative powers, is but a hot house precocity which is repaid by premature old age as in the years when the man and woman of more temperate climates are in the vigor of their prime, these

are already fast going in decay. This ceremony of marriage or betrothal is observed with great pomp among the higher castes of the Hindoos, and among the rich, sums almost incredible are lavished in vain display; it is a lingering remnant of the Oriental magnificence of the old days, and as such is cherished with a peculiar love and veneration.

Chitpore Road—We have turned from Chitpore Road, and now stand in a different locality from any we have yet seen. This is a poorer portion of the city; the habitations about us are nothing but bamboo huts roofed with earthen tiles; and where the door stands open and a light burns within we see that they are of the meanest description [fig. 16.28]. The chinks between the poles are plastered with mud or stopped with straw the floor is the damp ground and there is little or no furniture with the exception of two or three miserable bamboo bedsteads. Here the husband and father the wife and mother, and the children male and female repose promiscuously. Were it day now this narrow lane would resound with the shouts of childish mirth; from boys and girls from 3 to 10 years old, all in the most perfect state of nudity.

A Dying Hindoo—A perfect and unbroken silence reigns about us, but no! my ear catches a faint sound near. We turn the corner, and perceive in front of a hut, extended on a litter with a red cloth thrown over it, a human body. "Dead?" you ask. No, but dying. There is a sound of wailing in the hut, and as we stand gazing 5 or 6 natives come out and with a low chanting broken occasionally by short sharp cries raise the litter upon their shoulders [and] bear it away. And where?—to the bank of the river, to insure the after happiness of their friends. This carrying the dying to the bank of the Ganges is one of the peculiar superstitions of the Hindoo. Formerly they were left at low water and suffered to perish at the return of the tide. This is also done at present in the country districts, and by many in the metropolis; but as the authorities have forbidden this and erected a suitable building for the dying on the bank of the river, they are for the most part in Calcutta, carried there. After death the body is carried to the burning ghaut near by, is consumed on a funeral pile [pyre] and the ashes collected and thrown in to the water.

"This," then you say, "is enough for one night." Well let it be so, death is perhaps an appropriate closing for the scenes that have been presented before us, and we will return home. And now does not the thought present itself to you, that there has been no occasion for the use of your revolver or for any weapon of defence although in our perambulation we have passed through many dark and suspicious places and encountered many hundreds of heathen? It no doubt does; but you would probably experience no attempt at affront in any amount of nocturnal wandering about this great city from any of the natives.

Thoughts on Bigotry—Many blame the superstition and bigotry of the Hindoos without making the least allowances for their education or their position in the social scale. It is not considered that they have a right for their belief in the traditions handed down from their forefathers, and the instruction of their childhood, and many good simple souls go to India with the expectation of rooting out in a few months, or years at least, the observances and superstitions of ages. I have had a man remark to me, "Does it not appear more than strange that those natives are so bigoted!" when the person himself would scoff at the idea that anybody could go to Heaven or to any other place except the lowest depths of Hell unless they swallowed whole, and without winking, the entire creed of the Episcopal church,—kept all the fasts, abstained from meat and ate fish Fridays and pancakes at Shrovetide, and did many other things which would appear equally ridiculous to the Hindoos, as do many of their religious observances to us.

My reply to this was, that I was not surprised at the <u>belief</u>. For I could not call it <u>bigotry</u> of those in question, when I found a person educated in an enlightened country like the United States who believed because a man preferred roast beef to cod fish for his Friday's dinner that he would be damned to all eternity in consequence. Why that man would be a <u>dissenter</u> from the established church, and of course would go to Hell was the reply. Here is a point that should be understood. If many who think it strange that the Hindoos, will not at once imbibe their doctrines, were told that they must not expect to be believed at once they would exclaim "Why! we are Christians!" Well but so the others are Hindoos! who think at least they have as good reason for following the belief of their father as you have for following that of yours. So where is the difference; we have our traditions and they have theirs; we have a bible, and they their Vedas; and while we do not for an instant question the compar-

Fig. 16.28 *Native Houses*, Calcutta, c. 1850, from an album owned by Bostonian Thomas Wigglesworth, Jr. (1814–1907). Painting on mica, 9.2 x 13.3 cm; Peabody Essex Museum E82002.13, Gift of S. Dillon Ripley in honor of Evelyn Bartlett, 1986.

ative excellence of Christianity and Brahmanism can we reasonably expect that they will at once and forever throw their faith aside? Certainly we cannot unless we draw an argument contrary to all experience. Let us then beware while we censure bigotry in others we do not ourselves fall into the same error.

If we coolly examine for a few minutes, the subject before us we may perchance discover that these <u>heathen</u> are not so much to blame in their unreadiness to imbibe our faith as we commonly imagine. Our Christian missionaries tell them of our faith and of its institutions. They preach of our observance of every seventh day as a time of rest from labor, and tell them that in the happy countries beyond the sea, this sabbath is strictly kept and yet many of the Christian merchants from these same countries make no account of the sabbath while in the East, and not only transact business themselves but oblige others to work for them. The Hindoo is also told of the supreme God and of his only begotten son, and how they both should be revered and worshipped, as they are by the Christians, and yet every day they hear this being called upon in the way of swearing in the most indecent manner, to witness any slight occurrence. On the contrary, no threats no bribes can procure a Hindoo to work for you upon their religious holidays, no matter how poor or how much distressed they may be; these days belong to their gods alone. Nor do they swear by their deities or even mention them

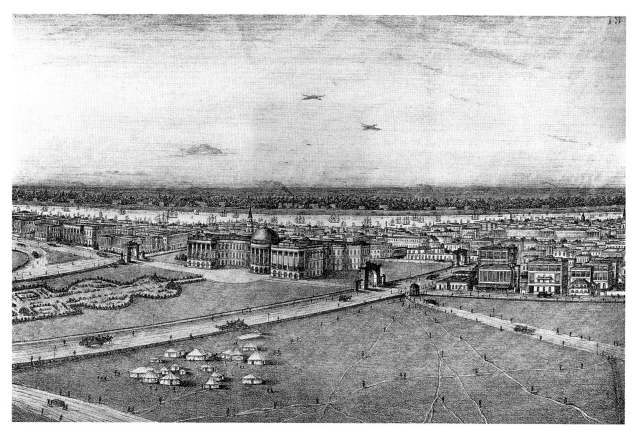

Fig. 16.29 Two views of a six-part panorama, taken from the top of Octherlony Monument by Frederick Fiebig, published by T. Black, Asiatic Lithographic Press, Calcutta, 1847. Lithograph, each 21 x 32.5 cm; By permission of the British Library.

except in the most devout manner. And so it is to a great extent in the social as in the moral virtues, the one violate all the principles that are taught by their brother Christians, while the others, follow to the letter the rule of conduct handed down to them. Here are the two examples before the Hindoo; he sees the practical working of Brahmanism, the every day violation of Christianity. Is it strange then that he does not always choose the last? . . .

Again, it should not be forgotten that I have been speaking of the lower classes; of the higher castes or educated classes among the natives there is another point to be considered. If a Brahmin forsakes the religion of his ancestors he is at once branded as an outcast. No one, not even a member of his own family can hold intercourse with him without contamination. I have talked with many of this high caste, priests even—upon the relative merits of Christianity and Brahminism and they have not denied the superiority of the first, as far as it develops the

social virtues, and yet there is but little incentive for them to profess the new faith, where by the change, although there is much to gain, there is everything as far as the enjoyment of this life is concerned, to lose. And this is also true of all the other castes.

Finally, let it be remembered that the conquerors of Hindoostan,—the nation that now rules them with an iron sceptre, that has imposed upon them, taxes, or at least a tax, enraging every principle of humanity, is a nation of Christians! Will it not then cease to be a wonder, when we view these point in all their bearings, that the term Christian has passed to almo t an expression of contempt among the Hindoos?

But here we are at the gate of "our house" again, and I ear that I have wearied you with my long lecture; but no matt r! It has at any rate done me some good to express my thought upon the matter, and allow to escape some of the choler I alw ys feel arise within me when I think of some conversations I ave had upon "bigotry" with persons who suppose the definit on of the

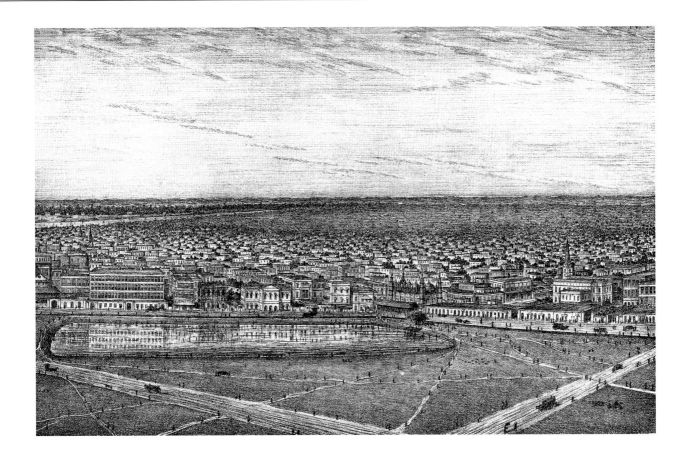

term to be a tenaciousness of a belief differing from their own.
—I have done—Ho! Derwan! carput bunkero! The door
swings open before us and we stand within the compound, well
besmeared with mud, and our clothes wet with perspiration.
Thus endeth our Evening Walk in Calcutta.[29]

The Battle Monument—Upon the public grounds near the Fort
and Chowringee, attracts some attention in coming up the river,
as it is seen above the surrounding objects. It is raised in memory of a general of the Anglo Indian Army who fell in some of
the battles of conquest.[30] It rises in a simple shaft to the height
of 112 feet. There is a spiral staircase ascending to the top inside,
and a good view from two galleries one above the other of the
surrounding country [fig. 16.29]. A native keeps the iron gate of
the monument, which he opens at sunrise and closes at sunset.
It was a clear morning shortly after my arrival that I ascended
to the upper gallery and spent an hour in viewing the varied
prospect which the elevated position I occupied presented to
my eyes. As far as vision could reach the ground was one
extended plain. At my feet a large open tract spreading about
Fort William, contrasted its rich green, here and there relieved
by a luxuriant tree, streams of water, and herds of sheep, goats
and asses feeding, with the dazzling whiteness of the houses of
the English town, sparkling in the rising sun, bordered by the
bamboo huts of the natives. Before me was the domed capped
roof of the Government House, and beyond, stretching far
away into the interior, its bosom freighted with water craft of
peculiar construction, the river celebrated in song and legend
from time out of mind in the writings and traditions of the
Hindoos. Upon my left the view was also inland; the eye
stretching over the same succession of huts and palaces, occasionally relieved by the tall form of a fruit capped cocoa nut
tree, till it was lost in the meeting of earth and sky. Upon the left
and south, over the bosom of the Hooghly upon one side and
the black walls and battlements of Fort William on the other, a
wild luxuriance of tree and jungle added variety to the scene.[31]

PALANQUIN and BEARERS

Fig. E.1 *Palanquin and Bearers* by William Haswell, bound in his *East India Journals*, 1801–03.
Peabody Essex Museum Library.

First Impressions

The chapters of this book have moved back and forth between wide-angle perspectives on the course of Indo-U.S. relations and close-ups on the exploits of individual Yankee mariners. Moving between broad developments and the experiences of individuals has brought into focus ways that mariners' encounters with India were shaped by the commercial and political climates in which they operated, and in turn how their responses to circumstances and events sometimes prompted them to see themselves and their world differently.

This zooming in and out has been possible because of the rich array of mariners' writings and mementos that have been preserved in public and private collections and survive as palpable records of the past. For readers today, these narratives and objects do more than link particular experiences to broad historical trends. Because they are survivors from long ago, writings and mementos are experienced as genuine links to the past, openings to the thoughts and responses of early nineteenth-century mariners and an opportunity to connect with objects that belong to earlier times. The journals, letters, pictures, and curiosities make the past feel present. Through mariners' writings, the responses of individuals become accessible and events and encounters that happened long ago can be seen through their eyes. Similarly, prints and paintings provide visual access to scenes of the past, showing how places and people of the time may have looked and how artists of the period chose to depict them. Of all these survivors, the mementos that project the strongest sense of connection to the past are those that were not intended to represent their time or place. Things that were made for actual use in very unfamiliar contexts—a hubble-bubble for smoking, a spindle to make cotton yarn, or an image of a deity for worship—are experienced as opportunities to meet something that truly belongs to another time and place, unmediated by the intentions of a narrator or artist.

The narratives, pictures, and objects presented in these pages create a dual effect. They provide a close encounter with the past as well as a means for understanding the relationship between history and people's lives. In *Yankee India*, it has been possible to explore how a group of mariners lived and understood their encounters with India. Their experiences, put side by side, emerge as highly individual and at the same time guided by certain cultural constructs that appear and reappear like motifs in a symphony, expressed in inumerable variations. In their encounters with India, these mariners were guided by belief in the preeminence of their religion, race, and civilization. Most of the time what they experienced could be comfortably fit into this framework. Now and then cultural expectations collided with experience, sometimes producing insight, a broader view, opening spaces for reconsidering their own society and their assessment of India and its people. This delicate process had the cumulative effect of building familiarity with Indian civilization and creating the possibility of deeper understandings.

In the ports of British India, as in most places they traded, Yankee mariners were identified as Americans. Their ships carried American papers and flew the American flag. On the open ocean, foreign privateers and naval vessels dealt with them as Americans. In the ports where they stopped, trading privileges were awarded or denied according to their nationality. For the mariners themselves, American identity had a range of meanings. William Rogers, whose journal was an exegesis on the failings of British monarchy set against the superiority of American republicanism, felt great pride in his country and was American to the core. For Benjamin Carpenter, who advocated forming an American East India company, national identity was a more pragmatic concern that could extend his business interests through the establishment of a nation-based mercantile company along European and British lines. Henry Lee, who placed commerce far above nationalist sentiment, was ready to secede from the union before he would see his business hamstrung by federal policy. While national identity was variably taken to heart, all Yankee mariners operated in a world where they were recognized as Americans and the salience of this identity was indisputable.

When they sailed into the ports of British India, these American merchant mariners came as men of commerce. For all of them, a handsome profit was the principal goal. Even Edwin Blood, nineteen-year-old supercargo's clerk, explained in his journal that his business activities took precedence in his narrative because business was the object of the voyage. The journals kept by Benjamin Carpenter and James Briggs were entirely taken up with commerce. Dudley Pickman, whose account was intended to be broadly descriptive of what he found in India, and William Rogers, whose journal was mainly an exercise in political discourse, both understood themselves first and foremost as men of business. They were guided in their dealings in port by certain readily transportable cultural constructs. They believed strongly that their religion was the true one, that the morality it entailed was universally applicable, and that their race was preeminent among humankind. These convictions of moral, spiritual, and racial superiority helped them adapt to the uncertainties and discomforts of the contact zone, and served them well in the business of trade.

In India, they shared the view that honesty was in very short supply among the "natives" with whom they dealt. In part this view was a standard of contact zones. Where no sense of community was shared and diverse moral systems coexisted, self-interest and pragmatism prevailed. Yankee mariners who entered these ports with their New England Protestant creed and firm belief in their own moral integrity were predisposed to view the motives of others with suspicion and to overlook their own pragmatic and dubious practices (and sometimes those of other Westerners). Benjamin Carpenter at Madras was indignant at the petty thievery of the boatmen but noncommittal about Europeans who swindled native buyers. On one page of his journal, William Rogers assailed the dishonesty of "natives" and a few pages later smugly reported fudging numbers and applying small bribes to get what he wanted. Their conviction that natives lacked honesty made it easier to deceive them in turn. Their sense of moral superiority provided protection against awareness of their own lapses.

From time to time, their business dealings with "native" merchants so surpassed their wary expectations that they were moved to genuine admiration of native perseverance, judgment, energy, and honesty. The portrait of George Washington (fig. 4.8) presented to Ramdulal Dey (fig. 4.7) was a tribute to Dey from a group of American clients who knew they owed to him much of their success in the India trade. Henry Lee, whose funds were lost in his banians' business failure, was deeply impressed at the lengths they went to make good on their debt to him. Edwin Blood was so affected by the kindness and sensitivity of the sircar Ram Rutton that he felt compelled to rethink his evaluation of native character. Experience from time to time escaped the structures used to contain it and precipitated new ways of thinking about India and its people.

Of all their shared orientations, their New England Protestantism was the most frequently and most self-consciously applied to their encounters in India. Their Protestant beliefs provided some clear and simple standards of evaluation. Idol worship was prohibited by the Ten Commandments and Hindus were known to worship images. Hindus recognized multitudes of deities; Christians were certain there was only one god. These facts were common knowledge. From its first year of operation, Americans could see for themselves at the East India Marine Society's museum, which displayed Hindu "idols" (see fig. I.3). The people of India were classified as "heathens." Some Americans thought they could be enlightened and saved by conversion to Christianity. In India, New England Congregationalists and Unitarians felt secure in their superior status as Christians.

A recognition of Indians as racially distinct also served to arrange people of the contact zone hierarchically. Like religion, considerations of race allowed mariners to position themselves as superior beings. Natives were black—and their blackness was emblematic of their racial inferiority. Race was well established as an organizing principle in British India. Madras and Calcutta had Black Towns where most of the native population lived. Dudley Pickman duly noted that blacks weren't allowed to enter the fort at Madras in palanquins. Acknowledging the inescapable presence of race in social relations of the contact zone, Rajinder Dutt in a letter to an American friend referred to himself with mischievous irony as the "black grandpa" of his correspondent's children. Sometimes Americans were surprised by the outstanding qualities of those purportedly of an inferior race. Edwin Blood, in relating his tale of the sircar Ram Rutton's kindly treatment, noted that it defied stereotypes of his race, and also observed that Ram Rutton behaved in an extremely generous manner despite the ill-treatment of his race by those of Blood's own. Rajinder Dutt's eulogist in the *New York Nation* wrote of him with great esteem, implying that Rajinder's fine character was all the more remarkable given his race.

The scanty clothing of Indians and the pervasiveness of beggars, jugglers, dancing girls, and snake charmers also disturbed Yankee mariners' New England sensibilities, signaling for them a compromised, even degraded morality. Pickman, Rogers, and Blood all commented on the near nudity of the laboring classes. The connection between near nudity and moral degradation was a powerful one, though Blood managed to make a little room for the appreciation of beauty as well. Given the close association between clothing, sexuality, and virtue that went back to the story of Adam and Eve, their remarks were far from innocent. Both Pickman and Rogers attended nautch (dance) performances and were confounded by the public acceptance of women of such questionable moral character. The established place of dancing girls as well as beggars and jugglers, who were subject to arrest at home, cast the moral character of Indians in a poor light.

Because Yankee mariners' firsthand experience sometimes defied their guiding beliefs about religion and race, many of them slowly came around to more complex views of Indian religiosity. Close encounters with "heathenism" sometime produced unexpected effects. William Rogers, who had been predisposed to think of natives of India as a "mild" people, was undone by the raucous behavior he witnessed during the celebration of Holi and by the observance of lingam worship at a Shiva temple. Yet even Rogers, when he went to the cremation ground expecting to enjoy a macabre spectacle, was nonplussed by the urbane civility of the Brahmin priest, especially as it contrasted with his own rather boorish behavior. It was not quite so easy to dismiss Hinduism and its practitioners. Both Dudley Pickman and Benjamin Crowninshield remarked on the devotion and solemnity they perceived in the practices of hook-swinging and sati, rites they expected to be merely horrific. Edwin Blood's observations contained both respectful descriptions of the piety of lowly Muslim laborers, and incomprehension that the likes of Jagannatha in the form he saw in the bazaar (fig. 16.27) could be a focus of devotion. Taking all he had seen into account, Blood came to the unanticipated conclusion that Hindu practices really could be genuine expressions of religious devotion.

Encounters that many Yankee mariners had with Christianity in India also moved them to reevaluate their views. They were surprised and disturbed that in India, Westerners routinely conducted business on the Sabbath. Missionaries they met seemed naive and inadequate as representatives of the true religion. William Rogers even alluded to allegations of adultery among the community of American missionaries in Bombay. Such disruptions and challenges to their preconceptions were instrumental in bringing about a more tolerant attitude toward religious difference among some of these New Englanders. Benjamin W. Crowninshield expressed this view in the speech discussed in chapter 8, strongly advocating respect for the intelligence of Indians and their divergent beliefs.

While these New Englanders may have questioned a wholesale low evaluation of "natives," instances of genuine esteem were noticeably rare. The pioneering banian for the American trade, Ramdulal Dey was very highly regarded by many of his American clients (if not by Henry Lee). When James B. Briggs described his 1823 donation of clay statuary to the East India Marine Society's museum, he referred to the figures as the work of a "distinguished native artist of Calcutta." This description is especially remarkable given that there was little recognition in the West that any kind of art was being produced in India at the time, let alone that an Indian sculptor could be "distinguished." Rammohun Roy's writings were widely read and he garnered great respect in America, especially in the emergent Unitarian movement, though part of the attraction was the hope that Rammohun Roy was opening the door to the reception of Christianity in India. Rajinder Dutt's character and intelligence were highly regarded not only by his eulogist in the *New York Nation* and those who nominated him for an honorary degree at Harvard University, but by Charles E. Norton, who wrote in a letter that he otherwise thought very little of "natives." The linguistic and cultural chasm that separated America and India was difficult to bridge. The attitude toward Indian civilization, the positive reception—in some quarters at least—of writings by Benjamin W. Crowninshield, Rammohun Roy, Ralph Waldo Emerson, and Henry David Thoreau, and the founding of the American Oriental Society all indicate a slow but discernible movement toward a deeper relationship.

Despite the complexity of America's encounter with India in the age of sail—banal and profound, simplistic and sophisticated, reassuring and disturbing—substantial connections were made and a process of incorporating elements of Indian civilization into American life was underway. The Transcendentalists adapted Indian philosophical and theological texts to their literary and intellectual projects. The

Unitarian movement garnered insights both from the works of Rammohun Roy and from Yankee mariners' experiences with Indian religiosity. At mid-nineteenth century, the encounter with India even became the source of perennial symbols for deeply held and often conflicting American values. Tensions between American love of freedom and equality and esteem for wealth and distinction, which animate so much of national political and social life, were instantiated in emblems with Indian origins. That archetype of American elitism, the Boston brahmin, was created by Oliver Wendell Holmes in the 1850s when he applied the Indian term for the high-ranking priestly caste to the ever more exclusive, endogamous, and privileged community of old wealth in New England. The designation stuck, and "brahmin" continues in use today for the nation's rich, cultured, and privileged elite. Bandannas, also originally Indian, have become emblems of the opposing tendency in American life. Originally silk handkerchiefs from Bengal, bandannas (figs. 4.10–11 and below) became identified with working folk—sailors, farmers, cowboys, laborers—and adopted nationwide to stand for American egalitarianism and rugged individualism. Today red and blue cotton squares decorated in white floral and paisley patterns are worn by rich and poor, young and old. Bandannas and brahmins, now fully Americanized, have been deployed to stand for principles at the heart of American culture.

America's encounter with India in the age of sail brought wealth, adventure, and experience of cultural difference. Mariners returned with fragments of Indian civilization and ideas about India and its people to share with family, friends, and fellow citizens, initiating an American experience of India that would expand and develop, sometimes taking root in unexpected ways, gradually becoming part of American life.

Fig. E.2 Bandanna handkerchief, American, c. 1998. Printed cotton, 54.6 x 55.9 cm;
Courtesy of Edith S. Rhoads.

INTRODUCTION

1. See Nicholas Thomas, *Entangled Objects* (Cambridge, Mass.: Harvard University Press, 1991), p. 126, and "Licensed Curiosity: Cook's Pacific Voyages," in *The Cultures of Collecting*, ed. John Elsner and Roger Cardinal (London: Reaktion Books, 1994), pp. 116–36.

2. *The East India Marine Society of Salem*, 2d ed. (Salem, Mass., 1831), p. 4.

3. For example, Caleb Wright, *Lectures on India* (Boston: published by the author, 1849), and David O. Allen, *India Ancient and Modern* (Boston: J.P. Jewett, 1856). Like these, most such publications were written by missionaries. A few had been published earlier, including Jedidiah Morse, *A New Gazetteer of the Eastern Continent* (Charlestown, Mass.: Samuel Etheridge, 1802); William Robertson, *An Historical Disquisition Concerning the Knowledge Which the Ancients Had of India* (Philadelphia: Bioren & Plowman, 1812); and Abbé J. A. Dubois, *Description of the Character, Manners, and Customs of the People of India* (Philadelphia: M. Carey & Son, 1818).

4. Robert G. Albion, *The Rise of the Port of New York* (New York: Scribners, 1939), p. 195; see also Philip C. F. Smith, *The Empress of China* (Philadelphia: Philadelphia Maritime Museum, 1984).

5. Holden Furber, "The Beginnings of American Trade with India, 1784–1812," *New England Quarterly* 11 (June 1938), p. 258.

6. James Duncan Phillips, *East India Voyages of Salem Vessels before 1800* (Salem, Mass.: n.p., 1943); also G. Bhagat, *Americans in India, 1784–1860* (New York: New York University Press, 1970).

7. Albion, *Rise of the Port of New York*, p. 204.

8. U.S. Congress, *American State Papers: Commerce and Navigation*, 1790–1836, continued as U.S. Treasury Department, *Commerce and Navigation: Foreign Commerce of the United States*, 1837–44.

9. Mary Louise Pratt, *Imperial Eyes* (London: Routledge, 1992), pp. 6ff, introduces this term, intending it principally for colonial encounters; here it is extended to encompass places and situations in which people from different social worlds interact. See also Philip Curtin, *Cross Cultural Trade in World History* (Cambridge: Cambridge University Press, 1984).

10. For example, a volume by Roderick Mackenzie, *A Sketch of the War with Tippoo Sultaun* (Calcutta: n.p., 1794), and reports in the *Salem Gazette*, July 12, 1799, November 5 and 20, 1799, and January 10, 1800, on the defeat and death of Tipu Sultan.

11. The first American missionary society, the American Board of Commissioners for Foreign Missions, was formed in Salem, Massachusetts, in 1812 and that same year sent missionaries to India.

12. See also a volume by Rammohun Roy, *A Conference Between an Advocate and an Opponent of the Practice of Burning Widows Alive* (Calcutta, 1823).

13. Henry David Thoreau, *Walden* (New York: Bantam Books, 1962 [1854]), p. 325.

14. When Massachusetts established its first house of correction in 1834, it was to put to work "all rogues, vagabonds, and all idle persons going about in any town or place in the country begging, or persons using any subtle craft, juggling, or unlawful games or plays, common pipers, fiddlers, runaways, stubborn children, common drunkards, common nightwalkers, pilferers, wanton and lascivious persons…" Robert W. Kelso, *The History of Public Poor Relief in Massachusetts, 1620–1920* (Boston: Houghton Mifflin, 1922), p. 127.

15. In 1999, a Southern Baptist guide for missionaries described Hindus as "more than 900 million people lost in . . . hopeless darkness . . ." *India Abroad*, October 27, 2000, p. 6.

CHAPTER I

1. Cited in M. V. Kamath, *The United States and India, 1776–1976* (Washington, D.C.: Embassy of India, 1976), p. 22.

2. E. B. Dexter, "Founding of Yale College," *Papers of the New Haven Colony Historical Society* 3 (1882), pp. 227–48; Gauri Viswanathan, "Yale College and the Culture of British Imperialism," *Yale Journal of Criticism* 7, no. 1 (1994), pp. 1–30.

3. Thomas Wentworth Higginson, *Descendants of the Reverend Francis Higginson* (Cambridge, Mass.: privately printed, 1910).

4. Joseph S. Davis, *Essays in the Earlier History of American Corporations* (Cambridge, Mass.: Harvard University Press, 1917), p. 113.

5. Philip C. F. Smith, *The Empress of China* (Philadelphia: Philadelphia Maritime Museum, 1984), p. 3.

6. *Essex Gazette* (Salem, Mass.), August 15, 1769.

7. Cotton Mather, *India Christiana* (Boston: B. Green, 1721).

8. *Boston Evening Post*, April 10, 1774.

9. Kamath, *The United States and India*, p. 23, cites a report published in Virginia in 1767: "It is said that the great riches acquired in the East Indies are not obtained by mere trade, but chiefly by rapine, and plundering of the poor innocent natives."

10. S. E. Morison, *The Oxford History of the American People* (London: Oxford University Press, 1965), p. 203.

11. The 1768–69 famine in Bengal.

12. *Life and Writings of John Dickinson* (Philadelphia: Historical Society of Pennsylvania, 1895), vol. 2, p. 460.

13. *Boston Evening Post*, January 24, 1774.

14. Cited in Kamath, *The United States and India*, p. 24.

15. Florence Montgomery, *Textiles in America* (New York: Norton, 1984), p. 262.

16. Montgomery, *Textiles in America*, provides numerous examples of the varieties of Indian cloth used in colonial American homes, from which the examples that follow are taken in order: pp. 185, 333, 304, 185, 143, 343, 199, 152, 333, 304.

17. Samuel E. Morison, *The Maritime History of Massachusetts, 1783–1860* (Boston: Houghton Mifflin, 1961 [1921]), pp. 29–30.

18. Morison, *The Oxford History of the American People*, p. 283.

19. Ralph D. Paine, *The Old Merchant Marine* (New Haven: Yale University Press, 1919), pp. 96–97.

20. See, for example, James Duncan Phillips, *Salem and the Indies* (Boston: Houghton Mifflin, 1947), ch. 5.

21. Ibid., p. 48.

22. Morison, *Maritime History of Massachusetts*, p. 38.

23. Ernest L. Bogart, *The Economic History of the United States* (New York: Longmans, Green, 1917), p. 122.

24. See Smith, *Empress of China.*

25. Samuel W. Woodhouse, "Log and Journal of the Ship 'United States' on a Voyage from Philadelphia to China in 1784," *Pennsylvania Magazine of History and Biography* (July 1931), pp. 251–53.

26. The exotic was also duly noted by Redman: "The first time I ever had an opportunity of seeing a camel was at Pondicherry, except the elephant it is the ugliest animal in the world . . ."

27. Perhaps carrying freight for the French at Pondicherry.

28. Home Miscellaneous Volumes, Series H, Madras Letters, vol. 4, January 30, 1785, Oriental and India Office Collections, British Library.

29. Holden Furber, "The Beginnings of American Trade with India, 1784–1812," *New England Quarterly* 11 (June 1938), p. 236.

30. Ibid., pp. 238–41.

31. Amales Tripathi, *Trade and Finance in the Bengal Presidency* (Calcutta: Oxford University Press, 1979), p. 30; Timothy Pitkin, *A Statistical View of the Commerce of the United States of America* (New Haven: Durrie & Peck, 1835), p. 185.

32. Tons were a measure of the capacity of a vessel calculated by a formula applied to its length, beam (breadth), and depth.

33. Patrick Crowhurst, *The Defence of British Trade, 1689–1815* (Kent, U.K.: Dawson, 1977), p. 217. A vessel needed a crew of about one man to every 15 tons. The proportion of officers to seamen was not less than one to five. See Morison, *Maritime History of Massachusetts*, p. 106.

34. Morison, *Maritime History of Massachusetts*, pp. 110–11; Kenneth Porter, *The Jacksons and the Lees* (Cambridge, Mass.: Harvard University Press, 1937), pp. 44ff. See also journal of the *Ruby*, chapter 3, which gives crew wages and other expenses for a voyage in the Indian Ocean.

35. Morison, *Maritime History of Massachusetts*, p. 77; Porter, *The Jacksons and the Lees*, pp. 53–68.

36. Crowhurst, *Defence of British Trade*, p. 222.

37. Bogart, *Economic History of the United States*, p. 122.

38. Furber, "Beginnings of American Trade with India," pp. 240ff.

39. Realizing three dollars for each dollar invested; see G. Bhagat, *Americans in India, 1784–1860* (New York: New York University Press, 1970), p. 9. See also Gertrude Kimball, *The East-India Trade of Providence from 1787 to 1807*, Papers from the Historical Seminary of Brown University, no. 6 (Providence, R.I.: Preston & Rounds, 1896).

40. Pitkin, *Statistical View of the Commerce of the United States of America*, p. 145.

41. Bhagat, *Americans in India*, pp. 13–14.

42. Porter, *The Jacksons and the Lees*, pp. 29–31.

43. Paine, *The Old Merchant Marine*, p. 96.

44. Kamath, *The United States and India*, p. 72.

45. Robert G. Albion, W. A. Baker, and B. W. Labaree, *New England and the Sea* (Mystic, Conn.: Mystic Seaport Museum. 1994), p. 59.

46. Tamil *tupash* is borrowed from Indo-Aryan.

47. *Banian*, derived from *baniya* ("merchant"), was first used by the Portuguese and adopted as the Anglo-Indian term for commercial agents in Calcutta. See Dilip Basu, "The Banian and the British in Calcutta," *Bengal Past and Present* 92 (1973), pp. 157–70.

48. See Francis Hutchins, *Mashpee, the Story of Cape Cod's Indian Town* (West Franklin, N.H.: Amarta Press, 1979).

49. On March 25, 1790, an entry in the log of the brig *Henry* at Madras (Peabody Essex Museum Library) records that Mr. Gibaut and his servant boarded. In November of that year, they had reached the West Indies. In Eustatia Road, Mr. Gibaut and servant transferred to a Derby schooner, Captain Orne commanding from Guadalupe. Joseph B. Felt, in his *Annals of Salem* (Salem, Mass.: Ives, 1845–49), vol. 1, p. 25, mentions on December 26, 1790, that Captain J. Gibaut arrived from India with a native of Madras who excited much "curiosity."

50. William Bentley, *Diary of William Bentley* (Salem, Mass.: Essex Institute, 1905), vol. 1, p. 228.

51. The passage continues: ". . . and saw other Gentoos suspended by hooks in their flesh and swing for a great while in the air, by order of their priests. The sufferers bear these things without complaining. He thinks their vegetable diet calms down their feelings and prevents emotions. The religion of the Gentoos consists, he says wholly in ceremonies. They comb their heads and put on their cloaths as a part of their religion. Morality is no part of their religion. They have neither probity nor benevolence." George W. Corner, ed., *The Autobiography of Benjamin Rush* (Princeton: Princeton University Press for the American Philosophical Society, 1948), p. 175. Cited in Carl T. Jackson, *The Oriental Religions and American Thought* (Westport, Conn.: Greenwood Press, 1981), pp. 15–16.

52. Log of the Brig *Henry*, Benjamin Crowninshield, Keeper, 1789–91, Peabody Essex Museum Library. Spelling and punctuation have been modernized.

CHAPTER 2

1. Benjamin Carpenter, Journal of the *Ruby* to Calcutta, 1789–90, Peabody Essex Museum Library.

2. The portrait, by an unidentified artist, was bequeathed by Carpenter's widow to the Salem Marine Society in 1860. It was appraised at her death (May 26, 1860) for $20; another portrait, of a Mr. Rogers, by Copley, was valued at $300. A cow was appraised for $25. (Probate Records, Probate Court, Cambridge, Mass.) The portrait was given to the Peabody Essex Museum in 1880.

3. This information is from an unsigned, undated manuscript in the Maritime Art and History Department, Peabody Essex Museum.

4. *Essex Institute Historical Collections* 45 (1909), p. 245; *Portraits of Shipmasters and Merchants in the Peabody Museum of Salem* (Salem, Mass.: Peabody Museum, 1939), p. 25.

5. Carpenter's obituary in the *Boston Patriot*, September 1823, relates that his arrival "puzzled the government there—whether to condemn the vessel, send her commander to Newgate as a rebel, or purchase his ship. They preferred the latter, and thus evaded the nice question of independence. The examination of Captain Carpenter by Lord Sandwich and other Lords of the

Admiralty, was curious, spirited and humorous, and ought to be preserved in history." The obituary also eulogized Carpenter for his "undeviating Republicanism."

6. *Boston Patriot*, September 1823.

7. Ibid. A natural child, a daughter, survived him. She is mentioned in his will, in which he expresses the wish that his third wife and heir to all his property might remember this daughter in her own will. She did not, though she left bequests to many individuals. Probate Records, Probate Court, Cambridge Mass.

CHAPTER 3

1. The Dutch took control of Pointe de Galle from the Portuguese in the mid-seventeenth century. Despite subsequent struggles with the Portuguese and the kingdom of Kandy, the Dutch retained Pointe de Galle until 1796, when they lost it to the British, who soon controlled all of Sri Lanka. Pointe de Galle was a source of coconuts, cinnamon, and, later, furniture.

2. The southwest monsoon blows from June to November, the northeast monsoon from December to May.

3. Coromandel or southeast coast of India.

4. Between June and November.

5. A town on the Coromandel Coast north of Masulipatam.

6. Maldah, a town on the Ganges in West Bengal.

7. Piece goods, silk or mixture of silk and cotton.

8. Radhanagar, a town in West Bengal.

9. A town near Murshidabad on the Ganges north of Calcutta, at which there was an important East India Company factory.

10. That is, arrive in early November, leave in December.

11. Prohibited to American trade since 1783.

12. Patna, upriver from Calcutta on the Ganges, was a major source of opium.

13. This trade was in fact begun in 1789. The ship *Columbia* was fitted out by a group of Boston merchants and sent to the Northwest Coast for furs and then to Canton. See Samuel E. Morison, *The Maritime History of Massachusetts, 1783–1860* (Boston: Houghton Mifflin, 1961 [1921]), p. 47.

14. The French set up a factory at Chandernagore in 1673.

15. A keelless barge with a passenger cabin.

16. William Bentley, *Diary of William Bentley* (Salem, Mass.: Essex Institute, 1905), vol. 1, p. 237.

CHAPTER 4

1. Presidential proclamation, *Salem Gazette*, May 7, 1793.

2. Anonymous (James Stephen), *War in Disguise: or, The Frauds of Neutral Flags* (New York: n.p., 1806), p. 17.

3. Robert G. Albion, W. A. Baker, and B. W. Labaree, *New England and the Sea* (Mystic, Conn.: Mystic Seaport Museum, 1994), p. 55.

4. Ernest L. Bogart, *The Economic History of the United States* (New York: Longmans, Green, 1917), p. 121.

5. A law was passed in 1789 to refund duties on re-exported India goods. James W. Gould, "The First American Contact with Asia," *Claremont Asian Studies* 7 (1960), p. 6.

6. Ralph D. Paine, *The Old Merchant Marine* (New Haven: Yale University Press, 1919), p. 99.

7. The treaty states in Article XIII: "But it is expressly agreed, that the Vessels of the United States shall not carry any of the articles exported by them from the said British Territories to any Port or Place, escept to some Port or Place in America …" and "It is also understood that the permission granted by this article is not to extend to allow the Vessels of the United States to carry on any part of the Coasting Trade of the said British Territories." *Treaties and Other International Acts of the United States of America*, ed. Hunter Miller (Washington, D.C.: GPO, 1931), vol. 2, pp. 255–56.

8. Albion et al., *New England and the Sea*, p. 73. In 1798, the U.S. Congress terminated the treaty of 1778.

9. Motto adopted in 1839 for the official seal of Salem, Massachusetts.

10. Adam Seybert, *Statistical Annals of the United States* (Philadelphia: Thomas Dobson, 1818), p. 93.

11. Bogart, *Economic History of the United States*, p. 122, estimates the value of this carrying trade from 1803 to 1807 to be $32.5 million per year.

12. Albion et al., *New England and the Sea*, p. 63.

13. Servants (i.e., employees) of the East India Company were permitted a certain amount of private trade in company vessels. Many of them exceeded the allowance and accumulated profits in private trade while in India. Foreign ships were useful in bringing this wealth home to England undetected.

14. The Board of Control's Collections F–4: 719, 1038, 2636, Oriental and India Office Collections, British Library.

15. Holden Furber, "The Beginnings of American Trade with India, 1784–1812," *New England Quarterly* 11 (June 1938), pp. 235–65; G. Bhagat, *Americans in India* (New York: New York University Press, 1970), pp. 28, 33ff, 42, quoting C.R.O. Bengal Commercial Reports, 1804–05. The Bengal government reported to the Home Office that this enormously favorable balance of trade was an "amazing advantage which the British possessions in India derive from our commercial Intercourse with America."

16. Bhagat, *Americans in India*, pp. 43–44, quoting C.R.O. Bengal Commercial Reports, 1806–07.

17. Furber, "Beginnings of American Trade with India," p. 258.

18. Samuel E. Morison, *The Maritime History of Massachusetts, 1783–1860* (Boston: Houghton Mifflin, 1961 [1921]), p. 166.

19. Jacob was also chair of a congressional committee on commerce and manufacturing. Later, his brother Benjamin served as President Monroe's secretary of the navy. Paul Goodman, *The Democratic Republicans of Massachusetts* (Cambridge, Mass.: Harvard University Press, 1964), p. 115.

20. John H. Reinoehl, ed., "Some Remarks on the American Trade: Jacob Crowninshield to James Madison, 1806," *William and Mary Quarterly* 16, no. 1 (1959), pp. 83–118.

21. Ibid., p. 110.

22. Ibid., p. 111.

23. David Rudner, *Caste and Capitalism in Colonial India: The Nattukottai Chettiars* (Berkeley: University of California Press, 1994).

24. *Times of India*, obituary, June 14, 1814, cited in Ruttonjee A. Wadia, *Scions of Lowjee Wadia* (Bombay: n.p., 1964), p. 70.

25. Probably a Kashmir shawl, which Americans sometimes wrongly designated as camel's hair.

26. William F. Mavor (1758–1837), *Historical Account of the Most Celebrated Voyages, Travels and Discoveries . . . ,* 20 vols. (London: E. Newbery, 1796–97).

27. George Nichols, *George Nichols, Salem Shipmaster and Merchant* (Salem, Mass.: Salem Press, [1914?]), p. 48.

28. A rupee was worth half a Spanish dollar; *lac* means 100,000. (Kenneth Porter, *The Jacksons and the Lees* [Cambridge, Mass.: Harvard University Press, 1937], pp. 53, 54.)

29. Ibid., p. 1164.

30. The portrait, in the style of Gilbert Stuart, is attributed to William Winstanley. The painting remained in the Dey family for two generations. It was then purchased by the Mulliks for their collection in the Marble Palace, Calcutta. In the 1960s, Eric Kauders of Marblehead, Massachusetts, purchased it. It was later acquired by Washington and Lee University, the present owners. In the 1980s, the portrait was returned for a few years to India, where it was displayed in the U.S. Embassy in New Delhi.

31. Grish Chunder Dutt, *A Lecture on the Life of Ramdoolal Dey* (Belloore: Bengalee Press, 1868).

32. Ibid., p. 18.

33. Porter, *The Jacksons and the Lees*, p. 619.

34. Ibid.

35. Beverly Historical Society. Oudh: a kingdom in central northern India, far upriver from Calcutta; *cossaes*: a fine, closely woven muslin, exported from Bengal (Henry Yule and A. C. Burnell, *Hobson-Jobson: A Glossary of Colloquial Anglo-Indian Words and Phrases*, 2d ed. [London: Routledge & Kegan Paul, 1985], p. 707); Marath: probably Maratha, a kingdom in western India; *sannoes*: piece goods exported from Bengal (ibid., p. 708); *gangy*: possibly from Hindi *ganj* ("store, store-house, market") (ibid., p. 403).

36. Lee Papers, Massachusetts Historical Society.

37. Porter, *The Jacksons and the Lees*, p. 891.

38. "Mergungee" probably refers to Mirganj, a town halfway between Patna and Gorakhpur in Bihar. Lee further warned: "There are ten different kinds or more of narrow and coarse mamoodies which go sometimes by one name and sometimes another" (ibid., p. 891). Evidently, Indian merchants played this name game too.

39. Nichols, *Salem Shipmaster and Merchant*, p. 48.

40. William Bentley, *Diary of William Bentley* (Salem, Mass.: Essex Institute, 1907), vol. 2, p. 235.

41. Abbé Raynal, *A Philosophical and Political History of the Settlements and Trade of the Europeans in the East and West Indies*, trans. J. O. Justamond (London: n.p., 1776).

42. Quotations are from the statement of purpose of the East India Marine Society as reissued in 1831. This statement also encourages the acquisition of "such books of history, of voyages and travels, and of navigations as they may think useful . . ." *The East India Marine Society of Salem*, 2d ed. (Salem, Mass., 1831), pp. 3–4.

43. Ibid., p. 8.

44. Walter M. Whitehill, *The East India Marine Society and the Peabody Museum of Salem: A Sesquicentennial History* (Salem, Mass.: Peabody Museum, 1949), pp. 18–19.

45. The letter quoted is from the donors of the palanquin to their "brethren" of the East India Marine Society. Papers of the East India Marine Society, Peabody Essex Museum.

46. See Pheroza Godrej and Pauline Rohatgi, *Scenic Splendours: India Through the Printed Image* (London: British Library, 1989), pp. 147–48.

47. Roderick Mackenzie, *A Sketch of the War with Tippoo Sultaun* (Calcutta: n.p., 1794).

48. *Salem Gazette*, May 10, 1791.

49. Carl Crossman, *The Decorative Arts of the China Trade* (Suffolk, U.K.: Antique Collectors' Club, 1991), pp. 38, 53.

50. The images in the East India Marine Society's collection are consequently rather singular—never meant to be preserved—and are rare surviving examples of the forms from which developed the naturalistic style of the Krishnanagar modelers.

51. The dangers of this passage, which remained the same throughout the era of sailing ships, are vividly recounted in the journal of Edwin Blood's voyage (chapter 16).

CHAPTER 5

1. *Salem Register*, November 9, 1846; *Essex Institute Historical Collections* 67 (1931), pp. 273–76.

2. Dudley Pickman's maternal forebears were also very respectable folk, if less wealthy. His maternal grandfather, Reverend Dudley Leavitt, was pastor of Salem's Tabernacle Church.

3. Crowninshield was a member of one of Salem's leading mercantile families. His journal of the *Belisarius*' voyage to India the year before, 1797–98, has been published in the *Essex Institute Historical Collections* 81 (1945) and 82 (1946).

4. James Duncan Phillips, *Salem and the Indies* (Boston: Houghton Mifflin, 1947), p. 82.

5. The *Salem Gazette* reported on December 24, 1799, that the *Belisarius* cleared for Tranquebar, the Danish port near Madras.

6. *Salem Gazette*, December 27, 1799.

7. The tea would have been produced in China; tea was not yet commercially grown in India. Information is from the log of the *Belisarius*, 1799–1800, Peabody Essex Museum Library.

8. Pickman Family Papers, Peabody Essex Museum Library.

9. Ibid.

10. Ibid.

11. Journal of the *Belisarius*, Peabody Essex Museum Library.

12. Although slavery had been abolished in Massachusetts in 1781.

13. Quotations in this paragraph, Journal of the *Belisarius*.

14. Ibid.

15. Ibid. This view became a central tenet of the Indian nationalist movement in the late nineteenth century and a central component of Gandhi's movement for independence in the twentieth century.

16. Ibid.

CHAPTER 6

1. On April 12, 1800.

2. Later Marquis Wellesley, who in 1799 defeated Tipu Sultan, the chief foe of British rule in southern India, and served as governor-general of British India from 1798 to 1805.

3. Edward Clive (1754–1839) was the son of Lord Robert Clive (1725–1774), who, by his victory at the Battle of Plassey in 1757, began the era of British colonial expansion in India. Edward Clive was governor of Madras from 1798 to 1803.

4. Ships carrying Danish flags were permitted to trade in some ports where the British were prohibited.

5. Handkerchiefs were large cloths, about a yard square, widely used by Europeans and Americans as neck cloths and bundle wrappers. Madras and Pulicat, north of Madras and Dutch from 1610 until 1825, were well known for their production.

6. Guinea cloths were made for export to West Africa.

7. Cloths about 18 yards long and 38 to 44 inches wide.

8. Usually white cotton, possibly distinguished as an export cloth for being longer than cloths made for domestic use.

9. From Persian for "trousers," probably the kind of cotton cloth used to make trousers or "pyjamas."

10. Very finely spun and woven cotton, highly sized, folded, and packed, resembling leaves in a book.

11. In the Third Mysore War, Cornwallis defeated Tipu Sultan, the East India Company's foe in southern India. Tipu ceded half his territory to the British in 1792.

12. From the Portuguese *gentoo*, a gentile or heathen; applied to the Hindus but not the Muslims, who were known as *moros* or moors.

13. The single red perpendicular line indicates devotees of Vishnu.

14. From Tamil *kari* ("sauce"), applied to highly spiced gravies.

15. Pickman's stay in Madras during April and May coincided with the spring season (*vasanta*), the beginning of the Hindu year and a time of many festivals.

16. The Muslim festival of Id-ud-Zuha commemorates Ibrahim's willingness to sacrifice his son as ordered by Allah. Ibrahim blindfolded himself to do the deed, and when he removed the blindfold found that he had sacrificed not his son, but a ram (or goat or camel). This is the same story that is in Genesis 22.

17. By 1800, the British had acquired large areas in Bengal and Bihar in the east, on the Coromandel and Malabar coasts in the south, and the island of Ceylon.

18. After Tipu Sultan's defeat and death in 1799, his kingdom was restored to a previous Hindu dynasty that ruled as a British dependency. The Mahrattas, to the north and west of Mysore, remained the only major obstacle to British expansion in the south.

19. Danvers, Massachusetts, adjacent to Salem.

20. Probably, he surreptitiously moved French property in and out of English ports on vessels flying the American or Danish flag.

21. The Danes ceded Tranquebar to the British in 1807. It was restored in 1814 and then purchased by the British in 1845.

22. Actually the *dargah* or tomb of the Sufi master Shahul Hamil. See S. Arasaratnam, *Maritime India in the Seventeenth Century* (Delhi: Oxford University Press, 1994), p. 268.

23. A port in eastern Bengal.

24. Near the southernmost tip of Africa.

CHAPTER 7

1. At the mouth of the Godavari River, about halfway up the east coast of India.

2. Baleshwar, off the coast of Orissa, from which point a pilot was necessary to continue the voyage from the Bay of Bengal up the Hooghly River to Calcutta.

3. North of Boston, near Salem.

4. Floodwaters of the river, from the monsoon rains, rushing to the sea.

5. Lord Mornington (later the Marquis Wellesley) led the army against Tipu in the Fourth Mysore War. Tipu was killed in 1799 and his kingdom became a dependency of British India under the rule of a restored Hindu dynasty.

6. Source for the quotation on nautch is unknown.

7. A dangerous sandbank in the Hooghly River below Calcutta.

CHAPTER 8

1. John Phipps, *A Guide to the Commerce of Bengal* (Calcutta: n.p., 1823), p. 213, reports that in 1817 and 1818, there were very significant shipments of cotton from Bengal to Boston; it is unclear if the *Tartar*'s cotton was for New England mills or, as Boston merchant Henry Lee suggests, it was intended for re-export to Europe. See Kenneth Porter, *The Jacksons and the Lees* (Cambridge, Mass.: Harvard University Press, 1937), p. 1269.

2. Timothy Pitkin, *A Statistical View of the Commerce of the United States of America* (New York: James Eastburn & Co., 1817), p. 33.

3. Adam Seybert, *Statistical Annals of the United States* (Philadelphia: Thomas Dobson, 1818), p. 60.

4. Ernest L. Bogart, *The Economic History of the United States* (New York: Longmans, Green, 1917), pp. 120ff.

5. Seybert, *Statistical Annals of the United States*, pp. 65–73.

6. Samuel E. Morison, *The Maritime History of Massachusetts, 1783–1860* (Boston: Houghton Mifflin, 1961 [1921]), pp. 168–69.

7. Ibid., p. 190. Edward Gray, *William Gray of Salem, Merchant* (Boston: Houghton Mifflin, 1914), p. 43.

8. John H. Reinoehl, ed., "Some Remarks on the American Trade: Jacob Crowninshield to James Madison, 1806," *William and Mary Quarterly* 16, no. 1 (1959), pp. 85–91; Ronald P. Formisano, *The Transformation of Political Culture: Massachusetts Parties, 1790s–1840s* (London: Oxford University Press, 1983), p. 163.

9. John H. Brown, ed., *Lamb's Textile Industries of the United States* (Boston: James H. Lamb, 1911), p. 409.

10. Ibid., p. 261.

11. James M. Burns, *The Vineyard of Liberty* (New York: Random House, 1983), p. 66.

12. Timothy Pitkin, *A Statistical View of the Commerce of the United States of America* (New Haven: Durrie & Peck, 1835), p. 472, citing the report of Secretary of the Treasury A. Gallatin.

13. The British, alarmed at this burgeoning of U.S. industry, hoped to nip it in the bud. Timothy Pitkin, writing on the American economy in 1835 (ibid., p. 474), took note of a British Parliamentarian's remark: "it was well worthwhile to incur a loss on the first exportation, in order by the *glut*, to *stifle* in the cradle those rising manufactures in the United States which the war had *forced* into existence contrary to the natural course of things."

14. Ibid., p. 474.

15. Ibid., pp. 188–89.

16. Porter, *The Jacksons and the Lees*, pp. 8–9.

17. Ibid., p. 969.

18. Ibid., p. 827.

19. Ibid., pp. 830–31.

20. Ibid., p. 834.

21. Ibid., p. 841.

22. Ibid., p. 848.

23. Ibid., p. 969.

24. Ibid., p. 1046.

25. Ibid., p. 1070.

26. Ibid., p. 1071.

27. Ibid., p. 1110.

28. Ibid., p. 1039.

29. Ibid., p. 1076.

30. Francis R. Morse, *Henry and Mary Lee: Letters and Journals* (Boston: privately printed, 1926), p. 132.

31. James F. Banner, *To the Hartford Convention* (New York: Knopf, 1970), p. viii.

32. Morse, *Henry and Mary Lee*, p. 126.

33. Ibid., p. 117.

34. Ibid., p. 145.

35. Ibid., pp. 161–63.

36. Ibid., p. 117.

37. Porter, *The Jacksons and the Lees*, pp. 1203, 1266.

38. Ibid., p. 1267.

39. Ibid., p. 1078.

40. Ibid., p. 1266.

41. Ibid., p. 1263.

42. Ibid., p. 166.

43. Ibid., pp. 1077–78.

44. Ibid., pp. 1088–89.

45. Ibid., pp. 1171, 1077–78.

46. Ibid., p. 34, citing William Bentley, *Diary of William Bentley* (Salem, Mass.: Essex Institute, 1914), vol. 4, p. 82 (February 2, 1812).

47. Mrs. Ann H. Judson and James D. Knowles, *Memoir* (Boston: Lincoln & Edmands, 1829). Henry Lee shipped indigo in the *Harmony* when it returned to Philadelphia in December 1813 (Porter, *The Jacksons and the Lees*, p. 1064).

48. Clifton J. Phillips, *Protestant America and the Pagan World* (Cambridge, Mass.: Harvard East Asian Monographs, no. 32, 1969), p. 48.

49. Ibid., p. 298.

50. Ibid., pp. 32ff.

51. Ibid., p. 32.

52. East India Marine Society Manuscript Register, 1799–1820, Peabody Essex Museum Library.

53. "Old Testament in the Sanscrit Language," "New Testament in the Sanscrit Language," "The Pentateuch in the Bengalese Language," and "The Psalms of David in the Bengalese Language," in *The East India Marine Society of Salem*, 2d ed. (Salem, Mass., 1831), p. 89, entry nos. 1550–1553.

54. Ibid., p. 157, entry no. 3724. Brahmins did not ordinarily wear beards, and the wisp of hair so designated seems to have been the long lock of hair Brahmins often kept on their shaved heads.

55. Judson and Knowles, *Memoir*, p. 63.

56. Morse, *Henry and Mary Lee*, p. 149.

57. Quotes in this paragraph, ibid., p. 150.

58. Phillips, *Protestant America and the Pagan World*, p. 293, quoting a letter from Hall to Samuel Worcester, April 16, 1818, ABC: 16.1.1 II, no. 75.

59. Crowninshield Family Papers, Peabody Essex Museum.

60. Quoted in Phillips, *Protestant America and the Pagan World*, p. 278.

1. William A. Rogers, Journal of the *Tartar*, 1817–18, Peabody Essex Museum Library.

2. George Granville Putnam, *Salem Vessels and Their Voyages* (Salem, Mass.: Essex Institute, 1930), vol. 4, p. 86.

3. Rogers Family Papers, Peabody Essex Museum Library.

4. Putnam, *Salem Vessels and Their Voyages*, vol. 4, p. 33.

5. Rogers Family Papers, Peabody Essex Museum Library.

6. Personal correspondence, Rogers Family Papers, Peabody Essex Museum Library.

7. Paul A. Varg, *New England and Foreign Relations, 1789–1850* (Hanover, N.H.: University Press of New England, 1983), p. 40.

8. This is Rogers family lore, related in a telephone conversation with a descendant of one of William's brothers. It may also be that the political situation in France during the disintegration of the Napoleonic empire had become inhospitable to foreigners. In William's letter to the artist Vanderlyn, quoted below, he alludes to Vanderlyn's forced return to the U.S. in 1815.

9. Letter from William A. Rogers to J. Vanderlyn, February 22, 1816, Senate House State Historical Site, Kingston, New York. Vanderlyn's biographer, William Oedel, kindly brought this letter to my attention.

10. Putnam, *Salem Vessels and Their Voyages*, vol. 4, p. 27, whose information was based on notes kept by William's grandnephew, Augustus D. Rogers.

11. "Valuable articles and curiosities" is terminology used by William's mother in a letter to one of his older brothers categorizing things brought home from a trip abroad (Rogers Family Papers, Peabody Essex Museum Library). The usage, common into the nineteenth century, distinguishes things of intrinsic intellectual interest from things of monetary value at a time when there were still many objects in the world that had not become commodities.

12. Letter dated October 22, 1811, Rogers Family Papers, Peabody Essex Museum Library.

13. He uses this phrase in his journal to explain his reason for going to sea. Putnam, *Salem Vessels and Their Voyages*, vol. 4, p. 26.

14. James Duncan Phillips, *Salem and the Indies* (Boston: Houghton Mifflin, 1947), p. 154.

15. A letter from Josiah Orne to Benjamin Pickman and John Derby, dated February 8, 1818, advises that if cotton cannot be sold it should be sent on to Liverpool in a British vessel, and warns that there is no market for Indian cotton on the Continent. Benjamin Pickman Papers, Peabody Essex Museum Library.

16. Rogers Family Papers, Peabody Essex Museum Library.

17. Thomas and William Daniell, *Oriental Scenery*, 6 parts (London, 1795–1808).

18. Rogers Family Papers, Peabody Essex Museum Library.

1. Richard S. Rogers, his elder brother and master of the *Tartar* on this voyage.

2. Enos Briggs, Salem shipbuilder, cousin of James B. Briggs; see chapters 12 and 13.

3. Claude Joseph Vernet (1714–1789), French marine painter and member of the French Academy, commissioned by the king to paint the seaports of France.

4. The underlining here and throughout appears in the original.

5. Large tropical sea birds, tame and easily taken and therefore considered stupid.

6. Bait fish caught in Massachusetts Bay.

7. The star located about 35° east from Arietis and 14° southeast from the Pleiades or Seven Stars.

8. The yard, or wooden spar, crossing the mast at the front of the ship from which the sail is set.

9. A mountain about 7,359 feet high and about forty miles inland from Colombo.

10. The upper section of the principal mast.

11. The third, aftermost mast of a square-rigged sailing ship.

12. A makeshift wooden support.

13. Serendib is the Arabic name for the island of Ceylon. Sieldendiva was the name given the island by Cosmas Indicopleustes, a Greek traveler and monk who wrote in the seventh century. Henry Yule and A. C. Burnell, *Hobson-Jobson: A Glossary of Colloquial Anglo-Indian Words and Phrases*, 2d ed. (London: Routledge & Kegan Paul, 1985), p. 181.

14. The treatment of the king of Kandy is given below. Seringapatam was the capital of Tipu Sultan, ruler of Mysore. Tipu was finally defeated in 1799 in the Fourth Mysore War by Wellesley, later Duke of Wellington.

15. This description was probably taken from a gazetteer on the ship. Rogers did not land at Ceylon.

16. The name of the mountain Adam's Peak and the sandbar Adam's Bridge were described in an early British account, which noted that it was "universally believed among [the natives] that Ceylon was either the Paradise in which the ancestor of the human race resided or the spot on which he first touched on being expelled from a Celestial Paradise." Robert Percival, *An Account of the Island of Ceylon*, 2d ed. (London: C. and R. Baldwin, 1805), p. 76.

17. Conde Udda (literally, "greatest mountain") was the name of the two preeminent districts of Kandy, site of the king's residence, located in an inaccessible mountainous part of central Ceylon.

18. This entry and others that follow as the *Tartar* sails up the Malabar Coast of India seem to have been adapted from a gazetteer kept on board, for example, Jedidiah Morse, *A New Gazetteer of the Eastern Continent* (Charlestown, Mass.: Samuel Etheridge, 1802) or J. E. Worcester, *A Geographical Dictionary*, 2 vols. (Andover, Mass.: Flagg & Gould, 1817), both of which contain wording very similar to Rogers' description.

19. Louis XVIII, an obese old man, was restored to the throne after Napoleon's defeat.

20. In fact, the king of Kandy deposed by the British was a Tamilian from India, the brother-in-law of his predecessor, the last of his line. Tipu Sultan, another example earlier mentioned, was the son of a Mughal commander who overthrew the Hindu dynasty of Mysore.

21. Note the change in attitude that occurs after Rogers has been in port at Bombay for two weeks.

22. Deserting to the other side.

23. King of Naples, 1808–15.

24. *Dony* or *dhony*, from Tamil *tooni*, a large wooden vessel of shallow draught and broad beam. Yule and Burnell, *Hobson-Jobson*, p. 323.

25. Dudley Pickman made a similar observation in his journal of the *Belisarius*; see chapter 6.

26. Owned by Benjamin Pickman.

27. Hindu ruler of Calicut.

28. Elsewhere the derivation is from Kolikodu, meaning "cock fortress." Yule and Burnell, *Hobson-Jobson*, p. 148.

29. Muslims of the Malabar Coast.

30. Nellore, a town north of Madras on the Coromandel Coast.

31. The Apennines, a mountain range running the length of Italy.

32. "Mountain region" is a more accurate translation. Yule and Burnell, *Hobson-Jobson*, p. 539.

33. I.e., "more or less."

34. The famous Greek statue of Apollo's priest and his sons being killed by serpents.

35. "The same rascal (mentioned on December 14) was taken out of his place for the time being having been found guilty of such crimes which are proof of the vilest and most abject character." An entry in French on December 14 relates that the same "miserable person" gratified his annoyance with Rogers by letting loose a captive black albatross, but Rogers wishes to be charitable about it because the "rascal" was "of a kind not well known in America." It seems likely that Rogers is alluding to a homosexual advance from the third mate.

36. Portuguese version of the Mughal title "Adil Khan." Yule and Burnell, *Hobson-Jobson*, p. 431.

37. Islands near Bombay.

38. Recently arrived on the *Malabar*.

39. Sons of Nusserwanjee (fig. 4.4).

40. A massive stone projection that serves as a breakwater for the harbor.

41. Or Caffer, Caffre, Coffree, from Arabic *kafir*, "an infidel, an unbeliever in Islam"; applied to blacks, mostly Africans. Yule and Burnell, *Hobson-Jobson*, pp. 140, 141.

42. Descendants of Portuguese and native Indians.

43. Probably the Irish poet Thomas Moore (1779–1852).

44. Timothy Dexter of Newburyport, Massachusetts, was famous at the time for his house and grounds, which were profusely ornamented with statues.

45. Coin equal to 1/64 of a rupee.

46. Yazdezard, the last Zoroastrian king of Persia. The Persian monarchy was overthrown by Arab Muslims in 641 A.D.

47. Hormuz, an island at the entrance of the Persian Gulf.

48. The place was Sanjan about 25 miles south of Daman, in 716 A.D. ruled by Jadi Rana.

49. That is, they built a fire-temple in which the sacred fire was kindled in 721 A.D.

50. Nowsaree: Navsari in Gujarat; Veirow: probably Variav in northern Gujarat; Occlicar: probably Anklesvar in northern Gujarat.

51. Mulla Feroz succeeded his father as dastur or high priest in 1802. Dosabhai Framji Karaka, *History of the Parsis* (London: Macmillan, 1884), vol. 1, p. 109.

52. The popular name for clerks and members of the Kayastha caste in Bombay. Yule and Burnell, *Hobson-Jobson*, p. 682.

53. Holi is the last major festival of the Hindu year. It marks the end of all misfortune in the passing year and makes way for the coming year with ribald song and raucous celebration, combining many of the more boisterous characteristics of American New Year's Eve, Fourth of July, April Fool's Day, and Halloween.

54. Priapus, the Roman god of male procreative power.

55. A New York ship.

56. English gothic novelist Anne Radcliffe (1764–1823).

57. George Whitefield (1714–1770), English Methodist-Calvinist preacher.

58. A servant who runs alongside a palanquin.

59. Italian sculptor Antonio Canova (1757–1822).

60. Mrs. H. Newell died at Île de France in 1812. Her husband went on to Ceylon and Bombay, where he died in 1821. Miss Thurston was his second wife.

61. From Arabic *hammal*, a porter.

CHAPTER 11

1. Robert G. Albion, *The Rise of the Port of New York* (New York: Scribners, 1939), p. 8.

2. Ibid., pp. 12–13.

3. Mitra Business Papers, Private Collection, Calcutta.

4. Adam Seybert, *Statistical Annals of the United States* (Philadelphia: Thomas Dobson, 1818), p. 213. Ernest L. Bogart, *The Economic History of the United States* (New York: Longmans, Green, 1917), p. 122, estimated the returns from the neutral carrying trade, in which India goods were prominent, at about $32.5 million a year.

5. J. R. McCulloch, *A Dictionary, Practical, Theoretical, and Historical, of Commerce and Commercial Navigation*, 2d ed. (London: Longman, Rees, 1834), p. 212.

6. U.S. Department of the Treasury, Office of the Secretary, *Commerce and Navigation*, 1820s and 1830s; McCulloch, *Dictionary*, pp. 203–12.

7. Albion, *Rise of the Port of New York*, p. 127. Boston in 1831 imported more than $6 million worth of goods from England, $685,000 from India, and $762,000 from China (McCulloch, *Dictionary*, p. 173).

8. Sugar, the other mainstay, had become more widely available, from Louisiana and the West Indies.

9. See Kenneth Porter, *The Jacksons and the Lees* (Cambridge, Mass.: Harvard University Press, 1937), p. 1431, and Susan S. Bean, "The Indian Origins of the Bandanna," *The Magazine Antiques* (December 1999), pp. 833–39.

10. Florence Montgomery, *Textiles in America* (New York: Norton, 1984), p. 304.

11. Frank Ames, *The Kashmir Shawl* (Suffolk, U.K.: Antique Collectors Club, 1986), pp. 161–62; Valerie Reilly, *The Paisley Pattern* (Salt Lake City: Peregrine Smith, 1989).

12. Amales Tripathi, *Trade and Finance in the Bengal Presidency* (Calcutta: Oxford University Press, 1979), p. 189.

13. McCulloch, *Dictionary*, pp. 137, 209, 774.

14. John Phipps, *A Guide to the Commerce of Bengal* (Calcutta: n.p., 1823), p. 109; McCulloch, *Dictionary*, p. 212; John H. Reinoehl, ed., "Some Remarks on the American Trade: Jacob Crowninshield to James Madison, 1806," *William and Mary Quarterly* 16, no. 1 (1959), pp. 83–118.

15. Francis R. Morse, *Henry and Mary Lee: Letters and Journals* (Boston: privately printed, 1926), p. 140.

16. Porter, *The Jacksons and the Lees*, pp. 1349, 1361, 1404.

17. Ibid., p. 1362.

18. When President Monroe visited Salem in 1817, Peabody, like Benjamin Pickman, had the privilege of entertaining him at home (see chapter 5).

19. Walter M. Whitehill, *Captain Joseph Peabody, East India Merchant of Salem (1757–1844)* (Salem, Mass.: Peabody Museum, 1962), p. 17.

20. Samuel E. Morison, *The Maritime History of Massachusetts, 1783–1860* (Boston: Houghton Mifflin, 1961 [1921]), p. 218.

21. Ralph D. Paine, *The Old Merchant Marine* (New Haven: Yale University Press, 1919), p. 144.

22. George Granville Putnam, *Salem Vessels and Their Voyages* (Salem, Mass.: Essex Institute, 1924), vol. 2, p. 49.

23. Ibid., p. 30.

24. Currier Family Papers, Peabody Essex Museum Library. By comparison, an auction in 1810 of the cargo of the *Sally-Ann* sold at Long Wharf Boston on April 6, 1810, included well over 12,000 pieces of cotton and silk textiles (Stark Papers, Peabody Essex Museum Library).

25. Binaya Krishna Deb, *The Early History and Growth of Calcutta* (Calcutta: Rddhi, 1977 [1905]), p. 104.

26. P. J. Marshall, *Bengal, the British Bridgehead: Eastern India, 1740–1828* (Cambridge: Cambridge University Press, 1987), pp. 108–09, cites H. R. Ghosal, *Economic Transition in the Bengal Presidency, 1793–1833*, 2d ed. (Calcutta: K. L. Mukhopadyay, 1966), pp. 291–92, for this statistic. Marshall also proposed that "there is a great deal of evidence which suggests that factories used coercion and intimidation both to persuade peasants to grow indigo and to fix the prices given for the crop" (p. 109).

27. Bogart, *Economic History of the United States*, p. 180.

28. J. Leander Bishop, *A History of American Manufactures*, vol. 2 (Philadelphia: Edward Young, 1864), p. 317.

29. Victor S. Clark, *History of Manufactures in the United States*, vol. 1 (New York: Peter Smith, 1949 [1916]), p. 333.

30. McCulloch, *Dictionary*, p. 172.

31. The industry employed more than 3,000 workers, about half of them female, and used nearly half a million dollars' worth of materials (Bishop, *History of American Manufactures*, vol. 2, p. 361).

32. Maurice Whitten, *The Gunpowder Mills of Maine* (Gorham, Maine, 1990), p. 3.

33. Each cord measured 4 x 4 x 8 feet. The *Tuscany*'s cargo of ice weighed 180 tons. See also C. Littlefield, "An Abstract . . ." (Peabody Essex Museum Library), which includes a brief account of the voyage of the *Tuscany* which he commanded, and Susan S. Bean, "Cold Mine," *American Heritage* (July–August 1991), p. 73.

34. Diary of Frederic Tudor, May 4, 1833, Tudor Company Collection, Baker Library, Harvard Business School.

35. Diary of Frederic Tudor, January 31, 1834, Tudor Company Collection, Baker Library, Harvard Business School.

36. Joachim H. Stocqueler, *Memoirs of a Journalist* (Bombay, 1873), p. 105.

37. David G. Dickason, "The Nineteenth-Century Indo-American Ice Trade: A Hyperborean Epic," *Modern Asian Studies* 25, no. 1 (1991), pp. 53–89.

38. *North American Review* 6, no. 17 (1818), p. 285.

39. From the report by Nathaniel Bowditch, July 5, 1820 (Walter M. Whitehill, *The East India Marine Society and the Peabody Museum of Salem: A Sesquicentennial History* [Salem, Mass.: Peabody Museum, 1949], p. 36). In *The East India Marine Society of Salem* (Salem, Mass., 1821), Dr. Bass's catalogue listed each object by its assigned number (painted in large numerals on the object so that visitors could easily identify each in the catalogue), and gave a brief description, noting its provenance and donor.

40. Whitehill, *The East India Marine Society*, p. 27.

41. From Anne Royall, *Sketches of History, Life and Manners in the United States (by a Traveller)* (New Haven: n.p., 1826), p. 360.

42. Minutes, September 6, 1838, East India Marine Society Papers, Peabody Essex Museum Library.

43. Caroline Howard King, *When I Lived in Salem, 1822–1866* (Brattleboro, Vt.: Stephen Daye Press, 1937), p. 29.

44. *The East India Marine Society of Salem*, 2d ed. (Salem, Mass., 1831), p. 126. Interestingly, Briggs' comment was the only mention of "art" in connection with any of the curiosities from India and indicates the appreciation Bengali artists could evoke when they produced for Western tastes. Based on genealogical information acquired at Krishnanagar in 1988, it is likely that the artist who made Briggs' statues was Kashinath Pal (1775–1860).

45. Later in the nineteenth century, Krishnanagar craftsmen would win numerous awards at world fairs held in Europe and America, where their work was recognized for its artistry and its perceived precision in representing Indian social types.

46. Probably intended as a transliteration of the Sanskrit for "To the High Dignity subject."

47. Papers of the East India Marine Society, Peabody Essex Museum Library.

48. Barton Family Papers, Peabody Essex Museum Library.

49. Letter dated February 27, 1836(?), Currier Family Papers, Peabody Essex Museum Library.

50. *The East India Marine Society of Salem*, 3d ed. (Salem, Mass., 1837), supp. p. 7.

51. Ibid.

52. Their ready facility for concrete visual representations of Indian types surely reinforced, if not contributed to, the model of a static, rigidly differentiated, and highly stratified Indian society that was constructed by the British in the nineteenth century.

53. Aberdeen Papers, Peabody Essex Museum Library.

54. Jagaddhatri's festival in the month of Kartiku (October–November) on the seventh, eighth, and ninth days of the increase of the moon, was an occasion of great celebration in Calcutta. Joguth Chunder Gangooly, *Life and Religion of the Hindoos* (Boston: Crosby, Nichols, Lee, 1860), p. 155; W. Ward, *A View of the History, Literature, and Religion of the Hindoos*, 5th ed. (Madras: Higginbotham, 1863), p. 80.

55. One contemporary report noted that on this day, "multitudes of clay images are worshipped." Ward, *A View of the History, Literature, and Religion of the Hindoos*, p. 134.

56. *The East India Marine Society of Salem* (3d ed.), supp. p. 18.

57. Letter dated May 26, 1836, Currier Family Papers, Peabody Essex Museum Library.

58. James Silk Buckingham, *The Eastern and Western States of America* (London: Fisher, Son & Co., 1842), pp. 270–75.

59. King, *When I Lived in Salem*, pp. 34–35.

60. See James Duncan Phillips, *Salem and the Indies* (Boston: Houghton Mifflin, 1947), p. 196.

61. Published privately in Northumberland. In the book, Priestly uses the translations of William Jones and the French scholar Langles to refute a theory then current that derived the five books of Moses from the five Vedas. See Spencer Lavan, *Unitarians and India* (Chicago: Exploration Press, 1991), pp. 17–18.

62. Ibid., p. 19.

63. See Carl T. Jackson, *The Oriental Religions and American Thought: Nineteenth-Century Explorations* (Westport, Conn.: Greenwood Press, 1981), p. 34.

64. Adrienne Moore, *Rammohun Roy and America* (Calcutta: Satis Chandra Chakravarti, 1942), pp. vii, 2, 3.

65. *Christian Disciple and Theological Review*, n.s. 5 (September–October 1823).

66. See Jackson, *Oriental Religions and American Thought*, p. 34.

67. *New York Review* 1 (1825), cited in R. K. Gupta, *The Great Encounter: A Study of Indo-American Literature and Cultural Relations* (Riverdale, Md.: Riverdale Co., 1987).

68. Moore, *Rammohun Roy and America*, p. 117.

69. Ibid., pp. 150ff.

70. Ibid., p. 149.

71. Ibid.; Van Wyck Brooks, *The Flowering of New England, 1815–1865* (New York: E.P. Dutton, 1936).

CHAPTER 12

1. Account books and shipping logs, Peabody Essex Museum Library.

2. Probate Records, Essex County, Massachusetts.

3. Obituary, *Salem Register*, December 10, 1857.

4. The journal was passed down from Thomas Saul, who was first mate on the voyage, through his son James Briggs Saul and his grandson Walter Saul, who gave it to the Peabody Essex Museum in 1921.

5. Amales Tripathi, *Trade and Finance in the Bengal Presidency* (Calcutta: Oxford University Press, 1979), p. 194.

CHAPTER 13

1. A flat-bottomed boat used for loading and unloading vessels not at a wharf.

2. The *Dover*, John Austin commander, owned by the Austin family, sailed from Boston to Calcutta in August 1832 and returned August 1833. Shipping logbook is in the Peabody Essex Museum Library.

3. Probably the mark for Austin's cargo.

4. James B. Briggs, Invoice & Letter Book, vol. 2, Peabody Essex Museum Library.

5. That is, a voyage of 126 days from Boston to the mouth of the Hooghly, where a pilot is taken on board to navigate the passage upriver to Calcutta.

6. The agency houses were heavily involved in the production, manufacture, and trade of indigo; a rash of speculation had led to a collapse of the market, resulting in a great scarcity of capital in the city.

7. Prices are given in rupees and annas (16 annas to the rupee).

8. All the goods listed are silk handkerchiefs.

9. Smearing with pitch or tar.

10. Knots that join ropes.

11. Masts are in three sections: the middle is the topmast, the uppermost is the topgallant mast. The yards are the cross spars from which the sails are set.

12. Probably Charak Puja, the festival when hook-swinging was performed.

13. Drain holes cut through the bulwarks (side planking above the upper deck) to allow water to run out.

14. Sprockets on the windlass, a device for lifting, to engage the anchor or other lines.

15. Owned by R. C. Mackay and J. S. Coolidge of Boston. Captain Webb may have been Joseph Webb, who donated the pair of hooks used at Charak Puja to the East India Marine Society's museum (see fig. 11.21).

16. Uppercase initials were used as owner's marks.

17. Swett, Swett, and Walsh owners.

18. A sandbank in the Hooghly below Calcutta named for an English ship wrecked there in 1694.

1. The project engineer was a Bengali, Shibchandra Nandi (Samaren Roy, *Calcutta: Society and Change, 1690–1990* [Calcutta: Rupa, 1991], p. 210).

2. James M. Burns, *The Vineyard of Liberty* (New York: Random House, 1983), p. 531.

3. By 1860, there were about 50,000 miles of telegraph. In 1861, a line was opened to San Francisco (Ernest L. Bogart, *The Economic History of the United States* [New York: Longmans, Green, 1917], p. 233).

4. *Gunny* is from Sanskrit *goṇi* ("sack"). Henry Yule and A. C. Burnell, *Hobson-Jobson: A Glossary of Colloquial Anglo-Indian Words and Phrases*, 2d ed. (London: Routledge & Kegan Paul, 1985), p. 403.

5. U.S. Department of the Treasury, *Commerce and Navigation*, 1854, pp. 170, 214, 216, 248, 250, 262, 301.

6. J. R. McCulloch, *A Dictionary, Practical, Theoretical, and Historical, of Commerce and Commercial Navigation*, 2d ed. (London: Longman, Rees, 1834), p. 582.

7. Roger W. Moss, *A Century of Color* (Watkins Glen, N.Y.: American Life Foundation, 1981), p. 10.

8. Benoy Chowdhury, *Growth of Commercial Agriculture in Bengal, 1757–1900* (Calcutta: R.K. Maitra, 1964), p. 196.

9. John H. Brown, ed., *Lamb's Textile Industries of the United States* (Boston: James H. Lamb, 1911), p. 195; Richard Temple, *Oriental Experience* (London: J. Murray, 1883), p. 216.

10. Burns, *Vineyard of Liberty*, p. 526.

11. Brown, ed., *Lamb's Textile Industries*, p. 195.

12. Samuel E. Morison, *The Maritime History of Massachusetts, 1783–1860* (Boston: Houghton Mifflin, 1961 [1921]), p. 284.

13. Mitra Business Papers, Private Collection, Calcutta.

14. Robert G. Albion, *The Rise of the Port of New York* (New York: Scribners, 1939), p. 204: "The average from India . . . was $9,800,000, which was almost equal to the China average of $10,600,000."

15. Morison, *Maritime History of Massachusetts*, p. 284.

16. *Other Merchants and Sea Captains of Old Boston* (Boston: State Street Trust Company, 1919), pp. 46–47.

17. See U.S. Department of the Treasury, *Commerce and Navigation*, 1854, pp. 32, 40.

18. Ibid., pp. 38, 40.

19. Morison, *Maritime History of Massachusetts*, p. 285.

20. First published in the 1859 *Atlantic Monthly* as an installment titled "The Brahmin Caste of New England."

21. These are the romanizations of their names they each used.

22. Haradhan Dutt, *Dutt Family of Wellington Square* (Calcutta: n.p., 1995), p. 42.

23. Autograph box, Peabody Essex Museum Library.

24. Personal communication from R. K. Mitter, January 7, 1986; Lokanatha Gosha, *The Modern History of the Indian Chiefs, Rajas, Zamindars, etc. Part II* (Calcutta: J.N. Ghose, 1881), pp. 263–64; Mitra Business Papers, Private Collection, Calcutta.

25. *Other Merchants and Sea Captains of Old Boston.*

26. Raj Kissen Mitter to John T. Coolidge, October 31, 1846, Peabody Essex Museum Library.

27. The Peabody Essex collection includes seven portraits of Mitter family members, all originally presented to Yankee clients: two of Radha Kissen, two each of his sons Raj Kissen and Gopaul Kissen, and one of an unidentified son.

28. Grish Chunder Ghose, *The Life of Ramdoolal Dey* (Belloore: Bengalee Press, 1868), pp. 53–54.

29. Joguth Chunder (Philip) Gangooly, *Life and Religion of the Hindoos* (Boston: Crosby, Nichols, Lee, 1860), pp. 155–56. Gangooly was a Calcutta Brahmin who had converted to Unitarianism. He visited the United States to help promote the Unitarian cause in India. During his stay in the Boston area, Gangooly visited the East India Marine Society's museum, where he saw the memorial post that had been donated a half-century before by Calcuttan Durgaprasad Ghose.

30. Dutt, *Dutt Family of Wellington Square*, p. 20.

31. Letter from Rajinder Dutt to C. E. Norton, February 4, 1853, Norton Papers bMSAm1088 (1830–1843), by permission of Houghton Library, Harvard College Library.

32. The family of Nobel laureate Rabindranath Tagore.

33. Harvard University Archives.

34. Not until Ananda K. Coomaraswami came to the Museum of Fine Arts in Boston in the early twentieth century was Indian art incorporated into American art museum collections.

35. Dutt to Norton, October 7, 1852, Norton Papers, by permission of Houghton Library, Harvard College Library.

36. Dutt to Norton, February 4, 1853, Norton Papers, by permission of Houghton Library, Harvard College Library.

37. Dutt to Norton, January 8, 1852, Norton Papers, by permission of Houghton Library, Harvard College Library.

38. Dutt to Norton, January 7, 185?, Norton Papers, by permission of Houghton Library, Harvard College Library.

39. Gangooly, *Life and Religion of the Hindoos*, p. 6.

40. Dutt to Norton, January 8, 1852, Norton Papers, by permission of Houghton Library, Harvard College Library.

41. When he had the opportunity to observe the sacrifice of goats to the goddess Jagaddhatri. Sara Norton and M. A. DeWolfe Howe, eds., *Letters of Charles Eliot Norton* (Boston: Houghton Mifflin, 1913), pp. 43–55.

42. Gangooly, *Life and Religion of the Hindoos*, p. 155.

43. Dutt to Norton, January 8, 1852, Norton Papers, by permission of Houghton Library, Harvard College Library.

44. Celebrated by Van Wyck Brooks in his Pulitzer Prize–winning *The Flowering of New England, 1815–1865* (New York: E.P. Dutton, 1936).

45. See Arthur Christy, *The Orient in American Transcendentalism* (New York: Columbia University Press, 1932); Carl T. Jackson, *The Oriental Religions and American Thought: Nineteenth-Century Explorations* (Westport, Conn.:

Greenwood Press, 1981); R. K. Gupta, *The Great Encounter: A Study of Indo-American Literature and Cultural Relations* (Riverdale, Md.: Riverdale Co., 1987); Dale Riepe, *The Philosophy of India and Its Impact on American Thought* (Springfield, Ill.: Charles C. Thomas, 1970).

46. Christy, *The Orient in American Transcendentalism*, pp. 63ff. In the 1840s and '50s, Sanskrit was first taught, if intermittently, at Yale and Harvard Colleges. Libraries were formed. Fitz Edward Hall, who had traveled and studied in India in the 1850s, gave or sold more than 2,000 manuscripts to Harvard.

47. James E. Cabot, *A Memoir of Ralph Waldo Emerson* (Boston: Houghton Mifflin, 1887), vol. 1, p. 290. The *Bhagavad Gita* is a discourse on religion and morality, the Puranas are stories about the deities, and the Upanishads are philosophical and religious commentaries.

48. Christy, *The Orient in American Transcendentalism*, p. 21.

49. Ibid., p. 188.

50. Henry David Thoreau, *A Week on the Concord and Merrimack Rivers* (Boston: Ticknor & Fields, 1868), p. 293.

51. Cited in Jackson, *The Oriental Religions and American Thought*, p. 66. In the Transcendentalists' magazine, the *The Dial*, a series of "Ethnical Scriptures" were published beginning in 1842 proclaiming their position that "Each nation has its bible . . . the grand expressions of the moral sentiment in different ages and races, the rules for the guidance of life, the bursts of piety and of abandonment of the Invisible and Eternal" (Emerson, quoted in Christy, *The Orient in American Transcendentalism*, p. 11).

52. Jackson, *The Oriental Religions and American Thought*, p. 69.

53. Herman Melville, *Moby Dick* (New York: Harper & Bros., 1851), p. 293. The *matsya* avatar of Vishnu is a giant fish, not a whale, and it is not depicted in the Elephanta Cave temple.

54. John Pickering, "Address," *Journal of the American Oriental Society* 1 (1849). During its first decades, India received by far the most attention in the American Oriental Society's journal. See Jackson, *The Oriental Religions and American Thought*, pp. 38–39.

55. Pickering, "Address," p. 47.

56. Ibid., p. 43.

57. Henry David Thoreau, *Walden* (New York: Bantam Books, 1962 [1854]), pp. 324–25.

58. Spencer Lavan, *Unitarians and India* (Chicago: Exploration Press, 1991), pp. 85, 91. Dall's first convert was Philip Gangooly, who visited Boston in the late 1850s and published a book, cited above, *Life and Religion of the Hindoos*, in Boston in 1860.

59. Lavan, *Unitarians and India*, p. 94.

CHAPTER 15

1. Blood Family Papers, Peabody Essex Museum Library.

2. *Newburyport Herald*, June 29, 1876.

3. John J. Currier, *The History of Newburyport, Massachusetts, 1764–1905* (Somersworth: New Hampshire Pub. Co., 1977 [1906]), vol. 1, p. 182.

4. John Dunn Davies, *Phrenology: Fad and Science* (New Haven: Yale University Press, 1955), pp. 38ff.

5. Blood Family Papers, Peabody Essex Museum Library.

6. Journal of the *Rockall*, Peabody Essex Museum Library.

7. When Edwin Blood sailed, the ship was owned by Samuel F. Morse, Frederick Gray, Henry Wainwright, Sewell Tappan, Benjamin E. Morse, William Rollins, E. William Rollins, and Joel Richards.

8. The letter continues: "The death of Captain Martin leaves me the last survivor of all those who set out in the cabin of the *Rockall* in 1854. The graves are wide apart. Mr. Burroughs, the second mate, died in Calcutta shortly after our arrival. Mr. Douton, who succeeded him as second mate and who went out in the ship before the mast and was the only one of the outward crew (several of whom died in Calcutta) who came back in her, died on the homeward passage and was buried at sea. Capt. Wilcox, the chief mate, died, many years ago, on the west coast of South America. Mr. Farnham, a passenger afterwards long U.S. consul at Bombay died there three or four years ago. Mr. Greenleaf, the other passenger (afterwards with the house of Foster, Rogers and Co. Calcutta) died in Philadelphia some years since."

9. Salem Public Library, "Books on India," 1891, is an extensive list of books, many published before 1860. The Salem Athenaeum also had at least twenty volumes on India published before 1860.

10. P. Thankappan Nair, *Calcutta in the 19th Century* (Calcutta: Firma, 1989), p. 752.

11. Ibid., p. 923.

12. Currier, *History of Newburyport*, p. 177.

CHAPTER 16

1. Owned by Charles and Augustine Wills of Boston and Newburyport; Charles Thurston, master.

2. The Crimean War.

3. Port (opposite to starboard), the left side of a vessel when one is facing the bow (forward).

4. A Salem ship owned by the firm Stone, Pickman, and Silsbee.

5. Owned by Robert C. Mackay of Boston; William Pierce, Jr., master.

6. A *dhoti*, a piece of white cotton approximately five yards by one yard, wrapped and tied; the lower garment of Hindu males in Bengal.

7. One of the landing places at Calcutta.

8. Built in 1833 by the Anglo-Indians of Calcutta to store the ice shipped regularly from Boston by Frederic Tudor and others.

9. Maria Taglioni (1804–1884), a famous Italian ballet dancer.

10. Ice cut at Wenham Lake and exported from Boston was esteemed and known by name in places as far away as London and Calcutta.

11. Passage omitted titled *A Native Holiday*, about the festival of Lord Jagannatha.

12. *Section Fifth, Business Life, Continued*, describing the method of conducting business and his experiences in the saltpeter bazaar, has been omitted.

13. Passage omitted on the importance of human muscle power in India and the operations at a screw house where cloth, hides, etc. are compressed for shipping.

14. Alexander the Great made his way to India and secured control over the northwestern part of the subcontinent in the fourth century B.C.E.

15. Passage omitted on the pleasant process of being bathed and dressed by servants.

16. A description of the housemates gathering and eating breakfast is omitted.

17. Passage omitted on Lady Dalhousie's death.

18. The Marquess of Dalhousie was governor-general of India from 1848 to 1856. He developed the railroad, telegraph, and road system in India. He pushed Western education and established the first three Indian universities. He also devised the doctrine of lapse (when a ruler had no direct heir) and other measures whereby Indian states could be taken over by the British.

19. A campaign initiated by Dalhousie concluded with the annexation of lower Burma in 1852.

20. The Sikh kingdom in the Punjab was defeated and annexed by the British under Dalhousie in 1849.

21. Robert Clive led the East India Company forces that defeated the Mughal ruler of Bengal at the Battle of Plassey in 1757, establishing the British as a political power in India. Sir Charles Napier conquered Sind for the British in 1843.

22. Descriptions of the customary evening promenade on the Strand, enter-tainment offered by a military band, and the foppish, outlandish behavior of a wealthy "native" gentleman aping European ways have been omitted.

23. Blood continues on the dearth of evening amusements in Calcutta; passage omitted.

24. Blood is probably referring to Mahmud of Ghazni, who took territory in northwestern India in the eleventh century. He was not the founder of the Mughal dynasty.

25. Cholera, a waterborne infection, is endemic to the deltas of the Bay of Bengal.

26. Lord Jagannatha is a form of Krishna whose main image is kept at the great temple complex at Puri, Orissa, with those of his brother Balarama and his sister Subadhra.

27. Probably egg-shaped lingas, forms of Lord Shiva.

28. The couple, though married, do not cohabit until of age. Blood knew this and had recorded a line later crossed out perhaps for drama's sake: "but the nuptials are consummated when the first menstrual flow shows that the age of puberty in the female has arrived."

29. Sections on morning walks and the Government House have been omit-ted.

30. This is the Octherlony monument, now known as Shahid Minar, erected in 1828 in honor of Sir David Octherlony, the Boston boy who served the East India Company in the conquest of the subcontinent (see fig. 1.2).

31. A passage on Fort William that followed is omitted.

Puri, Orissa, 189
Purvoos (clerks), 164
R
racial inequality, 21–22, 34, 90–91, 268
railroads, 211, 255
Ramakrishna, 219
Ramdulal Dey, *See* Dey, Ramdulal
Ramduloll Day, 72
Ramsey, William, 191
Rash Jatra, 218, 220
raw materials, 18, 121, 139, 175, 178–80, 196
Reaper, 126–27
Rebellion of 1857, 211
Redman, Thomas, 33–34
Reed, David, 193
re-export of goods, 36, 37, 40, 67, 68, 69, 70, 93, 126
religion
  see Christianity and Hinduism; Hinduism; Hindu religious practices; missionaries
Republican party, 70, 88, 122, 138
Revolutionary War, 16, 29–30, 33, 45, 177, 178
Rhode Island, 178
Rice, Luther, 130, 132
Rich, John, 35, 46
Rockall, 211, 212, 217, 225, 226
  journal of Blood's voyage on, 215, 226, 231–65
Rogers, John, 137
Rogers, John W., 137, 139
Rogers, Nathaniel L., 137, 139
Rogers, Richard S., 137, 139, 143
Rogers, William A., 12, 13, 22, 121, 125–26, 128, 135, 137–41
  American identity of, 19, 128, 267
  education and career of, 137–38, 195, 222
  journal of voyage on *Tartar* by, 16, 125–26, 128, 139–41, 143–71
  missionaries encountered by, 133, 170, 191, 269
  portrayal of Indian society by, 19, 268, 269
Rogers, William C., 180
Rogers family, 191, 214
Roy, H. C., 218
Roy, Rammohun, 19, 135, 191–93, 221, 222, 223, 269, 270
Royall, Anne, 182
Ruby, 12, 35, 37, 46, 49
  journal of Carpenter's voyage on, *see* Carpenter, Benjamin
rule of war, 1756, 67
Rush, Benjamin, 41
Russia, 212
Rutton, Ram, 228, 244, 245, 268

S
sailors *(lascar)*, 196, 231
Salem, 19, 45–46, 69, 88, 123, 212
  Crowninshield's Wharf , 10
  dedication of East India Marine Hall at, 182
  Federalists of, 88, 138, 139
  Indian visitor to, 40
  loss of trade by, 175, 177
  merchant families of, 12, 17, 69, 87, 122–23, 137, 177, 191, 214, 222
  missionaries ordained in, 132
  ships built in, 89, 139, 143, 195
  Unitarianism in, 191
  voyages from, 37, 41, 45
Salem Courier, 193
Salem East India Marine Society, *see* East India Marine Society
Salem Gazette, 83, 88
  store sale advertisement in, 19
Salem Marine Society, 195
Salem Register, 81, 182
  store sale advertisement in, 68
saltpeter, 18, 178, 179, 211–12
Sanskrit literature, 21, 23, 40, 193, 221, 226
Sanskrit texts, 135, 191, 192
Sanskrit translation of bible, 132
Santiago, Cape Verdes, 49
sati, 41–43, 125, 133, 189, 269
seersucker, 31–32
Serampore, 132
Seringapatam, 82–83, 88, 94, 146
servants:
  in Bombay household, 171
  in Calcutta household, 185–87, 240, 251
Seybert, Adam, 121
Shakuntalam, 78
shipmasters, *see* captains
ships, size of, 35–36
shoe manufacture, 178–79
silk handkerchiefs, 77, 124, 176, 212, 270
silks, imported, 17, 19, 31–32, 74, 77, 212
Silsbee, Nathaniel, 21, 69
Silsbee family firm, 89, 214
silver specie, 35, 36–37, 213
  British need for, 69
Simpson, John, 229
Simpson, Mary Elizabeth, 229
sircar (clerk), 18, 39, 73, 183, 185, 238
  Ram Rutton, 228, 244, 245, 268
Skerry, Samuel, Jr., 87
Slater, Samuel, 123
slavery, 21, 34, 90, 211
slave trade, 176
snake charmers, 22, 160, 269
Southeast Asia, 16, 28
Spain, 176
spindles, 31, 84

Spruzheim, Johann, 225
St. Helena, drawing of, 138
Stark, John, 130
statuary, displays of, 220
  see also clay statuary; Jaipur marble figures
steam transportation, 226
Stone family, 89, 214
Suez Canal, 226
Sultana, 37
Sumatra, 88, 89, 109
Sumner, C. P., 133
Sumner, Thomas W., 182
supercargoes, 18, 27, 35, 36, 37, 39–40, 68, 121
Surat, 40, 69
  governors of, 83, 84
syce (groom), figurine representing, 187, 188
T
talipot tree, 149
tariffs, 17, 89, 124–25, 175, 176, 177
Tartar, 12, 16, 121, 137, 139, 195
  journal of Rogers's voyage on, 125–26, 128, 139–41, 143–71
  Rogers's voyage to Calcutta on, 141
Tea Acts, 29
teak wood, 152
Tegh Khan Bahadur, Nawab Namdar, 83
telegraph, 211, 226, 233, 234
Tenerife, 49, 87
textile manufacturing, 16, 17, 89, 123–25, 175, 176, 178, 213
  printing and dyeing, 176, 178
textiles, Indian, 17, 19, 23, 27, 28–29, 31–32, 40, 74–77
  advertisements for, 19
  decline in U.S. market for, 121, 124, 175–76, 178, 212
  duty imposed on, 124, 175
textiles exported to India, 16, 175, 213
Thoreau, Henry David, 21, 221, 222–23, 269
Thorndike, Israel, 75, 123
Three Sisters, 88
Timur Shah , 217
Tipu (Tippoo) Sultan, 16, 29, 33, 82–83, 88, 152
Towne, Solomon, 83
Tranquebar, 22, 37, 90, 91, 93, 102–4, 106
Transcendentalism, 193, 222, 225, 269
Treaty of 1783, 105
Trent, William, 31–32
Trexel, 141
Tuckerman, Joseph, 193
Tudor, Frederic, 179–80, 181
Tudor, William, 135, 191–92
Tudor's Wharf, 212
Tuscany, 179–80
Two Brothers, 45, 195

U
U. S. trade with India, *see* Indo-U.S. trade
Union, 128?
Unitarianism, 19–20, 87, 134, 191, 222, 223, 225, 269, 270
Unitarians, 22, 135, 193, 228, 268
United States, 17, 33, 35, 36
Upanishads, 192, 221
U.S. foreign commerce, growth of, 68, 69, 121
V
Van Buren, Martin, 190
Varick, Margarita van, 31
Vedantic Hinduism, 193
Vishnu "idols," 261
Vivekananda, 22
W
Wadia, Nusserwanjee Maneckjee, 71–72, 79, 164
  portrait of, 79, 83
  portrait statue of, 184, 217
wages for seamen, 36
Walden (Thoreau), 21, 222–23
Waltham, Mass., 195
Ware, Rev. Henry, 193
War of 1812, 17, 121, 123, 127, 175, 176, 182
Washiad, The (Blood), 229
Washington, George, 29, 38, 67, 87, 88, 122, 123–24, 147
  commemoration of, 88, 220
  portrait of, 72, 220, 268
Waterloo, 88, 138
Watson, Marston, 125
Webb, Joseph, 189
Wellesley, Richard Colley, Marquis (Lord Mornington), 82, 88, 93, 112–13
West, Thomas, 89
West Indies trade, 33, 37, 67, 68
Wheatland, Henry, 182
Whigs, 225
White, Joseph, Jr., 84
Whitney, Eli, 124
Whittier, John Greenleaf, 221
Williams, Roger, 28
Williams, Timothy, 88–89
Willing, Thomas, 34
Willis, N. P., 219
Worcester, Samuel, 132
World Congress of Religions, 22
Y
Yale, Elihu, 27, 28
Yankee India, vision of, 40–41
Young Bengal, 218–19, 223
Z
Zanzibar, 89, 137